MR. HOUSE OF TEXAS

MR. HOUSE AND PRESIDENT WILSON IN THE DAYS OF "THE PERFECT
FRIENDSHIP"

Mr. HOUSE OF TEXAS

By

ARTHUR D. HOWDEN SMITH

FUNK & WAGNALLS COMPANY

NEW YORK AND LONDON

1940

TO
ROBERT M. TAPPAN

AUTHOR'S NOTE

As I write this, the worst consequences which Mr. House foresaw as possible contingencies of the errors of the Treaty of Versailles, and the failure of the League of Nations to correct them, have been realized. Twenty-six years of history, the lives of millions of people, billions of capital investment, have gone for nothing. The world is back where it was in August, 1914, with every likelihood that man's inventiveness in the interim will create more destruction in the coming months than he achieved in the period of 1914-18. We, of the Americas, are again at the crossroads of destiny, and again, as in 1914, '15 and '16, we are hesitating to assume the just burdens imposed upon us as the greatest of the democracies. I am sure that I do no injustice to Mr. House's memory when I say that his counsel today would be the same as it was in those years. We and our sister states are democracies. The nations which are frankly attempting to wreck the European democracies, and all that the world has achieved through democracy, are a throwback to the crass materialism of the Dark Ages. If they succeed, we must perish. This is not a question of one continent or another, of one nation or culture. It is a question of the continuance of freedom of religion and political expression. It is a question of the continuance of civilization, because civilization, as we have known it, could not continue to exist under the dominion of the totalitarian states. If we do not do our share to check them, we shall perish—and we shall deserve to perish.

A. D. H. S.

May 15, 1940.

Contents

Illustrations

MR. HOUSE OF TEXAS

Book 1

By Way of Explanation

THIS is, I suspect, a most unorthodox way to begin a biography. I employ it because I believe it furnishes the most intelligent means of setting the character of the subject, and explaining why I happen to have been familiar with him and his ideals and the part he played in an eventful period of American history. I make the explanation very humbly. It was mainly through the friendship which ripened between us, and from his patient and kindly teaching, that I learned whatever I came to know of the secret and conflicting motives and ambitions of human personalities, which, at all times and in all countries, influence tenaciously the course of human events.

Many people will dispute the desirability of the system of secrecy, even of concealment, which dominates politics and statecraft from the bickerings of the ward to the quarrels of nations. Both Woodrow Wilson and Edward M. House fought for "open covenants openly arrived at." They failed. Men, who claim to be wiser than they, have been fighting for the same objective ever since their defeat. I believe only hypocrites would pretend that the fight has been carried beyond the point they reached. It remains one of those ideals for which men and women reach hungrily toward the stars. And if humanity once abandons those ideals the day will be at hand when humanity must perish from the earth.

One more word of explanation. It will be noticed that in this book its subject is referred to as "Mr. House," unless he is addressed directly in conversation. The reason is that Mr. House detested the honorary title of Colonel, which he never earned and never sought, just as he detested all other titles, including the various knighthoods and patents of nobility foreign nations offered him. He regarded it—and endured it good-humoredly—as a political nickname. Those of his friends who used it did so in that sense. All who knew him familiarly addressed him formally, as did the members of his family, as plain "Mr. House." It was one of those little traits which furnish the essential clue to a man's inward being.

2

One evening, in the late spring of 1913, I happened to drop in at the old Herald Square Theater in New York. The play was the current musical success. After the first-act curtain had risen, two men strolled down the aisle and took seats several rows in front of me. Nobody noticed them, but I recognized one as William Gibbs McAdoo, Secretary of the Treasury in the new Administration. The other I finally identified, with some difficulty, as "the mysterious Colonel House," whose position as reputed advisor to President Wilson was arousing much public interest and more hostile speculation.

They seemed to pay little attention to the play, which was drawing gales of laughter and applause from the audience. Their heads were close together. They were deep in a conversation obviously absorbing to themselves. It was apparent to me, but to no one else in the theater, that they were there because they regarded a crowded theater as the safest of all places for a conference they wished to keep secret. The reason, of course, was equally apparent.

The country, as a whole, was chiefly interested in the Tariff Bill of the new Administration; but in the East, and in New York especially, a violent controversy was raging over the Glass-Owen Bill for currency reform, actually the more important measure of the two, which was to lead finally to the establishment of the Federal Reserve system and to revolutionize the American theory of banking. McAdoo was playing as important a role in moulding sentiment in Congress for this second bill as were its official sponsors in the House and Senate. Any newspaperman knew that if he left Washington in the height of the struggle to see Mr. House it could be only to discuss Currency Reform.

In the morning I told my city editor what I had seen and what I suspected. He shrugged his shoulders.

"I daresay you're right," he said. "But what of it? House sees nobody. He can't be reached. Nobody knows his address, and his telephone number is private."

I reached for *Who's Who*, which gave Mr. House's permanent address as Austin, Texas, but revealed the fact that he was married. The city editor was watching me with amusement.

"No go, eh?" he said.

"Wait a moment," I told him, and took down the *Social Register*, which lists all persons recognized by the mythical world of Society. And there he was, with an address in East Thirty-fifth Street.

"Glad for the information," admitted the city editor, jotting it in his notebook. "It won't get you anywhere, but trot up and see him, if you like. The news looks thin this morning."

The address in East Thirty-fifth Street was an unpretentious apartment house in an unfashionable block between Lexington and Third Avenues. The hallman telephoned my name upstairs.

"Very good, sir," he reported. "Mr. House will see you."

A maid let me in to a pleasant, sunny apartment, as unpretentious as the building. A slim, gray man, with warm, friendly blue eyes, came forward and received me with the courtesy which is the heritage of the old South.

"Glad to see you," he said. "How did you run me down?"

I told him truthfully, and he laughed.

"You're a smart young feller," he retorted. "Yes, McAdoo came over to talk to me about Currency Reform. They're having trouble in Washington. We didn't want the newspapers to know he was coming, so when he telephoned I told him I'd meet him for dinner with tickets for the theater." He laughed again, good-humoredly rueful. "I thought that would be the safest place to talk, but it seems I was wrong."

He led me into a tiny study off the living room, where we talked for an hour, he with the utmost frankness, of the difficulties in the path of the Currency Reform policy the Administration had adopted, largely at his suggestion. His desk was covered with papers, correspondence with bankers, merchants and business men in every State of the Union. He answered every question, and if it was necessary to elucidate what he said he produced documents and named names. In the beginning of our conversation I asked him if I might quote him.

"Not directly," he replied; "but you may use everything I say to you."

I have never met a man whose personality so strongly impressed me. His eyes were his outstanding feature, blue and luminous rather than bright, seldom winking. Ordinarily, they were friendly. I learned later that they could also be blank and stare disconcertingly. His head was narrow, with prominent, almost Mongolian cheekbones. His mustache was close-clipped. Oddly enough, he had almost no chin—and yet no man ever lived who had a more iron will. He had complete control over his facial muscles. When he wished it, his face was a mask; but it could brighten and reveal every shade of feeling or sentiment in moments of relaxation. He would have made an excellent gambler on the frontier of his boyhood—you couldn't have told whether he held a pair of deuces or a royal flush.

In build he was about the middle height, his frame compactly knit. Physically, he moved as quickly and surely as he did mentally—toward the end of his life he used to take my breath away by the daring with which he negotiated New York traffic, regardless of the signals.   His voice was low and clear, tinged agreeably by the slurring accent of his native State.   For instance, he always said "ye-eew" for you, not "yo'" or the variants of the rest of the South.   His choice of language, his nicety of phrase, were those of an elder day.   His manners were simple, and perhaps I cannot better characterize their perfection than by the statement that I knew no man of his generation who could match them but the immortal John Sharp Williams, of Mississippi.

When I rose to go—and it is significant of him that he made no move to terminate the interview—he shook hands with the firm grip of a frontiersman.

"I don't know why I let you come up," he said; "but come again, come often, come whenever you please.   Here, I'll give you my private number."

I remember that when I went away I had a feeling as of a clean wind blowing in my face across the open range.

"Why," I said to myself, "this man is a greater American than Theodore Roosevelt."

For, while I admired President Wilson and believed in his works, there was a cold aloofness about him which kept me, and I think many other Americans, from feeling anything warmer than intellectual admiration for him.   I once mentioned this to Mr. House, coupling it with the recitation of several small snubs I had received, and he understood.

"Yes, that is the President's misfortune," he said.   "But he never means to hurt.   I am sure he never meant to hurt you."

For one reason or another I did not see Mr. House again for some months.   Perhaps, as much as anything, I was loath to seem to exploit his courtesy, in which feeling I showed how little I appreciated him. When I did telephone him, his voice came reproachfully to my ear.

"Why haven't you been to see me?   I thought you were coming often?"

That day, after the conclusion of our talk, he said:

"I hope you'll understand now that I mean what I say."   He laughed— and, incidentally, he seldom laughed, though he often smiled.   "You know, Mr. Smith, I never could understand why I let you up that time. I think it must have been partly because of your paper, which I have always admired, but mostly because I wanted to see the young feller who hunted me down.   Come again, come soon, my young friend.   I like to keep in touch with the young men.   It's the young men who make the country's future."

I have described this incident in such detail because, as I have said, it furnishes a key to Mr. House's character, and it was the beginning of a friendship which continued without a break practically for twenty-five years—as fine a friendship, I believe, as could exist between two men who were separated in age by a generation, and marked on his part by a consideration as distinguished as that which he showed for men who were his equals in age and achievement. Indeed, when Mr. House bestowed his friendship upon young men, he invariably treated them as his equals. He never addressed us by our last names without the prefix "Mr." When we were received into intimacy—and a young man had to prove himself to attain that privilege—he called us by our first names. I am proud to say that he often asked my advice or opinion, and when he didn't take it, and events proved him wrong in the contrary course, he admitted it cheerfully and without pretense.

The incident is also interesting as illustrating the absurdity of the legend that he craved mystery, that he was secretive, that he was "hard to see," a legend which thrived until the close of his active career in politics. The truth was that he was too busy to allow himself to be bothered by the casual interviewers and favor-seekers who pester every public man; and in addition there was the mandatory fact that he was scrupulous in endeavoring not to divert to himself any of the credit that was due the President and members of the Cabinet for the legislation and policies they were supposed to create.

Any newspaperman, with a valid reason for seeing him, could obtain an interview; and as time went on, and his importance in national affairs began to be understood, probably many of them saw him as often as I did, his one stipulation being the same that he had made to me at our first meeting: he must not be quoted directly. Anyone who violated this stipulation, which applied equally to politicians and curious business men, immediately lost his confidence. There was no argument about it. He simply gave the offenders the "silent treatment." I remember one man, a leader in Wall Street and head of one of the important war agencies of the Administration, who begged me pathetically to "ask the Colonel" what he had done and make peace for him. His offense had been no more than the bad taste of quoting to others a statement of Mr. House's criticizing another official. He apologized and was received back into limited favor, but Mr. House never entirely trusted him again.

There were, by the way, definite disadvantages to possessing Mr. House's favor. I was continually being requested for "inside" information and interviews with him. Early in the war I was approached by a well-known mine operator, who was notoriously pro-German. He wanted to introduce me to an organization handling German propaganda in William Street. I was curious to learn all I could about their activities, and agreed to meet them. With some hemming and hawing, they offered me $50,000 outright and $10,000 a year to serve as secretary to their committee. I told them I wasn't worth any such price, and after a deal of further dodging about, their principal admitted that they wanted me in order to keep posted on what Mr. House was doing. I delayed a definite refusal until I had obtained from them a file of the official casualty reports issued by the German War Office, which I promptly dispatched to London and which furnished the first check-up for the British General Staff on German losses on the Western Front.

I was angry and indignant, at the time, that a man who had known me for several years, a man at whose table I dined, should have supposed me so dishonorable as to be willing to abuse a trust, even supposing I had been sympathetic with his prejudices. Now, I can be amused, as I can be at the brokers who complained because I had not given them an advance tip on a story which sent one of the "war baby" stocks zooming for a rise of sixty or seventy points.

"The next time the Colonel tells you something like that, pass it on to us," they said. "We'll take care of you."

Probably none of them believed me when I protested that I had not received my information from Mr. House, that I had developed the story by cobbling two facts to two facts, and that I had not made a dollar out of the deal. I was governed in this last circumstance, perhaps, because Mr. House had influenced me profoundly by his precept that no one occupying a position of public trust could honorably profit by knowledge he acquired as a consequence of that position—and the newspapermen who trained me had taught me that an honest newspaperman was a trustee of the public interest.

But I am still unamused by the popular conception evidenced by the corporation executive who asked me what kind of man Mr. House was, and in answer to my general statements replied irritably:

"Yes, yes, I know he's a great man. I wish I could use him. But what I want to know is: What's his game? What's he getting out of this? There never lived a man who worked for nothing."

I hope that I shall be able to make it clear, in the course of this book, that Mr. House was the most perfect exemplification we have had in this country of the man of moderate means who is willing to devote the substance he owes to the country to unselfish service in its interests. This quality alone would have made him a great citizen, a great gentleman. It was a happy accident that an unusual combination of political adroitness and intelligence made him also one of the greatest liberal statesmen who ever lived.

Book 2

The Young Texan

ANDREW JACKSON was President of the United States, apostle of a New Deal which was crushing the lifeblood out of the Federalists and smashing the tradition of aristocracy inherited from the Colonial era—the party and the tradition of George Washington. The frontiersmen of the Mississippi valley were in the saddle, and they and their leader were hell-bent on destroying Nicholas Biddle and the Bank of the United States, that ill-omened monster which had provided the country with its first sound credit system. Waves of bankruptcy swept over cities and farms, uprooting families and individuals by hundreds of thousands, tearing them from their homes and their occupations, drowning many, bearing more on the recurrent crests in the one direction which promised hope: westward. At the height of that depression Andrew Jackson paid off the National Debt with money obtained from the land warrants of the victims of his financial policy.

That was a century ago. The Great American Desert stretched beyond the Mississippi to the Shining Mountains, endless miles of buffalo grass, rising and falling in swales of tough verdure, unbroken by the wheel or the plow, its muddy rivers rimmed by growths of softwood timber offering precarious barriers to the mighty winds which scourged it. The only Americans who dared its challenge were those uncouth naturals, the Mountain Men, the trappers of the American Fur Company and the independent brigades who, between wrangles amongst themselves, were saving their scalps from the Blackfeet, discovering the South Pass, the Great Salt Lake, the wonders of the Yellowstone, and the road to California. But the true lords of the Desert—which Washington Irving decreed to be the limit of American expansion—were the free-riding Sioux, the Arapahos, the Pawnees, the Comanches, and a score of lesser tribes.

Southward lay Texas, an outlying dependency of the Mexican State of Coahuila. The Mexicans, harassed by their own difficulties in whittling a Republic out of the short-lived Empire of Iturbide, had mistakenly invited colonization of this rich domain, which they did not pretend to control beyond the line of missions on the Rio Grande. Wherever an Anglo-Saxon has set his foot on unoccupied land it has never been wrested from him. It was one thing to enlist the aid of a few riflemen to stand off the raids of the Comanches. It was something else again to bring in, and grant lands to, whole communities of Americans led by such men as Sam Houston, Davy Crockett, James Bowie, Mirabeau B. Lamar, Henry Smith, J. W. Fannin, James W. Robertson, Stephen Austin.

Texas was a promised land to Americans who had been driven from their farms by an outrageous mortgage system or to Englishmen whose country was convulsed by the agitation over the Corn Laws and the extension of the suffrage. All over the United States and the British Isles men locked their offices, closed their shops and hung the code sign on the door—"G. T. T.," Gone To Texas. Settlements sprang up along the upper Gulf Coast and in the valleys of the Nacogdoches, the Brazos and the San Jacinto. The Comanche was a pest, and was to be for nearly a generation to come; but the colonists handled him.

They handled the Mexicans in the same ruthless fashion, only more decisively. It was impossible for men of their traditions to adjust themselves to the administrative methods of a Latin dictatorship, and particularly the dictatorship of a Santa Anna. They declared their independence on November 13, 1835, and achieved it in a fierce, bloody war of four months. By the end of April, 1836, they had their freedom, a constitution, an organized government, and the imperishable memories of Goliad, the Alamo, and San Jacinto. And so the Lone Star Republic was born for an existence as brief as it was glorious, immense in territory, meager in population, but with an egotism that bounced to the moon.

One of the soldiers who fought under General Burleson, lieutenant of Sam Houston, was a young Englishman named Thomas William House, who had run away from home—"when a child," his son wrote long afterward—and gone to sea. Like so many of his type, the surge of adventure had landed him upon the shores of Texas. His services were rewarded with a grant of land in Coryell County, and presently he married Mary Elizabeth Shearn, daughter of one of the early jurists of the Republic. Hard work and an intellect beyond the average brought him prosperity. Before the Civil War, he was one of the richest men in Texas, which in 1845 united herself to the Union by a treaty negotiated as a sovereign power. He owned large holdings of sugar-cane and cotton lands and many slaves, and did a flourishing business as a private banker. It says much for his acumen that he was one of the few Southerners who came through the war years without any appreciable diminution of wealth.

His photograph, taken in middle age, reveals a broad, strong face, with kindly, intelligent eyes, a prominent nose and a firm, humorous mouth. The son, quoted above, said of him:

"He seems to me, now, among the ablest men I have ever known. I owe more to my father than to any person, living or dead. He not only made it possible for me to pursue the bent of my inclinations by leaving me a fortune sufficient for all moderate wants, but he gave me an insight into the philosophy of life that has been of incalculable value. . . . While he acquired what seemed to Texas a large fortune, he taught me not to place a fictitious value on wealth. It was with him merely a means to an end."

This son, his seventh, was Edward Mandell House, born in Houston, July 26, 1858.* Thomas William House lived until 1880. When he came to Texas no homestead in the Eastern counties was safe from the ravages of the Comanches. He lived under four flags, the Eagle and Snake of Mexico, the Lone Star, the Stars and Stripes, the Stars and Bars, and again the flag of the Union. The roads were traces. Any journey was a dangerous undertaking. Business was mostly by barter. When he died, the railroads were beginning to be a problem in State politics, but outside the Gulf counties the rancher was king, herds still thronged the Chisholm trail, and the cowboy wore his six-gun outside his chaps.

He was a great man in Texas, but his son lived to be a greater. His son "walked with Kings, and kept his virtue," played a tremendous role in world history, helped as a young man to curb the railroads and corporations, saw oil supplant beef as the leading product, Houston, where he was born, become a seaport and the cowboy, alas, a legend. In his lifetime Texas was transformed from a backward frontier State to one of the proudest of the commonwealths, fifth in population, with a dozen stately cities and an educational equipment second to none—thanks, in part, to his efforts—a vital factor in the nation's politics and economy.

Their two lives spanned more than a century of the development of Texas, yes, and of the United States, from the New Deal of Andrew Jackson to the New Deal of Franklin D. Roosevelt. And both of them,

---

* One of the malicious rumors whispered about Mr. House in certain quarters was that he was of Jewish extraction. He admired the Jewish people, and would have scorned to hide a Jewish origin. But he was not Jewish. My understanding is that his middle name, Mandell, was that of a Jewish merchant in Houston, who was one of his father's most intimate friends. The fact that the elder House conferred a Jewish name upon his son indicates the family's attitude toward the race.

essential aristocrats though they were, believed in the blind, dogged common sense of the masses as the surest antidote to economic fallacies which
might triumph for a while against every argument of reason.

2

No American boy of today can hope to grow up under the conditions
of danger and romance that spiced the boyhood of Ed House, as they
called him in Texas. The roar of gunfire was in his ears from infancy.
He himself thought that his gentleness of manner, the courtesy he showed
toward everyone, were learned in the tough school of the frontier where
the mildest questioning of a man's veracity was an invitation to "shoot it
out." The bad men of southern Texas, he maintained, were usually mild-
spoken, often delicate in appearance, and invariably polite.

"I think it is my memory of early times in Texas," he told me during
the World War, "which keeps me from being as shocked as some people
are at the dreadful slaughter of this war. To a man who can remember
when bad men killed for sport in open daylight in city streets, and des-
peradoes swarmed in bands and ruled whole tracts of country, the destruction of European lands is not so startling, after all."

He was a year old when Sam Houston made his last appearance on
the political stage as Governor. The ex-squaw man and hero of San
Jacinto had been his father's commander and idol. As a child, Ed House
heard the story of how he had fought to hold Texas in the Union, resigned in grief in '61, and died of a broken heart two years later. As a
small boy, he saw the Confederate soldiers tramping through the streets,
and the huge ox-carts laden with cotton on the road to Galveston where
the blockade-runners lay with steam up, biding a chance to slip out past
the Federal gunboats. This last was the true romance for him, and he
recalled it to the end of his life, for his father was active in the trade of
shipping cotton abroad and bringing back cargoes of arms, munitions and
medicines for the army.

The family had a house in Galveston, and he spent a considerable portion of the war years there. He had pleasant memories of its red brick
dignity, the tall white pillars of the portico, and the oleanders and orange
trees in the block-square grounds. There was a cupola on the roof, and
sometimes, when the afternoon was stormy, he would climb to it and
watch, fascinated, as his father peered through binoculars to study the
weather and count the gunboats tossing off the bar. That meant that a
blockade-runner would put to sea after dark. And in the morning he
and his father would climb the ladder again, and make a second count

of the gunboats; if there were as many visible as there had been the afternoon before, then the House cotton probably was safely on its way to
Havana or the Belize. But of course you could never be entirely sure
there hadn't been a misadventure—not until the lean, coal-blackened hull
showed off the bar in the glimmer of a false dawn, belching smoke from
her stack, and the guns of the harbor forts thundered a warning to the
gunboats pelting in her wake.

After the war came the nightmare of Reconstruction, when men went
armed and the fire-bells clanged at night, calling the citizens to quell riots.
It was a raw, hateful period of oppression, chicanery and injustice. Fortunately, it didn't poison Ed House, as it did so many other boys. He
didn't hate Negroes. As a man, he was one of the best friends they had.
But he remembered that he, like all his playmates, succumbed to the
atmosphere of recklessness and disorder created by their elders. Firearms
were toys to them, and accidents were common. Ed House's eldest
brother had one side of his face shot off, and he himself had two narrow
escapes from killing other boys by carelessness with weapons.

"I was a quarrelsome boy," he admitted to me once in that curiously
gentle voice of his. "I used to like to set boys at each other to see what
they would do, and then try to bring them around again."

He was also sturdy and robust, able to endure all normal hardships. He
could fork a bronco at the age boys today ride bicycles. He could follow
a trail, build a campfire in the open, take care of himself competently.
He was a dead shot with rifle or revolver; in fact, as he grew to manhood
he established a reputation for quickness on the draw. He was always
boyishly vain of that accomplishment. But he never did well with the
shotgun, and he explained this in terms which illuminate one of the fundamentals of his character.

"I think it was because I have never cared about shooting things, and
killing birds with small shot always has been repugnant to me. I have
hunted larger game with the rifle, but hunting is not a sport that appeals
to me. I learned to shoot because everybody in our country knew how to
shoot. It was something worth knowing, too, and I have never regretted
the time spent on it. There is always a chance it may be useful."

A year or so after the Civil War, when business conditions in Texas
had returned to an approximation of normal, Thomas William House
took his family to England for a protracted visit and settled in Bath. It
was a breathtaking experience, as disturbing as exhilarating, for a small
boy with an extremely sensitive mind. To him, as a matter of course,
the way he and other Texan boys played was the logical way for all
boys to play. But when Ed and his brother James, six years older, were

entered in an English school, the first thing they discovered was that their rough ways were not popular with their new classmates. They were continually in hot water, and Mammy Eliza, Ed's Negro nurse, was at her wits' end to keep him presentable.

There is a photograph of these two, young Ed and Mammy Eliza, taken at this time. Mammy Eliza is sitting, dressed in her Sunday best, even to mitts, staring into the camera lens with the calm inscrutability of the Negro slave to whom slavery was an honor not lightly to be held. One arm is clasped around the waist of the tense little boy who stands very straight beside her. His right hand is clenched in a fist. His beautifully modeled head is held proudly. His mouth is quirked into an expression of resentment and defiance, and this, too, is the expression of his deep-set eyes. He looks as though he might be nine years old. I wish I had asked him. But if you study the picture carefully you can discern something of what Ed House was going through that year in Bath.

What he learned from the unfamiliar routine of an English school was negligible. The Bath episode is important in his story only because here were planted the seeds of that partiality for Britain, his father's homeland, which undoubtedly exerted a profound influence upon his mental attitude in after years. He didn't enjoy it at the moment. Like his brother, he longed for the freedom and the wild, lawless vigor of frontier Texas. But when he sailed for home there was smoldering deep down within him that unconquerable nostalgia which was to fetch him back again and again, and lead him to serve Britain with a loyalty second only to that he accorded his own country.

3

He was growing fast in these pre-adolescent years, promising to match his stalwart brothers in height and strength. Then, in his twelfth year, he suffered an accident which affected his whole future life more drastically than anything which was to befall him. He was in a swing when a rope broke, and he fell heavily on his head. Brain fever developed. He was saved from death by a narrow margin, and on top of that he contracted malaria. He was never to be strong again. And as if this handicap were not enough, several years later a heat stroke gave warning that he must be cautious of the Texas sun. He was not an invalid. He refused to accept that status. But only by ceaseless vigilance over his health could he expect to grow to manhood and play a man's part in the world.

It is a tribute to his will power and self-control that he lived into his eightieth year, that he accomplished as much as any man of his generation, and that up to the last two years of his life he maintained a schedule of work which would have killed any ordinary individual by sixty-five. But he could never hope to hold political office, with its ceaseless pressure of obligations and demands for public appearances. Of course, he didn't realize at once all that this implied. He simply knew that it was no longer possible for him to meet other boys on equal terms. It was four years afterward that he accepted—without bitterness—the fact that it was useless for Ed House to plan to make himself Governor of Texas and President of the United States.

On top of his physical afflictions, a sore trial to a boy of his age, his mother died when he was fourteen. It was decided to send him to a school in the mountains of Virginia, with the idea that the bracing air would be beneficial to his health. It was a good idea, but he hated the school more keenly, apparently, than any person or institution that figured in his life. He would never identify it. What irked him most was the brutal hazing, which he denounced in terms unmeasured for him. He submitted once. Before he was attacked a second time he had equipped himself with a pistol and a large knife, and small as he was, succeeded in convincing the school bullies that he was quite prepared to kill anyone who laid a finger on him.

It was a relief to him to be transferred to Hopkins Grammar School at New Haven for preparation to enable him to enter the Yale class of 1881. He was seventeen, and he owned, in discussing this period of his life, that he was a very poor student.

"I have been called a great student. As a matter of fact, I didn't give a hang for my studies in school or college. I got through them as best I could. I wasn't interested in them. There were just two subjects that did interest me from my childhood—politics and history—and I read everything on those subjects that I could get my hands on. But I cared about nothing else."

There is no reason to dispute his own estimate of himself. At Hopkins he soon discovered that he was actually more deficient than he had supposed. All he had learned at the Virginia school was practically worthless—except what he had taught himself. He was conspicuously lacking in Latin and Greek, which were requirements at Yale; and as the school year progressed he became discouraged about the possibility of his being able to pass the entrance examinations. But with the resourcefulness which was one of his most remarkable traits he secured a compensating value. He made friends with a classmate, Oliver T. Morton, son of Senator Oliver P. Morton, who had been the great Civil War Governor of Indiana.

New vistas, infinitely more attractive than those offered by school or college, opened before him. Senator Morton was one of the leaders of Congress. He was also a prominent candidate for the Republican nomination for the Presidency in the campaign of 1876. Young Morton had the entrée into the inner circles of New York and Washington. He took his friend everywhere he went, and the political education of Edward Mandell House was fairly launched. House, naturally, was a Democrat, and his personal sympathy was engaged to Tilden; but with the hearty impartiality of youth he was almost equally partisan in his feeling toward Senator Morton, and shared fully the disappointment of young Morton when the telegraph operator at New Haven showed them the dispatch notifying that the Republican Convention had compromised on Rutherford B. Hayes.

That summer Ed House hung around Democratic Headquarters in the Everett House in Union Square whenever he could get to New York. He saw all he could of Tilden, and marveled that a man so frail could support a Presidential campaign. Perhaps it stimulated the secret ambition he continued to cherish on his own behalf. If it did, the ambition was to be quashed within the next few months. He attended every political rally he could reach, and listened with a precociously critical appreciation to the cloud-tearing spellbinders of the day. After the election he shamelessly deserted his studies, and accompanied Morton to Washington as often as possible to listen to the debates in Congress and the proceedings of the Electoral Commission which was canvassing the disputed ballots in the Southern States.

He met General and Mrs. Grant, and several members of the Cabinet, and always spoke appreciatively of the General as a very great and simple man and soldier, a conqueror who had known how to be merciful. It was at this time, too, I think, that Ed House became interested in Lincoln, the spell of whose authentic personality was still vibrant in Washington. One of his earliest recollections was of his father coming into the house in Galveston, and telling his mother of Lincoln's assassination, with the remark that it was the worst thing that so far had happened to the South. Now, as a reflective youth, he heard at first hand of the dead President from men who had known Lincoln in the years of his travail.

"Perhaps the greatest American who ever lived," was his mature judgment.

But I think, yet am not positive, that by this he meant the greatest American who was not formed during the Colonial period.

"The closest to the people," he added. "A consummate politician. But if he had lived he would probably have been the worst-hated of all the Presidents because he would not have permitted the persecution of the South. He would have been lucky to escape the impeachment that was brought against Johnson. And what would the Republican party have done without the Lincoln myth?"

Ed House learned more during those visits to Washington than he was to learn in college. For one thing, he learned to recognize his own deficiencies. He saw that few public men could speak well, and that of those who could, hardly one combined excellence in delivery with first-rate substance of material. He knew himself to be incapable of excelling in either quality, and he was determined not to attempt any role in which he could not be best. For another thing, privileged as he had been to consort with the national leaders of both parties, he saw that two or three men in the House, an equal number in the Senate, and the President, ran the Government. These two circumstances, plus his lack of physical stamina, confirmed him in the decision never to try for public office. Better far, he reasoned with uncanny shrewdness for a boy of eighteen, to shape his life so that he might become one of those policy-makers and counselors who sit behind the scenes and inspire the course of events. He was the more determined in this program because he was passionately interested in improving the efficiency of government. It seemed to him, even at this age, that it was more important to invent and build the engine than it was to run it.

But in the meantime he and his friend Morton were compelled to realize—not too suddenly—that they had devoted so much of their energy to studying practical politics, instead of Latin and Greek, that the Hopkins faculty were more than dubious of their ability to enter Yale with the class of '81. Possibly it was this very practicality of their recent surroundings which prompted them to a solution of their problem. They turned their backs on Yale, engaged a tutor, and had no difficulty in satisfying the entrance requirements of Cornell.

Here Ed House spent two of the happiest years of his life, satisfied to skin by examinations with a little intensified cramming at the last minute, and enjoying himself at leisure in the two subjects which absorbed him. The picture I have of him during the Cornell years I obtained from a classmate, a distinguished surgeon in New York, whose eyes sparkled as he talked:

"My recollection of Ed House as a college chum is that he always played the part of a quiet peacemaker in college rows, and established with us a high reputation for kindly diplomacy of a high order. He was an Alpha Delta Phi, I remember, and a valued member of our chapter. Whenever there was a disturbance Ed would silently appear, and in a few minutes—you wouldn't know exactly how it happened—the trouble would be over. He had an exceptionally sweet disposition, and got on with everybody. As I recall, he was not the friend merely of a set of men, but of many fellows of a wide range of tastes and habits. And he was everlastingly exploring some book. One of my earliest remembrances of him is that of a quiet youth, reading a ponderous volume of de Tocqueville's *Democracy in America* as he walked along the street. That picture has stuck in my mind for forty years, I suppose. He liked especially to start discussions on current topics in the news, political matters in this country or abroad, analyze what had been done, and then start out to develop a plan which would have worked better.

" 'They ought not to have done that,' he would say. 'Now, this would be much better. Listen to me, now.'

"And then he would launch into his own views, and he made us listen and debate them with him. He always liked to hear what other people thought."

It would be a mistake, however, to give the impression that Ed House had turned his back on Texas throughout the years at school and college in Virginia and the North. A part, at least, of each summer he spent at home, familiarizing himself with the details of his father's vast plantation, which spread into two counties, or, in the town house at Houston, sitting by and listening to the famous men who never passed through without stopping for a visit with Thomas William House—such men as Jefferson Davis, forgotten in the bustling North, but wearing with dignity in the dreamland of the Confederacy the martyr's crown his persecution had won for him in the esteem of the people who had called him President.

He was not as subject to heat prostration as he became afterward—or perhaps the arrogance of youth refused to admit it if he was—and traveled widely in the vast realm, really a nation within a nation, that was frontier Texas, already evolving, so imperceptibly men failed to notice it, into a land of law and order. He came to know men like Captain King, whose principality is still the largest area under family control in the United States, and other ranchers, tall, red-burned, slow-spoken men, with squinty eyes, who ranged countless herds in the far-away Panhandle. He knew the western end of the State when Judge Bean, of Langtry, was "the law west of the Pecos." He knew the old breed of Rangers, men like Captain Bill McDonald, to whom he was plain Ed so long as Captain Bill lived. He knew gamblers and buffalo hunters and town

MR. HOUSE AT THIRTY-SEVEN WHEN HE WAS ELECTING A DYNASTY
OF TEXAS GOVERNORS

marshals and bad men and good men—and he learned something from all of them.

He saw men shot down in cold blood, and he saw men, who deserved it, executed with impromptu efficiency in the street. And like all young Texans of his generation, he practiced the quick draw for hours in front of a mirror, although the only time he might have needed to put his practice to the proof he didn't have a chance to test it. He had gone to visit a college friend at Breckenridge, Colorado, a mining camp. He was wearing an overcoat, and for that reason carried his revolver in a side pocket. A man he had never seen before entered a saloon, and without warning commenced to vilify him in violent terms. Ed House had his gun cocked, and was about to shoot from his pocket, when the bartender vaulted between the two. It was a case of mistaken identity. "In five seconds more I would have killed him," he remarked of the incident in 1917.

That was in 1879. He was twenty-one years old, two years older than Billy the Kid when the greatest man-killer of the frontier died. And the self-control Ed House demonstrated in holding his fire in that situation was a forecast of the characteristic which was to lift him to a unique place in American history. He was never afraid to wait. He preferred to let "the other feller," as he said, make the first mistake. Then, if he had to move, he moved like chain-lightning. He always had that five seconds to spare.

Perhaps the reason was that he had seen so much of sudden death loosed by uncontrolled passions. He could remember two unpremeditated duels on his father's plantation, in which three men out of four were killed, in each case because of an idle word and the Texan frontier code that any slight must be wiped out in blood. A savage code, but one which, he used to say, prompted men to measure their words and practice courtesy.

Previous reference has been made to the sensitivity of his mind. All those who knew him closely must have marked this trait. His mind was like a photographic plate, registering every variation of light and shadow. He was keenly perceptive to shades of personality, and similarly, possessed the knack of sifting instinctively true facts from those warped by prejudice. I believe he owed this mainly to the bilateral scope of his education. He was as familiar with the easy, sheltered culture of the East as he was with the crude, raw life of the frontier. As a youth, he came to know the complex financial structure of the older-settled States just as he knew the more primitive economy of Texas. It was not strange that in maturity he could focus his mind constructively upon the problems of the United States as an entirety, differentiating their several aspects according to social and climatic conditions and historic background. He thought of his country not from the viewpoint of one State or region, but as an empire presenting as many conflicting needs and antagonisms as the continent of Europe.

4

Ed House's political studies at Cornell were cut short by the death of his father in 1880. Whether he liked it or not, the vague ambitions which had stirred him to restlessness on the campus beside Lake Cayuga must be postponed until he had mastered the task of managing his competence, a task in which, naturally, he was guided by the advice of his brothers, who were twelve and fifteen years older than himself. Thomas William House had built up a substantial and diverse fortune in the eventful years since 1836. In the final settlement of the estate, three of the sons bought out the other heirs, Thomas William, Jr., taking over the banking interests, John the sugar lands, and Ed the cotton plantations.

The youngest son's portion, carefully handled, brought in about $25,000 a year. It is significant of his attitude toward money—an attitude which he testified his father taught him—that he never tried substantially to increase this income while he was in public life, although its purchasing power diminished steadily throughout the ensuing forty years. The charge that he had profited financially from his connection with politics, both in Texas and in national affairs, touched him to the quick, and drew from him a statement, unsolicited by me, which set forth his actual standing in 1918, when his capital was relatively unimpaired, and sketched his personal philosophy of service. It is cited here, chronologically out of place, because it dramatizes so clearly his unshaken faithfulness to the ideals of his youth. The Edward Mandell House who, as a stripling, decided that $25,000 a year was ample to afford him leisure for impersonal service to his State and country, was the same person who attained a power second only to the President's and held it as a sacred trust.

"I have no more money today," he said, and he spoke with rare feeling, "than my father left me. They say I am a banker. That is not true, and it never was. I got out of my father's bank as soon as I could. At this moment I have about $3000 of stock in a bank in Austin and several thousands more in a bank in Houston. My bank-stock holdings may aggregate $15,000 to $20,000. I doubt if they ever exceeded $7000 after I disposed of the interests my father left me, until recently, when I sold my home in Austin and took in payment for it $12,500 of bank stock. Formerly all my money was invested in Texas cotton lands, but several years ago, when I found my time was becoming more and more occupied with the work of the Administration, I sold off most of my property, and the major portion of my income now comes from the interest on the notes I took in payment for my land.

"People talk about my connection with Wall Street and the big banking houses. They seem to think I must get some sort of a shady rake-off for my services. It is as pitiful as it is despicable. Why, I can show you without fear the source of every penny of my income! The only bonds I buy are those of public-service corporations over which municipalities have control. The only Government bonds I own are a small block of Liberties, purchased for the same patriotic reason which animated millions of other Americans.

"If I wished to make money out of my position, I could do it easily. With my knowledge of what is happening, and what is going to happen, I am in a far better position than the powers of Wall Street, themselves, to take advantage of market conditions. But I will have nothing to do with that sort of thing. If I wished to make money dishonestly, I could make plenty of it without Wall Street's assistance. It is difficult for some people to understand that I have enough money for my wants. I have never accepted any salary or retainer from any Government, except that when I have gone abroad for the President on official missions my expenses have been paid.*

"People ask what I get out of it. My answer is that the only work that is worth while, the only work that brings satisfaction, is the work that is unselfish. I say this without desiring to be ostentatious. Examine yourself, and you will find it to be true. Consider men like General Goethals or Charles W. Eliot. Imagine the wonderful pleasure, the heart-warming satisfaction, Goethals gained from building the Panama Canal on his meager salary of an engineer officer of the regular army. Or the satisfaction Dr. Eliot must have derived during the years he devoted to Harvard University. Take a man like Harriman. I have always thought that he was not guided solely by personal ambition in his career. Underneath all his achievements was the desire to do things, and his gratification in accomplishment would have been much greater if he had not had to acquire a fortune along with it.

"Some people who do not care for pecuniary rewards, on the other hand,

* As a member of the Commission to Negotiate Peace, having status as a Minister Extraordinary on Special Mission, he received $10,000 a year, the salary of the grade. On several previous occasions, when the Government paid the traveling expenses of his party abroad, he insisted that the State Department send with him an auditor in charge of disbursements.

do like the purely honorary badges of success. I happen not to care for the badges, either. Honors are all very well in their way, but I get more pleasure out of something I have done without reward, other than the appreciation of my friends, than I could from all the money and decorations in this country and Europe."

The next milestone in his life was his marriage on August 4, 1881, to Miss Loulie Hunter, of Hunter, Texas. A beautiful woman, charming, socially tactful, a hostess such as only the Old South produced, Mrs. House was reminiscent of the great ladies of the ante-bellum generation, women of the type of Mrs. Clement Clay, of Alabama, whose husband shared Jefferson Davis's imprisonment, or Mrs. Roger A. Pryor, wife of that gallant Virginian, last of the duelists under the Code, journalist, soldier and jurist, who had disdained to contest with Edmund Ruffin the dubious honor of firing the first shot at Sumter.

They traveled for a year in Europe, the first of many pilgrimages in search of personalities rather than landmarks, and on their return to Houston decided to move to Austin, partly for the sake of his health, partly to be closer to the Public Land Office in order that he might have better facilities for developing his holdings. But the major consideration in the back of his mind was that Austin, as the State capital, was the center of political activities and offered the best field for studying the methods by which men climbed to power.

It cannot be emphasized too strongly that at this early age he had decided that he preferred to conserve his fortune, to organize it so that, properly administered, it could be relied upon to produce the income he had fixed upon as necessary to his needs. He had no desire to add to it. He wished simply to be free to devote himself, with complete independence, to influencing the election to office of men of the highest possible integrity and intelligence, and the enactment through their efforts of the most constructive and progressive legislation the voters could comprehend.

That was the cornerstone of his personal philosophy in the twenties. Thenceforward he lived in harmony with a definite rhythm of purpose: Service. And he never wavered in loyalty to that purpose. It would take him more than thirty years to attain the final objective he had set himself, but he attained it. And then, glimpsing by chance a farther and a nobler goal, he preached its excellence to his fellows, and with his first and—as he thought—knightliest friend, he led them in the greatest of the Crusades to win it. But too many were denied the clarity of his vision, the selflessness of his faith. Or so History teaches us at this reading. He, himself, was never content with History's current page.

This, however, is looking into the future, of which Ed House in 1882 had only the faintest glimmer, even as we who have survived him are unable to see beyond our individual interpretations of the day's news. We *think*—we do not know. It is a tribute to his uncanny perceptiveness that so much of what he thought turned out to be the fabric of destiny.

Book 3

Four Governors

In Austin the Houses lived much the same life as other well-to-do young couples of the urban South. Two daughters were born to them, which added to their happiness, and they found ample relaxation from domesticity in the simple, easily conservative society of the little capital, where "everyone knew everyone else." Whatever chance there might have been of boredom was mitigated by summer trips North or abroad. Their comfortable home, with its wide porches, was a port of call for innumerable relatives, friends and acquaintances, for Mr. House maintained the tradition of hospitality established by his father, and was eager to explore every intelligent mind he encountered.

Ostensibly a cotton planter, he spent very little time on his land. He had a tiny office near the Capitol, its one sign of occupancy a calling-card pasted on the door, where Major Edward Sammons, his secretary and accountant, conducted the essential business of the estate. And with his habitual abhorrence of details, he hired the best agriculturist he could find, a man named William Malone, to supervise the work on his farms. It was the same system he afterwards employed in politics and diplomacy. He worked out broad policies for which he held himself responsible. The application of these policies he left to men he felt he could trust.

His spare time, which was ample, he devoted to books and the study of human nature and how most surely to influence it. This last was a subject which always absorbed him and of which he became a master. His interest in books was exceedingly catholic. He was well-read in history, biography, politics and economics. He had a nice taste in poetry and essays—Charles Lamb was one of his favorites. He liked purely conventional fiction, but he had no real appreciation for it outside the narrow groove of tradition. It was an amusing sidelight on his character that, although he was a genuine liberal—many people would say a radical— in politics and economics, he was highly conventional in a social sense. Rabelais and Lawrence Sterne were closed preserves to him, and he was unable to understand the modern realists.

I have always thought that one of the reasons why he and Woodrow Wilson sparked at their first meeting was his familiarity, not only with Mr. Wilson's monumental *History of the American People*—an essential point of view which charmed him—but with such favorites of Mr. Wilson's as Bagehot, Mill, de Tocqueville and Bryce. One of his greatest admirers and staunchest friends in later life was Sir Horace Plunkett, who might fairly be said to have ranked with Lord Bryce as among the foremost constructive thinkers of their period.

All his life he enjoyed beyond anything else the company and conversation of authors, playwrights and professors—not pedants, but those academic thinkers who put abstract facts to practical usage. It meant something that his intimates included Mark Twain, O. Henry, Augustus Thomas, Fannie Hurst, Albert Bigelow Paine and a myriad others. He often said that he wished he had turned to writing in his youth, and as a matter of fact, in 1912 he perpetrated anonymously a novel, *Philip Dru,* which is probably one of the worst ever published, but is nevertheless of abiding interest as a statement of his political philosophy as applied to the Government of the United States, and as a forecast of the important domestic legislation he helped the Wilson Administration to put through Congress within the next two years.*

I have said that "he was highly conventional in a social sense." That is one of those truisms which are dangerous when expressed as flat statements. In the politico-social sense he was highly radical, more than liberal, and he seems to have been so from his youth. He was a fearless thinker, utterly untrammeled by accepted conventions. For example, he was under no illusions as to the basic character of the American Constitution and the system of government it created. He believed that the Constitution, product of eighteenth-century minds and the quasi-classical, medieval conception of republics, was thoroughly outdated; that the country would be better off if the Constitution could be scrapped and rewritten. But as a realist he knew that this was impossible in the existing state of political education.

He realized, as do few Americans, that the Constitution, in practical effect, sets up a sovereignty of limited tenure, but limited only by the dangerous expedient of tradition. He did not find fault with the men who drafted the Constitution, because they were necessarily limited in their outlook by the historical knowledge available to them. There was no such thing as honestly responsible parliamentary government in the

* The apparent influence of *Philip Dru* upon Franklin D. Roosevelt's legislative program is discussed in a subsequent chapter.

eighteenth century. The English Parliament was the tool of the kings, their ministers and placemen. The prevailing conception of a Republic was essentially oligarchic. The one strikingly original idea the Constitution contained was the system of counterchecks and balances of power between the Executive, the Legislative and the Judicial divisions. And even this, he held, was dangerously topheavy in favor of the Executive. Given a strong Chief Executive and an emergency, and you had a concentration of dictatorial power in the hands of a President. This had happened in the cases of Jefferson, Jackson and Lincoln. It was to happen again in Mr. Wilson's second term. And before he died he was to watch with foreboding a similar exploitation of the Executive authority by the second Roosevelt.

He was concerned, too, by the lack of responsiveness to shifts in popular sentiment inherent in the American system, which made it possible for a President of one party to be faced by the impossibility of carrying out his policies because one or both houses of Congress had passed under the control of the opposition party. He was of the opinion that this was fair neither to the President nor to Congress nor to the people, who, since the President's election, must have reacted against his policies and yet be hamstrung in obtaining the measures they sought. It was, he believed, neither a republican nor a democratic system of government, and in the course of years he inclined toward the conviction that a parliamentary system would be preferable, provided the people could be brought to see the advantages accruing to them from prompt responsiveness to their desires at Washington.

He sums up this feeling in his book by having Philip Dru say that in the United States "we have been living under a Government of negation." The corrective measures he prescribed, through Dru as a mouthpiece, and occasionally in unwary moments of self-expression, were five in substance: the President's powers were to be limited—in effect he would become a figurehead, rather like the President of the French Republic; the active executive would be the chief of the Cabinet, appointed, of course, by the President; the Cabinet would be responsible to Congress; the members of the Cabinet would have seats in Congress, appearing in either House or Senate to debate legislation as required; the terms of members of Congress would be synchronized with the President's, but upon an adverse vote the Cabinet could advise the President to dissolve Congress and proclaim new elections.

The germs of these, and many other thoughts and speculations, were seething and bubbling in Mr. House's brain during the '80s and '90s. He loved to set up a theory and invite debate from hostile or critical minds. Sometimes an idea came to him clearcut and definite, and he hewed to it for years. More often its original shape was nebulous or inchoate. He scrutinized it from various angles, took it to pieces, refitted them together, offered it to be hammered by other men's conceptions, and perhaps either abandoned it or pondered it anew whenever occasion served. Throughout these years, as a young husband and father and landowner, he was carrying forward the self-education he had commenced in his youth. He was learning many things besides cotton planting and the technic of buying and selling land to advantage. And the sum of what he was learning amounted to practical politics, their application and practice.

He studied the political art from its lowest common denominator to the top, using the State of Texas as his laboratory. He studied the organization of the precinct, the voting district, the county, the city, with its peculiar problems; the influence of race and personality; the organization of committees and their operation; publicity and the psychology of the spoken word. He met and probed every politician, important and unimportant, who came his way. He made friends with as many people as he could, invariably sympathetic and unostentatious, more anxious to discover what they thought than to tell them his views. But each one who left any impression on him he ticketed in his mind for future reference. For he soon concluded that it was impossible to judge any man from what other people reported of him.

"Judging men you don't know is just like walking through a strange country," he used to say. "Every rolling swell in the land you see ahead of you looks more inviting than the hill you are standing on. But when you get to the next elevation, you find the view just the same—in fact, as like as not you will be disappointed because it is no better. I have found that if you allow yourself to become enthusiastic about a man you don't know, when you do come to know him he will seem disappointing. And that is your fault as much as his."

In 1892 he was ready to launch his first attempt. He had long since decided that it was a waste of time for his purposes to play small politics. He wanted to influence measures that would count in the evolution of Texas. Also, without any egotism, he felt that there were no foemen worthy of his steel in the limited arena of county and municipal affairs. He would reelect a Governor, who was conceded by his supporters to be doomed to defeat, who was opposed by the railroads and the big corporations, who had no money behind him and was being attacked by every daily newspaper in the State.

How? To quote one of the maxims he liked to toss off in casual conversation:

"Politics is largely a question of organization. You've got to have a good, clean feller to put before the voters. After that it's organization."

2

In Texas, in 1892, the railroads and the so-called "big" corporations were on the verge of obtaining complete control of the State government. The corporations were a minor factor in the situation. It was the railroads, and notably Collis P. Huntington's Southern Pacific, which threatened to transform Texas into a feudal appendage of their legal departments, exactly as Huntington had done in the case of California. Texas was saved from this fate by the intervention of Mr. House, who was then thirty-four years old.

The Governor of Texas was James W. Hogg, a large, fearless, aggressive and somewhat blustery individual, who had been fighting unsuccessfully through his first term for the establishment of a State Railroad Commission and a Stock and Bond Law to regulate the issue of securities against railroad property in the State. Mr. House liked him personally, and believed in what he was trying to do. In the summer of 1892 the feeling in political circles was that he would be defeated for renomination—in Texas, of course, the equivalent of reelection—although it was a custom in the State to renominate every Governor for a second term. His opponent, Judge George Clark, of Waco, had the support of the conservative interest, and as has been said, of the important newspapers, together with a generous field chest.

Mr. House went to Governor Hogg and offered to help in his campaign, with the one proviso that the help must be anonymous. Mr. House wanted the authority, not the credit. Governor Hogg accepted the offer. A committee was selected, with General W. R. Hamby, a friend of the Governor and Mr. House, as chairman, and Mr. House started to work. The railroads, the corporations, the bankers and a majority of the business men—in other words, the larger centers of population—were against them. But the Governor stood well with the farmers, and he was widely supported by the rural weekly newspapers. The lack of money was minimized by volunteer help, none of which was obtained by pre-convention promises of patronage, a principle Mr. House followed in all his subsequent campaigns. "It always makes trouble," he commented on this typical dodge of American politics. "The same office gets promised to two or more men, they meet and compare notes, and then you have enemies instead of friends."

The tactics Mr. House employed were the same tactics he used afterwards to elect and reelect Woodrow Wilson President of the United States, the second time against almost insuperable odds. He and his emissaries went into the counties and organized sentiment for the election of Hogg delegates in the primaries. They built up that sentiment practically vote by vote. No detail was too small to merit their attention. Yet up to the last minute it was taken for granted that Judge Clark would control the State convention. When his supporters discovered on the convention floor that a majority of the delegates were for Hogg they bolted and gave Clark an outlaw nomination, which was endorsed by the Republicans, likewise dominated by the railroad interests. The ensuing campaign was a bitter one, but Hogg was reelected by a decisive majority.*

This campaign, the first in which Mr. House was the guiding genius, is notable for several aspects. It was successful, as was every campaign he conducted; he worked independently of any existing political machine, a second feature to be found, in greater or lesser degree, in all of his campaigns; his participation was unofficial and unpublicized—fewer than fifty politicians in the State were aware of it; success was predicated on the basis of painstakingly elaborate organization of the precinct or election district, as it is called in the North; there were no advance commitments of the candidate. Finally, the measures in behalf of which he made the endeavor were enacted into law. The power of the railroads was curbed, and Texas had the honor of leading the van of States in securing such constructive legislation.

The Southern Pacific and its allies fought the constitutionality of the new regulatory laws up to the United States Supreme Court, and were defeated by the legal ability of Charles A. Culberson, who had been elected Attorney-General on the ticket with Governor Hogg. He was a young man of about Mr. House's age, whose father had served as chairman of the Judiciary Committee of the House of Representatives under

---

* It was Governor Hogg who conferred the title of Colonel upon Mr. House, much to his disgust. The Governor sent with the commission a dress uniform of the rank, aiguilettes, epaulettes, gold braid and all, which Mr. House bestowed upon Allen, his Negro coachman, who immediately rose to the supreme grand mastership of his lodge. Notwithstanding this infliction, Mr. House entertained a high opinion of Governor Hogg's abilities, rating him as superior to Sam Houston in the galaxy of Texas notables. He believed that the Governor would have risen to national prominence had he entered Congress instead of devoting his capacities to amassing a fortune.

Cleveland. When 1894 rolled around, and the question arose of a successor to Governor Hogg, Mr. House's choice was Culberson, as an outstanding liberal and the man best fitted to supervise the enforcement of the new laws. Governor Hogg, however, had chosen for his successor the veteran John H. Reagan, last survivor of the Cabinet of Jefferson Davis, who had patriotically resigned his office as Senator from Texas to accept the chairmanship of the State Railroad Commission.

It was a difficult situation. Judge Reagan represented what might be called the Old Guard of the liberal movement in the State, Culberson the Young Guard. Mr. House, possibly because of his age, thought that the future of the liberal movement could most efficiently be served by giving the nomination to the representative of the younger element of the party, who, also, was more intimately acquainted with the mechanism of the laws he considered all-important at the moment. Governor Hogg was indignant over this difference in opinion, and in a conference which was momentous—for Mr. House, at any rate—attempted to roar down his former manager. Mr. House countered with the quiet logic which was his forte, insisting that it would be wicked to divide the liberal element in face of a conservative opposition as strong and compact as it had been two years previously, and that of the two candidates Culberson was most likely to be able to make good the results for which they were striving. Governor Hogg demonstrated his magnanimity by abandoning his position and persuading Judge Reagan to withdraw. More, the man who had been chosen to nominate the veteran concluded a speech the Convention supposed to be in favor of Reagan with a peroration seconding Culberson.

Except for this demonstration of Mr. House's gift for conciliation, the Culberson campaign is chiefly significant as the only one in which he assumed the active chairmanship of the committee in charge. "For the life of me, I can't see why I did it," he said regretfully when he was telling the story. "The chairmen of political committees are usually figureheads. Most of them are forgotten by the public a few months after their candidates have won or lost. And the publicity was a nuisance to me."

Culberson was duly elected and reelected, but at the end of the four years Mr. House was dismayed to find himself again in conflict with his political protégé. Governor Culberson wished to advance the claims of his Attorney-General, M. M. Crane. Mr. House opposed the nomination, principally on the ground that there was growing to be a tradition in Texas politics that the Attorney-General of the retiring Governor should have first claim as his successor. Mr. House thought that this was a dangerous idea, tending to create a self-perpetuating, demagogic machine of administration. He was vigorously opposed to all self-perpetuating political machines, but particularly to machines of this type, which conceivably might become intrenched in the actual administration of government.

The problem posed for him by Governor Culberson's stand was an unusually embarrassing one, despite the absence of personal feeling on either side, inasmuch as he himself had violated his own precept in supporting Culberson as Attorney-General for reasons which still seemed to him at once extraordinary and sufficient. Furthermore, the evidence available indicated that Crane's position was all but unassailable. Mr. House was obliged to assume that the Governor's candidate had 80 per cent of the chances for success, while in addition to this fact the opposition vote within the party was split between Lieutenant-Governor Jester and Colonel Wynne, of Fort Worth. Mr. House decided to ignore both of the opposition candidates, and brought forward against Crane Major Joseph Sayers, a Confederate veteran with a long record of service in Congress.

Crane undoubtedly could rely upon a majority of delegates to the Convention, reckoning upon all the counties, but he labored under the disadvantage of being uncertain how many counties he could absolutely control. Major Sayers started from scratch with control of the delegations from the counties in his Congressional district and a few others in which Mr. House had personal interest. The Crane faction hesitated to call the county primaries, as was permissible under the State electoral law, in order to see what the Sayers faction intended. So Mr. House responded by calling primaries in one safe Sayers county after another until, toward the end of the Sayers strength, he had bluffed Crane into withdrawing his candidacy.

The Spanish-American War was being waged that year, and Major Sayers was unable to abandon his duties in the House of Representatives. Mr. House elected him without his making a single speech, without his presence in the State. And not a word was printed in the newspapers of the part the Austin cotton planter played in this, perhaps the most crucial of his political battles. I say most crucial because after that battle no politician in Texas seriously challenged Mr. House's dictatorship in State elections, and what was even more important, it made his name and talent known in the inner circles of the Democratic national organization. Governor Culberson revealed his own fairmindedness toward the man who had defeated his candidate by requesting Mr. House to direct his campaign for the United States Senate. He was elected to the first of four terms, and emulated his father by serving as chairman of the Judiciary Committee of the upper chamber.

Major Sayers was reelected Governor in 1900, and in 1902 Mr. House directed the campaign of W. H. D. Lanham, another Confederate veteran and member of Congress, who, with proper coaching, rode rough-shod over opposition. This was the last of the House campaigns in Texas. He had proved his political theories to his satisfaction, and he believed that it was unhealthy for the public good for one man to exercise supreme power for more than eight or ten years, a belief he applied likewise to the Presidency. "There is a natural law behind the two-term tradition," he declared. "No man can continue to produce original policies for more than eight years, and few men are good for four years of worthwhile ideas."

Another consideration was that he had inspired and helped in the enactment of all the progressive ideas in legislation he thought Texas was capable of digesting at the time. His State, he asserted proudly, had been foremost in implementing liberal laws in the 1890s. "We were ahead of all of them in railroad legislation," he declared. "Governor Hogg put through the Australian ballot for communities of more than 10,000 population. And you take municipal reform. Why, we had commission government in Galveston before Iowa or Wisconsin or any of the Middle Western States attempted it."

Above and beyond these reasons for relinquishing his dominance in State politics, he wanted to try his theories in a national campaign. Already in 1900, Hogg had written him to "go to the front where you belong." But he was determined, whatever else he did, not to work actively for any Presidential candidate whose ideals and policies failed to command his complete loyalty. He would vote for the nominee of his party, yes, but he would not go out and canvass the country for the nominee unless he believed that the nominee could and should be elected.

3

The period between 1902 and 1911 Mr. House described as the "twilight years" of his life. During this period he was seeking a man of sufficient independence and personality to break the spell which William Jennings Bryan exerted over the Democratic party. He liked and admired Bryan personally; the Nebraskan's staunch liberalism and progressiveness, his feeling for the common man, for the rights of labor, his hatred of the concentration of economic power in the hands of a group of New York bankers, all these qualities appealed to Mr. House. But he thoroughly disliked Bryan's currency doctrine, calling for free coinage of silver at the ratio of 16 to 1 of gold. He never ceased to dislike and distrust this doctrine. It was no more palatable to him at the end of his life when Franklin D. Roosevelt recognized it substantially by a policy of indirection; his answer was a quizzical look when you suggested to him that at least it insured the Administration the support of the silver States.

"I know, I know," he'd say.

He never needed the monosyllabic affirmative to imply his agreement with a proposition. He could use silence so that it was weighty with dissent or sound louder than a thundered "yes." And, radical as many bankers thought he was in his theories of currency control, he was as conservative as any of them in his belief in the gold standard, just as he was in his conviction that a promise by a Government to pay in gold was an obligation which could not be broken without the taint of dis- honor.

This mental attitude—frankly, the attitude of a man of moderate wealth, whose income depended upon the soundness of the nation's business structure—necessarily sapped the confidence he might otherwise have had in Bryan's fitness for the Presidency, despite the apparently contradictory fact that his view of party regularity led him to vote for Bryan in 1896, 1900 and 1908, and to acquiesce in, if not to approve, the sending of free-silver delegations from Texas to the 1896 and 1900 con- ventions. He analyzed his own feelings in these words:

"I didn't think Bryan could win on the free-silver issue. But at the same time I didn't think it was fair for me to refuse to play with Bryan's crowd just because they had gotten what they wanted, which happened to be what I didn't want them to get. I have always been a worker for the party, and perhaps as much for that reason as any other I have always been regular. I can't conceive myself voting anything but a Democratic ticket."

And here he paused, taking stock of what he had said.

"But that doesn't alter my conviction that the salvation of the country is the great body of independent voters. Where would we be if every man voted rigidly either a Republican or Democratic ticket? If we had no silent body ready to curb abuses of power, no matter what party was responsible for the evil? No, I am regular because, taking part as I do in the direction of the party's affairs, it is only right for me to abide by the party's decisions, its mistakes as well as its achievements. But the independent voter has my admiration and respect. He is the highest type of good citizen."

Mr. House first met Bryan in Houston in 1897. He had received an intimation in 1896 that his participation in the national campaign would be welcomed, but had declined for the reasons given above. At the same time he was anxious to determine more positively through personal contact whether his misgivings as to Bryan's political character were justified. He observed nothing to shake his original impression, and a second and more extended intercourse with the Commoner served to confirm rather than to weaken it.

This came about through the illness of the Bryans' daughter, Grace, which led them to spend the winter of 1898-99 in Austin. Governor Hogg and Mr. House secured them a home next door to Mr. House's, and there was continual visiting back and forth through the hedge which separated the properties. The intimacy between the two families created opportunities for long discussions of the impending campaign, in which it was certain that Bryan would be the Democratic candidate.

"I was amazed to see how lacking he was in political sagacity and common sense," Mr. House said. "Mrs. Bryan was much more practical than he. She was open to advice and suggestion. But I honestly believe that Bryan never altered an idea after he had formed an opinion on it. It was his weakness and his strength."

So again, in 1900, Mr. House resisted the urgence of Governor Hogg and other friends, and abstained from active participation in national affairs. He was a good waiter, one of the best in creation. He waited a third time in 1904 because he didn't approve of Alton B. Parker and the temporary triumph of the Eastern conservatives in the party's councils, which had alienated the sympathy of the West and guaranteed Theodore Roosevelt's election. He had no intention of squandering his energies upon a struggle which was hopeless beyond challenge, or upon a candidate who would be unresponsive to the current of liberalism he sensed to be rising higher beneath the surface of the nation's life with the passage of every year.

In 1908 Bryan's forces regained control of the Convention, and Mr. House stood aside for the same reasons which had influenced him in 1896 and 1900. The man who could lift the Democratic party out of the slough in which it had been floundering since Cleveland's retirement must be an intelligently constructive liberal, capable of appealing to both the sense and the imagination of men in all sections and of all classes. A man, to be sure, who would be accepted by the Solid South. But Mr. House, for a Southerner, entertained an unorthodox opinion of the Solid South. He thought—and the thought grew more positive as his experience broadened in later years—that the Solid South was an unhealthy

influence in the Democratic party. It was, as a unit, essentially conservative, and in a strictly party sense, the tail that wagged the dog. He had
a vision of his party's future in which the Solid South's support would
not be a prime necessity for Democratic success.

But this was very much a matter for the future. No man had appeared
on the political horizon by 1908 whose qualities matched the requisites
Mr. House had tentatively outlined to himself. Two years later it was
a different story. William J. Gaynor, who had made a deserved reputation as a Justice of the State Supreme Court, had been elected Mayor of
New York City the preceding November. Mr. House began to read
pithy, pungent statements by Mayor Gaynor, reports of municipal policies which indicated a clear-thinking, independent mind. A Democrat,
Gaynor had established his reputation as a young man by smashing the
John Y. McKane gang that had exerted a corrupt control over the old
city of Brooklyn before the consolidation of the Greater City.

He had been nominated for Mayor by Tammany Hall, but had waged
his campaign on the pledge that the nomination had come to him unsolicited, and that he was, and would be, independent of Tammany control. He demonstrated a picturesque, aggressive personality, a disregard
for precedents, a keen knowledge of the science of government, an adroit
flair for publicity and conspicuous wit as a public speaker. He was testy
and temperamental in disposition, in hot water continually; but he handled himself with a sang-froid which won the admiration of the cynical
population of the nation's largest city. His sympathy for the poor, his
ruthless repression of police brutality, his humanness, made him good
newspaper copy in the South and West. In short, he was that rarest of
New Yorkers, the man the remote States can understand. And best of
all, he was acceptable to Bryan, who had desired him for running mate
in 1908, a plan frustrated by hostile delegates who showed the Commoner
newspaper clippings purporting to prove that Gaynor had maligned the
Catholic Church, a traduction there was not time to disprove in those
hurly-burly days at Denver.

Impressed as he was, Mr. House abided by his political principle not to
form a definite judgment of any man's availability without a personal
inspection of him. When he was in New York, in the early summer of
1910, he arranged with the late James Creelman, president of the
Municipal Service Commission, to invite Judge Gaynor to a private
dinner at the Lotus Club. The evening was passed in intimate discussion, Mr. House seeking to estimate the qualities of the Mayor's mind
by probing his hobbies and special interests. Gaynor, as it happened,

showed at his best. He evinced none of the brusqueness and temperamental instability which were his chief faults as a public man.

"He was a most remarkable man," was Mr. House's verdict. "I have rarely met his equal for depth of learning in political and governmental problems."

Even more impressed than he had anticipated, Mr. House stated frankly to Gaynor his belief that the Mayor could obtain the Democratic nomination for President in 1912, *if*—and this if was all-important in Mr. House's opinion—he accepted the Democratic nomination for Governor that year and was elected. But right at this point in their deliberations Mayor Gaynor demonstrated the incorrigible eccentricity of his character. He would have nothing to do with the Governorship, he declared. The office of Mayor of New York City was infinitely more important than the office of Governor of the State of New York; he considered it the most important office in the country after the Presidency. And when Mr. House argued with him that, though this might be so, a majority of voters would prefer a Presidential nominee with the prestige of a triumph in a State election, Mayor Gaynor spiked the Texan's guns by asserting that Bryan had expressed agreement in his stand. He continued his objections, despite Mr. House's assertion that political history revealed not one President who had jumped from a Mayor's chair into the White House.

The two parted company in complete amity and mutual respect, but Mr. House had begun to doubt that the Mayor was of Presidential caliber. Then, on August 19, that summer, Gaynor was shot by a discharged city employee as he was standing on the deck of a liner bound for a vacation in Europe. The gallantry with which he withstood an almost fatal wound in the throat, plus the dramatic aspect of the episode, raised him in a week to the status of the most popular man in the country.

"He was shot into the Governorship," Mr. House put it.

As soon as Gaynor was well enough to give thought to a future beyond the foot of his bed of pain, Mr. House renewed the suggestion that he should announce himself a candidate for the Governorship. The effort was as fruitless as the first had been—and it is worth noting here that the Democratic candidate of that year, John A. Dix, by no means so strong or so well-known a personality, was duly elected. Gaynor would have swept the State with what afterward came to be known as "an Al Smith majority."

Mr. House, however, had acquired so much respect for the Mayor's courage and independence of thought, that he decided to forget his own doubts, and do what he could to make Gaynor more of a figure in the eyes of the South and West. Having first gained assurance that the suggestion would be welcomed, he called upon the Mayor by appointment, accompanied by Senator Culberson and Colonel R. M. Johnstone, subsequently Senator from Texas. They extended a formal invitation to address the Texas State Fair to be held at Dallas, as well as the Texas Legislature. These addresses, Mr. House knew, in the circumstances, would make Gaynor a household name in the Southwest, and would surely lead to similar invitations from other sections.

Perhaps only those who had any acquaintance with Mayor Gaynor can understand his conduct in this situation. His response to Mr. House's little committee was courteous and enthusiastic. He would be delighted to accept. It was left to him to answer formally the invitation from Dallas. But no written acceptance arrived, and after a lapse of some days a Texas newspaper editor wired the Mayor, inquiring if he was really coming. Gaynor's prompt response was that it was the first he had heard of the matter. This act of discourtesy wiped his name from the list of Presidential possibilities as soon as it was repeated in national political circles. Mr. House and his friends would have overlooked what they believed to be an error in political judgment in recognition of the Mayor's ability as a speaker, his really imposing manner and normally keen discernment of men's motives and capacities. But it was a horse of another color for a man in his position to insult so unnecessarily the people of a great State and their leaders. They knew that in existing conditions it would be fatal to the future of the Democratic party to put in the White House a man who could be guilty of such erratic conduct.

"It was one of the best illustrations I know of what instability can do to the fortunes of a really brilliant man," Mr. House said. "We elected Woodrow Wilson in 1912. There was no reason why, if he had been sensible, we couldn't have elected Gaynor. He was actually better known than Wilson."

4

Undiscouraged, and a little more certain of the kind of man essential to his purpose, Mr. House resumed his quest for a standard bearer. But this did not mean that during "the twilight years" he abandoned his primary interests in Texas or the extension of his ever-widening circle of friendships at home and abroad. It was in these years that he came to know, more or less closely, such men as Dr. Charles W. Eliot, of Harvard; George Lansbury, that staunch old Radical of England; Walter Hines Page, editor of *The World's Work* and a director of Doubleday,

Page & Company, the publishers; David F. Houston, president of the University of Texas; and Edward S. Martin, the wise and scholarly editor of *Life* in the great days of that magazine as a weapon of creative thought.

He took a great interest in the University of Texas and its problems, and made friends with many of its faculty, a member of which was his brother-in-law, Sidney A. Mezes. Dr. Mezes had married in 1895 Mrs. House's sister, Anna, and presently became dean, afterward president, and at a still later time president of the College of the City of New York, which he developed as a foremost custodian of liberalism. One of Mr. House's four Governors wished to appoint House a trustee of the university, an honor he refused because of his dislike for the routine of office.

This calls to attention the two corporation offices he held in these years, from both of which he disentangled himself as soon as possible. The first was with the Trinity and Brazos River Railway, a ninety-mile line which tapped the cotton country near Austin. Mr. House had perceived the need for a railroad to serve this area as a feeder for the main lines, but his chief idea in undertaking its construction was to give an object lesson to the big railroads in building and operating a road for profit, while at the same time remaining on neighborly terms with the people who bought and used its traffic facilities.

He raised the capital by the aid of his friend, Thomas Jefferson Coolidge, Jr., of the Old Colony Trust Company of Boston. The construction was directed and supervised by Mr. House, his own estate employees and a few friends. There was no graft in the construction, and as soon as operation commenced Mr. House established the rule that all damage claims could be settled directly, without litigation or delay. It was a money-maker from the start. Mr. House made thirty thousand dollars out of it, probably the largest sum he ever earned in a business operation.

"We had a lot of fun with that little road," he said, "and it taught me a good deal about railroading. I'll never forget how we enjoyed all the questions that arose, the fun we had naming the stations and making up time-tables, and so forth. It was new to all of us. But we sold it at a substantial profit to B. F. Yoakum and Edwin Hawley, who later disposed of it to the Denver and Rio Grande, by whom it is still operated. We did it to prove that a railroad could be built, and run, and make money, and still be fair to the people."

His second corporation experience was as director of the Equitable Trust Company of New York. He resigned when he discovered that it would be inconvenient for him to attend board meetings, and, as he put it, he "believed that directors were elected to direct." These two ventures are the sole evidence supporting the charge, frequently brought against him, that he was "a director and corporation magnate and a promoter of large business interests."

The truth is that he simply was not attracted by such enterprises as a permanent occupation. He learned something from each experience. Having learned what he wished to know, he withdrew—in the latter case, ostensibly, it is true, for the reason given above, but also because he had satisfied himself that most of the country's bankers had no appreciation of the need for drastic reorganization of the whole structure of banking.

Besides, something happened in 1911 to lead him to confine his efforts for the next decade to promoting the fortunes of one man. He had found the man he'd been seeking, the man, he was persuaded, who would lead the party out of the "twilight years."

Book 4

The Perfect Friendship

I

Just about the time Mr. House erased Mayor Gaynor's name from his political slate, another—and to the Texan a brighter—star rose on the horizon of Democratic hopes. Woodrow Wilson, born in Virginia, reared in South Carolina and Georgia, educated at Princeton University in New Jersey, had been elected in 1902 president of this conservative Presbyterian institution. Mr. House had been hearing of him from various friends, especially in the faculty of the University of Texas, who joined in praising the valiant struggle he waged for academic liberalism. But it had never occurred to Mr. House that he might be eligible political timber until, in 1910, he electrified the progressive wing of the Democratic party by winning election as Governor of the normally Republican State of New Jersey by an impressive majority of 49,000 votes.

Turning his attention from the irascible Gaynor to Wilson, Mr. House was intrigued by the forward-thinking policies this schoolteacher-governor proceeded to force through a none too pliant Legislature. Here was a man whose historical works had been esteemed a notable contribution to the understanding of American government, whose labors as a professor and a university president had been distinguished by a vigorously independent scorn of traditions, who had fearlessly resisted the opposition of a hostile board of trustees to the innovations he introduced in university discipline, and who, in addition to all this, had achieved the most startling upset of Republican strength at the very time when Mr. House's intuitions warned him that progressive men were turning toward the Democratic party as the means of realizing their ideals.

Mr. House was intrigued, but months passed before he was convinced that Governor Wilson was the man for whom he had been seeking. For a while he played with the idea of advancing the fortunes of his friend, Senator Culberson. But Culberson was not a physically strong man, and Mr. House believed that a Texan would meet resistance from the East and Middle West. Folk, of Missouri; Governor Harmon, of Ohio;

Speaker Champ Clark—all these, and men of substantially equal claims, including Representative Oscar Underwood, of Alabama, Mr. House was antipathetical to, either for reasons of political geography or because of alliances which induced him to doubt their freedom from conservative influence.*

His theory, as far back as 1910, was that Bryan, despite three defeats for the Presidency, would control the Convention of 1912, at least to the extent that any man Bryan opposed would be defeated for the nomination. In plain language, whoever Mr. House tried to have nominated in 1912 must be acceptable to Bryan. It was a terrific handicap for many men, and another consideration demanding reflection was the possible influence of the Tammany Hall-Hearst alliance in the East, strongly against any swing of the party to liberal doctrine. On the face of it, the problem of presenting, nominating and then securing the election of a prominent liberal seemed all but insoluble. The actual issue of the event produced more complications than had been expected.

Before Mr. House had made personal acquaintance with Governor Wilson he was very dubious that Wilson was the ideal man to run for President. As late as August 30, 1911, he was writing to his friend, Martin:

"The trouble with getting a candidate for President is that the man that is best fitted for the place cannot be nominated, and if nominated, could probably not be elected. The people seldom take the man best fitted for the job; therefore it is necessary to work for the best man who can be nominated and elected, and just now Wilson seems to be that man."

It was around this time, a Sunday in the late summer of 1911, that Martin and Walter Hines Page drove to Princeton to discuss the situation with Governor Wilson. One of them, in the course of the conversation, remarked:

"By the way, Governor, there is a man named House working for you down in Texas. You ought to meet him. He has ideas."

This was the first time the Governor had heard of Mr. House. His immediate reaction was to write to his unknown friend in Texas, expressing appreciation for the efforts being made and a desire for a meeting in the near future. Mr. House liked the tone of the letter. He liked more and more the mental attitude he was tracing out of the New Jersey Governor's speeches and legislation. He admired the way in which Wilson had compelled the State Legislature to carry out the will of the

* Strictly speaking, this was not absolutely true at this time of Speaker Clark.

voters, expressed in a referendum, and elect James E. Martine to the United States Senate instead of ex-Senator James Smith, one of the two Democratic bosses of the State. This victory of Wilson's gave substantial support to the impetus behind the constitutional amendment for direct election of Senators. Mr. House likewise approved the "Seven Sisters" law regulating corporations, a law considered unhealthily radical by Wall Street and the bankers; a direct primary law; a law making possible commission government for cities; and a law to punish corrupt practices at elections.

As a result of Governor Wilson's letter, Mr. House concluded to offer him the same chance of establishing himself in the eyes and minds of Texas voters as had been ignored by Mayor Gaynor. In September, 1911, Thomas Watson Gregory—afterwards Attorney-General of the United States—was sent to Trenton with an invitation for the Governor to address the citizens attending the State Fair at Dallas the coming October 28. Governor Wilson had a habit of keeping his engagements. He appeared in Dallas on October 28, and made a speech which was his first real bid for preference outside the borders of his own State. His theme was a demand for progress by evolution, not by annihilation of existing machinery, "a just, well-considered, moderately executed readjustment of our present economic conditions." He spoke of the States as "the political laboratories of a free people," a phrase and a philosophy which met with the enthusiastic approval of Mr. House, who had used Texas in precisely that fashion.

The Governor and Mr. House did not meet on this occasion. But the matter of the speech, no less than the unanimous reports of its hearers, endorsing the speaker's charm and personality, went far to confirm Mr. House in his predilection for the Governor. In this connection, it might as well be pointed out here that Mr. House was not—and never claimed to be—"the first Wilson man." He wasn't by several jugfuls. It is one of those subjects the introduction of which can always be relied upon to bring out the war clubs. But so far as I could ever determine from fairly close political contact with the inception of the "Wilson boom," the original effort in behalf of Governor Wilson was started by a little group of Princeton alumni, led by the late William F. McCombs, a young lawyer of New York, a man of marked intellect, of indefatigible loyalty, but one who labored under two defects: he was a cripple, whose health was not of the best, and his personal and business connections trended into Wall Street. McCombs' group was very much expanded later, and McCombs himself was recognized for his pioneer work by appointment as chairman of the Democratic National Committee, a post for which events demonstrated him not to have been fitted, although no man questioned his personal staunchness.

Other pioneers, although not of this group, were Colonel George Harvey, editor of *Harper's Weekly* and connected with the house of J. P. Morgan & Company, a man whose original motives have never been made adequately comprehensible, and whose support came close to resulting in Governor Wilson's defeat at the Convention; Mr. Page, who was rewarded with appointment as Ambassador to Great Britain; and Mr. Martin, who, with the delightful puckish quality which was as inseparable from him as his speaking trumpet, helped all he could unselfishly, retained the right of criticism and disapproval, and was content to be a leaven of common sense.

It was McCombs who was directly responsible for the first meeting between Mr. House and Governor Wilson. Mr. House had remained in New York when the Governor went South to Dallas; in his cautious way, he preferred to leave his tentative candidate entirely on the candidate's own until after that speech. When the Governor returned to Trenton he dispatched McCombs and William Gibbs McAdoo, a young financier from Tennessee, who had just made a reputation by constructing the Hudson River tubes connecting New York with New Jersey, to call on Mr. House at the Gotham Hotel where he was staying. It was the first time Mr. House had seen either of them. McCombs bore a message from the Governor, inquiring if it would be convenient for him to come to New York for a consultation on the management of his campaign, which was driving ahead at a rate demanding expert control. Mr. House replied that he would be delighted to see the Governor at any convenient time.

Several days later—the date was November 24, 1911—McCombs telephoned Mr. House to say that Governor Wilson would be in New York that afternoon, and would like to call on him at four o'clock. And so happened to be arranged the initial meeting between the small, gray Texan, whose background was the old, bloodstained frontier, the expert in practical politics, widely traveled, subtle-minded, and the tall, lantern-jawed college professor, son of a Presbyterian minister, whose background was the manse and the classroom, whose knowledge of the mechanism of politics was theoretical, who was ignorant of the art of meeting men as equals, and whose travels had been straitened by the routine of his existence.

They were a strange but not an ill-matched pair, for in essence they complemented one another. So long as their spirits were in harmony they accomplished infinitely more together than either one could have done alone.

2

I never heard any account of that meeting from Governor Wilson, and so far as I know, he never discussed it at length with anyone, unless it might have been his first wife, Ellen Axson Wilson, with whom he was used to talking fully and freely of what he did, the feeling between them having taken its inspiration from one of those piercingly beautiful personal relationships which add graciousness to lives otherwise austere. Mr. House talked of it frequently to me, and I am persuaded that his version is as fair as a remarkable memory could make it. Mr. House, as these pages will make clear, never cherished an atom of resentment for the final rupture in a friendship he liked to characterize as "perfect," a friendship based, as long as it lasted, upon a mutual respect, trust and affection almost unprecedented in history between two great men of marked strength of character and iron individualism.

His version is given here in his own words. I put them in writing, and submitted the transcript for his approval. As he left it, so it is printed.

Governor Wilson came over from the Hotel Astor, where he was staying. The two met in Mr. House's room at the Gotham. The Governor was promptly on time, and opened the interview by apologizing that his commitments for the day left him but an hour free; "but we used every minute of it," Mr. House remembered.

"We talked and talked," he continued. "We knew each other for congenial souls at the very beginning. I don't remember just what we said, but I know we hit the high spots—we talked in generalities, you know. We exchanged our ideas about the democracies of the world, contrasted the European democracies with the United States, discussed where they differed, which was best in some respects and which in others."

He smiled one of his rare smiles—all the more cordial for their rarity.

"I remember we were very urbane," he went on. "Each gave the other every chance to have his say. He would say what he thought, and then wait and let me say what I thought. We agreed about everything. That was a wonderful talk. The hour flew away. It seemed no time at all when it was over. I remember we both remarked that. We were very sorry we could not stay together longer, for each of us had many things he wanted to talk about which there had not been time to discuss.

Each of us started to ask the other when he would be free for another meeting, and laughing over our mutual enthusiasm, we arranged an evening several days later when Governor Wilson should come and have dinner with me.

"Our second meeting was even more delightful. We dined alone at the Gotham, and talked together for hours. We talked about everything, I believe, and this time we could go into details and analyze our thoughts. It was remarkable. We found ourselves in agreement upon practically every one of the issues of the day. I never met a man whose thought ran so identically with mine.

"It was an evening several weeks later, when he had been paying me a similar visit, that I said to Mr. Wilson as he rose to go:

" 'Governor, isn't it strange that two men, who never knew each other before, should think so much alike?'

"He answered:

" 'My dear fellow, we have known each other all our lives.'

"I cannot tell you how pleased I was with him. He seemed too good to be true. I could hardly believe it would be possible to elect him. You know, in politics you can almost never elect the best man—he has done something, said something, or has something about him, which prevents his success. You have to take the next best man or perhaps the next to the next best man. But here was the best man available, the ideal man. And he seemed to have a good chance of success. He rarely made mistakes; he acted always with sense and judgment. You could rely upon his discretion to do what was best in any contingency. But we despaired of being able to nominate him because it seemed too good to be true; and after he was nominated, we were constantly worrying lest he should be defeated for the same reason. But Roosevelt stood by us, and he won."

There is historical evidence in that last phrase of Mr. House's—"But Roosevelt stood by us, and he won." What Mr. House meant, as I gained from subsequent conversations with him, was that, in planning to run Woodrow Wilson as Democratic candidate in 1912, he had not anticipated the revolt from the Republican ranks of Theodore Roosevelt's Bull Moose party. Roosevelt carried with him the bulk of Progressive Republicans upon whose partial support Mr. House had reckoned. The liberal element in the country was split asunder, and the reactionary and conservative strength was concentrated behind Taft, with many Democrats of the same complexion either standing sullenly aloof or secretly voting Republican. It was a crazy, haywire campaign. What it would have been like had Colonel Roosevelt remained in the Republican organization and supported Taft with assurances, implied or forthright, of belief in his freedom from the Old Guard, is a matter for the judgment of any man who cares to study the prevailing state-of-mind of the mass of voters. Mr. House was inclined to think that Governor Wilson would have had a good chance of winning, but certainly not with so many votes as came to him from States in which the opposition was so evenly split as to make possible his overwhelming success in the Electoral College as a minority President. A definite issue for such a campaign could not honestly be proved today on the historical evidence. But certainly the shooting of Colonel Roosevelt in Chicago, and the gallantry with which he carried on his efforts, won him many wavering votes from those people who are swayed by hysteria.

After the first two meetings of the new friends in the Gotham which Mr. House described, they were constantly in touch. Mr. House had noticed that the Governor was not stressing the tariff in his speeches, and told him this was a mistake, as both Representative Underwood and Speaker Clark were making a feature of the subject, in which both were well-grounded. Mr. House was sure that Governor Wilson, with his lucidity of expression and flair for making understandable the most abstruse problems in economics, could handle it better than any of his opponents. The Texan suggested that the Governor should meet his friend, Houston, who was then chancellor of Washington University, and who was considered to possess an unusually thorough grasp of the controversial aspects of the tariff question, both industrially and agriculturally.

Governor Wilson agreed, with the humble readiness he showed toward criticism from Mr. House for nearly seven years afterward. So House arranged a dinner at the Gotham on December 7, which was attended also by Houston, Walter Page, McCombs and Martin, of *Life*. Mr. House, who privately rather fancied himself an expert on the tariff, revised Houston's data, which were shaped so as to be readily organized for public expression, and gave them to the Governor, who based all his tariff speeches on them. The Texan believed that this, as much as any other factor, dramatized Wilson before the country as the leading antagonist of the theory of high protection. As a matter of fact, this was literally not so. There were men in Congress who were really more familiar with the details of the subject than the future President ever became, and who wrought out tirelessly the revised schedules afterwards adopted.

It is interesting to find Dr. Houston, a few days later, recording the opinion that "Wilson is the straightest-thinking man in public life, and can say what he thinks better than any other man. He may not be a great executive officer, but neither was Lincoln, and I am for him."

3

In the first week of December, 1911, the American public was ignorant of the existence of a man named Edward M. House. There would have been excitement at many breakfast tables if a story had been printed, stating that he was known to the powers who work the heavy machinery of politics as one who must be reckoned with in all major decisions. Yet at this time he was not only outlining the preliminaries of Woodrow Wilson's campaign, but had been approached by an emissary of William Randolph Hearst with an invitation from the newspaper owner to conduct a fight planned to bring Hearst prominently before the 1912 Convention as a "dark horse" candidate. And he was also engaged in a protracted and involved stroke of diplomacy, designed to achieve the joint ends of eliminating Bryan as a Presidential possibility, and at the same time persuading the Commoner to remain benevolently neutral as to Wilson's candidacy.

As to this last matter, it is safe to say, in view of all that happened, that the influence Mr. House had gained over Bryan, during the winter the Bryan family spent as next-door neighbors to the Houses in Austin, was the crucial element in securing Governor Wilson's nomination. Without it, the Wilson talents would have gone for naught. But the snapper on the story was to be that the obligation of honor the Governor incurred—and political expediency entered into it as well because of the need of the new Administration for the support of Bryan's prestige in Congress—brought about the embarrassment of the President by the unpractical views of foreign relations entertained by his Secretary of State.

Bryan was very much on the fence during the maneuvers of the several candidates preliminary to the Convention. He consistently refused to consider Underwood, and he was hostile to Harmon, of Ohio, as friendly to Big Business. Champ Clark he liked for the reason which animated most of his political friendships: Clark had given him earnest support in his three campaigns. He was similarly partial to Mr. House's friend, Culberson, which would have seriously complicated the Texan's position had it not been for the good understanding between them. For Hearst, on the contrary, Bryan had no use at all, and felt the same toward any candidate Hearst supported. Indeed, there was a strong suspicion in Mr. House's mind, and it was widely shared by others, that Bryan secretly hoped to see the vote in the Convention so hopelessly split that at the last moment there would be a break to him.

But whether this was true or not, Bryan's personal attitude, during what must have been a time of great stress and uncertainty for himself, was always marked by a human tolerance and sincerity which redounded to his credit as an unselfish Democrat. Shortly before Mr. House's first meeting with Governor Wilson, the Bryans passed through New York on their way to the island of Jamaica. Mr. House called on them by appointment at the Holland House. The three sat down to breakfast together, and Mr. House went to work, with his usual bland persuasiveness, to present the case for the Governor.

"Mr. Bryan listened very attentively to everything I had to say"—so ran Mr. House's report of the interview. "He was rather noncommittal, but he did indicate that he had several objections to Governor Wilson, all of which I was able to explain away, except his enthusiastic support by Colonel Harvey, whose name meant to Bryan Wall Street, J. P. Morgan & Company, and a link with the Money Trust. I noticed that Mrs. Bryan, for whose judgment I had profound respect, endorsed all that I said about the Governor, and this encouraged me."

This was not the first intimation to Mr. House that Colonel Harvey's support of the Governor was doing more harm than good in several parts of the country. He reported Bryan's suspicions to Governor Wilson at their meeting at the Gotham, and also sent word to Harvey through their mutual friend, Martin, of *Life*. His intention, both in his report to Governor Wilson and his message to Harvey, was not to suggest repudiation of Harvey's support, but rather that it should be toned down— "softened" was his exact word. It is probable that he was unaware at the time that Colonel Henry Watterson, a few weeks previously, had suggested the advisability of the same procedure to the Governor and Harvey. The double reproof—or admonition—must have scraped Harvey's nerves, for a few days later occurred the famous encounter between Governor Wilson and Harvey at the Manhattan Club in New York.

Harvey put the direct question to the Governor: was the support of *Harper's Weekly* doing him harm? Governor Wilson replied, with the direct honesty which was frequently—and pardonably—taken for curtness, that some of his friends thought it was.

"Is that so?" Harvey commented, and withdrew, much hurt.

The story got about, and produced from Colonel Watterson a scathing denunciation of the manner in which Governor Wilson had replied to Harvey. McCombs, as the Governor's active campaign manager, made the mistake of replying publicly to Watterson, who, after all, had been animated only by a resentment that his advice, extended without any desire to humiliate Harvey, should have been so brutally, as he thought, translated into action. The resulting controversy was in some ways harmful to the Governor, but it did him good in two directions. Mr. House's lieutenant, Gregory, employed one of Marse Henry's vituperative phrases, "the austere truthfulness of the schoolmaster," to win for Wilson the support of forty thousand schoolteachers in Texas, and the incident operated to remove from Bryan's mind the doubt of the Governor he had expressed to Mr. House.

This last was an unusually lucky break for Governor Wilson, because he promptly put his foot in it again. Or it would be more correct to say that his foot was put in it for him by the publication by Adrian H. Joline, one of the trustees of Princeton who had been opposed to his academic policies, of a letter, written to Joline by Wilson, April 29, 1907, in which Wilson remarked: "Would that we could do something, at once dignified and effective, to knock Mr. Bryan once and for all into a cocked hat." It should be pointed out that this letter was written at a time when Wilson shared with Mr. House, as a loyal Democrat, an impersonal distrust of Bryan's influence in their party, which they jointly regarded as partly responsible for the temporary assumption of control by the conservative wing.

Its publication, however, was a matter of much concern to Governor Wilson's friends, and they wired Mr. House, asking him to meet Bryan, who was on his way North from Key West, and explain it to him. Mr. House, as it chanced, was prostrated in Austin with a bout of fever which kept him an invalid for two months. He was doubly sick to think of the possibility of the destruction of all his efforts with Bryan, who was being pressed by persons hostile to Wilson to exploit the letter to their advantage. Such a break could not have come at a worse time, for Bryan's errand in returning to the United States was to attend the Jackson Day dinner in Washington, January 8. Governor Wilson likewise had been invited to address this dinner, and any ill-feeling shown for him by the Commoner could not fail to impress the assembled political leaders of the party and be commented upon by the press.

The best thing Mr. House could do was to wire Josephus Daniels, editor of the Charlotte (N. C.) *Observer*, afterwards Mr. Wilson's Secretary of the Navy, a man very close to Bryan, to meet him and endeavor to mitigate the letter's effect. Daniels did so, and how satisfactorily may be judged by the tone of the statement Bryan issued upon his arrival in Washington:

"I have nothing whatever to say about that (the Wilson letter). I never heard of such a letter until I was informed of its existence by one of my newspaper friends (Daniels). I am not discussing Presidential candidacies at this time."

At the dinner, he went out of his way to show cordiality toward Governor Wilson, speaking to him and of him warmly and putting an arm around his shoulders in a gesture of comradely affection. Mrs. Bryan later explained his conduct by saying that he was too genuinely great of soul to exploit what he considered the illicit use of a private letter, while, for another thing, he remembered that in times past he himself had felt compelled to criticize Grover Cleveland and other Democratic chiefs. Whatever his reasons, he did not permit the letter to prejudice him against Governor Wilson. He did not single out the Governor for peculiar favor, but when Mr. House next saw him in New York in April, 1912, he suffered himself to be persuaded by his wife and the Texan that either Clark or Wilson would be an acceptable candidate. And this was a considerable advance from his previous wary pose of reluctance to agree that there were outstanding candidates.

4

Although Mr. House fell ill as soon as he returned to Texas in December, 1911, he was not idle. In fact, I never knew him to be idle during any of his sicknesses, and he had more than his full share. His correspondence continued copious, but his principal effort was devoted to building up an organization in the State to win the delegation to the Convention for Governor Wilson. He had been under no illusions as to the magnitude of this job. He had paid scant attention to State politics in recent years, and the actual control of the machine had passed from the hands of the men to whom he had relinquished it. Culberson's junior, Senator Joseph W. Bailey, and a band of allies owned the chairman and thirty of the thirty-one other votes in the State Executive Committee, and they were for Harmon and ardently against Governor Wilson.

Most men would have been disposed to pessimism in such a situation. Not Mr. House.

"How did we do it?" he replied when he began to outline his tactics. "We just picked the right people. That was all. We didn't use any brass bands. We went ahead quietly, secured control of the State Convention, and elected a solid Wilson delegation."

And the forty votes of the Texas delegation were the cornerstone of the Wilson nomination, standing by him for forty-six ballots!

"The right people," of course, were the answer to Mr. House's success. They were such men as Albert Sidney Burleson, afterwards Postmaster-General; Gregory, afterwards Attorney-General; Senator Culberson; Governor Campbell, who originally had been opposed to Governor Wilson; Cato Sells; M. M. Crane, who had been kept from the Governorship by House's efforts and bore no resentment; W. F. Ramsey, Cone Johnson, Thomas B. Love, T. A. Thomson, Moshall Hicks and Thomas Ball—every one a veteran of previous House campaigns, every one schooled in his methods of painstakingly detailed organization. Bailey, and all but four of the State's Congressmen, stumped the State against Governor Wilson, but the impromptu House machine rolled over the Bailey organization and crushed it. An amazing performance!

Mr. House even advised the Governor not to accept a second invitation to Texas. "You have already made your bow to Texas. That is enough. Leave Texas to your friends down there."

In the midst of the work which occupied his convalescence in Texas Mr. House found time, in odd moments of thirty days, to write the first draft of his novel, *Philip Dru: Administrator*. It is referred to here again because there seems to be something significant of the vaulting independence of Mr. House's imagination in the fact that the reforms he imagined in the whole fabric of the American idea were brought to fruition in his mind at this particular time, when he was preoccupied with the practical details of electing a man he expected would realize as many of them as were practicable.

It was published in the autumn of 1912, and the audacity of the ideas expressed by its anonymous author drew a volume of comment out of proportion to its sales—comment that was as often skeptical as friendly. As soon as the new Administration gave voice to the character of the legislation it wished enacted, this comment redoubled. Dru, as Administrator, proceeded to work out a tariff law abolishing the theory of protection, a graduated income tax, a banking law affording "a flexible currency bottomed largely upon commercial assets," and destruction of "the credit trust"; proposed making corporations share with the Government a part of their net earnings, decreed that labor was "no longer to be classed as an inert commodity to be bought and sold by the law of supply and demand," prepared old-age pension and laborers' insurance laws, and established the right of labor to have representatives upon the boards of corporations, with a percentage of earnings above their wages and a compensatory obligation to submit all grievances to arbitration.

Small wonder that members of the President's Cabinet began to comment upon the similarity between the Wilson program and Dru's. "All that book has said should be, comes about," wrote Franklin K. Lane, Secretary of the Interior. "The President comes to Philip Dru in the end."

Mr. House himself was loath to discuss his book, but he put on record that while he had revised his opinions as to some measures he recommended, he continued to consider most of them as expressing his political and ethical faith.

I know of no novel, including the works of H. G. Wells, which so deeply and positively influenced the trends of contemporary life. I always believed, personally, that Mr. House was a bit thunderstruck by the extent of the reforms he inspired, and came to believe that it would be better not to tinker too broadly with the foundations of the Republic. As in the case of all great men who attain responsibility for national affairs, the impatience with which he went at abolition of evils he perceived was minimized by a corollary perception of the very weight of this responsibility.

5

Back in New York in April, Mr. House resumed his personal contact with Governor Wilson and his ghostly supervision of the Governor's strategy. He was still unknown to the mass of political workers, not to speak of the general public; but there is an amusing story which indicates that the former were beginning to get a glimmer of his existence.

Governor Harmon's supporters were not yet aware of the overturn of their interests Mr. House had achieved secretly in Texas; but they must have been uneasy, for a Harmon manager in New York received a wire from Texas about this time:

"Everything fine down here, but will you please find out what Colonel E. M. House is doing? He is stopping at the Gotham."

This young man had been working diligently at his job for several years, and he was puzzled. House? House? The name was strange to him. So on his way uptown to the hotel he stopped in to see an older Southern friend.

"Know Colonel Ed? Why, of course, I know Colonel Ed! A mighty fine man, sir. He's a power in Texas—been running things down there since 1892. A great friend of Bryan's."

The Harmon man was impressed. He hastened to the hotel, and a clerk immediately satisfied him further.

"Oh, yes. Colonel House, of Austin, Texas. Here he comes, now."

The Harmon manager, as afterwards he described it in an interview in the New York *Sun,* saw "a slender, middle-aged man, with a gray, close-cropped mustache, well-dressed, calm-looking, who was coming quietly in, with an accent on the 'quiet.' He was not pussyfooting in or slinking in or gliding in, but while he walked firmly he walked quietly. He went up to the desk and asked the clerk a question in a quiet tone. He did not hiss the question nor did he whisper it; he asked it quietly, and when he got his answer he bowed courteously and walked quietly to the elevator, which, catching the infection, shot quietly out of sight."

Somewhat impressed, but recognizing no immediate occasion for misgiving, the young manager wired to Texas:

"Your Colonel House is up here and I understand he is going to stay here. I think he is devoting all his time to his personal business."

The answer flashed back:

"Never mind what you think. You'd better find out what Colonel House is doing and what he is going to do."

The young Harmon manager had no difficulty in securing an appointment with Mr. House, and got a direct and courteous answer. Mr. House was sorry; he admired Governor Harmon tremendously. But, speaking for himself alone, he favored the nomination of Governor Wilson.

And that afternoon there was more than sunlight in Texas. But not so much could be said for New York. Mr. House returned to be told that his candidate's fortunes were not going so happily as he had hoped. In a year which had promised well for a Democratic triumph the party was being split by factional strife almost as serious as the growing animosity between the Taft and Roosevelt wings of Republicans. The Wilson boom, thriving on the Harvey-Watterson controversies and the absence of Bryan's opposition, had gotten off to a flying start, snatching delegations right and left from the progressive States where Bryan's support had been firmest in the past. As a consequence, the conservatives had made a deal with Underwood's and Clark's backers to stop Wilson by concentrating in each State behind the locally strongest of the three candidates.

They had expected Harmon to profit by this strategy, but it was Clark, popular with the liberals and a known Bryan man, who leaped rapidly to the front, garnering votes on every side. The entire opposition, active and passive, to Wilson was gathered to him. He had gained a position which insured his being able to deadlock the Convention against Wilson. The chance of an early stampede to the Governor had vanished. In Mr. House's words:

"The honeymoon was over. We had hard work and plenty of it."

To make matters worse, McCombs' health was bad, and Mr. House had been so weakened by his illness of the last winter that he was obliged to go to his summer home at Beverly, Mass., on June 1, taking McCombs with him for a rest and a course of coaching in Convention tactics. The most promising aspect of these weeks was the continuing neutrality of Bryan, who, indeed, was weakening in his attitude as he realized that the conservative Democrats had been obliged to throw over Harmon and unite for Clark, which did not incline him to regard the Missourian with favor. Mr. House was optimistic, but not too hopeful. "It looked to me," he recorded, "as if Wilson had a good chance, but nothing more."

He was, however, encouraged by Governor Wilson's amenability to advice, and by the knowledge that many delegates, instructed for Clark or Underwood, really favored Wilson and would vote for him as soon as they were released from their pledges. The two main instructions he gave McCombs and Gregory, designated his lieutenants on the floor at Baltimore, were to divide the loyal delegations to work in units upon doubtful State delegations in which they had friends, and to make agreements with delegations instructed for candidates other than Clark that under no circumstances would they vote for Clark, which would have the effect of creating a bloc of more than one-third of the votes and if preserved would make Clark's nomination impossible.

Having done all that he felt he could for Governor Wilson, Mr. House sailed for a vacation in Europe on June 25, the day the Convention opened at Baltimore. He had mixed the necessary dynamic human forces in the political retort. He wanted them to simmer and boil into a certain concoction, but he could not be positive, any more than the next man, that they would. And he knew that his lieutenants, if they followed his battle plans, would succeed, if success was possible, while the heat and hysteria would only undermine his health and impair his future efficiency.

What happened in Baltimore was what Mr. House hopefully anticipated, but it didn't happen in the way he expected. It never does in politics. The liberal tendency of the delegates was demonstrated on the second day, when the Convention adopted the minority report of the Rules Committee, smashing the unit rule of voting upon which the conservatives had relied to obtain control of the nomination. The struggle also was clearly between two liberal candidates, Clark and Wilson. But the conservatives were playing a deep game in the earlier balloting, in the expectation that the liberal candidates would cut each other's throats and afford an opportunity for a stampede to Underwood or some unknown. Nothing like this ever could have happened. Clark, with his larger bloc of votes, preserved his superiority through day after tedious day; but the device of the House machine, in organizing an iron bloc of more than a third of the delegates committed against Clark, was an unbreakable obstacle to his nomination.

Next, then, Bryan turned against the Missourian, after the Tammany-Hearst controlled votes of New York were delivered to him accompanied by bitter attacks on Governor Wilson. After that, as Underwood's cause became patently hopeless, more and more delegates, who were instructed for Wilson as second choice, abandoned him. Mr. Wilson gained slowly on Clark. He passed five hundred votes on the night of July 1, but it was not until the opening hours of July 3, on the forty-sixth ballot, that he received the essential two-thirds, with 990 votes, 264 more than were necessary.

Without House, he could not have won. Without Bryan, he could not have won. And neither could he have succeeded without the Texas delegation, who, through forty-six ballots, thundered their pledge of "Forty votes for Woodrow Wilson, of New Jersey!"

Mr. House received the good news one day out from Liverpool. He did not let it deter him from a leisurely trip through Northern Europe. He never believed in squandering energy, and long campaigns he regarded as extravagant and boresome. But when he heard in August that the Bull Moose Convention at Chicago had nominated Roosevelt in opposition to President Taft and Governor Wilson, he hastened home. The opportunity was too precious to intrust to other hands. Defeat for the Governor seemed impossible. Still, he didn't believe in taking needless chances.

6

Mr. House regarded Governor Wilson's election as "in the bag." What he was most concerned about was preserving harmony in the Democratic organization. There were plenty of hates and grudges left over from the pre-convention struggles and the strident contest at Baltimore. Equally dangerous to unity of endeavor were the menacing feuds in the National Committee. Time, and a willingness to forgive, must be relied upon to heal the rivalries which had been displayed in the open. That is an old story of politics. But the situation which had developed in the National Committee Headquarters must be handled with prompt and diplomatic regard for the personalities involved.

The trouble in the National Headquarters was directly due to the physical, and resultant nervous, condition of McCombs, the new National

Chairman. McCombs had justly won the honor of titular leadership in the campaign, and no opprobrium attaches to the criticism that he was possibly the worst man who could have been selected for such a job, with its demands for poise, endurance and rigid self-control. All his life an invalid who pluckily refused to admit it, physically afflicted almost beyond bearing, hourly in pain, he had a naturally sweet disposition, but it was beyond expectation that he could have supported the toils of body and brain required by his position. He was a sick man, at one time absent from headquarters for six weeks. Someone had to carry on for him, and that someone was McAdoo, in accordance with his duties as vice-chairman.

McAdoo was one of the stormy petrels of politics for the next twenty-six years. He was gifted with extraordinary executive and administrative abilities. He had a talent for intrigue. He had a capacity for making men admire him and hate him, and there was seldom a tendency to minimize either feeling with those who knew him. His background, as a young financier in the transportation field, who had been obliged to carry through a gigantic enterprise on his own initiative, had inclined him to a contemptuous indifference to bosses, political and financial. He was the sort of man who appealed to Governor Wilson, while McCombs, as a corporation lawyer, had had close relations with Big Business and was disposed to conciliate established authority. He had steel nerves; McCombs was irascible, suspicious.

By the time Mr. House returned to Beverly at the end of August, there was open warfare between these two, which had divided the National Headquarters into jealous factions. McCombs came to Beverly from the Adirondacks, where he was taking an essential rest, and laid his case before Mr. House with a fiery eloquence which coated the venom beneath it. Mr. House had become fairly familiar with McCombs; he had seen McAdoo only twice. And he was disturbed by McCombs' threat to resign the National Chairmanship. He was even more disturbed to perceive that the idea of the Democratic leaders seemed to be that they could win the campaign by oratory and fireworks. Oratory and fireworks were regarded by Mr. House as window-dressing. It was his custom to win campaigns by organization as thoroughly worked out as a G.H.Q. battle order.

He placated McCombs to the extent that the threat of resignation was withdrawn, and urged Governor Wilson by letter to press McAdoo to adopt a more conciliatory attitude. He also recommended that an attempt be made to attract conservative Republican voters by placing one Taft Republican on every precinct committee, winning them over with the appeal that Wilson offered the surest means of stopping Roosevelt. It was a bait that caught many bewildered fish.

Despite the disorganization of the Democratic campaign and the disharmony amongst its leaders, Mr. House had no serious doubt as to its success. But this was by no means the conviction of many of those who worked with him, and the country as a whole was in a mood to believe that either Wilson or Roosevelt would be elected. The Rough Rider was trumpeting his hastily concocted social doctrines—most of which he afterward forgot—with the vivid energy and colorful phrase of which he was a past master. Wherever he went he raised a great wind of politico-religious hysteria. Who that knew those days will ever forget the delegates of the second Chicago Convention dispersing to their self-appointed task, singing "Onward, Christian Soldiers"? Or Roosevelt's ringing clarion-call: "We go to Armageddon to battle for the Lord!" Nobody has yet discovered the means by which "T. R." received his divine commission as Field Commander, but there can be no question that he sincerely believed himself to be a Man of Destiny, "a mighty hunter before the Lord." He was almost as familiar with the Creator as his friend, the last German Kaiser. And, make no mistake about it, he was honest. I know from personal experience that he could call a man a liar when he knew very well that the man told the truth—and make the man like it. Small wonder that many intelligent political observers disagreed with Mr. House in 1912.

As soon as the weather moderated in the middle of September, Mr. House came to New York. I think he was more disturbed to find his name on the door of an office in the National Headquarters suite in the Fifth Avenue Building than he was by the feuding atmosphere which surged through the corridors. He ordered his name removed, and conferred with Governor Wilson, who set him right on the facts of the McCombs-McAdoo situation, and advised him to confirm them for himself by personal observation. Two weeks sufficed to convince Mr. House that he had been wrong. He was compelled to agree that the chief fault was McCombs', who was jealous, dictatorial, and galled, especially because his own enforced absences from headquarters had brought McAdoo into closer touch with the newspaper reporters, with a natural increase in publicity for the hardworking vice-chairman. Mr. House thought McAdoo's attitude relatively generous, and was impressed when, at a later stage of the controversy—which seethed just under the boiling point until after the election—with McCombs threatening to create a public scandal, McAdoo assented to taking a back seat and declared his willingness that Governor Wilson should ignore him in all future communications to the National Committee.

This incident is another of those object lessons furnished by practical politics. McAdoo, not a little bitter at what he had a right to consider injustice, still continued to give his best to the Wilson cause, and asked nothing but leave to retire at the end of the campaign. McCombs confidently expected a Cabinet appointment. What happened was that McAdoo was appointed Secretary of the Treasury because he had shown capacity and willingness to consider the interests of others. McCombs' heart was broken by the purely conciliatory offer of the Embassy to Paris. He died soon afterward, one of the saddest, and in a way one of the most gallant, figures in American political history.

The McCombs-McAdoo row was involved with another and more serious aspect of the campaign. This was the question of the policy to be followed by Governor Wilson as to the Democratic nomination for Governor of New York. McCombs was inclined to tolerate the authority and prestige of Charles F. Murphy, boss of Tammany Hall. Governor Wilson, remembering the hostility of Murphy toward his nomination and inspired by his instinctive hatred for political bosses, refused as a gesture to endorse the renomination of the Tammany incumbent at Albany, John A. Dix. Murphy's unspoken proposition, which everyone understood, amounted to an offer of Tammany support in return for Wilson's endorsement of Dix. Otherwise, Wilson would be "cut" by the Tammany organization in New York City, and the Tammany-controlled votes thrown to the Republican State Committee in return for a gentlemen's agreement as to patronage. An old, old story in New York.

McAdoo sided with Governor Wilson, wanted him to come out publicly against Murphy and Dix. Mr. House detested Tammany Hall as much as his candidate; but he knew from experience the danger of antagonizing so powerful an organization in a campaign in which, however promising the outlook, an unforeseen shift in national sentiment might influence the fate of the election. He worked out a compromise through which Murphy assented to a demand from Governor Wilson that no man should dictate its choice to the New York State Convention. The Convention thereupon nominated Representative William Sulzer, another typical Tammany product, who afterwards refused to obey the orders of his superiors and was impeached and found guilty. Governor Wilson certainly carried New York in the election, but a study of the vote does not inspire the belief that he received marked support from Tammany Hall.

The most dramatic incident of the national campaign was the shooting of Colonel Roosevelt by a crazy man in Milwaukee on October 14. A wave of sympathy swept the country, one of those hysterical outbursts which were typical of the year. Mr. House didn't exactly believe that it might alter the result he had foreseen, but his sense of chivalry, as much as hard common sense, persuaded him to advise Governor Wilson to issue a statement announcing that he would make no more speeches until after his opponent's recovery. The Campaign Committee were opposed to this advice, and Governor Wilson himself doubted its wisdom; but he finally agreed, perhaps influenced by realization of the success of another policy Mr. House had urged upon him, which was to refrain from any personal attacks upon President Taft, but rather to direct his criticisms toward the reactionary advisors of the National Administration.

An amusing sidelight on the Roosevelt shooting was that Mr. House was seriously concerned for Governor Wilson's safety. The Government Secret Service men of that day were all right, but they lacked the experience in rough-and-tumble gun-fighting of the frontier. So he wired his friend, Captain Bill McDonald, of the Texas Rangers, one of the last great gunmen of the Old West:

"Come immediately. Important. Bring your artillery."

"I'm comin'," replied Captain Bill.

Mr. House loved to tell the story of Captain Bill's arrival in New York a few days later. Cap'n Bill, who had known Mr. House since boyhood, had jumped to the conclusion that some people in the East were "pickin'" on his friend, and he stepped off the train with blood in his eye. He had borrowed carfare from a friend, and hadn't stopped even to shave.

"I can see him now," Mr. House said, in describing the incident, "and thinking of meeting him that evening reminds me of another time I met him with Albert Bigelow Paine, who wrote for him the story of his adventurous life. He wore his old yellow slicker and a slouch hat. We took him to a little hotel near the Players Club, and I shall never forget the look that dawned on Paine's face when Captain Bill slipped off his slicker and coat and calmly unhitched his six-shooter and automatic from either hip. He carried those guns for ballast, you might say. He couldn't have walked straight without them. And he took them off just as you might take off your watch and key ring."

Captain Bill, incidentally, was scornful of Governor Wilson's Secret Service guards because they carried .38s. They claimed you could kill a man as easily with a .38 as with a .45, to which the rawboned old Ranger retorted: "Yes, if you give him a week to die in."

His presence beside Governor Wilson was a great comfort to the candidate and his family. He added a bit of color, which was not unhelpful to the Governor's personality.

The campaign was as good as over. As late as October 25, eleven days before the election, McCombs was in a panic, fearful they would lose such key States as New York, Illinois and Wisconsin; but Mr. House was assured by reports from his confidential agents that nothing could stop Governor Wilson's sweep. The chivalry with which the Governor had acted toward Colonel Roosevelt, withholding his own efforts until the Rough Rider was able to appear at the big Bull Moose rally at Madison Square Garden, had quenched the last hopes of the new party. Mr. Taft, unfortunately advised and poorly served, had not had a chance since the day of his renomination.

On November 5, Governor Wilson received 435 electoral votes to 88 for Colonel Roosevelt and 8 for President Taft. For him were cast 6,303,063 votes, as compared with 4,168,564 for Colonel Roosevelt and 3,439,529 for President Taft—1,305,030 less than the combined totals of his opponents. He was to be technically a minority President, but he had large majorities in the House and Senate, and for the first time in twenty years the Democratic party was effectively in the saddle, able to enact the legislative and economic reforms it had pledged to the people.

Mr. House was more than satisfied, and personally pleased that the man he had selected as best fitted to lead in the achievement of these results expressed to him, two days later, his own appreciation of the part the Texan had played in making it possible.

7

One result of the campaign of 1912, which Mr. House may have foreseen, but which nevertheless dismayed him, was the loss of his prized anonymity. He spent more time at National Headquarters than he ever had at State Headquarters in Texas or than he did in the campaign of 1916 when he was so largely absorbed in international affairs. It was impossible for him, in the fierce light which beats upon a center of such activity, to escape the attention of politicians and newspapermen, and there developed a natural curiosity concerning the small Texan, who came and went unostentatiously, but was known to have the ear of everyone from the candidate down through the upper ranks of the Organization's hierarchy.

People talked and gossiped about him. He became known as "the mysterious Colonel House," a title he accepted with amused distaste. Conjectures, comments, attacks, humorous witticisms commenced to appear in the newspapers. Newspapermen from his home State accepted him for what he was, but not the cynical commentators of the larger journals of opinion, always vigilant to assay the inside-pressure men and musketeers who grind their livings on the political fringe.

The public, which takes its political information at second hand, was supplied with a deal of misinformation and conjecture. It was said of him:

"He is a noiseless millionaire. House is a mental equilibrium, a gyroscope, a sounding-board, and an ambassador, ex jure, of the Presidential mental slant. He knows what the President's thought emanations are, and how to feed them upon what they seek. No one has to 'see' Colonel House. No one can 'see' him, because upon approach he would dive into a hole and pull the hole in after him, if possible. He detests and fears publicity. He gets nothing out of it, except the satisfaction of honestly believing that he is serving his country and his party."

Politicians who met him were besieged for news about him. One committeeman, who was a better judge of character than most, contributed a sketch which is an accurate summary of his working methods in contactual relations:

"Colonel House would come into the office and say a few words quietly," quoth this gentleman, "and after he had gone you would suddenly become seized by a good idea. You would suggest that idea to your friends or superiors and be congratulated for it; it would work first-rate, beyond your wildest dreams. You might forget about it. But sometime, as sure as shooting, in cogitating pridefully over it, you would come to an abrupt realization that that idea had been oozed into your brain by Colonel House in the course of conversation.

"You did not know it at the time—because the Colonel did not want you to know it. He is never anxious to gain credit by his ideas; anybody who can make 'em work is welcome to them. Well, sir, as a matter of fact, before the campaign was over some of us had come to the conclusion that Colonel House was about the biggest man in the works. He never held any position; he wouldn't take one. He didn't seem to represent any person or persons. Nobody ever thought of declining to listen to him. You were always anxious to talk to him; he had a quiet way of making you feel that it was a personal interest in your particular welfare that prompted him. Besides, you knew that he had no ax to grind, that he was working for Wilson, and through Wilson for the country. And anyway, after you had listened to him once, you knew he was worth listening to."

Mr. House was genuinely embarrassed by the attention he was receiving. The day before the election his mail was loaded with applications from office seekers. He would have nothing to do with such matters, nor did he ever, save when the President-elect called upon him voluntarily for advice, which otherwise he never proffered. It was a theory of his—utterly impractical, as he was to learn—that he could be of greater service to the country and his friend if permitted to remain in the shadows. He may have been correct in this theory, but he came to realize that so long as mankind was constituted as it was he could not escape public attention, that if he overdid the attempt his attitude would be seized upon as an excuse for malicious rumors and assertions, which would work to the disadvantage of the man he was trying to help carry the awful burdens of the Presidency.

Of himself, I can say truthfully that he was the most completely unselfish man I have known, in or out of public life. I might, perhaps, qualify this by saying that one or two great churchmen, Cardinal Gibbons, for one, possessed this quality.

"What is your ambition?" I asked him once, before I knew him well. "What do you really want?"

And he answered like a shot, without pausing to deliberate:

"I am working for what I conceive to be right, and if I contribute in any measure to the success of public affairs, I am satisfied with the accomplishment of my object."

He expressed this feeling more abstractly, but possibly more compellingly, in his dedication of *Philip Dru,* which might well be his epitaph:

"This book is dedicated to the unhappy many who have lived and died lacking opportunity."

During the campaign, and for some time afterward, there was no definite understanding between Mr. House and Governor Wilson. They worked on a simple basis of friendship. Mr. House wished to serve; Governor Wilson appreciated the unselfishness of that wish. Indeed, their relationship was never formal. But more and more, in the days following election, the President-elect eagerly accepted the opportunity to share his responsibilities with the man who had declared that he did not, and never would, ask any favor for himself.

Governor Wilson was anxious that Mr. House should enter the Cabinet, offering him any post except that of Secretary of State, which they had agreed, back in September, must be reserved for Bryan in recognition of the Commoner's generous support. Several years afterward, in discussing with me his unyielding refusal to accept office, Mr. House said of this:

"I never wanted office, anyway. But even if I did want it, I know that I should be signing my death-warrant to accept any office of worth, with its requirement of rigid hours and unremitting application. When I was a young man I used to think that I could do anything, ride and tramp in the sun like a Negro farmhand. But I did it once too often, and I had something like a heatstroke. Since then I have not been able to stand the Texas summer climate. When I entered Texas politics this handicap stared me in the face, and I knew it would be foolish of me to consider accepting any State office which would have required my year-round presence in Austin.

"For the same reason I could not hold any Cabinet position which would demand my presence in Washington during the summer. The climate in Washington is almost as hard on me as the Texas climate during the hot months. The kind of work I am doing is very different. For one thing, I always have the knowledge at the back of my head that if I wanted to drop it, I could quit tomorrow. I am not bound down. For another thing, I am not held to regular hours, and I can work when, where, and how I choose, in New York, for instance, instead of Washington. I don't mean by this that I have ever seriously thought of dropping my work; but that, after all, I have the comfortable feeling of being able to do so if I ever felt the burden was too great."

The increasing warmth of the friendship between Mr. House and Governor Wilson is indicated by the change in their form of addressing one another, which dates from the fall of 1912, when their visits back and forth to Trenton and New York attracted the attention of the newspapermen assigned to cover the movements of the President-elect. Governor Wilson's letters, now, began: "My dear Friend," and were signed "Affectionately yours" or "Very affectionately yours," as were Mr. House's, who addressed his letters: "My dear Governor" instead of "My dear Governor Wilson," a form he continued to employ until the termination of their intercourse.*

The President was always a lonely man, in a spiritual no less than a physical sense, aloof by habit, reserved and perhaps unduly conscious of his dignity. Marse Henry Watterson struck shrewdly home when he

* Woodrow Wilson's letters and telegrams to Mr. House, all of them written by himself, either in longhand or on his portable typewriter, are sealed in the collection of House Papers deposited in the Sterling Library at Yale University. By one of those strange quirks of the law, they are the physical property of the Library, under Mr. House's deed of gift, but the right of publication belongs to President Wilson's estate, the executor of which is his second wife. She has deemed it right to refuse to have them published, although they are one of the finest testimonials to the true nobility of Woodrow Wilson.

coined the phrase "austere dignity of the schoolmaster." Austerity, icy and remote, was the touchstone of his character, although we have the testimony of his family and Mr. House that he could be gay and affectionate, and rather liked to affect a touch of illiterate English in his "hours of ease." It was not in him to hail a friend, however dear, by a first name—for which he rates more pity than censure. At any rate, the form of address he used with Mr. House—and in personal conversation as well as correspondence—represented real, heartdeep affection. It was the form he used until the sad moment, more than five years hence, when alien influences pried a gap in "the perfect friendship" and supplanted it with a barrier never to be broken down.

Nobody who knew them would have considered this conclusion possible in those days of the fall and winter of 1912-13, when Governor Wilson's favorite relaxation was a visit to the apartment in East Thirty-fifth Street, where he could lay bare his perplexities and harassments to Mr. House's luminous vision, and cobble his own ignorance of practical politics with the aid of the Texan's years of experience.

"Colonel House," he told a group of newspapermen who inquired the reason for his marked partiality for his "mysterious" advisor, "can hold a subject away from him, and examine it and analyze it as if he had nothing to do with it, better than any man I ever knew."

Book 5

The Fruitful Years

THE first task of the President-elect is to choose the members of his Cabinet. It is, in a sense, the most important task he must master, for the success or failure of his Administration, in all probability, will stem from the quality of the men he invites to join his official family. The Grant and Harding Administrations were branded corrupt, not because of any misdoings by the Chief Executives, but because of the dishonesty of men who owed their offices to them. On the contrary, the success of Presidents like Cleveland and Theodore Roosevelt was due as much to the public confidence inspired by their Cabinets as to their own qualities of leadership. Yet probity is not the one quality essential in a Cabinet officer. He must be competent, if the machinery of Government is to operate efficiently, and the Administration's program of legislation is to be made to realize the desired results.

Woodrow Wilson's problem in 1912 was complicated by the fact that during the fifty-two years since 1860 the Democratic party had been in control of the National Government only for Cleveland's two split terms. There had never fallen to it a sustained period of power in which to train men for the higher positions. Young, ambitious men, who turned to politics, either as vocation or avocation, usually adopted the Republican creed as offering the most advantageous opportunities for advancement. Even the leaders in Cleveland's second Administration had grown too old for office in the intervening sixteen years. The men the President-elect must appoint to the ten departments of the Executive branch would have to be untried in the peculiar duties awaiting them, their fitness determined, as approximately as possible, by their performances in Congress, business, education, science, journalism or the law.

Mr. House, thanks to years of studying the practical aspects of politics, understood this better than did the President-elect, although Governor Wilson had given more than casual thought to it, and was guided, theoretically, at least, by his academic studies in constitutional and political history. But it is safe to say that the Governor had no conception of the partisan difficulties raised in his path by the sectional character of his party, and the quarrels and feuds engendered during the last campaign, let alone those still festering from the antagonisms created by Bryan in his three campaigns. Jealous eyes were watching his slightest move. Suspicious minds were ready to decry whatever he did, whomever he appointed, on the slightest excuse of favoritism. It was impossible to please everyone—no President ever did. It was certain that the opposition parties would belittle his appointments, however wise and considered. The one thing he might be able to do to give stability to his Administration was to appoint men with sound records promising adequate performance, who would be representative of the various groups that had elected him.

Mr. House was keenly aware of all these circumstances, much more keenly than Governor Wilson, who showed appreciation of his own deficiencies by leaning on the Texan's advice to the exclusion of all others. It was the cause of a good deal of ill-feeling against Mr. House. Governor Wilson, of course, conferred with many men about Cabinet appointments, listened silently to advice which was more often than not unsolicited. But he decided upon no appointment without consulting Mr. House. It was a remarkable instance of one man's trust in another man's sagacity and honesty of purpose, as is shown by the fact that of the ten members of the first Wilson Cabinet, Mr. House had a definite voice in the selection of seven, and of four of these it might be said that he was directly responsible for their inclusion. There is no parallel case in American history.

Mr. House himself was inclined to belittle his work as a Cabinet builder, especially while he was still actively associated with the President. It embarrassed him to have it emphasized, although he was not aware that as early as 1917 influences were at work to undermine the President's confidence in him. His embarrassment was due, rather, to the disposition in quarters hostile to the President to represent Mr. House as having practically crammed the Cabinet down Mr. Wilson's throat. This was not the truth, as anyone knew who knew anything of Woodrow Wilson. The truth was that the new President found himself in a position which was unfamiliar to him. He was not used to meeting and sizing up men of all kinds and pretensions. He was excusably ignorant of the innumerable currents, counter-currents and whirlpools beneath the surface of the party's affairs. And with a humble thankfulness, surprising in one of his intellectual arrogance, he accepted, first, and afterwards asked for, Mr. House's advice and suggestions.

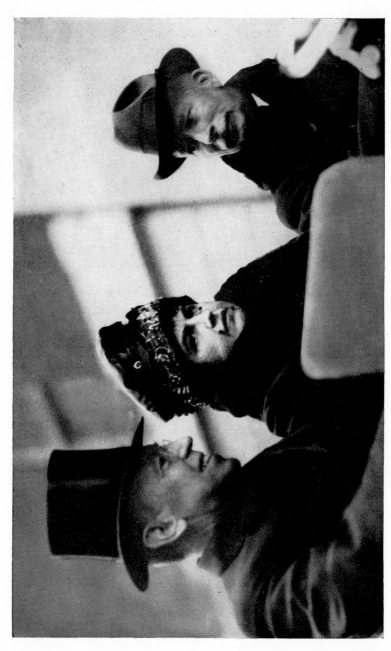

MR. HOUSE AND PRESIDENT WILSON, WITH THE PRESIDENT'S SECOND WIFE, IN WASHINGTON

That they never disagreed in this work of choosing a Cabinet was as much to his credit as to Mr. House's. It was his Cabinet. He was responsible for it. He would stand or fall by it in popular estimation. It may be taken for granted that he would never have suffered Mr. House to have a voice in its composition had he doubted for an instant the quality of the men whose merits the Texan sifted for him.

Bryan was the keystone of the Wilson Cabinet. It will be remembered that in the September preceding the election, Mr. House had suggested, and Governor Wilson seemingly had agreed, that Bryan's generous assistance should be rewarded by giving him whatever post he wished. Mr. House knew that the Nebraskan preferred the State Department, partly because he wanted to advance his ideas for world peace, partly because it was the senior Cabinet portfolio, and partly, perhaps, because the Secretary of State was second in succession to the President after the Vice-President. Bryan never got over his itch for the Presidency until he died of overwork—and possibly of humiliation in apprehending vaguely the spectacle he had made of himself—at the Scopes trial in Tennessee.

After the election, Governor Wilson was less enthusiastic about offering Bryan the State portfolio. He never said that he didn't want to do it. His hesitancy was revealed in reiterated questions as to whether Mr. House really thought it advisable to include Mr. Bryan in the Cabinet. Mr. House gathered the idea that he was afraid Bryan would use the position to attempt to advise him on matters concerning which he had formed opinions that were certain to be at variance with Bryan's. It was Mr. House's belief, however, that this was an objection of secondary importance—if, indeed, it was true that Bryan was disposed to criticize the President-elect's ideas; and, as it turned out, Bryan proved to be considerate and self-effacing, outside the realm of foreign affairs. The point that House enforced to Wilson was that Bryan's inclusion in the Cabinet was vitally necessary to assure a united party in Congress. Mr. Wilson could not have put through his legislative program during the first year of his term without Bryan's tacit support. At the end of that time, his own valid achievements and his demonstrated capacity for leadership had made him nominally independent. But it is nonetheless a tribute to Bryan's virile personality, and the confidence he had inspired in the Western Democrats, that his support was essential to whoever was President in 1913, and decreasingly so in 1914 and the beginning of 1915.

Invariably reluctant to press his personal opinion against another man's judgment, Mr. House led his friend to realize the strength of Bryan's

ambition for the State Department by suggesting that the offer be coupled with the choice of the embassies to London and St. Petersburg. Mr.
House was confident that, no matter how much importance Governor
Wilson attached to these diplomatic appointments, Bryan would express
his preference for the State Department. This was what happened when,
several days before Christmas, Bryan called on the Governor at Trenton.
They got along together better than Wilson had expected, but the
President-elect was distinctly surprised to hear Bryan respond to his
offer with a mere tentative acceptance. Mr. House knew, if Mr. Wilson
didn't, that Bryan would not join any Cabinet unless he was satisfied
with the character and political integrity of the men with whom he would
be called upon to serve. He had a keen appreciation of the value of his
prestige to the Administration.

Governor Wilson's indecision over the Bryan appointment was the
first clue Mr. House obtained to one of his friend's negative qualities:
Mr. Wilson's reluctance to attack, with his customary boldness, any
problem which had personally disagreeable implications. This was a
trait which amounted almost to a vice, although Mr. House was constrained to admire the courage and mental agility with which the new
President addressed himself to these problems once he had weighed and
dismissed his distaste for them. It seemed to be conditioned by the bul-
wark of vigorous prejudices Mr. Wilson had reared around himself, and
its most unfortunate aspect was the importance it assumed in influencing
the course of history.

The three other men whose names were suggested for the Cabinet by
Mr. House were Albert S. Burleson, Postmaster-General; Franklin K.
Lane, Secretary of the Interior; and David F. Houston, Secretary of
Agriculture. Burleson was a bluff, blunt, businesslike person, a very old
friend of Mr. House, with a long and excellent record in the House of
Representatives. His uncle, as has been noted, was one of the founders
of Texas. Houston has been described in these pages. It might be said,
in addition, that he combined the learning of a scholar and the skill of
a scientific agriculturist with the practical ability of a man of affairs.
Lane was a large, even-tempered man, who probably never had a personal enemy in his life. "Lane might have been President of the United
States, if he hadn't been born in Canada," Mr. House used to say. He
was defeated for election as Governor of California in 1902. In 1905,
President Roosevelt appointed him a Democratic member of the Inter-
state Commerce Commission, of which he was chairman in 1913. He
was one of the most delightful men of his time.

The presence of these three in the Cabinet may be traced back to a dinner which Mr. House gave in Austin in 1902—the year in which Woodrow Wilson was elected president of Princeton University. Lane was taking a vacation after his defeat in California, and stopped off in Austin to visit Dean Mezes, Mr. House's brother-in-law, with whom he had studied at the University of California. Houston, who had just become president of the Agricultural and Mechanical College of Texas, had studied later at Harvard with Mezes. Mr. House's dinner was given for these three. It was also attended by Burleson and Gregory. So here, eleven years prior to the event, you had four future members of the Wilson Cabinet, and the President's closest advisor and friend, sitting around a dinner table in Austin discussing plans for dragging the Democratic party out of the ante-bellum slump. Gregory, by the way, did not join the Cabinet until the fall of 1913, taking the place of James C. McReynolds as Attorney-General after McReynolds was appointed to the Supreme Court.

Mr. House was mainly, but by no means entirely, responsible for McReynolds' original inclusion in the Cabinet. As an attorney, practicing in New York, McReynolds had been appointed special counsel by President Taft to prosecute the Government's suits against the American Tobacco Company and the so-called Anthracite Coal Trust as conspiracies in restraint of trade. He had won the tobacco suit, and the preliminary decisions in the coal case. Mr. House recommended him for the Department of Justice after objections eliminated Governor Wilson's first choice, A. Mitchell Palmer, of Pennsylvania. Palmer was then asked to accept the War Department, which his scruples as a Quaker led him to refuse. It was just as well for Mr. Wilson's fortunes that this should have been so. As Alien Property Custodian, in the President's second term, Palmer's conduct of his office was prolific of criticism.

Josephus Daniels, who had been delegated by Mr. House to wait upon Bryan and soften the blow of the Joline letter, was appointed Secretary of the Navy, not so much because he knew nothing about naval affairs as that it was deemed advisable to have one dyed-in-the-wool Bryan follower in the Cabinet. He was a kindly, well-meaning man, whose misfortune it was to be placed at the head of the department he was least fitted to administer. Mr. House's theory, about which he had no reason to be proud, was that it didn't matter what department suffered from Daniels' fads. The thing to do was to have him in the Cabinet and conciliate Bryan.

Mr. Wilson was always more or less partial to McAdoo for Secretary of the Treasury, and Mr. House cordially endorsed the choice. There was bitter opposition to McAdoo in Wall Street and in banking circles

generally; but the sterling work he had done in the campaign had earned
Mr. Wilson's gratitude, and the two friends believed—rightly—that he
could be relied upon for loyal and constructive collaboration in the
framing of the Currency Bill they regarded as the biggest project ahead
of the Administration.

Lindley M. Garrison, Vice-Chancellor of New Jersey, was appointed
Secretary of War on the sole recommendation of Tumulty, Governor
Wilson's secretary at Trenton and afterwards at Washington, one of the
most steadfast friends the President ever had, who was rewarded, like
Mr. House, by the enmity of the little cabal that poisoned the President's
mind after he had been crippled by illness and disappointment. Mr.
Wilson talked with Garrison and liked him. He was a highly efficient
administrator, and parted company with the President on the subject of
preparedness.

The appointments of W. C. Redfield, of New York, as Secretary of
Commerce, and W. B. Wilson, of Pennsylvania, as Secretary of Labor,
were the results of a broad canvass in each case. No one man, no several men, sponsored them. Redfield was considered one of the ablest
members of Congress on the subject of tariff legislation, and had a record
as a successful business man. Wilson was a labor leader representing the
more conservative union sentiment.

If attention is concentrated here upon those who actually became members of the Cabinet, it is because in the case of everyone, except Garrison,
their names were always to the fore in the endless discussions which
went on between the President-elect and Mr. House and a number of con-
fidantes whose advice they sought. Scores of other men were considered,
several of whom would have been preferred had they been available. For
instance, Mr. Wilson was anxious to secure Justice Brandeis as Attorney-
General, a selection which Mr. House enthusiastically approved, in spirit,
while he felt that it might arouse a certain amount of ill-feeling amongst
party workers. He was particularly concerned by his friend's tendency
to favor independents as against Democrats who had been distinguished
by party regularity. The independents, he thought, should be represented
in the Cabinet, but only in proportion to their significance in the success
of the campaign. In other words, he was thinking practical politics, with
every disposition to idealism within limits, while Mr. Wilson was thinking, as he always thought, idealistically and not practically. Mr. House
did not believe Justice Brandeis would be willing to abandon the work
he was doing in liberalizing the construction of the law. Mr. House was
right. The future first lieutenant of the Great Dissenter delivered a courteous refusal.

At one time there was talk of switching Lane from the Department of the Interior to the War Department, and making Walter Page Secretary of the Interior; but—and this is a commentary on the difficulties of framing a Democratic Cabinet—Northern politicians objected that it would make trouble to have a Southern man in control of pensions. Then an attempt was made to secure Newton D. Baker, Mayor of Cleveland, for the Interior; but Baker refused to leave the job he was doing in cleaning up his city. Later, of course, he was appointed Secretary of War when Garrison resigned. Like Daniels, he was psychologically a misfit for the post. A pacifist by conviction, he hated the very idea of war, and was antipathetical to army ways; but, unlike Daniels, he had the faculty of readjusting his point of view, and in the drastic emergency of the war years he earned the reputation with military men of having been the greatest Secretary of War in American history. He was a complete justification of Mr. House's theory that in ninety-nine cases out of a hundred the office makes the man.

By the end of January, 1913, the Cabinet had been roughly framed, and Mr. House suggested that he should visit Bryan at Miami, and make a conciliatory gesture by showing him the list of men definitely selected and those still under discussion. It was the kind of gesture, Mr. House believed, which would minimize any resentment Bryan might otherwise develop over the fact that but one of his friends, Daniels, was to be included. This was exactly what happened. Bryan was led to feel by this empty courtesy that his inclinations had not been ignored, whereas in fact the contrary was true. He offered no criticisms on the men destined to be his associates for more than two years. "He showed a fine spirit," Mr. House wrote Governor Wilson. The one suggestion he made—and it was typical of the man's broad humanity—was that the Cabinet would be stronger for the inclusion of a Catholic and a Jew. Mr. House was able to tell him that an effort had been made to appoint a Jew, and that a Catholic did not appear on the list solely for the reason that none of the men brought to the attention of the President-elect happened to belong to that creed. He pointed out, too, that this defect was mitigated partially by the Catholicism of Tumulty, who, as Secretary to the President, might be said to approximate Cabinet rank.

It cannot be said that the composition of the Cabinet pleased the country. There was much adverse comment, regardless of party. It was called mediocre, commonplace, makeshift, "a Cabinet of unknowns," this last scarcely fair, unless it be taken as meaning that there was not a member of previous Cabinet experience. The reasons for this last circumstance already have been touched upon. Mr. House himself had no hallucinations about the capacities of the ten men whose advice and cooperation were to be available to his friend; but he thought that, by and large, they were representative of the best material available to the new President. Four years afterward, surveying in retrospect the men he and Mr. Wilson had sweated their brains to choose, he was inclined to believe that, as a group and allowing for individual defects of temperament, they had more than justified themselves.

"The President was frequently attacked in the early days of the Administration," he said, "for picking unknown and untried men. I was as much to blame as he was, and as a matter of fact, I think that the trial furnished by the war, let alone the four years of governmental progress and evolution, demonstrated the Cabinet to be an unusually competent body of men. Other Cabinets may have contained more individually brilliant men, but I doubt if many Cabinets have shown a higher level of efficiency and conscientious labor. Consider that the Democratic party had been out of office for sixteen years, and that we had practically no trained men available. Our case was very different from the Republicans'. They had plenty of men who had held office and were known quantities. But the generation of Democratic office-holders who had been employed in Cleveland's last Administration had grown too old for active service, and the President had to go into the ranks and select men who had never held high executive office under the Federal Government.

"In the course of his search for the best men available, some of my friends were selected, because, upon analysis, they seemed to be among the best. Every one of those men with whom I was acquainted before the Administration came into power has done splendidly."

It was Mr. House's pretense, as has been said, as long as his friendship with President Wilson endured, that his part in shaping the Cabinet was much exaggerated. I think the best proof of the facts set forth here—and they are facts—is that Houston complained after he, Houston, had been in office some time, that he had never received any notification of his appointment as Secretary of Agriculture, except Mr. House's statement to him that he had been chosen. Houston added that he and his wife had debated whether they should go to Washington. Their doubts were resolved by a letter inviting them to luncheon at the White House after the inaugural ceremonies. Lane never met the President until the day of the first Cabinet meeting, when he was obliged to go up and introduce himself to Mr. Wilson—"My name is Lane, Mr. President. I believe I am the Secretary of the Interior."

The selection of the Cabinet definitely established Mr. House as the most important private citizen in public life, if that solecism may be permitted. It was a matter of course that his power should arouse resentment. No man ever had occupied a position such as his in this country.* It was the sort of thing which had happened frequently in Europe and the Far East, but to Americans it was a novelty, and all novelties seem dangerous. More, it really was a dangerous position, dangerous for Mr. House and for the country. An unprincipled man, a selfish man, with the influence he possessed over an American President, could have been a source of evil. For he was in no way responsible for what he did, as he must have been had he accepted office. But it is difficult to imagine what Woodrow Wilson would have done without him. The two happened to fit, each satisfying the other's deficiencies. If they failed at last in their greatest endeavor, it was because one of them broke beneath the burden and allowed his intelligent affection to be poisoned by those in whom he had a right to trust.

2

It was typical of Mr. House that he did not attend the inaugural ceremonies. He took Mrs. House to join the Wilson party at the Shoreham, and himself went to the Metropolitan Club and, as he recorded, "loafed around with Wallace"—H. C. Wallace, afterward Ambassador at Paris. He loathed crowds and ceremonies with an intensity which may have derived from claustrophobia. He couldn't think straight in a crowd, he complained, which wasn't exactly true, because when he had to participate in large gatherings abroad he handled himself unconcernedly, and once made an important speech, of which he was very vain, in the ingenuous way which was one of his most lovable traits. "It was a damned good speech," he said of it reminiscently. And that was another amusing trait of Mr. House's. He was an unusually clean-mouthed man, especially if you consider the frontier atmosphere of his youth, but he loved an occasional judicious "damn" or "hell," spoken drawlingly and without undue accent, to color a phrase.

* Men like Martin Van Buren in Andrew Jackson's Administration, and Mark Hanna in William McKinley's, served their chiefs as intimate advisors; but the situation of neither of them can be compared to Mr. House's, inasmuch as both held office. McKinley persuaded the aged and dying John Sherman to resign his seat in the Senate and accept appointment as Secretary of State so that Hanna might succeed him, a step which delayed, but fortunately did not avert, John Hay's accession to the McKinley Cabinet. Van Buren's role was even less definite and exclusive than Hanna's, since Jackson had several other friends upon whom he leaned almost equally with his chief political advisor and successor. In the cases of both these men—and this is not said derogatorily—the chief interest was personal aggrandizement.

During the spring of 1913, before he went abroad toward the end of April for his annual survey of European sentiment, Mr. House probably spent more time proportionately in Washington than he did in any other period of the Wilson Administration. He lent some help to the drafting of the Tariff Act, but most of his attention was given to the Currency Bill, the Glass-Owen Act, as it is known in history. He felt strongly that this was destined to be the most important piece of domestic legislation initiated by the new President; but it is illustrative of his breadth of mind that he refused to share the prejudice, common to most of the leaders of his party, against the Aldrich Currency Bill of the preceding Administration. He cheerfully admitted that the work of Senator Aldrich and the Monetary Commission had laid the foundation for the Democratic legislation which created the Federal Reserve System. Mr. House was never a ghost chaser. He thought that financial power was too highly concentrated in the East and in the hands of the great private bankers, but he was not led to extremes by such denunciations of the "Money Trust" as resulted from the Pujo investigation. What he was after, and what he was largely instrumental in securing, was a dispersion of central banking facilities, allowing for recognition of regional needs, ample credit based on commercial paper and securing fluidity of resources, and a minimum of political control.

His one fear was lest Bryan should go off the reservation, as he put it, and lead a wild onslaught of Western radicals against any form of banking legislation which would be acceptable to conservative business men of both parties. He knew, from past probing of the Nebraskan's mental attitude, the pugnacious, unshakable hostility Bryan entertained for every degree of non-political banking administration. It was impossible to argue with Bryan on this question, and Mr. House decided that the only alternative choice was to ignore him. It was for this reason he insisted upon Bryan's inclusion in the Cabinet, reckoning upon the joint influence of the sop to vanity involved and the man's unquestioning submission to his pet creed of party loyalty.

"Mr. Bryan never understood the currency question," Mr. House once told me. "He was entirely ignorant of banking. He knew nothing of the problems involved. He knew nothing about economics. He never tried to master the subject or any of its phases. I doubt if he ever read the Glass-Owen Act. Most of the members of Congress never bothered to read through either the Aldrich Bill or the Glass-Owen Act. Bryan had his own views on how the country's banking business should be conducted, and he refused to alter them. If he had remained outside the Administration, undoubtedly he would have opposed our bill, and I am quite sure he would have defeated it. As a member of the Cabinet, however, he was constrained by loyalty to remain silent, although he never concealed his opposition in personal conversation.

"I recall that the first time I met Carter Glass, who was chairman of the House Banking and Currency Committee, some weeks before the inauguration, he told me that he was afraid Bryan would resist any attempt to legislate along the lines of the Aldrich Bill. I advised him to go ahead, regardless of Bryan, because I was convinced he would act as I have said. The President also was distrustful of the Aldrich theory, but I early succeeded in talking him out of that. I told him that it would be physically impossible for us to produce at one stroke an ideal bill. We could only frame one as close as possible to the ideal, and trust to time to amend its mistakes.

"As a matter of fact, a great many men, bankers, economists, business men, merchants, editors and others, had a hand, directly or indirectly, in shaping the philosophy of what we call the Federal Reserve System. Their work went back behind our time into the Taft Administration. I have always thought Senator Aldrich should receive due credit for his part in blasting the road for us. His bill was less ideal than ours, but we learned from his mistakes. One man, who is practically unknown today, who gave us many ideas, was my friend William Garrett Brown, of *Harper's Weekly*. I am glad that I was able to assure him on his deathbed that the bill would go through, substantially as he wished it.

"And I remember another thing about Glass," he added. "He told me in dismay at that first interview that he knew absolutely nothing about banking and currency. I answered him that he was in much better case than the men who thought they knew everything. And see what he did, being honest. He went ahead and studied the question, and became one of the best authorities in the country."

The bill, as it was introduced, was substantially the work of Representative Glass, Senator Owen of Oklahoma, and Secretary McAdoo, each of whom went at its drafting from different angles. But their ideas were modified, just as Senator Aldrich's had been, by suggestions from men of wide business and financial experience—such men as Victor Morawetz, one of the greatest corporation lawyers of his day and former chairman of the Finance Committee of the Santa Fé; Major Henry L. Higginson, of Boston, a traditional banker of the old school, who refused to be influenced by the jealousies of other men of his generation and training; Paul Warburg, of New York, who was to serve on the first Federal Reserve Board, and who, while doubtful of the political influence brought to bear on banking, was largely instrumental in making the new law work; Otto Kahn, Frank A. Vanderlip, Henry Frick, and Samuel Untermyer. The younger J. P. Morgan was as hostile to the theory of the bill as his father had been. It was a direct blow at the power of private banking houses. But his objections to it were frankly stated, and he was never underhanded in his opposition. Once it was the law, he gave it faithful support, and afterward applauded its success. He was only typical of the great majority of the big Eastern bankers.

President Wilson himself knew nothing of the practical aspects of banking. Theoretically, he was in favor of a liberal bill, which would throttle the dominance of the mythical power known as the "Money Trust," actually, the control over banking of the larger financial institutions, concentrated in the East. What he learned about the subject Mr. House taught him, with some help from Glass, Owen and McAdoo.* He had next to no financial or business friends. He did not like rich men. He had too many bitter memories of the way a group of them had thwarted him at Princeton.† But he did contribute the leadership he had won over Congress—with Bryan's tolerance—and the clarity with which he expressed arguments other men had devised for him. He did all that he could, and lacking the spell of his personality, the conviction of his honesty of purpose, the realization by Congress that the public supported him—again, because Bryan kept silent—the bill could not have passed. An interesting commentary upon the precariousness of legislative reform! To secure a modern, efficient banking and credit system, it was neces-

* Mr. House insisted that in my book, *The Real Colonel House* (Doran, New York, 1918), I should say of President Wilson's part in the drafting and passage of the Glass-Owen Act: "But none of them contributed more to it as finally enacted than the President. Indeed, without the President's keen brain and helping hand, the measure might well have failed, or at least gone through in feebler form." Strictly speaking, this was not the truth, or, at any rate, was one of those partial truths which are deceptive units of history.

† The defeat of Mr. Wilson's projects for reorganization of the academic structure at Princeton by the conservative element in the Board of Trustees, led by Moses Taylor Pyne, seems to have left an impression upon him which amounted to an obsession. He confessed to Mr. House that he frequently had nightmares about it. He had a tendency to brood over the incidents. At first, he said, everything had gone well with his administration of the university. Then trouble had succeeded trouble. His nomination and election as Governor of New Jersey had saved him from the alternative of resigning his position. He speculated over the possibility that the same mischance would befall his Presidency. Whether the deduction was justified or not, Mr. House was disposed in after life to believe that Wilson's difficulties at the university sprang from the same defects of temperament which clouded the last half of his second term at Washington: inability to mingle freely with his intellectual peers, and to adjust his mind to compromises of policies fiercely disputed.

sary to silence the opposition of one man who knew nothing about the subject, and to exploit the vicarious leadership of another man who was almost equally ignorant.

A determined effort has been made in recent years by a group of bankers and economists to diminish the significance of Mr. House's contribution to the enactment of the Glass-Owen Act. It is true that his efforts were directed chiefly toward coordinating the thoughts and ideas of others, and organizing or winning over support for the measure; but this does not alter the fact that he had one of the clearest conceptions of an Act that was practicable of enactment, and that without his influence as a human catalysis its achievement might have been considerably delayed. Certainly, its structural efficiency would have suffered. It was he who labored tirelessly to mitigate the opposition of bankers by correspondence and personal interviews. His little study in East Thirty-fifth Street was visited daily by the greatest figures in the banking fraternity, only a few of whom have been named here. He answered hundreds of letters. In Washington he soothed the fears of Congressmen who sought only a plausible excuse to vote against the bill. It was he who advised Glass, when the bill was finally introduced, to agree to no amendment of its essential features in the Senate, where the opposition to it was strongest. At his suggestion, after he and McAdoo had whipped Glass's draft into definite form, the President handed it to Owen as his own bill, the idea being that Owen would be much more respectful toward it as a Presidential measure than if it came from the House without the President's insistent endorsement. Mr. House knew well the Senate's jealousy of the House's prerogative of initiating such legislation.*

But the general public did not know for years of Mr. House's part in securing currency reform and the creation of the Federal Reserve System. The day he was assured of the bill's passage, he left Washington without waiting to attend the ceremonies incident to the President's attaching his

---

* It is an amusing commentary upon human nature that the dynamic and peppery Carter Glass in after years was disposed to be belligerently contemptuous of Mr. House's participation in the drafting and passage of the Act which bears his name, jointly with that of former Senator Owen, who, it should be said, never attached undue significance to his own conspicuous efforts. Senator Glass demonstrated the same irascibility toward other distinguished men who contributed ideas to the synthesis which was the Glass-Owen Act. It is fair to add that Senator Glass—as he became, after serving all too briefly as Secretary of the Treasury at the end of the Wilson Administration—more than justified Mr. House's prediction to him that a man honest enough to confess ignorance could become as good an expert on banking as anyone. But the groundwork of what he accomplished, and the strategy which made possible the enactment of his bill, were the work of other men as deserving of credit as himself.

signature. He would not even permit the newspapermen, who were aware of what he had done, to mention his name, all those who had his confidence having pledged themselves never to print it or to quote him. Yet it is probably not too much to say that his share in this reform—without which the country would have suffered more drastic economic shocks than it was fated to experience—exceeded in value the President's, Glass's, Owen's and McAdoo's. He had been going up and down the country for years, preaching the cause in his quietly reasonable, persuasive way, never arguing, battling selfish objections with facts difficult to answer.

The psychology of his efforts is illustrated by two statements he made to me:

"The whole trouble was that most of those bankers who opposed the bill had not taken the trouble to study it. If they had done so, they would soon have seen that the objections they claimed it possessed were not susceptible of proof. The measure is easily understood by one who has the faculty of absorbing such matters, and who is willing to devote a little time and study to it.

"I corresponded with bankers and others throughout the country, and I am persuaded that the opposition to it was never so general or so pronounced as some persons would have had us believe. The backbone of the element which opposed the measure was constituted of the small groups of powerful banking interests in Philadelphia, New York, and Boston. At the same time, I know of one well-known banker of Boston,* a typical representative of the old-school conservative spirit in banking, who took a broad-minded, patriotic, public-spirited view of the bill. And there were others like him in Philadelphia and New York.

"It was not possible at the time to segregate the opponents and favorers of the measure, as some people tried to do, and assert that the bankers who did favor it were to be found in the smaller cities and the rural communities. Many bankers in the big cities, outside of the groups I have mentioned, favored the bill. I remember a paper came out once with the assertion that 2000 bankers opposed the bill, and it made rather a sensation. But a great many more than 2000 bankers favored and supported the bill, and, what is more important still, the merchants and business men of the country, who were the most affected by it in the long run, were overwhelmingly in favor of it. The same was true of the farmers, although I do not think that they then realized, so well as they do now, that they would benefit more in proportion by the bill than the merchants and business men."

* Major Henry L. Higginson.

And then he told of an experience he had in attending a dinner given by the members of the Boston Clearing House Association on July 24, 1913, just after he had returned from several months in Europe, a change, rather than a vacation, dictated by the fatigues of his labors. The one object of the dinner was to afford the bankers present an opportunity to exchange ideas with him about the bill, which was in the throes of passage. The friend of whom he speaks, I believe, was Thomas Jefferson Coolidge, Jr., of the Old Colony Trust Company.

"A friend of mine went with me," said Mr. House. "On our way to the dinner he was very gloomy and had little to say. Afterward, he confessed that he felt very sorry for me. Well, will you believe me when I tell you that at the dinner not one of the bankers present had a word to say on the subject of the bill? The entire conversation was conducted between myself and the only other person present who was not a banker. They let him do all the talking, and he was not a person of any special knowledge regarding banking methods or problems. They were very courteous to me, but they seemed to know nothing about the bill, other than that they did not like it.

"A few days later, my host of the dinner called me up and told me that he and his friends, after considering the matter, had decided that they would adopt a resolution condemning the bill and make it public for its effect upon Congress and public opinion. I told him that I hoped he would not pass it for the sake of himself and his friends. 'As a matter of fact,' I said, 'as we stand today, your passing this resolution will be of inestimable help to the men who want the bill adopted by Congress. Your resolution will be telegraphed all over the country, and the people in the West and South will look upon it as another proof that the banking interests of the East are the sole obstructors of this legislation. Your opposition is of more help to us than would be your assistance, but my friendly advice to you is to drop your resolution.'

"He said nothing more, but I noticed that the resolution was not adopted and was never made public. Three years later—just a few months ago—this same banker invited me to his house to dinner again; many of the same group of bankers were present. We talked about our previous meeting, and he admitted freely that he had been all wrong in his estimate of the bill. His view had been that they had got along all right under the old financial structure, and they wanted to continue on the same basis. They were afraid of anything new, just because it was new. I asked him if he had not known that our old banking system was the most antiquated in the world, always liable to collapse. He conceded that this was so, but he said we had always managed to weather every storm, notwithstanding, and he dreaded a change. This attitude of mind was the chief obstacle."

The state of mind of these bankers is revealed by the fact that the day before the dinner Mr. House had been asked by Josiah Quincy, former Mayor of Boston, what would happen if the National banks, opposed to the bill, surrendered their charters and took out State charters. Mr. House replied that the threat was puerile, that he would not discuss it, and that the currency bill would be passed in any case. The real state of popular opinion, outside professional banking circles in restricted areas, was demonstrated when the bill became a law, December 20, 1913. It was received with applause and relief by Republican newspapers equally with Democratic organs.

In the selection of the first Federal Reserve Board Mr. House's part was as important as in the selection of the Cabinet. All of the five men appointed were chosen jointly by himself and the President, with most of the initiative in his hands. I formerly had in my possession a piece of scrap paper on which were written by himself and the President a group of alternative names divided by geographical sections. It was Mr. House's contention, in which the President agreed, that it was essential to divide the nominations in this way and also to give adequate representation to Republicans. The Board, as constituted, included two Democrats, two Republicans, and an independent. Mr. House contributed Paul Warburg and W. P. G. Harding, of Alabama, both bankers. McAdoo, most of whose suggestions were rejected by the President because he thought the Secretary wanted to make it "a social club"—that is, a board of men congenial personally to himself—nominated his Assistant Secretary, Hamlin; A. C. Miller, a professor of economics from California, seems to have been suggested to Mr. House by Lane and Houston; and F. C. Delano, of Chicago, a substitution for H. A. Wheeler, of the same city, was winnowed by Mr. House and the President from the alternates on the basis of his sponsors' reliability. As a board, these men successfully withstood the tremendous burdens imposed upon them.

And so, almost a century after Andrew Jackson destroyed the Bank of the United States, the country was provided with a central bank, operating through branches representing the sectional areas in recognition of the people's spread across the continent. Credit, bottomed on commercial paper, was assured of liquidity. Gold assumed its proper economic significance as the psychological guarantor of trade. The United States, at last, had the opportunity to realize its destiny as an imperial power, the opportunity it could capitalize only limpingly after California's gold gave us our first breath of economic freedom from the bankers of London, Paris, and Amsterdam.

3

If Mr. House's principal concern during the early months of the Administration was with the prompt passage of the Federal Reserve Act, it must not be supposed that this one piece of legislation absorbed all his attention. He was equally interested in the Tariff Bill and the Income Tax provisions, which were designed to produce revenue to replace the losses incurred by a lower schedule of import duties; but this was a field which had been studied intelligently by the Democratic leaders in Congress, as well as by many progressive Republicans, and he was able to confine his supervision to questions of general policy.

A considerable portion of his time was occupied in advising on appointments in the several departments of government, a task at once tedious and requiring the utmost tact, notably in the case of Bryan, whose unswerving acceptance of the spoils system would have loaded the key positions in the Diplomatic Service with "deserving Democrats," regardless of their intellectual or personal qualifications. It says much for Mr. House that he managed to thwart the Secretary of State's more dangerous suggestions without incurring the Nebraskan's displeasure or hurting his feelings. And in the midst of all these harassing, time-wasting activities, Mr. House was also planning diligently the preliminary steps in the most ambitious foreign policy the country had envisaged up to that time, a policy with the triple intent to enhance the prestige of the United States as a world power, to further its imperial destiny, and to strengthen the fabric of international peace and goodwill.

Revenue legislation actually preceded currency reform in enactment. In its first nine months in office the Administration had completely reorganized the country's financial structure, incidentally, strikingly in accordance with the conceptions outlined by Mr. House in *Philip Dru*. If, at first, there was a certain amount of dislocation and unrest in business, largely a product of economic conditions inherited from the Taft Administration, the events of the future were to justify more than amply the value of the achievement. Well might Walter Hines Page write from his new post as Ambassador at London to congratulate Mr. House on the work of the first year. In those nine months the President had accomplished more than Mr. Taft in four years, and the country was equipped to withstand the strains which—foreseen partially by Mr. House alone—were to vex it some seven months later.

In the Diplomatic Service Mr. House had been able, in addition to the appointment of Page to London, to overcome Bryan's prejudices to the extent of having James W. Gerard sent to Berlin, William G. Sharp to Paris, Brand Whitlock to Brussels, and Thomas Nelson Page to Rome. The other embassies and legations were filled with Democrats, deserving or otherwise, who compared favorably with their Republican predecessors—even Peking, which Mr. Bryan succeeded in confining to a church-going Protestant in obedience to missionary pressure. The President, perhaps, was disturbed for a while because several of his own choices, dignified gentlemen of academic backgrounds, somehow or other were lost in the shuffling of political recommendations and financial capacity; but his interest in foreign affairs at the moment was purely theoretical, and in the result he had no cause to find fault with those of his representatives who had managed to pass Mr. House's rigorous tests as to fitness.

Few people, outside the circle of Mr. House's personal friends, were aware in 1913 of the extent of his knowledge of international politics and personalities. He was considered then, and until 1915, even by well-informed newspapermen, as a practical politician whose interests were bound up with the resuscitation of the Democratic party. Important men who had occasional access to him considered him a "fixer," the President's representative in the distribution of appointments and favors. He was a small-town Texan with a flair for getting out votes and conciliating opposing political cliques. It was generally taken for granted that he was simply another Mark Hanna, and of course "he was getting his"—"somebody owned him." Industrial leaders, bankers, corporation lawyers, were always asking questions on these points.

The fact was that nobody in the United States was so widely informed as Mr. House about the conflicting currents of national interest in the world or had so complete a grasp of the country's concern in what was going on beneath the surface. Mr. Taft, Elihu Root, Nicholas Murray Butler shared his vision to some extent; but, unlike Mr. House, most of their contacts were with the political chieftains of other nations, and none of them had traveled so widely or encountered so broad a cross-section of international thought. Mr. House did not, at this time, know the chiefs of government abroad; but he knew many, if not most, of the original thinkers, radical and conservative, in the British Isles and on the Continent. By 1913, too, he was familiar with the more important foreign representatives in Washington. And, what was of more immediate importance, as a Texan he was acquainted at first hand with the thorny problem of Mexico, which, currently, was the most dangerous menace to peace in the Americas.

The Wilson Administration had taken over the Mexican problem from the Taft Administration, which had been able to handle it with an attitude of stiff-armed neutrality because, as yet, the revolution had developed along lines of definite and more or less orderly procedure. Now, however, a condition of anarchy was threatening, and presently would encompass the whole tortured country. The Border seethed with unrest. Citizens of the United States, who had the misfortune to be property-holders, were being robbed, murdered and raped by outlaw bands operating as patriot columns. British and German interests were intriguing with the shaky central Government at Mexico City to undermine their American rivals, whose reiterated appeals for intervention were supported by an organized campaign of propaganda by no means confined to the Southwestern States, geographically, or to the Hearst press and the oil companies.

Mr. House's contacts on the Border, and with Americans in Mexico, inclined him to lend a sympathetic ear to suggestions of intervention. He knew that the system of dictatorial authority constructed by Porfirio Diaz was crumbling, and that it would be many years before the rabble of military politicians, struggling with one another to succeed him, would throw forward one of themselves sufficiently powerful to consolidate a new government capable of enforcing respect for law in all parts of the Republic. But he was likewise conscious that Mexico was a sealed book to the vast majority of his fellow citizens. From a practical point of view he believed that Mexico's own fate would be easier if Washington adopted a vigorous attitude, stopping short, if possible, of active intervention, but making plain the readiness of the United States to compel orderly elections and the installation of a stable government. Common sense, political perspicuity, again, told him that the people of the United States were not prepared for so drastic a step, as, likewise, that such a policy must be expected to encounter the jealous disfavor of all other Latin-American countries, not to speak of Britain, Germany and France.

As always in a difficult situation, Mr. House tried to devise as satisfactory as possible a compromise between the ideal and the practical: joint mediation of Mexico's internal strife by the United States and the ABC powers of South America, Argentina, Brazil and Chile. The negotiations he started personally, and through the State Department with the ABC embassies at Washington, were unduly protracted, partly because of the astounding events which shook the world after August, 1914, largely because of the reluctance and final refusal of Chile to cooperate.

His plan came to nothing. But there can be no doubt that the indication by the United States of its willingness to share the curbing of its unruly neighbor with the sister powers to the south was a potent influence in earning the trust of Latin America, both during the World War and afterwards. And even when Mexico's continued turbulence made necessary the temporary occupation of Vera Cruz, the mobilization of a large army on the Border, and Pershing's expedition in pursuit of Villa, the Latin-American Republics were reminded that the United States had spared no effort to avoid active intervention by itself.*

It is possible that had Mr. House not become so absorbed in European affairs he might have been able to push his Mexican policy to a conclusion, and so saved the Mexican people from years of agony and misapplied effort. The State Department, as conducted by Bryan, made no consistent headway in Pan-American negotiations. The Secretary of State was absorbed in the series of futile arbitration treaties he depended upon to outlaw war. Formulas were the Bryan solution for every problem. Words rather than ideas. The active policies Mr. House developed, the schemes of approach he outlined, were left hanging in air. When Bryan was replaced by Lansing, a statesman with an orderly, if legalistic, mind, it was too late to mobilize Latin-American opinion in favor of immediate and definite solution of the Mexican problem. The United States did not dare to commit itself to a large-scale military adventure below the Rio Grande. All that could be done was to make the Border safe against bandit forays, and utilize the opportunity to train the National Guard for field service in France.

One aspect of the Mexican problem Mr. House was able to turn to good and immediate account. Not only did every move of the United States in Mexico City meet the opposition of British and German commercial and banking interests, but likewise the more subtle hostility of the legations of these two countries. In the case of the German intrigues there was nothing to be done except to counter them as opportunity served. The psychology underlying them is reminiscent, in perspective,

---

* For simplification, I have consolidated in these paragraphs a sequence of events, reflecting Mr. House's efforts to terminate the Mexican revolution, which continued from the beginning of 1913 to October 19, 1915, when the United States recognized Carranza as the *de facto* chief of government, and afterwards until Villa's revolt against Carranza in the spring of 1916, and his Border depredations, precipitated the operations of Pershing, which in turn aroused the suspicions of Chile and other Latin-American republics to the extent that they were unwilling to adopt joint intervention. These suspicions, as will appear in the next chapter, had much to do with the frustration of Mr. House's project for a Pan-American pact of non-aggression, which provided the germ of the idea of the League of Nations.

of the Germany of Hitler. They were to prove a boomerang in the final result, facilitating the alignment of the United States on the side of the Allies in the war of 1914-18. But British hostility to the United States was based on what Mr. House considered a valid cause of complaint: the refusal of the United States to honor the terms of the Hay-Pauncefote Treaty providing for equal terms to all nations using the Panama Canal.

Traffic through the canal, the treaty stipulated, should be "on terms of entire equality" to all nations. Yet notwithstanding this solemn affirmation, subscribed to by Hay as Secretary of State and upheld by the Government's legal advisors, Congress had enacted legislation exempting from tolls this country's coastwise shipping, and repassed the enabling act over President Taft's veto. Mr. House, as will presently appear, was deeply sensible of the menaces inherent in the European situation. Almost alone amongst responsible American statesmen he foresaw the implications of the Balkan Wars. Partially influenced, no doubt, by his English ancestry, he believed that the world's best hope for peace must lie in a community of endeavor between the British Empire and the United States. But Anglo-American harmony was impossible of attainment so long as British feelings were outraged by what British statesmen stigmatized as American treaty-breaking. Remove this obstacle, he was persuaded, and the Foreign Office could be relied upon to curb the intransigeance of the Cowdray oil interests in Mexico.

President Wilson was in complete agreement with Mr. House on this point. The question was how to go about the triple tasks of acquainting the British Government with the difficulty of persuading Congress to rescind its action, convincing the Foreign Office that its tolerance of British diplomatic and commercial hostility in Mexico was a hindrance to this effort, and lastly, cajoling Congress into abiding by the provisions of the Hay-Pauncefote Treaty. Mr. House realized more vividly than did the President the seriousness of the obstacles in their path. First, the trust of the Foreign Office must be won. Second, the President's leadership must be clearly established, for it was impossible to rely upon the assistance of Bryan in bringing Congress to heel—the Nebraskan was a confirmed twister of the lion's tail.

The first obstacle Mr. House hoped he could remove by his own efforts. The second would be implemented by the passage of the Tariff and Currency Bills. By the end of April, 1913, he was persuaded that the two bills were safely on their way to passage, and he sailed for England on his first mission as unofficial representative of the President of the United States, to convince Sir Edward Grey that it would be to Great Britain's profit to cooperate with us in Mexico. Mr. House's departure was unpublicized. His purpose was known only to the President, Sir Cecil Spring-Rice, the British Ambassador at Washington; Ambassador Page, in London, and Grey. It was, if you like, secret diplomacy. But, as a mission, Mr. House's visit to London more than justified itself. Indeed, in the issue, it turned out to be of paramount importance, for, aside from ironing out the differences which had alienated British sympathy, it established a lifelong intimacy between Mr. House and the Foreign Secretary and secured the prestige of his influence in London. It might be said to have marked the turning point in his career. Up to this time he had been content to play a role strictly political. After April, 1913, he was a statesman whose vision embraced the world, and whose poised mind was brought to bear upon every aspect of international affairs which concerned the United States.

In London, Mr. House found a sympathetic collaborator in Grey, who was prompt to understand the attitude of the Administration. The British Minister in Mexico City was instructed to alter the antagonistic policy which had been prescribed for him, and, in the subtle manner characteristic of British Governments, Lord Cowdray was given to understand that he must be aloof in his attitude toward factions of which the United States disapproved. In the following November, Grey sent his secretary, Sir William Tyrrell—afterwards Permanent Under-Secretary of the Foreign Office, later raised to the peerage and Ambassador to Paris—to Washington to consult with the President and Mr. House, so that there might be no missteps in British compliance with the Mexican policy of the United States. In March, 1914, his leadership now unchallenged and independent of Bryan, Mr. Wilson sent a message to Congress urging the repeal of the Panama Tolls Act "in the national interest," and in June Congress complied.

Thus, on the eve of war and while Mr. House was launching what he liked to call his "great adventure" to avert the struggle he sensed to be impending, the one possible cause of a breach between the English-speaking democracies was averted. The prestige of the United States was immeasurably heightened, and with it the international conception of the sanctity of treaties. It is not too much to say that Great Britain's own willingness to go to war for "the scrap of paper" which had been Belgium's safeguard, was intensified by the readiness of the United States to honor, however reluctantly, the terms of a treaty it had signed to its disadvantage.

"I have always considered President Wilson's action on canal tolls one of the bravest acts of his life," Mr. House said in discussing this episode. "It was a landmark and an object lesson in treaty observance. It made the world a better and a safer place to live in. The terms Hay signed were explicit. We could not ignore them without shamefully dishonoring our word. The fact that the canal was built with American money and skill, that it was our canal and not in any sense an international canal, such as the Suez, had nothing to do with the situation. We had agreed with the British that all traffic should share equal terms. There was no justifiable argument to support a contrary course."

He smiled one of his slow smiles.

"I'm glad that treaty wasn't signed by a Democratic Secretary of State," he added.

4

The year 1913 ushered in the most satisfying period of Mr. House's life. From November, 1912, to October, 1918, his influence was paramount in American politics, and his voice, beginning as a mere whisper, was listened to with increasing respect by European statesmen, who regarded him as the most intelligent representative of his country in foreign affairs. With a confidence surprisingly naïve, considering the keenness of his mind and his ability to read human nature, he pressed ahead in the program he had set himself, believing that his policy of self-effacement, his inclination to yield popular credit for his ideas to the men who carried them to execution under his direction, would be accepted at face value by those who worked with him. It was literally inconceivable to him that he might be acquiring enemies or that his motives could be misconstrued by honorable people. Had he known what was in store for himself he must have been thoroughly miserable, but it is probable that he would have continued on the course he had projected.

At the end of 1913 he could see no reason for misgivings for the future. All his major objectives had been attained. The basic framework of the national economy had been reorganized on lines which combined elasticity with efficiency. The growls of conservative apostles of Big Business were smothered by a chorus of optimistic satisfaction from Republicans and Bull Moosers as well as Democrats. His candidate, who had begun office as a minority President, was firmly seated in the White House, and Mr. Wilson's stature as leader of the party was growing from month to month. Bryan, his egotism adroitly coddled, had been immunized as a contending force, and without realizing what was being done to him. Congress was becoming accustomed to seeking guidance from the White House—and from the small, gray, poker-faced Texan, whose rare appearances in Washington brought the Moguls of Capitol Hill scurrying for audiences. The summer's trip abroad—which hadn't

stirred a rumble even in the State Department, where Bryan fussed over
the political eligibility of Third Secretaries and Vice Consuls—had assured
British cooperation in Mexico and driven an entering wedge for the more
ambitious project the coming summer.

More than anything else, however, Mr. House was pleased because,
within the span of those fourteen months, he had come to know Woodrow Wilson sufficiently well to assure himself that the man he had
chosen to be the Moses of the Democratic party was as soundly idealistic
as he had dared to hope for. To most men Woodrow Wilson was cold,
aloof, stilted, proud. Or so they said. To Mr. House he seemed to be
one of the warmest, friendliest, best-tempered, simplest human beings
imaginable. Shy, to be sure, disappointedly conscious at times that he
thought on a plane above most of his fellows, but always enthusiastically
delighted to find someone who could share his loneliness of spirit. And
above all else, Mr. House was impressed by his humbleness of spirit, his
search for rightness, for the conviction of purpose which was a heritage
from his Presbyterian ancestors.

On the other hand, Mr. House—being Mr. House, and used to estimating personalities and bending them to his own purposes—was quite
aware of the failings of the President. He made a point of studying the
Wilsonian idiosyncrasies, defects of temper, mental peculiarities, habits of
thought and speech. And he did this with the impartiality and ripe logic
which he could bring to bear upon anyone, no matter how much he
cared for the person concerned. I do not think it is too much to say
that nobody, with the possible exception of the first Mrs. Wilson, ever
came to know so closely as Mr. House the strange, contradictory bundle
of nerves, instincts, prejudices and inhibitions that was Woodrow Wilson
—starved for companionship, yet incurably remote from most of his
equals; proud as Lucifer, yet capable of a lofty humbleness; intellectually
an aristocrat, yet dogged all his days by the narrowness of outlook bred
into him by his forebears, petty tradesmen or divines of the dour Scotch-
Irish strain.

In this connection it should be added that Mr. House had the greatest
respect for the first Mrs. Wilson, whom he came to know, scarcely less
intimately than the President, in those throbbing, soul-stirring months of
1913, when the Democratic party was being revitalized and the country
provided with modern machinery of government capable of withstand-
ing the racking years just seven months ahead over the rim of Time.
Ellen Axson Wilson, in Mr. House's estimation, was one of those occasional women born to be helpmates of great men. He owed much of
his influence with the President to her instinctive trust in him and his

motives, and he never ceased to testify to her helpfulness and wise counsel in moments of stress. Her death, in 1914, brought the two friends still closer together. So long as memories of her counsel echoed in Mr. Wilson's consciousness their friendship was safe against disruptive efforts, no matter how insidiously maneuvered.

I never heard Mr. House speak unkindly or in a hostile tone about the President, either before or after the so-called "break," which was really a gradual rupture, so gradual, indeed, that it is doubtful whether Mr. Wilson appreciated the deliberate intent to poison his mind against his friend; but Mr. House's refusal to permit himself to be inimical in any degree toward Mr. Wilson did not deter him from blunt comments upon what he considered to be Mr. Wilson's temperamental shortcomings. In every instance they were made, not to justify himself, but to illustrate the effect of individual psychologies upon the trend of events.

The first thing Mr. House discovered about the President was that, while their idealistic philosophies were very similar, their theories of reaching the ends they sought were very different. The President, as a matter of fact, had only the simplest conception of how to give practical force to the policies he favored. He would make speeches, stating what he believed to be essential to the national interest; he would discuss those speeches in somewhat greater detail with the leaders of Congress. But beyond this he had no definite plan of campaign. He shrank, for instance, from meeting and talking with business men, for whom he seemed to have an instinctive aversion such as animals feel for creatures of a different breed. The one notable exception to this attitude of mind was his classmate, Cleveland H. Dodge, a man whose socially dangerous copper millions were offset in Mr. Wilson's estimation by a conventional religious bias, a genuine concern for philanthropy and the vague nostalgia of youthful days shared in common. Men who could not hope to match millions with Dodge were anathema because they were not so fortunate as to have lounged on the Princeton campus with the future President or to have been able to draw to his attention their gifts to institutions of the type of Beirut College or the Y.M.C.A.

Mr. House, however, by virtue of years of business and agricultural experience and political training, was disposed to consider always how to turn worthy policies into effective laws. He was used, as has been made plain, to consorting with all kinds and conditions of men, in this country and abroad. For example, his friend Houston, in the Department of Agriculture, was trying to educate American farmers in greater productivity and to extend the numbers of men owning, rather than renting, their farms. Mr. House happened to know that there was an

Irishman named Plunkett who had made a deep study of these subjects with a view to assisting small land owners and tenant farmers, and during his trip abroad, in the summer of 1913, he made a point of meeting Sir Horace Plunkett and arranging for him to visit the United States and swap the results of his endeavors with the President and Secretary Houston. Mr. Wilson was almost pathetically grateful for this contact with a man whose thoughts were capable of marching with his, but whom he would never have thought to go out of his way to meet.

Early in the Administration, Mr. House abandoned the idea of inducing the President to receive familiarly the men who might be regarded as the spokesmen of business, finance, industry and labor. The President was congenitally ill at ease, suspicious, of men of this stamp. They did not speak his language. Technically a scholar before he was a politician, he was accustomed to speaking in rounded, inclusive phrases. His mind was not habited to statistics, which is odd when you stop to consider that the academic mind is supposed to be schooled in the facts and figures of life; but Mr. Wilson's mind was not that of the classroom professor. He thought "in the large." He was not concerned with details; statistics bored him. His historical works, upon which rested his fame as a scholar, were distinguished by an absorption in problems of general policy and purpose. He was fundamentally a great theorist. In politics he must always have leaned upon a man or men capable of reducing his theories to practical application. Without Mr. House or someone like him, Mr. Wilson would have been lost. Certainly it is incredible that he could have been reelected to office.

But this failing—if it was a failing—did not bother Mr. House, who, so long as his friend trusted him, was confident that he could more than make good the President's deficiencies of temperament and inclination— as was the fact for six years of inspiring cooperation. And perhaps it is right at this point to state a deficiency of Mr. House's temperament, which was the chief factor in making possible his removal as the President's all-powerful advisor. Mr. House, it will be remembered, had never been defeated in any important project upon which he embarked. This was to be true until the fall of 1918. He had, not unnaturally, acquired a self-confidence which tended ultimately to an assumption that the power did not exist which could overthrow his influence. He was inspired, of course, by the knowledge that he was entirely selfless in his efforts. He had no smirch of guilt upon his conscience. He knew that he was trying solely to build up the achievement and reputation of Woodrow Wilson; and the singular loftiness of his own personality made it difficult for him to take into account the hostility of lesser persons or to credit the possibility that they could persuade his friend to separate from him.

In this state of mind, I think, there was at least a trace of arrogance. It was so obvious to Mr. House that Woodrow Wilson would be relatively helpless without the talents of Edward M. House, as likewise that Edward M. House sought no reward for himself, other than the opportunity of service to his friend, that it never entered his head that a contrary picture might be painted for the consideration of a man whose natural quickness of perception and straitness of understanding had been diminished by mental exhaustion beyond human endurance. Furthermore, Mr. House seems never adequately to have appreciated that if he himself was necessary to President Wilson's success, no less was the President essential to Mr. House's continued influence in affairs. Mr. House was not an orator. He could not sway continents by a few apt phrases and a resonant voice. His power was absolutely dependent upon the President's favor. He held no office during most of the term of his performance as the President's alter ego—at the end, he was no more than a Minister Plenipotentiary on Special Mission, outranked by any Ambassador. The very favor the President allowed him of taking and using power, without the burdens of elective or appointive office, was indicative in its character of the ease with which it could be withdrawn.

So, however reluctantly, it seems reasonable that Mr. House should be charged with a portion of the blame for the breach between himself and the President. His one excuse—and I know this to have been honestly offered—was that he always refused to believe that the President could be disloyal to him, even as he was persuaded that he had not been disloyal to the President. This feeling, I gather, was based mainly upon the readiness with which Mr. Wilson accepted his advice through the years of their sympathetic intimacy. But here again Mr. House failed to reckon upon the tactics he admittedly employed in bending to his purpose a man so stiff-necked and egotistical as Woodrow Wilson, for it must always be emphasized, in analyzing the President's character, that his humbleness was of a strictly impersonal nature. There was nothing humble about him in his individual contacts. Rather, his tendency was to think things out for himself—or at any rate to believe that he did so. He was self-willed, "sot" in his ways, impatient of forthright advice. And this characteristic Mr. House soon appraised and allowed for in their intercourse.

It was a lifetime practice of Mr. House's never to argue with a man whom he wished to influence. He had a way of stating objectively the several aspects and methods of solution of a problem, with a manner implying that he took it for granted that there could be no ultimate disagreement over its settlement. He was anxious, first of all, to develop the President's ideas on the subject, or, if the President had not as yet given it reasoned consideration, to stimulate an interest. If the President was flatly opposed to the approach he favored, he took one of several courses, depending upon the vehemence of the opposition encountered: he either let the subject drop for the time being without comment; or he asserted temperately his own point of view in terms which did not invite argument; or he endeavored to plant in the President's mind an alternative solution which would have the same general result as he thought desirable. He never, in any case, told the President that he (the President) "should" do this or that. For that matter, he never told anyone who asked his advice positively to adopt a certain procedure. The formula he used was always based on a variation of the phrase: "Now, if I were you, my friend—"

I know what I am talking about here, because I was much interested in the psychological methods he employed, and at one time wrote extensively on them, with the result—which amused us both—that we were widely quoted by the enterprising gentry who make a profitable living out of advising ambitious young men how success may be attained despite the uncertainties of life.

"It was invariably my intention with the President, as with all other men I sought to influence, to make him think that ideas he derived from me were his own," Mr. House said. "In the nature of things I had thought more on many subjects than had the President, and I had had opportunities to discuss them more widely than he. But no man honestly likes to have other men steer his conclusions. We are all a little vain on that score. Most human beings are too much guided by personal vanity in what they do. It happens that I am not. It does not matter to me who gets the credit for an idea I have imparted. The main thing is to get the idea to work.

"Usually, to tell the truth, the idea was not original with me. I read of it or obtained a glimpse of it from other men, whose thoughts I adapted or moderated or enlarged. The most difficult thing in the world is to trace down any idea to its source. We often think an idea to be original with ourselves, when, in plain truth, it was subconsciously absorbed from someone else. I daresay it is a realization of that fact which has kept me from being particularly gratified when, after having outlined to the President, without stress, a way to handle some thorny question, I have heard him, several nights or a week later, propound that same idea to me as his own. He was entirely innocent in doing so. His mind was constantly groping for assistance, but he was instinctively wary of accepting ideas voluntarily offered. He preferred to think them out for himself—at any rate, to ponder them before he was willing to adopt them, and by that time they seemed to him his own.

"I know that people said I had the faculty of always agreeing with the President. They said I found out what he wanted to hear, and then said it to him. That was ridiculous. How long do you suppose I—or anybody else—would have lasted with a man like Woodrow Wilson had I played the part of echo? He could have found ten, a hundred, a thousand men, more agreeable personally than I. It is preposterous to suppose that a man of the President's disposition would have tolerated an acquaintance based on such conditions. The person who gives heed to gossip of this kind confesses his ignorance of the President's character.

"It is true that we did not disagree very often because our minds ran parallel on most subjects; but we did disagree. The President never saw eye to eye with me on the Mexican situation, and he felt so deeply about it that I did not feel myself authorized to argue with him, once I had sensed that he was being guided by his own conceptions of right. What more can a man of honor say to another honorable man, after he has been answered gently that the course proposed, and for which the man being advised must be held responsible, does not seem one for which he can assume responsibility?

"We disagreed again upon the issue of Preparedness. I urged him to increase the Army and Navy soon after the war began in Europe, and continued to advise him along this line after attacks were made upon him by Theodore Roosevelt and others. But I did not push my arguments after I had appreciated that his opposition was inflexible in the circumstances. In this case I knew I was right, and history has justified me. It is quite possible that had the United States begun to arm early in the conflict we could have so strengthened our voice that we might have been able to compel a peace. At the least, our intervention would have been more immediately effective. But as to Mexico he may have been right. I was closer to the problem there, but it is also true that I may have been too close to it. I am not sure. I believe that Mexico would have been saved much suffering had we intervened, preferably with the cooperation of the ABC powers—although in the event that did not work out as I anticipated—and a favorable issue there would have been another factor to discourage Germany from an arbitrary submarine campaign. But I am not sure.

"I never argued with the President when we disagreed, any more than I did with other men, beyond a certain point. When we talked over a matter and found we were in disagreement upon it, I let it drop—unless, and until, I came across some new piece of evidence to support my views. A great deal of time is lost in useless argument. If two men, each reasoning conscientiously from the same basis of fact, reach conflicting viewpoints, then it is usually impossible to dissuade one or other of them, without the development of new facts or of some eventuality from the facts previously known. This is a general theory of conduct with me."

A typical instance of how Mr. House indirectly influenced the President's mental processes is to be found in a conversation, recorded in his diary, which began with the statement by Mr. Wilson that Alexander Hamilton was the greatest of the Colonial generation of statesmen, and that Washington's willingness to take his advice was a convincing bit of testimony to the first President's greatness of soul. "Yes," returned Mr. House, "but it is a common faculty of all great men to take advice, for only a really great man is willing to admit that he needs advice."

Mr. House's friendship with President Wilson, considered in perspective, was perhaps more of a tribute to his tact and self-sacrificing loyalty than to the emotional relief it undoubtedly furnished a man whose habitual loneliness was augmented in the austere atmosphere of the White House. Except for an intense nationalism and a tenderness for the ideal in democratic government, their minds were dissimilar. Mr. Wilson was a true idealist, with a suspicion of the apostolic complex. A teacher, he might very well have been a preacher, and many of his speeches savor more of the sermon than of the close-joined summation of integrated facts. Mr. House was a practical idealist. He cared nothing for martyrdom. If he had a chance of service by following the middle road of compromise, it seemed foolish to him to choose, instead, crucifixion, for an ideal beyond the comprehension of the public. He wanted, as he frequently said, to make the wheels go round.

And yet the most amazing conflict of personality between the two hinged upon the essential daringness of Mr. House's mind in contrast with Mr. Wilson's conventional acceptance of constitutional law and procedure. Mr. House, the practical idealist, the politician essentially, was one of the most revolutionary thinkers in matters of government since Thomas Jefferson died. Mr. Wilson, the pure idealist, the scholar, who privately loathed the machinery of politics, who preferred the higher levels of philosophic thought, was all for accepting the framework of the Founders and tinkering with it as little as possible.

The two men threshed out their opposing theories at the beginning of their intimacy, and apparently decided—or, more probably, Mr. House decided—to ignore their antipathetical ideas. Mr. House reports in his

Diary—and frequently discussed in personal conversation—Mr. Wilson's opinion that the Constitution might be relied upon to adjust itself to modern requirements and left alone substantially as written. The President was fond of quoting, in support of his opinion, the abandonment of the original right of the States to secede, which he maintained was inherent in the structure of the document as written. He was inclined to skip by the corollary implication that four years of civil war had been necessary to establish this modern conception. He believed, too, that the clumsier functions of the Government could be made efficient by personal leadership, pointing to the achievements of such Presidents as Jefferson, Jackson, Lincoln and Theodore Roosevelt.

Mr. House, whose heretical constitutional ideas have previously been discussed, flatly disagreed with the President. He was mistrustful of dependence upon personal leadership in a democracy, in which laws, rather than men, were supposed to govern. It imposed too much responsibility upon the leader, he thought. He foresaw the possible emergence of a dominant personality, who, by a combination of circumstances—popularity, ruthless ambition, hard times, the diffusion of erroneous ideas—might seize dictatorial power under the terms of the Constitution, which, he pointed out, had been written by men ignorant of the nineteenth-century conception of parliamentary (democratic) government, and for a raw country of yeoman farmers, sparsely populated, predominantly rural and innocent of the problems of the industrial era.

He was inclined to believe with the President—as he disclosed in *Philip Dru*—that only through personal leadership, under the Constitution, could genuinely efficient government be realized or any national emergency be handled. But he did not fancy the idea. And the trend toward the dictatorial form of government in Europe during the latter years of his life confirmed him in this opinion. He did not consider it safe to rely upon reinterpretations of the Constitution at the risk of civil war. He distrusted such distortions of the law as must be imposed by decisions under the "due process" clause. He thought that the Constitution should be redrafted and simplified, brought up to date to meet the requirements of modern life. Above all, he thought that it was an anachronism, in a democracy, to have a sovereign ruler and a Government so constituted as to be able to nullify a shift in popular sentiment as evidenced in mid-term Congressional elections.

It is indicative of Mr. House's character that he did not air these opinions to Mr. Wilson. There was plenty of work to be done at the moment upon which he and the President could agree. Also, practically speaking—and Mr. House was ever practical—the country was nowhere near being ready to consider a new Constitution.

Four of the President's traits profoundly disturbed Mr. House and gave him cause for uneasiness throughout their association together. One was Mr. Wilson's reluctance to share his responsibilities with his Cabinet and other officials of the Government. When Mr. House returned from Europe in July, 1913, he discovered that the members of the Cabinet were indignant and perturbed because their meetings had been cut to one a week. On this point he frankly told the President he was wrong, and in December induced him to restore the Friday meetings by representing the harm in hurting the feelings of his department heads. But this inclination of Mr. Wilson to avoid all the human contacts he could, outside the narrow circle of people with whom he felt at ease, was ineradicable.

So, too, was his disposition to avoid any decision which was disagreeable to him, regardless of how important it might be or how essential its dispatch to the country's interest, while even in matters which did not arouse his keen, almost feminine prejudices, he was disposed to be deliberate in making up his mind. He was a slow thinker, and academic surroundings had induced an exaggerated sluggishness in his mental processes. Once he reached a conclusion, he was capable of working it out, as a matter of policy—an appointment, his attitude toward a piece of legislation or a speech—with lightning speed and precision. Mr. House never ceased to marvel over the clarity of his mind. Few men have ever lived who could state so simply, so inclusively and in such finely honed prose, a subject which plumbed the depths of ethics or laid open to the understanding of elemental intelligences the most abstruse questions of economics or statecraft.

Another trait which led him into much trouble and earned him many enemies was his vigorous outspokenness about men he did not like. Let it be stated definitely here that there was nothing passionless about Woodrow Wilson. Behind his calm, scholarly features, conveying to the observer an effect of cold self-restraint, lurked a raging, fiery temper, impatient of control and never too safely disciplined. He was a good hater, and when he hated a man he talked about that man in very definite language, and refused to receive him, whoever he was, unless, in extreme cases, the utmost pressure was brought to bear upon him. One of Mr. House's meanest chores was coddling the feelings of Senators, Representatives and other people who thought themselves important, and whose feelings had been exacerbated by remarks of the President duly repeated to them by kind friends. This trait, also, Mr. House decided

was irremediable. He did what he could to mend the damage, and consoled himself with the thought that in most instances the men who received a Wilsonian blasting, or were cuttingly ignored in public, were
safer in the enemy's camp.

The fourth of the President's traits which aroused Mr. House's misgivings was his habit of making extemporaneous speeches, often in moments of great significance. This was—not for the first time—brought
home to Mr. House when he was driving through New York with the
President in the funeral procession of the sailors and marines who had
been killed at Vera Cruz. Mr. House inquired the topic of the speech
the President was to deliver at the services in the Brooklyn Navy Yard,
and was startled to be told casually that the remarks would be extemporaneous, keyed, of course, on the solemnity of the ceremony for these
boys, whose lives he felt heavy upon his own conscience as the superior
who had ordered them to their deaths.

The fact that many of the President's most felicitous addresses were
extemporaneous did not prevent Mr. House from urging his friend
against the danger of being carried away in a moment of emotion by
some phrase capable of misinterpretation. But here again Mr. Wilson
was incorrigible in habit. Why, it is difficult to say. Of all things, he
certainly was not mentally lazy. He claimed that he could think better
on his feet, and no doubt it was usually so. But "too proud to fight"
remains as the outstanding sample of several slips Mr. House felt should
have been avoidable.*

"I never could understand that failing of his," Mr. House remarked
of it. "It wasn't true that he had to think on his feet, as he said. His
State Papers are the answer to that."

The happiest commentary on their relations, this first year they worked
together, is their reaction to the initiation of what came to be known in
the inner circle as "the September breaks." Mr. House, in 1913, as in
following years, stayed away from Washington during the summer
months because he could not stand the heat. Inevitably, there were
rumors. Congress was sitting, hot and uncomfortable, and gossip is
always boiling during a summer session. The wiseacres nodded their
heads, and said: "Sure, the Colonel's through. It was too good to last.
They come and they go in this game. It's a break."

It is doubtful if Mr. House or the President appreciated how widespread was this impression amongst politicians and newspapermen. But
it was in consequence of the spread of such rumors that the President

* Both the incidents here cited, of course, happened subsequent to 1913.

wrote to a man who had asked him, in effect, to what extent Mr. House represented him:

"Mr. House is my second personality. He is my independent self. His thoughts and mine are one."

And Mr. House responded to an apology from the President for an interval of silence after they had been separated for months:

"I never worry when I do not hear from you."

Afterwards, when they met and discussed the gossip, they laughed tolerantly, as men do who trust each other unhesitatingly. Neither would have believed in 1913 that a "break" could ever come between them. And when the President sat of an evening in his study, and slipped a piece of scrap paper in his portable typewriter to tap off one of his frequent, heartfelt letters to the man who was proud to be his servant in the common cause, the first words which took shape under his nimble fingers were, "My dear friend."

5

The dawn of the year 1914 saw the President seated firmly in the saddle, his prestige growing from week to week. Business, which had been vexed by the uncertainties always attending novel and drastic regulatory legislation, was gaining confidence. The personnel of the Administration had settled into their collars for the four-year haul. But the demands upon Mr. House's time continued as pressing as ever. He was still "the eyes and ears" of the President, and the Cabinet members and heads of other government agencies sought his counsel upon almost every question of importance. Candidates for appointments poured into the apartment in East Thirty-fifth Street in a steady and somewhat monotonous stream. Legislation must be drafted, amended, steered to limbo or accomplishment. Questions of policy, frequently "importantly unimportant," often trivial, must be analyzed. And in so far as the President was concerned, Mr. House's burden was increased by his friend's preoccupation with Mrs. Wilson's failing health throughout these months. Fortunately, however, Mr. House was an omnivorous worker, endowed with mental capacities out of all proportion to his slight body, and in his secretary, Miss Frances B. Denton, he had a helper as tactful and indefatigable as himself. He never complained, although the volume of his labors exceeded in scope the responsibilities of anyone else associated with the Administration.

"I know I am appreciated," he said quietly in explaining how he was able to see people the day long at intervals of from five minutes to half an hour. "That's the best salt to savor any dish."

Most men in Mr. House's place would have been occupied sufficiently with domestic affairs, but, with the Administration operating as smoothly as was possible for a political organization, he diverted his attention more and more to spadework for his "great adventure," which he planned to launch in the approaching summer. Briefly, his idea, which had the President's approval—although it is doubtful whether Mr. Wilson as yet fully realized its significance—was to concert with the Foreign Ministers of Britain and France and the Kaiser a means to dissipate the international atmosphere of suspicion by a program of mutual exploitation of the world's undeveloped areas. His ultimate objective was an agreement on restriction of armaments, bulwarked by pledges of non-aggression. He designed to appeal to these several governments by stressing the material, rather than the ethical or sentimental, interests of all of them. He was confident that the adoption of such a policy by the Great Powers would win the adherence, willingly or otherwise, of Russia, Italy and Austria-Hungary, and would have the practical effect of removing the everlasting threat of war.

Few men have had so splendid a vision. It is a tribute to Mr. House, no less than a commentary upon human nature, that he missed, by a hair, achievement of it, not once, but twice. Few Americans, for that matter, had anything like so perspicacious a grasp of the international situation in his time as Mr. House. He saw clearly, in 1914, the dangers accumulating in the European tinder box, the devastating possibilities contained in the mounting jealousies of Germany and Great Britain— jealousy, on Germany's part, of Britain's lion's share of world trade, and on Britain's, of Germany's naval might. He had not missed, either, the implications of Germany's persistent attempts to humble France by interference in North Africa and the enforced resignation, as Foreign Minister, of Delcassé. He had perceived, with intelligent comprehension, the menaces to peace in the sequence of events flowing directly from the Young Turk Revolution of 1909—the irritation of the South Slavs by Austria's annexation of Bosnia-Herzegovina and Novibazaro; Bulgaria's declaration of independence of the Sultan's suzerainty; Italy's seizure of Tripoli and the Turkish-Aegean Islands in 1911; the formation of the Balkan Alliance by the efforts of Eleutherios Venizelos and Boucher, the London *Times* correspondent at Sofia; the successful war of the Alliance against Turkey, and the seizure of most of European Turkey; and the resultant war of the Allies, in which Bulgaria, which had done most of the fighting, was crushed, in 1913, by a combination of

Serbia, Montenegro, Greece and Rumania, and deprived of her share of the spoils.*

It was equally apparent to Mr. House that the expansion of the South Slavs, and Serbia's ebullient nationalism, had aroused the fears of Austria and the protective instinct, racial as much as political, of Russia. Both of these powers had mobilized in 1912. War on the grand scale was in the air until after Sir Edward Grey succeeded in bringing the Balkan belligerents to settlement of their various claims in the Treaty of London. Even then, the smoke clouds drifting over the Rhodope hills and the plains of Macedonia left a lingering distaste in the nostrils of the medieval-minded gentry of the chancelleries of Vienna and St. Petersburg. Vienna, especially, was provoked by the rise of the hated South Slavs, and was plagued by the specter of Slavs of any tribe ensconced upon the Golden Horn, never forgetting that Bulgaria's first rush had carried her armies to the Chatalja Lines, and that, but for the lack of siege artillery, the Bulgars would have occupied Constantinople before the Great Powers had had time to apply pressure in Sofia, Belgrade, and Athens. Russia, by contrast, was licking her chops in 1914, confident that her pups, who had missed so narrowly, would some day reach the objective she had been balked of in 1878 by Disraeli's fleet.

It has been said that few Americans grasped this situation. A number did, but none so comprehensively as Mr. House. Elihu Root and Nicholas Murray Butler were sent to Europe in 1912 by President Taft— at least, with President's Taft's good wishes—on a nebulous and quite unofficial mission to discuss with statesmen of their acquaintance a vague and unspecified project for some kind of conference to lay the ghosts of international animosity. Their well-meant efforts obtained no results. Conservative in outlook, hampered by their party's traditional aversion to "foreign entanglements," based upon an erroneous interpretation of Washington's doctrine framed for a weak, newborn nation of three and

---

* I served with the Bulgarian chetniks against Turkey in Macedonia in 1907, and came home convinced that a Balkan war was certain in the immediate future and that a general conflagration thereafter was inevitable. I found Englishmen who understood this situation, but Americans of position or influence were wholly unconcerned by it. Most intelligent business men and politicians in this country had only a hazy knowledge of the geography of southeastern Europe, and no conception of the consequences of war in this field. I had ridicule for my pains, and a reputation as a romantic youngster. The same mental attitude prevailed after the assassination of the Archduke Franz Ferdinand, but the most amazing thing about this event is that a year of European peace had lulled the sensibilities of the Foreign Offices in London, Paris and Berlin, and of the War Offices in the first two capitals—*but not in Berlin.*

a half million farmers, they discussed tentatively, and without definite authority, the desirability of doing something to make war more difficult. It would be interesting to speculate on what might have happened had it been possible for President Taft to entrust their errand to his former friend, Theodore Roosevelt, whose dynamic personality was capable of riding roughshod over precedents and formulas.

Roosevelt, be it remembered, was in essence as much of an internationalist as Mr. House in his conception of the true role of the United States in the twentieth century. It was to Roosevelt that we owed our first intervention in European politics by his nomination of an American delegation to the Algeciras Conference, which adjusted the conflicting claims of Germany and France in Africa. He was moved to this unprecedented departure from American policy by his apprehension that the United States, since the consolidation of its continental territory, the tremendous growth of its trade and the war with Spain, had become a world power, whether its people liked to admit the fact or not. And being a statesman of realistic bent, he understood that the possession of world power carried with it a share in the responsibility for what went on in the world. He had written a history of the War of 1812. He knew that in the first international conflict after our emergence as a nation we had not been able to avoid entanglement, and he foresaw that any future conflict of the same proportions would have precisely the same effect.*

It is probable, too, that Theodore Roosevelt was among the handful of Republicans who had read with comprehension the last speech of his predecessor. William McKinley, despite the tradition which has grown up around what little remains of his memory, was not one of those third-

---

* If more proof were needed of Theodore Roosevelt's ability to "see across the Atlantic," in Mr. House's phrase, it could be found in his stiff opposition to Britain's proposal to blockade Venezuelan ports in an attempt to collect debts of her nationals; in his intervention in the Russo-Japanese War, in the nick of time to save Japan, financially and morally exhausted after the struggle for Port Arthur and the battles for Mukden; and in his compensatory policy of dispatching the Battle Fleet around the world as a deterrent to Japan's expanding ego—a policy which held Japan in check until after President Harding and Secretary of State Hughes initiated the Treaty of Washington of 1922. Similarly, Roosevelt's Panama Canal policy illustrated his relentless determination to establish the authority of the United States in Asia as well as Europe. He always maintained that the ruthlessness of his attitude toward Colombia was justified by the continuous imminence of a possible national emergency. Mr. House never underrated Theodore Roosevelt. He knew that the man who fulminated hysterically against Woodrow Wilson after 1914 was not the same individual as the man who had gone to Brazil in 1913, and been prostrated by jungle fever.

rate Presidents—the Pierces, let us call them—who clutter the pages of American history. He was a plain, simple, Middle-Western American, a soldier with an excellent record, a Congressman known for sincerity and determination. He was not an imaginative man or a great leader; but he was not merely the voice of Mark Hanna. He tried to be real, to see the truth—and when the truth was elusive, he grappled for it. Elected to office on the wave of antagonism to Bryan, a high-tariff man, he seems to have had the faculty of learning from his own mistakes by the ancient test of trial and error.

Before he went to Buffalo to address a meeting in celebration of the Pan-American Exposition, September 5, 1901, he determined to make a speech, which he told Myron T. Herrick, George B. Cortelyou, his secretary, and Mrs. McKinley, he wished to be "truly 'epoch-making.'" And after a poor, crazy man named Czolgosz had shot him, the first question he asked was: "How did they receive my speech?" Not unnaturally, the speech was all but forgotten in the turmoil following his death and the reorganization of the Administration. But it is to be commended to the attention of those Republicans and Democrats alike who assert that the interests of the United States should be guided by a policy of isolation from world affairs. It was a frank appeal for abandonment of that policy, for acceptance of our role as a world power.

This was the meat of it:

"Isolation is no longer possible or desirable . . . God and man have linked the nations together. No nation can longer be indifferent to any other . . . Our capacity to produce has increased so enormously, and our products have so multiplied, that the problem of more markets requires our urgent and immediate attention. Only a broad and enlightened policy will keep what we have. No other policy will get more . . . By sensible trade arrangements that will not interrupt our home production, we shall extend the outlets for our increasing production. . . . Reciprocity is the natural outgrowth of our wonderful industrial development under the domestic policy now firmly established. The period for exclusiveness is past."

When this speech was delivered, the automobile was still an expensive, unreliable toy; good roads were unknown, the motion picture and the radio were raw ideas seething in the brains of their inventors, the telephone and the typewriter were luxuries; not for another twenty-five months would the Brothers Wright, greatly daring, soar for a precarious twelve seconds, in a flimsy object like a mammoth box kite, from the summit of Kill Devil Hill. But William McKinley saw the true vision of the future, and so did the obstreperous young man who was to succeed him in office a few hours later. Can it be that in their ignorance they were wiser, if not better, Republicans than their successors a generation later? Certainly, ignorant or not, enlightened or blind, they understood that their country could not attain to a degree of world power neither dreamed possible, holding one-half the wealth of civilization, without assuming the attendant responsibilities.

I never discussed this speech of McKinley's with Mr. House, but I know that he was an intimate friend of Herrick's, and I think it may be taken for granted that Herrick had brought it to his attention. Of President McKinley himself Mr. House remarked to me, in illustrating a pet maxim of his own:

"You take McKinley, now. He wasn't a great man, but he grew. He was another case of the office making the man. I never knew that to fail, if the man was honest. I have wondered what people would think of him if he had lived to serve out his second term."

It was on this occasion, by the way, that he made the comment that Lincoln, had he lived, and however undeservedly, would have been one of the most unpopular of the Presidents.

His attitude toward the first Roosevelt was a compound of admiration and whimsical tolerance.

"He was a great man, but one of those fellers who can't see that four years is a long time for a President to be able to have original ideas, and eight years is four years more. But he did see things in a big way. I don't see any Republican who can take his place. I mean any Republican who has the qualities he had. I sometimes think his energy was his worst handicap. He didn't know when to stop. Yes, he was an able politician, and the best campaigner I ever saw. And he could see across the Atlantic Ocean. He was much like the Kaiser. They both liked to be doing things, but they saw farther than most men. Too partisan? Yes, but most of us can't help that, if we stay in politics. It takes partisans to put parties in power—and independents to put the fear of God into parties. There can't be too many independents to suit me."

6

There was nothing spontaneous about the inception of Mr. House's "great adventure." The idea had taken shape gradually over a considerable period of time, the result of his studies of past and contemporary history and of countless conversations with thinking men and women at home and abroad. One of the reasons why he ignored Woodrow Wilson's political amateurism, in selecting him as the preferable Presi-

dential candidate in 1912, was his belief that Wilson's background of historical study, his warm feeling for humanity in the large, his gift for the
broad, inclusive phrase, all combined to fit him to take a leading role in
international affairs. But Mr. House soon came to realize that the President had given very little thought to the existing situation in Europe and
its bearing upon the future of the United States. So he set himself, cau-
tiously and deliberately, to the task of awakening his friend's perceptions,
dropping suggestions whenever opportunity served. It was typical of
their unusual relationship that his exploring mind led the way in developing the policy which was to be the President's chief claim to abiding
fame.

He prepared himself for his mission with his habitual thoroughness,
never losing a chance to probe a mind alert to what was going on in the
world—the minds of people like Jane Addams, Norman Hapgood, Dr.
Eliot, Walter Page, his friend Martin, for whose opinion he had much
respect; and abroad, such Englishmen as Lansbury, Sidney Brooks the
journalist, Plunkett. On May 9, 1913, he lunched with von Bernstorff,
the German Ambassador to Washington, and sounded him on Germany's attitude toward Britain, so that two months later, when he talked
to Grey in London on the specific subject of the Panama tolls controversy, he was able to inform the British Foreign Secretary that Germany
was pleased with Britain's conciliatory policy in the current Balkan situation. In December of that year, when Tyrrell was in Washington as
special representative of the Foreign Office—nominally, to supervise the
British Embassy, which was handicapped by Spring-Rice's illness—he discussed his plan in detail with that adroit diplomat, and was pleased to
find Tyrrell wholly approving of it. Grey's secretary agreed with him
that the Kaiser was the key man of those who should be interviewed,
and advised Mr. House to make the approach to him as unofficial as
possible.

In January, 1914, Mr. House arranged with Gerard, in Berlin, to make
the appointment with the Kaiser. Gerard, who, without any diplomatic
training whatsoever, already was proving himself one of our most efficient representatives abroad, advised Mr. House that the best time would
be early in June, after the Kaiser's return from his annual spring holiday
in Corfu and before he sailed upon a long-planned yachting voyage to
the Scandinavian fjords—this last a junket which was to have far-
reaching consequences nobody at the moment could have anticipated.
About this time, too, Mr. House obtained from Benjamin Ide Wheeler,
one of the two most intimate American friends of the German Imperial
family, valuable data upon the Kaiser's hobbies, personality, opinions and

prejudices. In April he canvassed the political line-up in Germany, and its implications, with Irwin Laughlin, who had been First Secretary of the Berlin Embassy. He also talked to Count von Moltke, cousin of the Chief of the General Staff, and to Prince Münster, both of whom were fellow voyagers to Europe when he sailed with Mrs. House and Miss Denton on May 16. He had the satisfaction of knowing that Gerard's notification to the Wilhelmstrasse of his visit as the President's personal friend, "the power behind the throne," had been followed promptly by a cable to Bernstorff asking for a complete report upon him.

The stage had been set as auspiciously as possible, not only in Berlin, but in Paris and London. In the last-named capital, Sir Edward Grey was awaiting him, anxious to support whatever headway he could make in neutralizing Germany's suspicions. But Sir Edward Grey, no more than Mr. House, was aware that the authorities at Vienna were insisting with a bureaucratic stubbornness, which some authorities have termed sinister, upon a visit by the Archduke Franz Ferdinand, heir to the Austro-Hungarian thrones, to Serajevo in Bosnia on the coming June 28, despite the warnings of the provincial police of terroristic activities by disgruntled Serbians. And surely neither the Englishman nor the American was sufficiently conversant with the gossip of Paris to suspect that Madame Caillaux, the wife of the Minister of Finance, was accumulating a hatred of an editor named Gaston Calmette, which would lead her to purchase a pistol to use against him, and thereby precipitate another in the series of Cabinet crises which had racked France in recent months.

So many little human things, all seemingly avoidable had destiny so willed it, happened in those mid-months of 1914. Suppose Franz Ferdinand had not been so eager to show his morganatic wife, Sophie Czotek, in state, because of his ambition to see her son succeed him one day as ruler of the Dual Monarchy. Suppose the Kaiser had elected to spend the hot weather in one of his mountain castles. Suppose Calmette had retracted the slurs which drove Madame Caillaux to a fury of revenge. Suppose a man as strong as Clemenceau—or Clemenceau himself—had become President of the Council of Ministers in Paris. Suppose, even, France had not been a prey to the bickering of a mess of petty parties such as torment her today. Suppose the Ministers in London had not been so distracted by domestic quarrels as to be blinded to the menace brooding in southeastern Europe. Suppose Mr. House had been able to launch his "great adventure" in the summer of 1913. If any one of these "supposes" had been translated into accomplished fact, August, 1914, might have been a warm, peaceful month promising no more than abundant harvests to a Europe eager to make comfortable its young men's lives.

Mr. House often thought of these mischances, as he did of other unforeseen events which blunted his efforts in 1919 and 1920. "You can only see ahead just so far," he said. "And then you can't be certain you are seeing what you think you do. I have never believed that some things have to happen, but sometimes it's almighty hard to stop them from happening."

Mr. House arrived in Berlin the last week in May. He had no fault to find with Gerard's provisions for his entertainment, unless it was that the genial Ambassador did not take too seriously his pleas for informality and the abjuring of his fortuitous title of Colonel, which, as Mr. House had feared, let him in for difficult half-hours with literal-minded German officers, who looked to find in him a brother professional. Gerard had made an appointment for him with the Kaiser, not without opposition from the Foreign Office, which was jealous of Mr. House's stipulation that it must be *tête-à-tête,* without the presence of a representative of the Civil Government. Gerard's diplomacy, and probably the strong recommendation of Bernstorff, overrode this opposition; but it may have been the latent hostility of the Wilhelmstrasse officials to the idea of risking Wilhelm's notorious loquacity which fixed the interview to take place immediately after the ceremony of the *Schrippenfest,* Whit-Monday, June 1, on which occasion the Kaiser dined in company with the common soldiers of the Imperial Guard at Potsdam. They might reasonably have figured that the conversation would have to be held under conditions insuring as little privacy as possible and in a minimum of time. If such was the case, their calculations went wrong. Nobody overheard what was said; the Kaiser gave Mr. House ample time—indeed, ignored attempts by the Kaiserin to interrupt their conversation—and showed the utmost cordiality and interest. It was Mr. House who indicated by silence when he had completed his say.

The substance of this conversation need not be detailed here. It is contained in Mr. House's minute, printed in *The Intimate Papers of Colonel House* (Houghton Mifflin Company, 1926).* For the purpose

* The secret of Mr. House's mission in 1914 was so closely kept that the first information about it was published by the writer in March, 1918. The reason for withholding from the public the President's offer to aid in a settlement of European antagonisms, on the eve of war, was the fear that publicity might undermine the persistent efforts of Mr. Wilson and Mr. House to develop a formula for peace. The Government of Great Britain, equally with the Imperial German Government, would have been embarrassed in explaining to their peoples why they had not profited by such an offer when the test of time had proven how imminent was the

of this narrative it suffices to state briefly that the Kaiser was entirely sympathetic with Mr. House's idea. He was, of course, disposed to see the prevailing situation in terms of Germany's interest, but Mr. House regarded his theories as reasonably moderate and intelligent. He declared that Germany needed peace. He professed to be eager for a better understanding with England, and thought that England, America and Germany were natural allies because of their racial kinship. On the other hand, he spoke rather contemptuously of the Latins and Slavs as "semi-barbarous," asserted that Russia was "the greatest menace" to England, and said that Germany was the barrier between Europe and the Slavs, stressing the fact that he, personally, was a friend to England and was doing her a service by holding the balance of power against Russia. England had nothing to fear from Germany, he insisted.

He agreed with Mr. House that because of the European nations' distrust of one another it would be better for the United States to lead the way in attempting to bring about such a cooperative alliance as Mr. House had in mind. One significant statement he made, which Mr. House did not appreciate at the moment, was that the reason why Germany had refused to sign Bryan's Arbitration Treaty, providing for a "cooling-off" period of a year before signatories might declare hostilities, was that Germany's superior mobility made it impossible for her to delay action in an international rupture, since, by so doing, she would forfeit her principal advantage. It seems, once again, an indication of Mr. House's *naïveté* that he should have been surprised to hear this expression of the first rule of German strategy, which was known to every statesman and journalist in Europe.

In conclusion, the Kaiser asked Mr. House to keep him informed of the progress of the American negotiations, remarking that letters would reach him "through our friend Zimmermann here in the Foreign Office." Mr. House was highly satisfied with his interview, and optimistic for the future, notwithstanding that a previous talk with von Jagow, the Foreign Secretary, had left him dubious of that personage, although Zimmermann, the Under Secretary, was "quite responsive" to the Texan's ideas.*

peril Mr. House had foreseen. Manifestly, publication of the facts in the United States would have been of assistance to the President in his campaign for reelection in 1916.

* How "responsive" Zimmermann was, is indicated by the fact that, as Foreign Secretary, he became the author of the note to the German Minister in Mexico City —intercepted by the British Secret Service—offering, as a bait for an alliance with the *de facto* Mexican Government, German assistance in recovering the territories lost to the United States in the war of 1846-48. This note, coming on the heels of Germany's declaration of an unrestricted submarine campaign against neutral

More significant for the future, in so far as the United States was concerned, was a long discussion with Admiral von Tirpitz, the Minister of Marine. Mr. House had been advised to stay away from von Tirpitz, since he was an advocate of war as a means to Germany's ambition of increased wealth; but, discovering that the Admiral was considered to be the most forceful man in the Empire next to the Kaiser, Mr. House tackled him after a dinner at the Embassy.

Von Tirpitz impressed Mr. House as possessing a dislike for the British which amounted to hatred. He also complained of anti-German feeling in the United States, as evidenced in newspaper editorials, and notably in the books and articles on naval subjects of Admiral Mahan. He disclaimed any ideas of conquest behind Germany's program of naval expansion, but declared that the best way to secure peace for Germany was to "put fear into the hearts of her enemies." Plainly, to von Tirpitz, the British were enemies. He hoped that Mr. House was right in believing that an understanding could be reached with them, but they were not "reliable," "they looked down upon Germans, and considered them their inferiors." One amusing comment he advanced was that the German Government had no control over the press, while the English seemed to be able to swing their newspapers around to the Government's point of view whenever that was desirable. Mr. House held his first premise to be as fallacious as his second was justified.

The interview was baffling in its connotations. Mr. House was obliged to admit to himself that if von Tirpitz was the most extremely anti-British of the Germans he had met, it was nonetheless true that all the men he talked to in Berlin shared this feeling in some degree, so markedly that he was led to write the President, May 29, before he had seen the Kaiser: "The situation is extraordinary. It is militarism run stark mad. Unless someone acting for you can bring about a different understanding, there is some day to be an awful cataclysm." But the Kaiser's relative sanity of outlook buoyed him up. If Wilhelm had made no promises, he had shown a readiness to seize any worthwhile chance to avoid the cataclysm.

Mr. House quitted Berlin for Paris that evening with the conviction

shipping, was the final straw which impelled the United States to enter the war of 1914-18 on the side of the Allies. Zimmermann, in fact, was a typical German diplomat of the unprincipled school that returned to power under Hitler, masking, beneath a suave exterior and a glib readiness to give lip service to humanitarian ideas, a ruthlessness as extreme as that which ruled—and rules—the projects of the General Staff. One of Mr. House's weaknesses, which he learned to control, was a disposition to grant European statesmen credit for an intelligence few of them possessed.

that he had been as successful as was possible in the circumstances. It would take more than one half-hour's chat with the head of the Hohenzollerns to snatch Europe back from the brink of the abyss toward which the nations were drifting for lack of a leadership above their 'mutual fears and suspicions. The great danger, he reasoned, was not that Germany or any other nation was deliberately planning war, but that the mood of tension created a tendency to react hysterically to any sudden incident. In Germany's case, this was complicated by the conviction of the High Command that the war machine in that summer of 1914 had been brought to a maximum of efficiency over their potential enemies, in consequence of the past year's capital levy. With the passage of time, France and Russia could augment the equipment of their armies, and Britain outbuild them increasingly afloat. But still there was hope. The Archduke Franz Ferdinand had not started for Serajevo, and the tuberculous lad, Gavrilo Prinzep, had not received his orders from the Pan-Slav terrorists in Belgrade.

In Paris, that first week of June, Mr. House found *l'affaire Caillaux* the one topic of interest to the exclusion of every other subject. It had upset the Ministry, a body as shaky as its predecessors, and now various political chieftains were trying to scramble together a substitute to perch as precariously on a toppling pyramid of parties and personalities. The Government was being run by the permanent officials, bureaucrats with whom it would be useless for Mr. House to confer. He reported to Ambassador Herrick, who confirmed his conclusions, and kept as much to himself as he could, an undertaking rendered easy by the presence in Paris of Theodore Roosevelt, a figure of much greater importance than the quiet Texan to Frenchmen and visiting Americans alike.

One fact Mr. House did learn from the responsible Frenchmen of his acquaintance who called by invitation at his hotel. The France of June, 1914, that is, France of the politicians, had forgotten Alsace and Lorraine. The statues on the Place de la Concorde were draped in their usual emblems of mourning, but that was no more than a gesture in memory of the brave men who had died for the Lost Provinces in 1870. *Revanche,* as a real factor in the national life, was as dead as Napoleon III. The thinking Frenchmen who talked to Mr. House were agreed upon that one point, no matter how much they differed on internal questions. Alsace and Lorraine were gone. Let them be forgotten. France's future lay in developing the Empire overseas. Germany? All Frenchmen wished was to live in peace with her. France in June, 1914, had no thought of war. Ah, but this Caillaux, with his infernal financial heresies! And this woman of his, with her pistol! That such atrocities could occur in a community of order! In your America, of course—

Mr. House took the boat train for London on the 9th, negatively encouraged by what he had observed in Paris. If he succeeded in London as well as he had with the Kaiser—and he had no reason to anticipate a contrary reaction—he was confident that the French would be willing to join in his plan for an international conference, which, ostensibly gathered to partition and regulate financial investments in backward countries, might be steered dexterously into a mutual undertaking to restrict armaments and adjust difficulties by arbitration. He was looking far ahead of Bryan in this respect. He wanted to make it practically worthwhile for the nations to abstain from war. His appeal was to be through their pocketbooks rather than their ethical concepts.

In London, his reception was as cordial as he could have desired. Sir Edward Grey "was visibly impressed" by his report, "a willing listener and very frank and sympathetic." But London, like Paris, was distracted at the moment by domestic politics. England was in a social uproar over the suffrage agitation and the disorderly activities of "the wild women." Ireland seemed to be on the brink of civil war. The Ulstermen of the Northern counties, led by Sir Edward Carson and "Galloper" Smith— afterwards Lord Chancellor Birkenhead—were arming to resist incorporation with the South under Home Rule. Gun-running, mainly from Germany, was prevalent on the coasts. Men were marching and drilling on both sides. Conservatives in England were openly backing the Ulstermen, and the War Office was disturbed by the partisan attitude of many officers, a disaffection which culminated in a military mutiny at the Curragh cavalry camp near Dublin, commanded by Sir Hugh Gough, one of the most popular of the younger generals.

For these reasons the Foreign Secretary was unable to give immediate effect to the sympathy he freely expressed, other than to stress to the German Ambassador his approval of Mr. House's purpose and the friendly disposition of his Government toward Germany, sentiments he begged to have transmitted to the Kaiser. More he could not do without securing, first, the considered approval of his colleagues in the Cabinet, whose absorption in the domestic situation inclined them to belittle the significance of European politics. He was also hampered by the feeling that before committing himself to formal negotiations with Germany he should consult the French and Russian Governments, and this was impossible until there was a Ministry in Paris which was sufficiently established to be able to look beyond the current month's agenda.

Mr. House appreciated Grey's difficulties, and was not disposed to be impatient in the circumstances; but he was uneasy over the Foreign Secretary's apparent failure to comprehend the tension in Berlin. Grey seemed apathetic to Mr. House's description of the importance attached by German officers to the aeroplane, and to their boast that modern invention had placed them within striking distance of England. At the same time, he was generous in his profession of willingness to conciliate Germany's ambitions, and assured Mr. House, as did other British statesmen, that there was no written alliance with France and Russia, and no determination on their part to forge around Germany the "iron ring" which plagued the Kaiser's dreams.

Mr. House was perplexed. He was all for striking while the iron was hot. He sensed urgency in the air—and was obliged to admit to himself that he was unable to convey the validity of his sensation to Grey. When he suggested that the two of them should go to Kiel during Yachting Week at the beginning of July, and talk informally to the Kaiser, pressing the lead he had started at Potsdam, Grey indicated approval; but nothing came of it beyond a subsequent message, conveyed by Tyrrell, that the Foreign Secretary was studying how to make a direct contact with the Germans in a way that would not offend the susceptibilities of the French and Russian Governments. The Entente might not rest upon a formal document, Mr. House reflected, but it seemed to operate to hamper free initiative as efficiently as a treaty signed and sealed.

It would be unfair to convey the impression that Mr. House thought Grey's deliberateness was due to any lack of candor on the part of the Foreign Secretary or the Cabinet. To Mr. House's mind, it was simply a reflex of the turgid cross-purposes which were playing hob with the relations of the Great Powers. Europe's statesmen had lived so long on the verge of war that they had been nursed into a false sense of security. The specter which had been so often invoked had lost its potence to create an impression of reality. "They felt like the countryman in the story the President liked to tell," Mr. House remarked of this situation. "I mean the feller who was shown his first giraffe at the circus, and turned away, saying: 'There ain't no sich animile.'"

If Grey was unwilling, himself, to go to Kiel, he nevertheless urged Mr. House to take advantage of the Kaiser's invitation to report progress, and also suggested that at a convenient time it might be advantageous for Mr. House to repeat his visit to Berlin. Mr. House, on consideration, decided not to seek another appointment with the Kaiser, at least until he had something more definite to talk about. But he did, on July 7, write the Kaiser, outlining the results of his visits to Paris and London and pushing open wider the door for a resumption of confidential communications. This letter reached the German Foreign Office while the Kaiser was absent on his Scandinavian cruise. When he was summoned home at the end of July, in time to lend his countenance to the mobilization order, Mr. House's worst fears had been realized.

"The Emperor took note of its contents with the greatest interest," wrote Zimmermann in his acknowledgment of August 1. "Alas, all his strong and sincere efforts to conserve peace have entirely failed. I am afraid that Russia's procedure will force the old world and especially my country into the most terrible war!"

The avalanche of steel had been started like many an avalanche of natural forces by the flick of an insignificant object—in this case, the steel-jacketed bullets discharged by Gavrilo Prinzep into the bodies of Franz Ferdinand and Sophie Czotek, the Bohemian noblewoman who was saved the possibly double annoyance of seeing her native race torn from Austrian rule and then dissected for the benefit of a resuscitated and hungrier Germany. Certainly the statesmen of Vienna and Budapest were saved from the problem of what to do about Sophie's sons after old Franz Joseph died. As it was, they raged and fumed prodigiously. The Balplatz was raucous with threats against the infamous Serbs. But wise observers on the spot thought they detected an undercurrent of relief. Franz Ferdinand had been neither loved nor popular, and the aristocracy had hated his unfortunate wife.

Europe seemed to accept the incident as just another Balkan outrage. People recalled how an infamous group of army officers had murdered King Alexander and Queen Draga in Belgrade in 1903. The German press was justly indignant, and the Government, very much on the quiet, gave Austria authorization to exact amends from Serbia for a crime which surely was plotted upon her soil and, in all probability, with the knowledge of elements in the Serbian War Office. But nobody dreamed that the thunderheads hovering over the Balkans would sweep beyond the Danube. People, great and small, went about their business as before. Business was good; the weather was wonderful. The Kaiser enjoyed himself at Kiel, only regretting to Gerard that the death of the Archduke made it necessary to cancel an invitation to sail a race with him; and presently departed in the *Standart* for the fjords. President Poincaré, also, saw no reason why he should postpone his state visit to St. Petersburg. Gerard, returned from Kiel, wrote to Mr. House, July 7, that the Kaiser and von Tirpitz "were both most enthusiastic about you," and added, almost as an afterthought:

"Berlin is as quiet as the grave."

In London, too, Mr. House saw no reason for extending his stay, and booked passage for home July 21. It was the middle of The Season, and people were trying to forget the suffragists and the income tax and the Irish situation—"Oh, the Irish are always making trouble!"—in the accustomed relaxations of a smart, well-bred society, which was used to considering its own interests above all others. Everybody was in town, and Mr. House turned his visit to account by meeting men who might be of use to him in the future, if not the present. He had breakfast with Lloyd George, the Chancellor of the Exchequer, whose appetite amused him, and who seemed to be "peculiarly ill-informed regarding America and its institutions." He lunched with Premier Asquith, "who cast the usual slur upon Mr. Bryan" (Mr. House had to explain the Nebraskan to practically every statesman he met abroad). He had illuminating talks with Plunkett, Lord Bryce, Curzon, Henry James, the Bishop of London, John Sargent, Lord Chancellor Haldane, Lord Crewe, and Spring-Rice, who was over from Washington and very thankful for the privilege. He saw a great deal of Tyrrell, and of many other men in and out of politics, the arts and journalism.

And to all these men, he remembered later, the Marne was merely a wistful tributary of the Seine, winding through an attractive countryside within easy motoring distance of Paris. Few of them could have located a town called Mons on the Belgian side of the French frontier. Any of them would have applied for a lunacy commitment for a man who told them that within a few weeks one hundred thousand British soldiers would be fighting on its outskirts. Yet, on the evening of July 20, as Mr. House was preparing to sail for Boston the following day, he recorded in his diary:

"Tyrrell brought me another message from Sir Edward Grey, which was to the effect that he wished me to know before I sailed that the Austro-Serbian situation was giving him grave concern."

Mr. House occasionally wondered afterward—uselessly, as he confessed—whether it had been too late, then, to launch openly his "great adventure." Probably, it was, he thought. The underground preparations of the Austro-Hungarian and German militarists had been carried to an extreme which would have led them to attempt to override any checks interposed by the German Civil Government. Personally, he never subscribed to the charge that the Kaiser was responsible for the outbreak of war. He was convinced that the Kaiser neither expected war nor wished it. He did, however, believe that the Kaiser had helped to bring about the situation in Germany which made war possible, by encouraging the militarists and the financiers in their attitude of suspicious belligerence. He thought, also, that the Kaiser was "foolish" in encouraging Austria-Hungary to develop the controversy with Serbia to so acute a stage, and in believing that Britain would hold herself aloof and that Russia would not force a show-down in support of Serbia, which must, in effect, have lost her independence had she yielded to the Austro-Hungarian ultimatum.

He never knew quite what to think of Spring-Rice's opinion that it was his talk with the Kaiser which had forced the hand of the militarists in Berlin and Vienna by making them realize that war very soon might become impossible. Spring-Rice contended that the militarists knew the contents of Mr. House's letter to the Kaiser before their sovereign did, as well as the tenor of the talks which Grey had had with the German Ambassador in London during Mr. House's visit there; and that these had animated their misgivings, previously aroused by what the Kaiser had told his entourage of Mr. House's interview.

"You came so near making a general war impossible that the war party in Berlin and Vienna became alarmed," Spring-Rice wrote to Mr. House. ". . . It was now or never."

Whether Spring-Rice's deductions were sound or not, it is interesting to note that years after the Treaty of Versailles had become a dust-catcher and a source of controversy, the Kaiser said to George Sylvester Viereck, an American friend:

"The visit of Colonel House to Berlin and London, in the spring of 1914, almost prevented the World War."

If Mr. House blamed anybody specifically for the failure of his "great adventure," it was Grey and his British colleagues for their refusal to take action prior to the Kaiser's departure from Kiel, although it should be emphasized anew that the Texan fairly gauged the perplexities which had encompassed them and the reasons for their dilatory tactics. There is a note almost of bitterness—a note seldom detectable in what he said or wrote—in his letter to the President, written upon his arrival at his country home, Pride's Crossing, Mass., July 31, immediately after the storm had burst upon a bewildered world:

"They [the British Ministers] seemed astonished at my pessimistic view, and thought that conditions were better than they had been for a long time. While I shook their confidence, at the same time I did not do it sufficiently to make them feel that quick action was necessary; consequently they let matters drag until after the Kaiser had gone into Scandinavian waters for his vacation before giving me any definite word to send to him. It was my purpose to go back to Germany and see the Emperor, but the conservative delay of Sir Edward and his confreres made that impossible. . . . If the matter could have been pushed a little

MISS FRANCES B. DENTON, "MISS FANNY"—FROM A DRYPOINT

further, Germany would have laid a heavy hand upon Austria and possibly peace could have continued until a better understanding could have been brought about."

Whatever bitterness Mr. House cherished at this time soon passed away. He realized that Grey, and the men associated with the Foreign Secretary, had been honestly unable, so rapidly as was necessary, to bring their minds into focus with a method of diplomacy so strange to them, and a view of their world contrary to the interpretations their understandings had reached. It was unfortunate, but it was one of the unavoidable mischances of life. He honestly had no fault to find with his own efforts. And the experience confirmed him in a belief he never lost that there was always a way to avert war, if the way could be found in time by men who had reason to trust each other.

7

Mr. House landed in Boston July 29, and established himself for the summer, as was his custom, at Pride's Crossing on the North Shore of Massachusetts. Although circumstances prevented him from seeing the President for another four weeks, he may be said to have been the principal factor in shaping the foreign policy of the United States from this date until Mr. Wilson returned to the Peace Conference in Paris in March, 1919. Much was not done that he would have preferred done, but those measures to which the President was willing to commit himself were, in the main, the product of the Texan's nimble brain. Bryan, as titular Secretary of State, was deprived of actual responsibility with a deftness which produced no personal resentment, but in the course of nine months culminated in his resignation. Robert Lansing, his successor and a sound lawyer and able diplomat, was a more intelligently compliant lieutenant to the two men who formulated the country's definite policy—a role which Lansing's spiritual greatness tolerated, despite its occasional irksomeness to his pride.

During Mr. House's voyage home the storm he had hoped to avert had burst with a fury exceeding his worst forebodings. It is unnecessary here to do more than sketch the opening moves of the Powers in that tense week at the end of July and the beginning of August. Mr. House was one of those who believed that an instant declaration of Great Britain's intention to support France against German aggression would have prevented hostilities. He was the more inclined to blame the Cabinet in London for delaying this announcement because he felt that he had given ample warning to the Foreign Secretary of the dangerous tension in Berlin. It was, he thought, a typical instance of the English tendency to muddle and procrastinate. But the harm had been done. The armies were marching, and for the first time he appreciated fully the significance of the Kaiser's warning that, once Germany had ordered mobilization, she would not, could not, hold her hand.

Austria's declaration of war against Serbia on July 28 had been followed by the bombardment of Belgrade. On August 2, German troops crossed the French and Belgian frontiers, and Russian armies began their advance into East Prussia—prematurely hurried in order to relieve the pressure on France—which was to end disastrously the last week of the month in Hindenburg's (really Ludendorff's and François') classic victory at Tannenberg. On August 7, Liége fell to the thrust of the German right wing in its wide sweep to outflank the French armies based on Verdun and Nancy, and nullify their invasion of Lorraine. Sir John French's army landed in France on August 16, and within a week was involved in the battles along the Belgian frontier resulting in the costly retreat to the Marne.

In the first five weeks of the war Germany swept all before her. Never again, except in the two black weeks following Ludendorff's desperate offensive of March 21, 1918, were the fortunes of the Allies to be at so low an ebb. Belgium was obliterated. A Teutonic wedge was driven deep into the heart of France. Preparations had been made to evacuate Paris by September 1. Uhlan patrols were within sight of the outermost suburbs. And then, when all seemed lost, the tide turned— not so much by reason of the stubborn stand of the French and the pitifully small British Expeditionary Force on the line of the Marne and northward to Verdun, but rather because of the inevitable dislocation of the German armies by the speed of their advance, and the withdrawal of several corps from the right wing necessitated by the unexpected vigor of the Russian penetration of East Prussia.

There was no "miracle of the Marne" any more than there were ghostly "bowmen of Mons" to guard the British retreat with flights of clothyard shafts. Foch's famous repulse of the Prussian Guards in the marshes of St. Gonde was simply one of a loosely jointed series of actions on a front of more than one hundred miles. It was important because it secured the French center. But the Allied victory was clinched when Samsonov compelled the German General Staff to withdraw corps needed to strengthen von Kluck's exposed flank. If the French had not wasted so many good divisions in Lorraine, they might have converted the Marne into a disaster comparable with Tannenberg.

As it was, they had the forces of Nature on their side, stronger than their strongest battalions. The Germans were physically exhausted; they had outrun their transport trains. Their bid for fortune was not good enough. As the future was to prove, they lost the war in the days between September 6 and 10, not because of any flaw in their plans, but because they lacked the men, the *matériel* and the time to exploit those plans—and, too, because the French, short of heavy field artillery and machine guns, were yet possessed of an *élan* which made up for deficiencies in equipment. Throughout the forty-nine months after September 10, the War in the West was a stalemate and nothing else, despite the ebb and flow of success, until the Americans helped to wreck Ludendorff's last offensive in the Soissons salient in July, 1918, pinched out the St. Mihiel salient, and so brought Metz and the mine fields of Lorraine within threat of French guns, and drove forward in the Argonne against the jugular vein of German communications.

This, substantially and in brief, was how Mr. House viewed the war in perspective, disregarding the various remote spheres of operations. He was not a "Westerner" in the strict sense, as the term came to be understood in England. That is, he did not subscribe to the cast-iron principle that the war could be won only on the Western Front. But he did believe that the one possibility of overwhelming defeat for the Allies consisted in a German victory in France so colossal as to entail the capture of Paris and the Channel ports, and consequently the destruction of the British armies. If this happened, he did not see how France and Britain could continue the struggle, no matter how successful they might be on other fronts. And it is typical of the man's steely nerve that he never once conceded the probability of such an event, although he freely admitted, more than once, that the ineptness of Allied generals, and their misapplication of resources, made such a catastrophe possible, if neither probable nor inevitable. Time and again, he saw the Allies with victory in their grasp, and unable to develop it. But he refused to despair of their ultimate success after the chaotic battle of the nations at the Marne had frustrated the demoniac energy of the first German offensive.

For it cannot be stated too positively that the key to the policy Mr. House adopted instinctively in that first week of August, 1914—and the policy he endeavored to implant in the President's mind, and in the collective mind of the American people, as rapidly as any considerable proportion of them were able or willing to admit the conception—was that victory for the two great European democracies was essential to the future safety of the United States and of the weaker sister democracies of Latin America. He was far more firmly of this conviction than Theodore Roosevelt, and infinitely more intelligently committed to it than the pro-Ally rabble-rousers and propagandists, who were stridently impatient of the inability of the bulk of the American people to think internationally. As a Texan and a man who had grown up in a small town, he knew how little used were his countrymen to thinking politically beyond the bounds of their own frontiers. Just as he knew that they must be educated patiently in a realization of their vital interest in a conflict which transcended their imaginations. Any different conception, he felt, would have indicated stupidity on his part and a want of patriotism. A victory for a militantly aggressive Germany, then, or at a later date, must be a defeat for everything for which the United States had stood, or would stand, he hoped, in the future. Mr. House was as wholehearted a partisan for the Allies as King George V or Clemenceau. To him, more than to any other one individual, must be attributed responsibility for our ultimate participation in the war. Next to his conception of the League of Nations, this was the greatest achievement of his life, and he never lost faith in the rightness of both policies, nor would he be less sure of them were he alive today to witness the collapse—temporarily, he would say—of the prestige of the edifice he had reared, no matter how willingly he admitted the defects inherent in man-made things.

Mr. House, it is scarcely necessary to say, was not singular in his feeling. It is true that his father had been born a British subject, that he had spent much of his childhood and adult life in the British Isles, and that many of his friends had been British. But anyone who was familiar with him knew that he was essentially American in his habits and outlook. The Old West had set its stamp upon him. No, his sympathy for the Allies, and especially for Britain, sprang from a source more elemental than the accident of an English-born father. To him it was as apparent as it was to the average intelligent American that the social organization of the United States was modeled on Anglo-Saxon-Celtic traditions of behavior. It was not unimportant, he thought, that Louisiana was alone in using the Code Napoleon as the basis of the State's laws, while the legal systems of forty-seven States were founded on the Common Law of England, and Blackstone and Coke remained the cornerstone of every law library. He considered it equally important that our political philosophy stemmed from the elaborate machinery for protecting the rights of the Commons which had grown up on the slender foundation of Magna Charta. Most of all, he saw a similarity in our jealousy of military supremacy in the State, our consistent attempts, however fumbling—in this, like England's—to demonstrate fairness toward weaker nations, our emphasis upon individual freedom of initiative.

The link between our interests and Britain's was so plain to him that he could not believe in the intellectual sincerity of an educated man who disputed it. Forget that we spoke the same language, and still there were innumerable racial and cultural traditions, jointly nourished, that pointed to the one goal: the preservation of democratic government. In this respect the two countries shared a responsibility of paramount importance, Britain to her dominions, colonies and dependencies, the United States to the many feebler nations which had emulated the system she had created, the system of republican sovereignty, that most amazing of man's efforts to curb his own propensities by counterchecks between the branches of government, and a limited tenure of executive authority.

It would be a mistake, however, to convey the impression that Mr. House was blind to the black spots in Britain's record, to the selfishness of her imperial policy, to the creakiness of her age-worn social fabric. He believed that the British might learn much from the United States, even as the United States might improve the efficiency of the American brand of democracy by adaptation of the more responsive features of parliamentary government. But, to put his philosophy in a nutshell, he considered any kind of Anglo-Saxon-Celtic democracy preferable to the military imperialism and concentration of power which characterized—and characterizes—Germany.

It may be a surprise to many Americans to know that his feeling was shared by the President, who stated to him in their first conversation after his return, that if Germany won it would change the course of our civilization and make the United States a military nation. Mr. Wilson did not see the situation as clearly as Mr. House. He could not have done so. He had not sufficiently studied it, and he was bewildered by the responsibilities of his office and the realization that the people had not "thought through" on the problem. But his instinctive reaction to the values at stake was the same as Mr. House's. *Woodrow Wilson always wanted the Allies to win.* He never lost this prejudice against Germany. "German philosophy is essentially selfish, and lacking in spirituality," he told his friend. But more than he wanted to see the Allies win, he wanted to keep the United States out of war. He was hag-ridden by memories of the long row of caskets, draped in the Stars and Stripes, which had been brought up from Vera Cruz in April. It was torture to his sensitive soul to reflect that he must hold himself responsible for every American he ordered into danger.

Mr. House had an acute perception of his friend's dilemma. In the months succeeding the outbreak of the war he came to know the President more intimately than ever, for, after Ellen Axson Wilson died, on August 6, no human being was so close as he to the grief-stricken, soli-

tary man in the White House, who had been denied by the exigencies of
the international tempest the barren satisfaction of surrendering himself
completely to absorption in his wife's last moments.

"I don't know how he kept his sanity," Mr. House said, in describing
the President's condition. "I was not well, myself, and the heat prevented me from going to Washington, so I did not see him until he came
north—he had taken Winston Churchill's place at Cornish for the summer. The trouble with him was that he shut up his grief so much within
himself. And he got worse instead of better. I was worried about him.
I remember one time, in the fall of 1914, I think it was, he came on to
New York unexpectedly to stay with me. That night, about ten or
eleven o'clock, he announced suddenly that he wanted to go out for a
walk, and he insisted that he would not have the Secret Service men or
the police dogging him. I argued with him, but it was useless. So,
without saying anything to him, I put a revolver in my pocket, and we
left the house by the service entrance. Nothing would do but that we
must walk on the main streets. I remember we went up Fifth Avenue
and through Forty-second Street and Times Square. The theater crowds
were out. We had people jostling all around us, but not a soul recognized him. It was an extraordinary experience. I wouldn't have believed it could happen, particularly when you consider how striking was
his face, and that he was the most widely photographed man in the
country at the time. If anyone had attacked him, I don't know what I
could have done. People were so thick around us that it would have
been difficult for me to shoot, although I seldom had my hand off my
gun. I thought at that time, and on several occasions afterward, that the
President wanted to die. Certainly his attitude and his mental state indicated that he found no zest in life. Yet it always seemed strange to
me that, feeling as he did, he never relaxed in application to his duties." *

Neither the President nor Mr. House anticipated in the summer of
1914 that the United States might be dragged into the war. Like other
statesmen and most military men, they subscribed to the popular theory
that a prolonged war was impossible within the complex structure of
modern industrialism. They looked for a peace before the end of the
ensuing winter. Their primary concern was for the after-effects of the

* The New York police official in charge of arrangements for covering President
Wilson told me, after Mr. House's death, that as a matter of fact the President and
Mr. House were shadowed on this walk, the officers on duty having been instructed
to make themselves as unostentatious as possible. "There were two detectives always
within reach of them," this official stated. "We knew that the President liked to
get away from his guards, and were on the watch for him."

struggle upon the United States. Both of them held the opinion that Russia's emergence as a substantial victor would be as dangerous to the democracies as a German triumph, and their objective of the moment was to do whatever was possible to bring about a peace which should leave in its train a minimum of evil consequences.

8

The world convulsion which Mr. House had striven to prevent exerted a profound, and in many ways a sinister, influence upon President's Wilson's health and personality, as well as upon his political fortunes. In this last respect, it must be remembered that in the summer of 1914 the President had attained a degree of popularity he was destined never again to be granted by a baffled and harried public. His domestic program was proceeding successfully, his leadership of his party was unchallenged, business confidence was restored, and a period of normal prosperity was in sight. But the war, and sorrow over his wife's death, upset him so drastically that by the fall of that year he was telling Mr. House that his great work had been done and he wished he might not have to run for reelection. He was bewildered by a situation with which he was not fitted by mentality or character to cope. To him war was not merely hateful in theory, as it was to Mr. House. It was loathsome. It exacerbated every fiber of his being. He dreaded the responsibilities it laid upon him, exactly as he dreaded promiscuous physical contacts and meetings with men of antipathetical disposition. And he was spiritually tormented by the conflict between his detestation for such episodes as the German rape of Louvain, his sympathy for the Allied cause, and his conviction that he must use every effort to prevent his country's entanglement abroad.

"His attitude all through the war was a tribute to his greatness," was Mr. House's judgment long afterward. "But if there had been no war, if we had been able to negotiate the international arrangements we had in mind, he would have stood foremost today in people's memories. He would have been easily reelected. Men of both parties would have admired him—and I believe his party would still be in power. Our prosperity would have been established on the sound bedrock of peaceful progress. It was his misfortune to be called upon to handle, with unsurpassed honesty of purpose, a situation which no man, however great, could have handled to the satisfaction of everyone. I think he deserves credit for having done as well as he did. He made mistakes. It is sad to think of them. But so any President would have done. No man can be always right."

One consequence of the war, and of the problems it created for Americans, was to bring out in high relief the primary differences in the characters of Woodrow Wilson and Edward M. House. Both of them hated war. Both hoped to be able to set up international devices for making it as difficult as possible. But their backgrounds and upbringings created in them radically opposite mental reactions toward the means of controlling this scourge which springs from man's eternal acquisitiveness. Mr. Wilson had been raised—to use the good old American folk word— in the peaceful security of a Presbyterian manse, in an atmosphere of religious austerity and intellectual detachment. He had encountered no wider experiences in youth and manhood. His only battles had been waged with brains. He had never seen a man killed or held a weapon in his hand. Mr. House, on the contrary, as has been made clear in these pages, was a product of the Frontier. Combat and death were an old story to him. He knew men in the rough. The Civil War had touched his childhood with a peremptory firmness Mr. Wilson's had escaped. Where Mr. Wilson's youth had been sheltered and directed in oft-traveled paths, Mr. House had ventured far afield. Academic influences had surrounded and perceptibly colored the character of the former president of Princeton. There had been no uncertainty in his career, up to the time university intrigues impelled him to run for Governor. When he went to England it was to slip into an identical atmosphere—it was Wordsworth's Lake Country which most interested his curiosity.

Consider, in opposition, the varied experiences which had shaped Mr. House's character. As a young man he was acquainted with every facet of American life, North and South, East and West. He had known what it meant to be obliged to carry a six-shooter for self-protection. He knew the raffishness of the Border, and the suave sophistication of society in New York and Washington and Boston, in London and Paris. Abroad, he was not so much interested in the traditions of the past as in the ideas that were molding the present and forecasting the trends of the future. He had inherited money, to be sure, had been presented with a financial security beyond anything Mr. Wilson had enjoyed; but he had employed this good fortune, with daring skill, to accomplish more than his own prosperity. He was practical, definite in his mental processes, where Mr. Wilson was idealistic and visionary. He was, it is fair to say, also an idealist. But it cannot be too strongly insisted that he was a *practical* idealist. He had no use for an ideal which could not be made to work. There were plenty of ideals which could be turned to account. So why waste time on those as yet unadaptable to human progress?

In this analysis, sketchy as it may be, I think you have a sufficient clue to the differences in habits of thought which governed the psychologies of the two friends in their separate interpretations of the problems thrown up by the war. Mr. Wilson was prepared to accept any recourse, short of national disgrace, to avoid committing the United States to hostilities. He would not even prepare for such an eventuality, lest an increase in American armaments should be branded as provocative in Germany, the one country which he could so much as picture in his imagination as meriting ultimately a declaration of war. Thus, in November, Mr. House's earliest attempt to persuade him to recommend large naval increases to Congress met with flat failure. Although a year later he veered around completely, and embarked upon a program which would have exceeded Britain's, at this time he refused to agree with his friend that a threat to national security could be most surely discounted by proving that the country was ready to resist aggression with preponderant might.

To Mr. Wilson, in 1914, Germany was a misguided nation, but it was incredible that she might contemplate harming the United States; indeed, sympathetic as he was with the cause of the Allies, his ire already had been stirred by the interruptions in trade resulting from the British blockade, and there is no doubt that this feeling mitigated to some extent his indignation with Germany. To Mr. House, while he labored to keep the peace between Downing Street and the State Department, Germany and Great Britain were never on all fours in their controversies with the United States and other neutrals. He regarded Germany as in the same category as a cattle rustler—and he had learned in Texas that hot lead was the one safe defense against a rustler's depredations. He did what he could to ease British pressure on American exports to the neutrals, but he thought such restrictions were pin-pricks compared to the menace of Germany's aspiration to dominate Europe. And once supreme in Europe, he was assured, her next grasp for power would be directed toward Latin America.

He had not forgotten her meddling in Mexico. When his policy of conciliating Britain on Panama Canal tolls finally had borne fruit in July —on the verge of the European crash—in the flight of Huerta, it was the German cruiser *Dresden* which had rescued the dictator from Vera Cruz. He would have been amused, had he been able to look forward twenty-four years, to find her up to her old tricks again, scheming and plotting to undermine the Monroe Doctrine. But he was not amused to note, shortly before his death, Hitler's attempt to hamper the influence of the democracies by an alliance with Japan. He remembered too well the Kaiser's dictum in 1914 that within twenty years the Western nations must reckon with the expanding imperialism of the yellow islanders.

Before the end of the year Mr. House was convinced that the United States must be dragged into the European struggle—if for no other reason than because of the weight of her own economic power—unless the embattled nations could be induced to accept a peace by compromise. But in this belief he knew that he was one of the farsighted few. He had too many sources of information to be ignorant that Americans beyond the Alleghanies had not the slightest perception of the possible consequences to them of the defeat of Britain and France.

"The people in California hardly knew there was a war, then or later," he said once. "And I suppose I'll have to admit that the people in Texas thought of Mexico, if you talked war to them. Even now, after two million of us have been in France, people have forgotten what it was about. You know, there really is something in the idea that this country is almost too big to think the same way. But we have gotten them steamed up twice. The other time? I mean the Civil War." He smiled. "Yes, I know they didn't all think alike, but they all *thought*. I suspect when it's necessary, and near to being too late, we can get them to think together again. But it isn't easy. People ought to remember this when they criticize Wilson. My lord, he had them coming at him from every direction in those years. And I have sometimes thought that he leaned backwards in holding out against war because he knew he was pro-British. He felt responsible about that, there were so many people who were anti-British. And he tried to be President of the United States, not President of one faction."

Bryan, who was anti-British and anti-preparedness, represented the sentiments of millions of Americans, especially in the West. Presently, but for Mr. House's intervention, he would bring the country to the threshold of a diplomatic break with Britain; and of his attitude toward an increase of the Army and Navy Mr. House recorded in his diary, November 8: "He did not believe there was the slightest danger to this country from foreign invasion, even if the Germans were successful. He thought *after war was declared* there would be plenty of time to make any preparations necessary. He talked as innocently as my little grandchild, Jane Tucker."

Despite his own predilections, Mr. House labored more tirelessly for peace than any other individual, including the President. The Ambassadors abroad did much of the spadework—Page, in London, cantankerous, compunctious, embarrassingly Anglophile; Sharp,* in Paris, calm, vigilant, always dependable; Gerard, in Berlin, one of the wisest and sanest men in the starred roster of the Diplomatic Service. But it was Mr. House who had the initiative in what was done. He conceived and outlined the strategy of the campaign against war which was soon being fought in every capital. The State Department was relegated to the status of an intermediary for his ideas, a depository of public records. Much of the more confidential diplomatic correspondence passed directly through the little apartment in East Thirty-fifth Street. The Ambassadors of the belligerents in Washington called on him when they wanted to influence the Administration or sought assistance in the web of intrigue that was being spun across the Atlantic. In South America, the embassies at Rio de Janeiro, Buenos Aires, Lima and Valparaiso were dinning away at his attempt to organize the democracies of the Americas in a solid front against imperialistic invasion, a generation before Franklin D. Roosevelt sent Cordell Hull to Lima to concert a similar opposition to a similar threat. If Mr. House were alive today, and could read this, I am sure he would smile gently, and say, as he often did: "The one trouble with democracies is that they learn slow, and forget fast."

Already on September 5 he had written Zimmermann, in Berlin, feinting for an opening to launch *pourparlers* with the several belligerents. The stalemate which succeeded the Marne made it plain to him that both sides were bogged down for the time being. This was true of the Eastern front no less than of the Western. The German victory in East Prussia had been offset by stunning Russian triumphs over the Austrians. All that was stopping the Russian armies from overrunning the Dual Monarchy was lack of transport to supply more than two million men at the front. Arms and munitions were lacking, of course, but had they been available it is doubtful whether the Russians could have used them to much advantage. In the circumstances, both sides were in a waiting mood, each disposed to leave it to the other to make the opening move.

Mr. House had "to walk on eggs," as he put it. He was in touch with the Germans, the Austrians, the British and the French, not to speak of emissaries of the secondary powers. They all wanted to use him, and except for his British friends, who told him what they honestly believed—and had to be discounted proportionately—they told him as little of the truth as they could. The most important element in the situation, however, was that all trusted him, with the possible exception

* Sharp took over the Paris embassy from Myron T. Herrick just before hostilities began.

of the Russians, more than they did any other neutral statesman. The informality of their meetings with him tended to make them more confidential than they could have been with officials of the State Department. For example, Dumba, the Austrian Ambassador, did not hesitate to reveal to him, in August, a distaste for the war which indicated to Mr. House the growing realization of the Vienna authorities that in their lust for vengeance upon Serbia they had incurred a higher risk than a paltry Balkan adventure. The aftermath of the Marne, likewise, left Bernstorff no longer "so cocksure" as he had been. The unpleasant truth was beginning to dawn on everyone that the war wasn't going to be concluded in a single smashing campaign. Page wrote from London, September 22, quoting Kitchener: "The war will begin next spring"; and several months later was citing French as admitting that it would take two years to drive the Germans out of Belgium, and four years to get into Germany. Gerard, in Berlin, testified with greater accuracy to the confidence of the officials he met. Sharp wrote from Paris of the widespread belief that time fought on the side of the Allies. The French had a confidence, which seems pathetic in retrospect, in the "Kitchener Armies" and the mythical "Russian Steamroller"; mythical, that is, when it encountered German, not Austro-Hungarian, opposition.

But out of the mass of conflicting evidence, the truths, half-truths, and lies which sometimes gave a valuable hint to truth, certain facts gradually became apparent to Mr. House. Both sides were afraid of the issue. Both sides would welcome peace. Each side, because it was afraid, was demonstrating an arrogance designed to conceal the underlying misgivings. Each side was determined not to yield enough to bear down its prestige. Mr. House believed—and never found reason to alter his belief—that in the winter of 1914-15 it was practicable to make a compromise peace, based substantially upon the *status quo ante bellum*. The obstacle, as was proved in the result, was the intransigeance of France and Russia, stung by their first defeats and swollen with confidence in the future. Nobody, of course, could have foreseen the stupidity of the British high command, which nullified the Empire's splendid effort. And weren't Italy and Rumania coming in to help?

On September 18, Bernstorff called on Mr. House in a mood which impressed the Texan as anxiously conciliatory. Mr. House had been warned before the war by his British friends to be wary of Bernstorff, who was alleged to have acquired a record for trickiness and insincerity in his diplomatic work, notably in Belgrade. But Mr. House detected nothing to confirm these allegations. Rather, he thought Bernstorff manifested a more straightforward and realistic attitude toward the situation than any other German. His ultimate judgment was that Bernstorff consistently had refused to be misled by the spell of Germany's tactical victories in the field, and did all he could at every turn to prevent his country from forcing American intervention.

Now, at Mr. House's suggestion, he agreed to a secret meeting with Ambassador Spring-Rice in Mr. House's apartment. Spring-Rice, however, was suspicious of Bernstorff's intentions. The British Ambassador, a most kindly, scholarly man, of impeccable honor, had the defects of a nervous, fussy disposition, complicated by ill-health and an exaggerated sense of his country's dignity. He was doubtful of the propriety of such a meeting, thought that, if it ever came to be known, it would be regarded in France and Russia as having been prompted by disloyal intentions. But on Mr. House's urgence he agreed to refer the decision to Grey.

In the meantime, about the middle of December and while they were waiting to hear from London, Mr. House received a letter from Zimmermann, dated December 3, in answer to his letter of September 5. It was written with cagey indefiniteness, but the important feature of it to Mr. House was that it welcomed his proffered assistance in starting peace feelers. A second talk with Bernstorff encouraged him by the Ambassador's admission that he saw no difficulty in accepting, as a basis for further discussions, the principle of evacuation and indemnification of Belgium and a treaty of general disarmament. But when Grey's cable arrived on December 20, it contained only an expression of the Foreign Secretary's personal belief that it would not be "a good thing for the Allies to stand out against" such a proposal. This was supplemented three days later by a second cable, emphasizing the fact that Grey had not seen fit to discuss the matter either with his colleagues or the Allies, and that he anticipated "great difficulties" from the latter. Spring-Rice gave it as his own opinion, which Mr. House naturally assumed to be a reflection of Foreign Office views, that France would demand a part of Lorraine and Russia Constantinople as a sop to peace. The idea of an informal discussion between Spring-Rice and Bernstorff was abandoned.

The response was not so favorable as Mr. House had expected, but Grey, like Zimmermann, left the door open for renewed suggestions; and President Wilson, who from week to week was becoming more sensitive to the dangers confronting the United States, redoubled his urgence that Mr. House should go abroad again as his unofficial representative to endeavor to devise a formula for negotiations which would win the approval of the belligerents. Mr. House was not so optimistic at the moment as his friend. The United States was unpopular with both sides

to the conflict. The Germans resented the increasing flow of American
munitions and foodstuffs to Britain and France, and the hostility of the
bulk of the American press and informed opinion. The British were
outraged by the reiterated protests pouring from the State Department
against the blockade's interference with our Scandinavian and Dutch
commerce, and our insistence upon their recognition of the Declaration
of London, which had exempted as contraband such sinews of war as
rubber and cotton. At the end of September there would have been a
severance of diplomatic relations, if Mr. House had not altered the texture of a draft of instructions to Page which Bryan had sent to the
White House for the President's approval.

"The devil of it was that there was right on both sides in these controversies with the British," Mr. House said in a conversation afterward.
"Our people were hot about what they regarded as unjustifiable interference with our trade with neutrals. It meant nothing to them at the
time that the neutrals were simply brokers for the Germans. The stuff
imported was shipped straight into Germany. But that didn't alter the
fact that Great Britain had signed the Declaration of London, that she
was violating international law. Bryan was technically right. So were
the British. If they hadn't stopped this trade in contraband, which
wasn't contraband under the Declaration, Germany would have been
stronger than ever. The truth was that in modern war everything was
contraband; everything, including food, went to bolster a nation's fighting
strength. It was a nasty situation. The Foreign Office did what they
could to placate us, but they couldn't control the Admiralty. It was the
old story of war all over again. You couldn't fight and avoid injustices.
And as far as we were concerned, Bryan didn't help any by his legalistic
attitude, and Page got so pro-British and anti-Bryan that the President
wouldn't read the long letters of protest he wrote."

The President's face "became gray" over these problems, Mr. House
recorded in his diary. In the same place one finds also a wistful comment by the President that he and Monroe, both peace lovers and the
only two Princeton men to hold the Presidency, had been confronted by
identical situations of world war and interference with American commerce. He hoped, he said, that he would have greater success than
Monroe in avoiding entanglement in the conflict.

After hearing again from Grey that the British Government would
welcome a visit from Mr. House, and a further series of exploratory conversations with Bernstorff, Dumba, Spring-Rice, Bakhmetieff and Jusserand, the President and his friend decided on January 13, 1915, that Mr.
House should sail at the end of the month. From London, if all went

well, he was to proceed to Paris and Berlin. Bakhmetieff and Jusserand were eager for him to go to Petrograd, but Mr. House concealed his mental reservations on this point. He had scant sympathy for Russia and her ambitions, and believed that if he could persuade the British to put pressure on France to be reasonable, and supposing Germany's peace professions were sincere, it would be relatively easy to bring the Czar's government to heel. But he had no illusions as to his chance of success, which, he was convinced, depended upon the willingness of the Allies to forego territorial gains not justified by the current military situation, no matter how overpowering might be the forces they hoped eventually to bring into the field. Germany wanted peace, but not with the desperation of a nation facing inevitable defeat.

9

Despite his preoccupation with European affairs, Mr. House found time in the fall of 1914 to push forward his long-range project for welding the South and Central American Republics with the United States in a pact to uphold the Monroe Doctrine, to guarantee mutually their independence and territorial integrity and to provide for settlement of differences amongst themselves by arbitration. This idea, as we have seen, had come to him before the war, largely as a consequence of study of the problems arising out of the Mexican Revolution. It was not entirely original with himself, inasmuch as it was merely a definite extension of ideas advanced by James G. Blaine, when Secretary of State, to a Pan-American Convention at Washington in 1889—which came to nothing; but it was important for two reasons: first, it provided the inception for the existing Pan-American organization; second, it was the germ cell from which grew the structure of the League of Nations.*

In November, Mr. House brought his plan to the President's attention in detail, taking advantage of the opportunity to pry Mr. Wilson's mind away from absorption in domestic policies by describing the beneficial results of uniting the democracies of the two continents. The President endorsed it enthusiastically, and several weeks later, when Mr. House was visiting him, sat down and wrote out with a pencil a short draft of the points to be covered in the preliminary discussions Mr. House advised with the ABC Ambassadors:

"1st. Mutual guarantees of political independence under republican form of government and mutual guarantees of territorial integrity.

* For clarity's sake, this project is outlined here regardless of the sequence of parallel events.

"2nd. Mutual agreement that the Government of each of the contracting parties acquire complete control within its jurisdiction of the manufacture and sale of munitions of war."

The first point was practically identical with the wording of Article X of the Covenant of the League of Nations. The second was discarded from consideration in future discussions with Latin-American representatives for the same reason that a similar article was dropped from the League Covenant: distaste for the commitment of governments to munitions manufacturing plus doubts as to the idea's efficiency. But the tentative pact, as finally written, embodied completely the spirit of the Wilson draft.

Mr. House showed the draft to Bryan, who heartily approved it, but thereafter showed no interest in advancing the project. The ABC Ambassadors also were cordial toward it, so that when he was obliged to leave for Europe in January, 1915, he considered his plan to be safely in train, one of his last acts being to urge its development upon the President and Bryan. But after his return in June he was dismayed to learn that practically nothing more had been done, partly because of Bryan's lack of interest, partly because of Chile's suspicion that it cloaked a plot of intervention in Mexico. Lansing, when he took office in July, wrote Mr. House that he could find nothing about the plan in the State Department files, but offered prompt cooperation in resuscitating it. He was as good as his word, and in addition adopted a suggestion by Mr. House to call upon the Latin-American powers for assistance in trying to straighten out the Mexican situation.

In August, representatives of the ABC republics, Bolivia, Uruguay and Guatemala, met in Washington and issued an invitation to the leaders of the several Mexican factions to join in a conference to arrange for orderly elections. Carranza alone, as chief of the Constitutionalists, refused. He did, in fact, hold the balance of power, and on October 19 the Administration was obliged to swallow its pride and recognize his government as the *de facto* régime. Still, the gesture had its effect in Latin America, and although Chile persisted in her attitude, it was not because of any overt act by the United States or for want of intelligent efforts by the State Department, operating under Lansing and Frank Polk, his Assistant Secretary, with an orderliness which produced paeans of praise from hard-driven envoys, who had been brought to the verge of despair by Bryan's casual ways and unpredictable prejudices.

By November 18, too, Lansing had whipped into comprehensive legal form a revised draft in four articles of the bare outline produced by the President and Mr. House, and could report the approval of it by the Argentine and Brazilian Ambassadors. The Chilean Ambassador, Suarez, professed to be satisfied, but his government held aloof, and matters drifted along without a conclusion being reached until Villa's foray of March 8, 1916, on Columbus, New Mexico, sent Pershing across the Border and brought about the mobilization of the National Guard along the Rio Grande. Then Argentina joined Chile in suspicion of the United States, and an *impasse* was reached. Too much was happening in the world for Mr. House to give the pact the help it needed. On August 8, Polk wrote from Washington that it "seems dead for the moment." Argentina at last was willing to sign, but difficulties arose with Brazil. In the fall of that year Mr. House reluctantly put the project out of his mind. Yet that it had been worth the efforts expended upon it, he thought, was demonstrated by the unanimity with which Latin America rallied to the Allied cause after the United States flung down her gage of battle to Germany. Nor did he ever lose faith in his idea. He would have been among the first to endorse Franklin D. Roosevelt's attempt to establish a similar alliance in defense of American democracy in December, 1938.

10

Mr. House sailed from New York, January 30, 1915, on his third mission abroad, with a *quasi* official status, in that, while he refused to accept diplomatic rank, he bowed to the President's insistence that his expenses should be paid out of the contingent fund of the State Department. Again, however, he had no definite instructions, and no credentials other than a brief note, written personally by Mr. Wilson, who did not take so much as a carbon of it, requesting him to do what he could, by consultation with leading statesmen, to enable the United States to proffer its services for peace. He had, too, Bryan's blessing in his efforts. The Commoner, with the unselfish manliness which characterized his attitude toward Mr. House, showed no jealousy of the Texan's choice as the President's representative, bidding him farewell as the man best fitted for the enterprise.

If Mr. House was not so optimistic as he had been the previous summer, he had reason to hope that he might accomplish something of moment. But an evil star hung over the world in those distraught months of 1915, an evil star which, to tell the sad truth, was to shine but little dimmed, at rare intervals, for many years to come, and which hangs imponderably in the heavens today. In London, the talk was all of war. Britain echoed the tramp of armed men. Industry was keyed with increasing tensity to squander materials in battle. There was an atmosphere of belligerent optimism. The new "Kitchener Armies" were taking the field. The Dardanelles fiasco was in the making. The members of the Cabinet were almost to a man, consciously or subconsciously, hostile to talk of peace, except in the abstract. Grey was a notable variation from the pattern, but even he was obscured in his judgments by the fervor of patriotism, the ceaseless jangle of propaganda, which dinned at men's mentalities. Of King George Mr. House recorded, after their first meeting: "He is the most belligerent Englishman I have encountered."

The situation was additionally complicated by the Germans' proclamation, February 18, of a submarine "war zone" around the British Isles, with their announced intention of destroying all enemy commerce within these waters, a step to which they had been driven by the disarrangement of their land campaign by the unforeseen success of the Russian attack on Austria. Mr. House perceived the certainty of trouble for the United States in such use of the submarine weapon, and he welcomed the President's prompt response that the United States would hold Germany to "strict accountability" for any resulting harm to her citizens. But the move had served mainly to whip up Britain's fury in the same way as the Zeppelin raids. Mr. House saw himself getting nowhere, and like the conjuror he was, pulled out of his hat a trick rabbit he called the Freedom of the Seas, which he had devised as a possible stop-gap for just such an emergency, a bait to arouse the peaceable instincts in both groups of belligerents, but especially the British and the Germans.

The doctrine of the Freedom of the Seas afterwards became one of the most momentous, as it was one of the most hotly debated, theories constituting the ideology of a machinery for World Peace. Many men's brains contributed to it, but perhaps none shaped it so effectively as Mr. House's. Briefly, as he first envisaged it, it provided that all sea-borne commerce, except actual munitions, that is, weapons and ammunition, should be immune to interference in time of war. But the conception broadened as he discussed it with other sympathetic minds, until it took on the sweeping formula that all commerce, of whatever description, should pass freely, save into ports effectively blockaded. In other words, as he told one statesman, who asked of what use navies would then be, warships would function only in battles between themselves—navies would be valuable essentially as weapons of defense. His complementary theory to this was that a great but isolated sea power like Great Britain would gain by the immunity of her sea commerce, and that Germany, in the same way, could secure the materials she needed, provided she had a navy sufficiently strong to keep her ports clear.

The propagation of this doctrine had much to do with bringing Germany to her knees. It had a conspicuous part in the debates and the motives behind them, which created the League of Nations. It had a good deal to do with the series of naval limitation treaties initiated by Charles E. Hughes, as Secretary of State under Harding. In the light of what has since happened in the world, it would be folly to argue that those treaties—and certainly Mr. House's doctrine—achieved the results which were anticipated for them. It may be significant that Grey himself, who ostensibly favored Mr. House's doctrine, seems, on the evidence, to have considered that the idea of outlawing war, as stipulated in the Covenant of the League, for which President Wilson justly claimed responsibility, rendered the idea of the Freedom of the Seas superfluous. If there was to be no more war by international agreement, then there was no necessity for Freedom of the Seas. It is a fact that he brought Mr. Wilson to acceptance of this theory.

Nowadays, when the unescapable logic of events has challenged the whole theory of the possibility of outlawing war, when all the nations have armed as never before and are feverishly increasing their armaments, when the submarine and the airplane are used as a matter of course against neutral as well as enemy commerce, it may well be asked whether there was ever any more chance that the Freedom of the Seas might become practicable than that the League of Nations might be able to prevent the raping of an Ethiopia or a Czecho-Slovakia. Mr. House did not live to be a witness to the last violation of international honor, but his answer to those who advanced it as a reason for believing that there was no such thing as honor between sovereign states would have been the same that he always made to criticisms of his theories in practice:

His theories never had been applied in practice as he and President Wilson and other honorable statesmen intended that they should be. A League of Nations, to be effective, must include all nations, and above all, the most powerful nation on earth, the United States. The Freedom of the Seas could be erected as international law only by the adoption and guarantee of it by all nations. Limitation of armaments could be effective only in the degree attained. It could not be substituted for disarmament. And world confidence and peace could be established only by universal acceptance of an international code of honor and obligation, on the part of all nations, to punish and curb any transgressor at whatever cost. There could never be such a thing as World Peace, unless the United States accepted her obligation as a member of the Commonwealth of Man. This was the price of peace, to take or to leave.

He died, I am sure, in the belief he always entertained, that the day would come when the United States would assume her burdens because of that same unescapable pressure of the logic of events. Otherwise, he felt, the world would continue, as in past centuries, like a group of property owners mutually predatory, and the spoils of civilization would go to the ones best armed, least scrupulous, and perhaps most favored by their neighbors' laziness or lack of courage and virtue. The test of this belief of his is presently confronting a world bewildered and dismayed.

In February, 1915, such a doctrine as the Freedom of the Seas attracted intelligent, forward-thinking men by its novelty and suggestion of a security the more dazzling for its contemporary absence. Grey indicated his personal acceptance of it. He agreed that Mr. House should try it on Berlin, whence Zimmermann had written, asserting that the main thing Germany wanted was permanent peace, "the same cry in each of the belligerent states," Mr. House noted.

In Paris he saw Delcassé, the Foreign Minister, the stormy petrel of Franco-German animosities, whose resignation the Kaiser had forced after the Agadir incident. Delcassé was suavely pleasant and conciliatory, but so outspoken in his belief that it was futile to talk peace before the Allies had won a substantial success on the Western Front that Mr. House was content to talk generalities and passed on to Germany. In Berlin he tendered his bait, savored by the hint that he "might" be able to persuade the British to accept it, to von Bethmann-Hollweg, the Junker Chancellor—whose capacity for beer astounded him—and his friend Zimmermann. They fell upon it with an avidity which impressed him as evidence of the growing concern of the Kaiser's Civil Government, struggling to maintain its authority against the arrogant chiefs of the fighting services. It offered, Zimmermann said, an excuse to the German people for evacuating Belgium, since adoption by England of such a doctrine absolved his Government of the necessity of clinging to the Belgian ports menacing the Narrow Seas.

Mr. House was encouraged to believe that perhaps he had found the magic formula to bring a crazy world to its collective senses. He hoped so more than ever, for all that he himself saw in Germany, all he learned from Ambassador Gerard—as keen an observer as himself, and much more familiar with the underlying intrigues and cross-purposes of Imperial politics—disposed him to pessimism as to the future. Resentment against the United States for supplying munitions to the Allies was so bitter that he was warned not to speak English in the streets. The Kaiser, restlessly parading from front to front, more and more under the influence of the Army and Navy Staffs and losing authority to them along with the Civil Government, was too anti-American to be talked to, Gerard warned him. The confidence of the German people in their armies had rallied since the fall of 1914. And if the Admiralty, dominated by von Tirpitz's hatred of England, ran amuck with their submarines in the proclaimed "war zone," it must be only a question of time before incidents happened which would involve the United States.

But despite the blackness of the outlook he left Berlin more hopeful than when he had entered Germany. The core of the problem, as he saw it, was to free the responsible statesmen of the belligerents from the Frankensteins of their own creation, the monstrosities of national egoism, hatred and blind lust, which mowed and gibbered in every hamlet of every land. The statesmen had become the puppets of the propaganda they had sowed to drive their peoples to the desperation of self-slaughter. Zimmermann freely admitted that peace, on the mere basis of the *status quo ante bellum,* would mean the expulsion of the Kaiser and the death or exile of the Government. Delcassé and President Poincaré, interviewed by Mr. House on his return journey to London, tacitly admitted as much for themselves. The Cabinet in London was about to be reorganized for the same reason. "Smash Germany!" was the slogan. Yet in each capital the few important individuals who cherished a remnant of sanity listened eagerly to Mr. House's gentle voice. There was a will to peace, he felt, if only it could be aroused.*

Then the German diplomats kicked his foothold from under him with the stupid ignorance of primary psychology which seems to be a trait of German diplomacy under any form of Government. On his return to London he was greeted with the information that German propagandists in New York and Berlin had seized upon the Freedom of the Seas as their own idea, and were boasting that it was the implement with which they had put England in the wrong. It was one thing, Grey pointed out, for Britain to be asked to accept so revolutionary a doctrine from the neutral source of America; but how could the Allies be brought to con-

---

* Mr. House was much impressed by Walter Rathenau, the great German Jew, who was the soul of Germany's economic defense during the war, and who, as Secretary for Foreign Affairs, was the first victim of National Socialist bigotry in 1922. In London he was impressed by the pacifism of men like Sir Francis Hirst, editor of the *Economist,* Lord Loreburn, and Lord Morley. De Casenave, of the French Foreign Office, also seemed to him less extreme than most Frenchmen; but, as was perhaps natural in the circumstances, he found little trace of moderation in most leaders of opinion. He considered Rathenau one of the greatest statesmen of the war period, perhaps the greatest of all Germans. There is no need to speculate on what his sentiments would have been toward the ferocious crucifixion of the Jews which was started by the Hitler machine in the fall of 1938.

sider it when it was put forth by a Germany which had bluntly stated its belief that a treaty was "a scrap of paper"? The Freedom of the Seas was temporarily suspect.

Mr. House sadly realized that his work was all to do over again. But he refused to be discouraged, and pressed his interviews with British leaders of all shades of opinion through April and the first week of May. On May 7 he had appointments in the morning with Grey—with whom he made a visit to Kew to see the flowers and hear the blackbirds sing— and the King. Both spoke of the dangers of submarine warfare, and inquired what the United States would do if American citizens were killed. That evening, at dinner at the American Embassy, the news came that the *Lusitania* had been sunk, without warning, at two o'clock in the afternoon off the Old Head of Kinsale, with a loss of American lives, 124, as was later determined. This was the eventuality which Mr. House had feared. A direct challenge had been delivered to the United States by the forces of German ruthlessness.

He was not in doubt as to the proper policy of the United States, but he waited to ascertain the indisputable facts before he acted. Then, on May 9, he cabled, with a forthrightness which could have left no doubt as to his feeling:

"It is now certain that a large number of American lives were lost. . . . I believe [it was typical of him that he did not use the word advise] an immediate demand should be made upon Germany that this shall not occur again. If she fails to give such assurance, I should inform her that our Government expected to take such measures as were necessary to insure the safety of American citizens. If war follows, it will not be a new war, but an endeavor to end more speedily an old one. Our intervention will save, rather than increase, the loss of life. America has come to the parting of the ways, when she must determine whether she stands for civilized or uncivilized warfare. We can no longer remain neutral spectators. Our action in this crisis will determine the part we will play when peace is made, and how far we may influence a settlement for the lasting good of humanity. We are being weighed in the balance, and our position amongst nations is being assessed by mankind."

On the original draft of this document is scrawled in the handwriting of the American Ambassador to Great Britain: "Page agrees, and considers political effect will be excellent at home." Mr. House, who was as fond of Page as he was aware of that estimable gentleman's occasional lapses of understanding, did him the favor, without telling him so, of eliding these words from the version cabled. They could only have emphasized the President's growing distaste for Page's Anglophile tendencies, and added to the consequent doubt as to his ability to continue to hold his post.

"Can you imagine," asked Mr. House, in showing the original document, "how the President would have been offended by a suggestion that he might make political capital of a situation which I knew, as anyone must have known who really knew him, was tearing his heart with dismay and calling upon him to sink every prejudice in consideration of what he believed to be for the common good? Page was a good feller, but sometimes he didn't use his head."

I asked him—this was shortly after Mr. Wilson died—if he still believed that we would have done better had we entered the war immediately after the *Lusitania* tragedy.

"I think so," he answered. "Italy was about to come in, and Rumania and Bulgaria and Greece were on the fence. If we had broken with Germany then, it seems plain that Italy would have been in better shape when she declared war against Austria a month or so later. I believe, too, that Bulgaria would have switched to the Allies, although already she was receiving loans from Germany to influence her, and Greece would have come in in time to help the British to success in the Gallipoli campaign. As for us, surely it would have cost us less, rather than more, had we begun our efforts at a time before the Allies were approaching exhaustion. It might even have staved off the Russian Revolution, at least until later. Something was bound to happen in Russia, but probably not Bolshevism, and if Russia had won Constantinople the world's future problem might have been Czarist imperialism instead of German militarism. You can't have everything you want. But, lordy, lordy, think of the lives and suffering and waste that could have been saved if the war had ended a year sooner! It would have meant a better peace, more prestige for us, our influence in the League. It seems a pity. But the President did what he thought was right at the time, what he thought was best for Americans. How many of us thought differently at the time? You must remember, I knew more than most people of what was going on. I tried to make the President see things as I did. If I didn't succeed, I can't blame him for it. The responsibility was his more than anyone else's." *

It is only fair to say that, although Mr. House thought the time had come for a flat showdown with Germany, he had no fault to find with the tenor of the President's *Lusitania* note of May 15. Its effect upon

* Mr. House made these remarks before Hitler was more than a joke, the forgotten "hero" of the Munich beer putsch of November, 1923.

Germany might have been much more satisfactory but for two almost incredible blunders, one committed by Mr. Wilson himself, the other by Bryan, both bafflingly typical of the two men. The President, in a speech at Philadelphia, permitted himself to be trapped by his habit of extemporaneous speaking, against which Mr. House had warned him, into the use of the unfortunate phrase: "There is such a thing as being too proud to fight." As a matter of fact, there was no such thing as Woodrow Wilson ever being "too proud to fight." He simply had succumbed to the orator's temptation of the tricky, unusual phrase, which, as often as not, turns out to be the unfortunate phrase.

Bryan's blunder was infinitely more mischievous. Mr. House heard of it from Gerard, who cabled from Berlin: "Zimmermann told me yesterday that Dumba, Austrian Ambassador, had cabled him that Bryan had told him that America was not in earnest about *Lusitania* matter." Heartsick, Mr. House cabled Gerard's message to the President, adding: "Of course, Mr. Bryan did not say that, but I think you should know what Zimmermann told Gerard." "Of course," as came out in due time, Bryan had said just what he was quoted as saying. He had also prepared the draft of a covering letter for the President's note, stating that it was to be taken in "the Pickwickian sense." The President killed it.

It was not strange that after two such statements, coming from the President and the Secretary of State of the United States, the German Government felt safe in offering a minimum of concessions to the President's demands. It is, by the way, an amusing commentary on human nature, as well as a testimony to Gerard's alertness, that Zimmermann's admission of the Dumba cable was a consequence of his being a "two-bottle man" at luncheon. Thus three indiscretions made an historical fact which otherwise might not be on the record.

In the meantime, and prior to the *Lusitania* incident, Mr. House had been pushing a substitute compromise for the Freedom of the Seas: a suggestion that Germany should abandon submarine warfare against commerce in return for a British concession admitting foodstuffs through the blockade. This the British Government, overriding the objections of the Admiralty, were willing to grant. But on May 25 Gerard was obliged to cable Mr. House at London that the Germans, their confidence increased by the President's reluctance to force an immediate issue, and equally by the failure of the Allies to make headway on the Western Front, would entertain the proposal only if raw materials were added to foodstuffs, which meant that the British blockade would become a joke.

Mr. House did not bother to mention the counter-proposal to his friends in London, except as an illustration of the state of mind prevailing in Berlin; but he never again had sympathy with the claims of the German propagandists that the Allies were starving Germany's civil population. The truth was that the German Army and Navy Staffs were willing to risk the discomfort of the civil population in their confidence that their submarines would break down civilian morale in the British Isles. Gerard testified to this in a letter of June 1.

By May 30, Mr. House had decided that war was inevitable, booked passage for home on the *St. Paul,* sailing June 5, and turned his attention to concerting with members of the British Government the measures the United States could take on short notice which would be of most assistance to the Allied cause. Italy had declared war against Austria-Hungary on May 23, and he was more sanguine than the event warranted of the success of the Dardanelles operations, initiated by the brilliance of Winston Churchill's imagination. He did not know, any more than did the British at the time, that Churchill's naval attack, branded a failure, actually had been successful; that when the British and French fleet withdrew to await the arrival of Sir Ian Hamilton's army there was not ammunition for more than an hour's firing in the Turkish magazines. Neither could he nor anyone else have anticipated the stupidity of the British War Office in failing to send Hamilton the troops needed and promised for the campaign.

"The British missed a great chance at the Dardanelles," he said, in talking about it. "But then they were always missing chances. Their failure to supply high explosive shells for the first Somme offensive was incredible, considering the information they had from their own people at the front. They might have had a break-through in the first tank attack at Cambrai, if they had been prepared to take advantage of their success. The trouble, as I got it, was mainly with Kitchener. He was a great soldier, but he always had been used to working on his own. He had no idea of sharing responsibilities. They all [he meant the Cabinet] complained about that. I talked to him for an hour before I left London, that June, at his request. He spoke of the Army as 'his' Army, as if he had been a sovereign. It was 'his' war, 'his' plans. No doubt he was a competent organizer, but his work should have stopped there or at least he should have shown more ability for working with the Staff. But he was a fine feller, a noble feller. I remember how he talked about our coming into the war. He said frankly it would mean everything to the Allies, but he wouldn't urge any people to come into such a war."

II

The *St. Paul* docked at New York June 13, with a hullabaloo of publicity such as Mr. House had managed hitherto to avoid, but which would attend his comings and goings from that day forth. The ship's company were excited over the naval escort the British had provided her through the submarine zone, an unprecedented attention, and there was a deal of speculation over the nature of the "dispatches" carried by the President's friend. There were no dispatches, of course. The British Government had taken this precaution solely because of the importance they attached to Mr. House's continued existence.

Upon his arrival in New York Mr. House heard two pieces of news which, separately, were to have considerable influence upon his future. One was that Bryan had resigned as Secretary of State because of his disapproval of the President's second *Lusitania* note of June 9. The second was that official Washington seethed with gossip over the friendship which had sprung up between the President and Mrs. Edith Bolling Galt, widow of Norman Galt, a Washington jeweler.

If Mr. House gave more than passing attention to this second item— and social gossip about people's personal affairs was taboo to him—it was merely to find satisfaction in the thought that the lonely man in the White House at last had freed himself from the painful isolation in which he had lived socially since the death of his wife. Mr. House did not then, nor did he for several months afterward, imagine that the President contemplated remarriage. Yet the fact was that after first meeting Mrs. Galt—a friend of Commander Grayson, his personal physician, and of his cousin, Miss Helen Bones, who had been his wife's secretary—in March, Mr. Wilson had become sufficiently attracted to her to propose marriage on May 9. This offer Mrs. Galt had conditionally declined, pleading the recent death of Mrs. Wilson as one excuse. She was spending the month of June at the President's summer home at Cornish with his daughters and several other members of the Wilson household, including Commander Grayson, who was pressing his own suit for the hand of Mrs. Galt's ward, Miss Altrude Gordon.*

Mr. House received the news of Bryan's resignation without a shadow of regret. Despite the great human qualities of the Nebraskan, no man could have been worse fitted for the complex duties of the State Depart-

---

* *My Memoir,* by Edith Bolling Wilson; Bobbs-Merrill Co., Indianapolis, 1939. The engagement of the President and Mrs. Galt was announced October 7, 1915; they were married in Mrs. Galt's residence in Washington the following December 18.

ment, especially in a time of international conflict. His absorption in the petty details of politics, his unthinking pacifism, his complete ignorance of world affairs outside the missionary activities of the Protestant churches, had completely disorganized the department's routine. He had been appointed by the President in the full knowledge that he would become an encumbrance upon the Administration. Since August, 1914, he had been a menace to the country and a source of irritation abroad. Nobody knew this better than Mr. House, who considered himself directly responsible for Bryan's inclusion in the Cabinet, and who, moreover, was genuinely appreciative of the fine understanding with which Bryan had accepted the Texan's quiet usurpation of many of his prerogatives.

In the circumstances, it did not come as a surprise to Mr. House to be informed that his own name was being mentioned as Bryan's successor. Indeed, he was assured that the office was open to him by the Collector of the Port before he left the *St. Paul*. But the idea never entered his head of asking for, much less accepting, an administrative post which would necessarily restrict the scope of his activities; and the President, he knew, had not the slightest intention of requiring of him the assumption of a burden that he lacked the physical stamina to support. But he was deeply touched when Attorney-General Gregory came over from Washington on June 20 to tell him that he, Gregory, and Postmaster-General Burleson had agreed to offer their resignations as the two Texas members of the Cabinet, in order to forestall adverse comment in the event that he cared to become Secretary of State.

"That's what I call friendship," Mr. House said of the offer, his eyes luminous with feeling as he spoke.

The President's inclination, of which Mr. House fully approved, was to promote in Bryan's place the Counselor of the Department—there was not then an Under-Secretary, as there is today—Robert Lansing, of New York, son-in-law and former law partner of John W. Foster, who had earned renown as Secretary of State under Cleveland. It was typical of the future Mrs. Wilson's habit of mind that she testified that when the President told her of his intention at this time she objected that Lansing was "only a clerk." Secretary Lansing may justly be said to have been one of the eminent constitutional lawyers of his generation; his name will surely rank in history with the long roll of his most distinguished predecessors. As Counselor to follow Lansing, the President appointed, again with Mr. House's hearty concurrence, Frank L. Polk, Corporation Counsel of New York in the Administration of Mayor John Purroy Mitchel, a great-nephew of President Polk and Leonidas Polk,

Episcopal Bishop of Louisiana and Lieutenant-General in the armies of the Confederacy.

Lansing and Polk were to prove themselves an excellent team. They combined intelligence with legal acumen and personal dignity. They were broadminded and courageous. Polk, in particular, had demonstrated extraordinary physical courage when he stepped in front of Mayor Mitchel to take a bullet in the neck from the pistol of an irresponsible assassin. Mr. House, like the President, could have asked for no better collaborators in the arduous task of maintaining the prestige of the United States, against not only the insolence of German aggression, but the scarcely less difficult arrogance of British sea power—this last destined to furnish a source of trouble in the near future, which would have been impossible to tolerate but for the greater menace of Germany's attitude.

12

From New York Mr. House reported to the President by telephone and letter, but they did not meet for some months to come. One of the most remarkable aspects of their friendship, it cannot be too frequently stressed, was its independence of direct intercourse. Often they were separated for weeks or months, but never, during these fruitful years, was there any interruption in the current of warm, tolerant comprehension of motives and purposes which united them in all their efforts. Tale bearers and backbiters might intrigue and deprecate. The two friends held themselves aloof from such pettiness, at the most conceding a degree of lofty amusement, each assured of the other's loyalty and disinterestedness.

Mr. House was sympathetic with the President's desire to avoid a break with Germany. As must have been made apparent again and again in these pages, he was convinced that nothing short of a miracle could keep the United States out of the war, unless it was possible to persuade the belligerents to a discussion of peace. But even so, he was assured by Gerard, writing from Berlin June 16, after the receipt of the President's second *Lusitania* note—which the Ambassador hoped would bring the Imperial Government to terms by its cold detachment and refusal to abate or debate American rights—that "Germany will never agree, directly or indirectly, to any freedom of land or disarmament proposal." In other words, Germany would discuss peace in certain contingencies, but not on the basis of future arrangements the President had laid down as essential.

The problem, as Mr. House saw it—from a background of information

perhaps more inclusive than any other human being's—was to convince
an overwhelming majority of the American people that only by a very
strong stand could the preponderant authorities in Germany—the military chieftains—be brought to a realization of this country's determination to make good its interpretation of its rights at sea. Failing the
establishment of this realization, the single resource of the United States
was armed resistance to aggression. If he dreaded this less than Woodrow Wilson, it was because his was not the final responsibility; he was
more intimately acquainted with the situation at home and abroad, and
his sense of realism inured him to the perception that war occasionally
was unavoidable for a proud people, an idea from which the President
instinctively revolted.

Similarly, he was as alert as the President to the rising indignation
in the United States, assiduously nursed by citizens of German and Irish
extraction, against the interference of the British blockade with our
Dutch and Scandinavian commerce. It was relatively unimportant, he
believed, both economically and legally, as compared with the threat
offered by Germany to the fabric of democratic civilization. But he
had striven to convince the British of the need to exert their strangle
hold with diplomacy and moderation. He continued to do so, and
presently advised Grey, as one means to lessen the tension between the
two countries, to throw upon France's shoulders a larger share of the
ignominy of intercepting American ships.

It would be difficult to estimate how often he returned to this theme
during the crucial months of 1915 and 1916. He never failed to stress
it to me.

"We must not have a falling out with England. God knows what
will become of the world if we do. They have their backs to the wall,
remember. The blockade is their most effective weapon. They say they
cannot allow the neutrals to reexport goods and food from us into Germany. Anyone can see what is going on by contrasting the normal
imports of Denmark, say, with those she is ordering from us. We must
find a way to satisfy our people and not help Germany." *

He was bolstered in this feeling by his knowledge, which he kept to
himself, that Germany had refused to abandon the submarine campaign
in return for unrestricted food imports.

It is illustrative of the unique position Mr. House had attained that
both the British and German Ambassadors hastened from Washington
to confer with him—as, likewise, it is of the difficulties besetting them

* Needless to say, such remarks were never printed, and were repeated only in
the quarters for which they were intended.

that he was able to give each information of the intimate condition of affairs in their respective capitals. Spring-Rice, abnormally nervous, sensitive as a woman, really too ill for his duties, received a wigging for having advised the Foreign Office that in estimating the President's intentions it must be taken for granted he was pro-German. His defense was that he had done it for "the President's protection"! Von Bernstorff, Mr. House noted satirically, still cherished the belief—or claimed to— that his Government would consent to peace upon the principle of evacuation of Belgium and a joint indemnity to her. Mr. House was able to assure him that, while the German Civil Government would welcome this solution, there was small probability they could induce the Army and Navy to accept it, and that even if they did such a repudiation of their wild promises to the German people would precipitate a revolution. Of the two Ambassadors, Bernstorff was far the abler. A realist, a Junker of Junkers, a master of intrigue, unscrupulous, he was yet one German who saw concretely from the beginning the disastrous consequences to Germany which must flow from active American hostility. It was not his fault that von Tirpitz prevailed in Berlin.

Assured that von Bernstorff would do his best to secure a satisfactory reply to the President's note, Mr. House left New York the last week in June to spend the summer at Manchester, near Boston, on the North Shore of Massachusetts. The German reply was received July 8, and was not satisfactory, as Mr. House had anticipated. Laying stress upon the British trade restrictions, it suggested that Americans should cross the Atlantic on neutral ships or upon four enemy vessels specially designated for passenger traffic. It ignored the President's demand for a pledge against repetition of the *Lusitania* incident. Mr. Wilson's prompt response was stiff, but not in the terms of an ultimatum, concluding with the flat assertion that "actions in contravention of these rights [referring to his previous refusal to abate or debate American rights at sea] must be regarded by the Government of the United States, when they affect American citizens, as deliberately unfriendly." *

* It is strange that Mr. House seems never to have appreciated, in connection with German submarine warfare, the remarkable immunity of the vessels of the French Line in the North Atlantic. Both the Hohenzollerns and the Hapsburgs held large blocks of stock of the Compagnie Générale Transatlantique. Whether justified or not, it was the belief of the American Army's Intelligence Service that this factor had something to do with the escape of such slow liners as the *Rochambeau*. Our General Staff in France also were suspicious of Rothschild influence in the sudden decision of the French High Command to divert the St. Mihiel offensive to the Argonne after the mine fields adjacent to Metz came within range of our railroad guns.

Mr. House had no fault to find with the texture of his friend's communication, but he was convinced, with Bernstorff, that only harm could be produced by continued diplomatic wrangling. "We must *certainly* stop publishing sharp and unsatisfactory notes," the German Ambassador wrote him July 27. It was merely a question of time, he believed, before Germany would commit an "overt act" which would produce a definite issue of peace or war. He was appalled—this is not an exaggeration—by the President's failure to realize the gravity of the situation, and endeavored to bring this home to Mr. Wilson in a letter of July 14: "If war comes with Germany, it will be because of our unpreparedness and her belief that we are more or less impotent to do her harm." It cannot be overemphasized that after August, 1914, he preached at every opportunity the policy of building up the Navy for its effect on all the belligerents.

"It would have been money well spent," he said afterward, "so much less than the cost of war."

The "overt act" Mr. House looked for occurred on August 19, when the White Star Liner *Arabic,* outbound for New York, with no contraband, in the German sense, in her cargo, was sunk off Fastnet. Two American lives were lost. Two days later the badgered, bewildered man in the White House wrote to his friend for advice on how he should act. Mr. House replied by implying three possible alternatives of action. The President, he said, might (1) break with Germany and hand von Bernstorff his passports; (2) summon Congress in special session, and place the issue squarely before the House and Senate; (3) privately inform Bernstorff that the United States must receive a disavowal and complete surrender on submarine warfare, or, failing that, break relations. Personally, Mr. House favored the first alternative, although he believed it meant war; but, in accordance with his custom, he did not press it upon the President beyond advising against the dispatch of another note. "Further notes would disappoint our own people, and would cause something of derision abroad."

In his diary that day Mr. House wrote: "I am surprised at the attitude he takes. He evidently will go to great lengths to avoid war. He should have determined his policy when he wrote his notes of February, May, June and July." This was the closest to a criticism of the President which ever came from Mr. House's tongue or pen. In the light of what happened, its cogency is unanswerable.

For several days, then, in the humid heat of midsummer, Woodrow Wilson sat in spiritual torment, trying to steel himself to a decision. Mr. House believed, privately, that he would have adopted the second alternative and laid the responsibility of the national policy upon Congress, as the branch of Government constitutionally authorized to declare war, however cumbersome and involved the procedure must have been, with its certainty of tedious and controversial debate. But he was saved from the necessity of a decision, which must have been distasteful to him in any respect, by the sudden intervention of Bernstorff, alert to the danger to his own country in the situation. The German Ambassador appealed to Secretary Lansing for time to persuade concessions from his Government, and on August 25 the President wrote Mr. House again, asking what he should do. Should he trust Bernstorff at all, and if so, how long a delay might be granted? Mr. House sensed how his friend's mind was working, appreciated the agony which beset him, and considering all the factors, advised a reasonable delay.

In the meantime, and while Bernstorff was keeping the cables hot with frantic appeals to the Wilhelmstrasse to bear down for once on their military and naval chiefs, Mr. Wilson at last was aroused to the necessity for additions to the country's armed forces. The day he wrote Mr. House, Secretary Daniels, a cheery, warmhearted, lackadaisical humanitarian, arrived at Manchester in the *Dolphin,* with instructions to find out from Mr. House how much money was needed for the Navy. Mr. House told him that what was needed was a fleet second only to Britain's. Secretary Daniels protested that such a gigantic building program would demand more than $200,000,000. Mr. House retorted that this was of no account, that he should spend three or four hundred millions, if necessary, and that he might rely upon the backing of the Administration, a sure majority in Congress and the sympathy of most of the American people.

This was the germ of the post-war Navy, which was destroyed by the well-intentioned—a hateful word—disarmament treaties of President Harding and Charles E. Hughes, as Secretary of State. The United States is paying for those treaties today. It will be fortunate if it doesn't continue to pay for them for many generations to come. Those treaties were a concession the United States yielded to the rest of the world for its refusal to adhere to the Covenant of the League of Nations, a policy to which Mr. House always attributed most of the subsequent economic and political ills of the world, and in particular, Germany's.

Naturally, the news that the Administration was projecting a naval building program seeped through the net of German spies to Bernstorff's ears, and encouraged him to redouble his efforts—although, in fact, he did not require additional incentive. On September 1, he produced a letter to Secretary Lansing, which was equivocal in tone, contained no positive security for the future, and was by no means satisfactory in its method of composition and delivery—as, in effect, simply an *aide mémoire* from an Ambassador, rather than his chief—but which was sufficient to save the face of the United States in its implied promise of orders to be issued to submarine commanders. The President relaxed, and Mr. House sighed with the realization that the inevitable conclusion again had been postponed. Bernstorff, however, justified Mr. House's none too implicit confidence in him by capping his first achievement by securing, on October 5, from a reluctant Foreign Office, a disavowal of the sinking of the *Arabic*.* This feat strained even his colossal self-assurance, for he telephoned Mr. House that at the last minute, on the insistence of the President and Lansing, he had taken the responsibility of eliminating from the Foreign Office draft a demand for arbitration of the conflicting evidence on the assertion of the submarine commander that the *Arabic* had attempted to ram. This was a real diplomatic victory for the United States, but it was still unsatisfactory in that it gave no definite commitments for the clouded future. Well might the President remark pathetically to Mr. House when they met in Washington in September: "My chief puzzle is to determine when patience ceases to be a virtue."

With the German controversy temporarily out of the way, Mr. House turned to the disagreeable task of aiding in formulating a policy calculated to convince the British Government of the necessity of curbing the operations of their own naval people. It must be admitted that he obtained much less cooperation from Spring-Rice than he did from Bernstorff, as was natural in the circumstances, since nobody seriously supposed there was any possibility the United States would go to war or yield to the demands of the anti-British factions to place an embargo on the munitions traffic. On October 14, in an interview at Washington, Mr. House finally brought the Ambassador to terms. Spring-Rice opened the discussion intemperately, finding fault not alone with the

* Bernstorff's diligence was stimulated by the President's action in dismissing Dumba, the Austro-Hungarian Ambassador, whose complicity in the sabotaging of munitions plants was proven by dispatches seized by the British from the luggage of an American newspaper correspondent. Von Papen, the German Military Attaché—afterwards one of Hitler's Junker lieutenants—was cited in these same dispatches. Several months later, he and Boy-Ed, the German Naval Attaché, were likewise sent home. To give Bernstorff his due, he used these incidents as arguments to try to impress his Government that they could not go too far with the United States. Bernstorff denied that he had a part in the activities of his attachés, and no proof ever was deduced to the contrary. Not strange, of course. He was much smarter than Dumba.

President, but with Mr. House for so much as associating with Bern-storff. "I lost my temper," Mr. House recorded in his diary, "and told him I regarded his remarks as an insult." Poor Spring-Rice apologized, and Mr. House forgave him.

"Spring-Rice wasn't a well man," Mr. House commented on this incident. "And so far as his personality went, he was the last man they should have had in Washington. He was the soul of honor, and sweet-tempered when he wasn't too everlastingly badgered; but he made plenty of trouble for us and his own Government. The next time I went abroad I half-intended to ask for his head, but Walter Page was making himself just as unpopular with the President by his pro-British letters and dispatches, and I was all the time trying to save him, too. They were nice fellers. I couldn't bring myself to it. And of course they were right in their feelings. The trouble was, they didn't know how to be right."

Spring-Rice's peculiarities of temperament disturbed Mr. House much less than the despair reflected in Grey's letters to him from London. That was a bad summer for the Allies. The Western Front was bogged down; the Gallipoli venture was getting nowhere; the German armies were driving through Poland; Bulgaria had come in against the Allies, and Serbia had been conquered.* Grey himself had been on the point of losing his sight when he took an enforced vacation from mid-June to mid-July. He admitted frankly that if the British blockade restrictions on neutral commerce were relaxed the Allies must lose the war. "It looks as if the United States might now strike the weapon of sea power out of our hands, and thereby insure a German victory," he wrote on November 11, 1915, a date Mr. House in later years recalled with dubious reflections as to its ultimate significance. In truth, the American note of October 21 was curt and peremptory, drafted with the keen incisiveness for which Lansing was justly famous. A storm of anti-American feeling broke in the British Isles, and spread to France. Page submitted a diatribe of twenty-three autograph pages in supplement to the reply which was engaging the attention of the legal advisors of the Foreign Office. But unyielding as was the President's attitude, and steadfast his determination to maintain American rights against British usurpation, he continued to share Mr. House's desire to do all that was possible to avoid a drastic step which might play into Germany's hands. It was as obvious to both of them as it was to Grey that the one barrier to German victory on the Continent was relentless pressure of Britain's naval power.

* This sentence has an oddly familiar ring to it in May, 1940.

On the surface the outlook was black, as black for the United States as for the European democracies, Mr. House thought. But in October he conceived a new plan, which he hoped, and the President with him, might avert the disaster threatening civilization. His attempt to implement this plan belongs properly to the year 1916, which was destined to be one of the busiest and most effective in his life.

Book 6

1916

A BLACK year, 1916. So was 1917. In 1918 the world won a chance to make a fresh start, and reorganize the civilization of the machine age, the civilization which had grown up more or less successfully on steam power, but which could not—apparently—handle the phenomenon of electricity. It is the problem which confronts the world today. It is the problem which must be solved if civilization, as we know it—the theory of mass production for the greater good—is to prevail. So far, we have failed—and most of us will admit it. We have failed, Mr. House thought, because we have never, as a planetary unit, solved the corollary problem of joint endeavor. We have not learned to feel that Americans, Britishers, Frenchmen, Germans and others can be brothers, that the problems of Asia, Africa and Australia are the problems of the Americas and Europe. That was what the war of 1914-18 was fought for. Men lost the idea in the brawl of fighting battles and whittling out a peace. And perhaps 1916 was the crucial year because what happened in those twelve months resulted in bringing the United States, and most of the other American republics, into the hostilities; and the United States, if not their Latin-American sisters, failed to live up to the obligations they undertook to assume.

It was a year of flux, in which the flow of events tended steadily against the European democracies, which, if you please, ignorantly, stupidly, selfishly, fought to restrain the attempt of the Central Empires to establish medieval, militaristic autocracies as valid anachronisms in the modern industrial world. The sequence of events was upon such a stupendous scale as almost to defy dramatization. To thoughtful men like Mr. House it seemed as though the ancient European world was bent upon destroying itself. The recurrent shocks were so drastic that they numbed people's imaginations. Headline writers threw up their hands in despair; they lacked type big enough to emphasize the news. Lives and money and property were squandered at a rate which appeared unprecedented to the average individual, although it is to be questioned whether the wastage exceeded, proportionately, that of the titanic struggles of the past: the first Moslem sweep, the Crusades, the Mongolian invasions, the Hundred Years' War, the Thirty Years' War, the War of the Austrian Succession, the Seven Years' War, the Napoleonic epoch. The truth is, of course, that since the beginning of recorded history man has sought, at periodic intervals, to destroy himself. Perhaps he never sought so more determinedly than in the period immediately under review.

The German attempt to capture Verdun was launched on February 21—and 500,000 Germans were sentenced to death. On March 9, Pancho Villa raided Columbus, New Mexico, and the American Border was set aflame. Pershing was sent after him into Mexico on the 15th, and was only prevented from catching the bandit leader by Wilson's reluctance to force an issue with the Carranza Government, partly because of his instinctive aversion toward intervention in Latin-American affairs, partly because of the European situation. The incident is chiefly important today for the reason that it diverted a large share of American interest in the World War to the Rio Grande, where more than 100,000 troops were concentrated. On Easter Day occurred the Dublin Rising, which distracted Britain's attention from her main jobs in France and the Near East. The great battle of Jutland was fought in the North Sea mists on May 31, and definitely crushed Germany's bid for sea power, despite the fact that British ineptness permitted Germany to fool most of the world into believing that it was a victory for the High Sea Fleet.

The matchless valor of the French at Verdun enabled the British armies in France to open the bloody and fruitless third battle of Ypres on June 2, and the scarcely more successful battles of the Somme, July 1. Meantime Kitchener had gone down in the *Hampshire,* June 5, very likely by accidental contact with one of the mines strewn broadcast in connection with the Jutland battle five days previously—it might even have been a British mine. It seems fair to say that the results of his death were chiefly psychological. He had fulfilled his mission of organization; the British commanders in France had come to look upon him as an arbitrary superior with little knowledge of the peculiar problems of trench warfare. The Brusilov offensive, Russia's last major effort, overran eastern Hungary early in the summer, and brought Rumania into the war upon the Allies' side, with promptly disastrous results for her ill-trained armies. Already, Russia was crumbling, sapped from within. In December, Prince Felix Yussoupov would murder Rasputin, in a madly desperate attempt to break the stultifying influence of the Court camarilla upon the pitiful Czar and Czarina. Few people, except

Mr. House, had appreciated from the opening of hostilities how unhealthy were the social and political conditions in Russia—yet he had
never heard of two men named Lenin and Trotsky, he admitted afterwards.

Everything was going against the Democracies and their Allies. The
attempt to aid Serbia had made no headway; the meager rescuing armies
were immobilized in the entrenched camp at Salonika. Defeatism was
rampant in France, despite the glory of Verdun. Petain's cliché, "They
shall not pass," was a wisecrack to be laughed at by war-weary, dis-
heartened soldiers. In London, sane British leaders no longer wrote to
Mr. House of "winning the war." They prefaced their statements with
"ifs." There was bitter criticism of the Cabinet, some of it certainly
justified. On December 5, Asquith was compelled to resign, and
was supplanted by fiery, aggressive, superficial Lloyd George. Winston
Churchill's head had long since fallen, as a concession to the hidebound
War Office faction, whose members had failed to comprehend the grand
strategy involved in his suggested Dardanelles campaign, and demanded
his sacrifice to cover their own blunders. It is a testimony to the British
sense of fair play that the injustice done him was realized by Lloyd
George, who recalled him to office.

At home, the American people's bewilderment over the foreign situation was accentuated by a series of startling events. German sabotage
was rampant. On Preparedness Day, July 22, in San Francisco, a bomb
was hurled at a parade, and ten people were killed, precipitating a social-
political controversy, which had not been settled twenty-two years afterward by the pardoning of the men found guilty of the atrocity. Eight
days later came the Black Tom explosion, which blew up $22,000,000
worth of property and munitions. The maunderings of the politicians,
who gabbled about the country's safety from foreign attacks, received a
setback with the arrival at Norfolk, July 9, of the German commercial
submarine *Deutschland,* and as if this were not a sufficient shock to
Americans' self-confidence, early in October the naval submarine U-53
put in at Newport, was sent to sea, and sank six vessels off Nantucket.
The British naval authorities accused us of responsibility, a ridiculous
charge, as Mr. House forced them to admit. The exploits of the U-53
were a disturbing demonstration of the increasing range of action of the
German raiders, but she had been scrupulous in observing the rules of
cruiser warfare. Then, to jar us further, on November 1, the plucky
Deutschland made a second visit to New London, landed her cargo,
shipped much-needed essentials for her country, and again dodged past
the British men-o'-war lying in wait for her.

While all this was going on, while every day men found in their newspapers reports of events which they had never previously envisaged as possible, the United States were convulsed by the Wilson-Hughes campaign for the Presidency. That campaign, as the Duke of Wellington said to Creevey, the diarist, the morning after Waterloo, was "the nearest run thing you (I) ever saw." The Democratic tactics and strategy were developed and largely controlled by Mr. House, who, at the same time, was bending his energies to the endeavor to work out a formula of peace which would be acceptable to the belligerents abroad. It was a source of endless wonder to those who knew him that he sustained the burdens imposed upon him as healthily, cheerfully and placidly as he did.

2

It was obvious to Mr. House, by the fall of 1915, that the Allies were stalemated in their efforts to force Germany to her knees by operations on the Western Front, while Germany's arrogance was swollen by the ease with which she had resisted them there, as well as by her triumphs in the East. The polyglot Austro-Hungarian armies were helpless before the Russian masses, but the staff work and technical efficiency of the Germans always managed to redress the balance. With a leaven of German divisions, the Austro-Hungarians forged ahead on any front. Unless there came a turn in the tide, he foresaw but two alternatives: a war of exhaustion, ending in disaster for everyone, or a German victory, not necessarily complete, but based on terms which would preserve the German military system intact. In the latter case he had no doubt that Germany would turn her attention next to the rich loot to be gained in the Western Hemisphere. Indeed, if he had had any doubts, they must have been resolved by Ambassador Gerard's report to the President of an interview with the Kaiser at Grand Headquarters—"he would attend to America when this war was over," Wilhelm had asserted.

Dismissing, as unworthy of consideration by a great power, the choice of a policy of drifting with events, Mr. House saw only two definite courses open to the United States. We could break with Germany on the issue of the *Lusitania* and the *Arabic,* or the President, speaking on behalf of the neutrals, could demand a conference on terms which would end the threat of overbearing aggression by any power, with the implied alternative the determination of the United States to enter the war against those powers which refused his invitation. Mr. House believed that Germany would not accept such an invitation, and his thought was to secure in advance the secret assent of the Allies to do so. The hitch in his plan was that both the Allies and the Central Empires were contemptuous of the military strength of the United States; but he did hope that by skilful preparation the British and French Governments could be brought to realize that they had everything to gain, and nothing to lose, from accepting it. He might have thought differently had he realized—as he did later—how fantastic were the ambitions of the French and British leaders, and the scope of the Secret Treaties uniting their nationalistic avarice. And it is likewise a commentary upon one of the most intelligent of statesmen, and one of the best-informed, that he seems never during these years to have foreseen the impossibility of establishing a new world order, however liberal in purpose, which would require the rest of the nations to tolerate the existence of three or four gigantically rich empires upon which all others must be economically dependent. He lived to know better.

Basically, it was a shrewd plan, well timed, and probably would have obtained the results he desired had it been adopted. The story of what happened to it offers a disheartening parallel between the acuteness and farsightedness of the statesmen of 1915-17 and their successors of the years 1936-39. And it does not lighten the responsibilities of the men of the latter era to admit for them that they owed their plight, in its genesis, to the mistakes of their predecessors. There were men in 1936 who saw what needed to be done, just as there were men like Mr. House who understood, in 1915, how the structure of civilization could have been maintained with a minimum of suffering. But in both instances clarity of vision was overbalanced by lack of determinate power.

Mr. House, in his own mind, rejected the first of his two tentative policies because it seemed to him that Germany's unsatisfactory responses to the President's extended series of notes of protest, in the *Lusitania* and *Arabic* cases, had been allowed to hang fire so long as to vitiate the effectiveness of extreme action by the United States. He hesitated for some time to communicate his second plan to Mr. Wilson for the reason that he doubted the President's readiness to adopt a policy which, in all probability, would lead to war—although perhaps not. His doubts were cleared by a casual conversation with his friend at the White House in September, 1915, in the course of which Mr. Wilson remarked that "he had never been sure that we ought not to take part in the conflict." Mr. House was agreeably surprised and encouraged, but decided to allow the facts of the situation to incubate a while longer in the President's deliberate mind. A few weeks later, however, after he had developed his conception of the plan, he explained it in detail to Mr. Wilson in a short interview in New York. His diary relates that Mr. Wilson "was startled," but "seemed to acquiesce by silence"—an habitual reaction of Mr. Wilson's toward Mr. House's suggestions.

Throughout this period Mr. House was in constant, intimate communication with Sir Edward Grey. During the second week of October he received a letter from Grey, dated September 22, inquiring whether the President would be willing to go so far, in an appeal for peace, as to propose a League of Nations, binding its members to refrain from war and outlawing violators of the pledge. He promptly took this letter to the President, who was impressed by it and authorized a favorable reply. Grey's answer arrived near the end of November, and was disappointing in its note of uncertainty. He questioned the willingness of the Allies to commit themselves in advance to a plan as drastic as Mr. House's, unless they knew its precise terms, and were assured positively of the aid of the United States. The reasons for his wavering? One, we may take for granted, was his knowledge of the terms of the Secret Treaties. A second, his acquaintance with the belligerent attitudes of his colleagues in the Cabinet, and the Ministers in Paris, Rome and Petrograd. A third may have been due to the fact that he shared, to a remarkable degree, Mr. Wilson's aversion to positive action. They were alike in that they were men of instinctive delicacy of thought, who loathed violence in all its connotations, who were accustomed to reasoning calmly and slowly toward logical solutions of problems.* A fourth reason, of course, was his adherence to the British tradition, which forbids a Minister to commit his colleagues without advisement.

Mr. House refused to accept the *impasse,* as did the President. It was plain to both of them that the doubts in London were due, to some extent, to the unsatisfactory work of Page in the British capital, and Spring-Rice in Washington. Mr. Wilson was so irritated that he was tempted to recall Page, and actually sent Mr. House abroad a few weeks afterward with *carte blanche* to ask the Foreign Office for Spring-Rice's scalp. It was Mr. House, alone, who saved the pair of them from the termination of their careers. He knew they were both honorable men, highstrung and working under tremendous pressure. Of the two, Spring-Rice was easiest to understand. He was an Englishman, and an invalid, who kept at his job by sheer nervous courage. Yet, regarding their conduct in perspective, it seems that the sensible thing to do would have been to recall both. Other men were constantly remedying their mistakes of temperament. They simply were not fitted to their posts.

* Many authorities have claimed that had Grey definitely acquainted Germany with Britain's intention to stand by France when the Balkan crisis first developed, the war would have been postponed, if not averted.

To complicate matters—and Mr. House's life in those years was guided by humorous acceptance of the self-perpetuating qualities of complications—the President found it necessary to send home the German military and naval attachés, in consequence of proven responsibility for sabotage and espionage in this country. The first was the notorious Franz von Papen, who has distinguished himself as the chief diplomatic *saboteur* in the Hitler machine. Karl Boy-Ed was the naval attaché, equally efficient. Their dismissal petrified Bernstorff, but Berlin received the snub quite mildly. Mr. House was inclined to give the German Ambassador's representations to his Government some credit for this circumstance. It is more likely that the German Ministry retained sufficient authority over the High Command to be able to persevere in its ambition to obtain a relatively profitable peace through the efforts of the United States. This view is bolstered by the fact that when Mr. House asked Bernstorff, in the middle of December, to ascertain if the German Ministry would welcome an exploratory visit from him, he received a prompt and enthusiastic response from Berlin.

The President decided that his friend should go. As an excuse for the mission, and to conceal its real nature, the press was informed that conditions abroad forbade the temporary recall of our Ambassadors to make their occasional personal reports to the State Department, so Mr. House was to advise them at first-hand of the policies and intentions of the Administration.

Mr. House sailed on December 28. He was optimistic of success. He knew, by now, the personalities of the men with whom he would have to deal. They were friends. They trusted him personally, although to them the President was an alien and enigmatic personality. He was confident that he could either lure the Germans into acceptance of his policy of restitution and reparation, in return for an assured economic future, or else maneuver them into a situation which would enable the United States justifiably to throw its strength into the balance against them. The assent of the British he took for granted. They were getting a great deal for practically nothing.

3

Mr. House landed at Falmouth, January 5, 1916. So close were his contacts in London that he was able to cable the President, January 7, that he had talked with both Grey and Balfour—who was destined to become Grey's successor at the Foreign Office eleven months later—and

had satisfied any doubts of theirs as to the sincerity of his friend's intentions. But, he added, he could not be so certain of the sympathies of
their colleagues, a suspicion of which he was only partially disabused in
the next two weeks. The President replied to Mr. House in a cable
of historic import, pledging himself generously to cooperate in "a policy
seeking to bring about and maintain permanent peace." It was a long
step forward for Mr. Wilson to take, and for him, a bold one. It marked
his definite abandonment of the isolationist attitude which had hampered
his official conduct; it impelled him upon the course of active intervention in foreign affairs, which resulted in the United States becoming a
belligerent; and it would, had it become known in subsequent months,
most certainly have cost him reelection.

At the moment, it strengthened materially Mr. House's position in his
conversations with Grey and Balfour, and it was certainly no more the
fault of the President than of the Texan that he found himself, in so far
as other Ministers and leaders were concerned, brought up short by the
traditional phlegm and caution of British public men, the centuries-old
tendency to look upon Americans still as Colonials. "I'm damned if
some of them ever did come to believe that there was such a thing as
an American statesman," Mr. House once said. "They hated to make
a decision. Grey was almost as bad as the rest of them. They were
frightened of anything different, anything that hadn't figured in the
past. They had a sort of feeling that our job was on one side of the
world, and theirs was anywhere they chose. Lawd, lawd, when I think
of the chance those fellers finally missed!" *

During the two weeks Mr. House spent in London, before proceeding
to Berlin, he met practically every man and woman of political significance in British society; but Lloyd George and Lord Chief Justice Reading were the only others, besides Grey and Balfour, with whom he
discussed the project of his mission, and he no more than hinted at his
purpose to them. He was surprised to find that Grey had come around
to a complete belief in that nebulous doctrine, the Freedom of the Seas,
which he had devised as a bait equally tempting to Germany and

---

* It would be futile to burden this narrative with the complete documentary details of Mr. House's several diplomatic missions. They are accessible to anyone
interested in *The Intimate Papers of Colonel House* by Dr. Charles Seymour, president of Yale University, and published by Houghton Mifflin Company. My purpose is not to repeat matters of record, State papers or events, but to clarify them,
in so far as I know, by bringing out the human motives which underlay the scenes
in which Edward M. House played a part. In order to do so, I must occasionally
use a portion of some material or incident which has been previously described.
Then, perhaps, I can add something to the picture.

Britain.* Lloyd George also was converted to this doctrine after Mr. House described its implications and owned to its authorship; he had been led astray by the Germans' stupid adoption of it as their own. Mr. House was more favorably impressed by Lloyd George than he had been previously. He liked the Welshman's bounce and energy. Lloyd George had more of that mental alertness and originality, which Mr. House admired, than any other British statesman. And perhaps it was due mainly to a suggestion from Lady Paget—in whom, as an American who had not ceased to be loyal to her own country, he had much confidence—but Mr. House presently came around to the belief that the British Government would be easier to work with if Lloyd George became Premier in place of Asquith, with Grey as a less trammeled Foreign Secretary.

It is extraordinary, in this connection, to note in Mr. House's diary how often he foresaw the occurrence of events. He told Lloyd George that the great danger of the Allies lay in the possibility of a broken Russia making a separate peace, and that Britain would do well to withdraw from Asia to avoid the bloody conflicts sure to follow the dissolution of China.† He privately laughed at the pacifists, who assured him that all the belligerents were war-weary. He told the people he met not to be unduly disturbed by German frightfulness at sea and in the air. It did more to build up moral indignation and determination to win

---

* Nebulous, that is, in the light of the intervening years. I doubt if Mr. House ever entirely lost faith in his doctrine. Despite the fact that he was a realist, he believed until his death that, if it were possible to bring the nations into a complete and honorable accord, it would be possible to restrict sea warfare to such limited operations as used to be practised by the professional armies, say, of the eighteenth century. And it is only fair to add that he made a great impression upon Englishmen of liberal views, men who began by challenging him: "What do you mean? Is that not what England always has fought for since the Armada came? Or do you mean that we should surrender our coaling stations and ports, which are open to the nations of the world, and give up our shipping to some world trust?" The former Lord Chancellor, Loreburn, was one such, who ended by exclaiming heartily: "The Freedom of the Seas, as you outline it, would be of 60 per cent advantage to the United States, 100 per cent advantage to Germany, and 120 per cent to the British Empire." But a few statesmen of all nations had illusions in those days.

† He was not so confident of the breakup of China in his later years. The Government of the Chinese Republic sent a mission to consult with him on questions of internal polity, economics, etc., and he remarked afterwards that he was hopeful they would succeed in creating the beginnings of a modern state, notwithstanding the persecutions of Japan. Mr. House would have been strengthened in this hope had he lived to behold the extraordinary courage and determination displayed by Chiang Kai-shek's armies and the civil population.

than successful battles, and furthermore was excellent propaganda against
Germany in the United States. He was not especially impressed by
Lloyd George's boast that the British would have 4,000,000 men for the
field in the spring, nor by the Welshman's insistence that after the summer's battles the President would be the only man who could force both
sides to terms. Mr. House's theory was that the United States ultimately would have to fight Germany into submission because of Germany's scorn of our unpreparedness—and because she was too strong
for the disjointed efforts of the Allies.

He ended his visit disturbed by two local factors: the innate conserva-
tism of most of the Cabinet, which, he feared, would lead them to postpone too late for effective action the plan he had outlined fully to Grey
and Balfour; and the possibility Grey stressed to him, that, if the President pressed the British too hard on the blockade issue, it would end
in Grey's being sacrificed by the Cabinet. On the first point, everything
he heard indicated that the British were so sanguine of the success of
their new armies in the approaching campaigns that they would be
unwilling to talk peace before September. This, he feared, would probably lead the Germans to proclaim unrestricted submarine warfare,
which would deprive the President of the opportunity to intervene as
a neutral, and must prolong hostilities. As to the second point, he did
his best by explaining to the King, and all responsible statesmen and
newspapermen, the difficulties of the Administration; and he wrote
Mr. Wilson, advising of Grey's situation, and urging that Lansing go as
easy in his protests as was possible in view of American indignation.

Much, of course, depended upon the reception he met in Berlin. He
hoped for the best—but not too hopefully.

4

Mr. House crossed the Channel to Boulogne on January 20 as the
guest of the British Government. Similar courtesies were accorded him
in France. He spent several days in Paris, but refrained from official
contacts at this time, preferring to postpone them until after his visit
to Berlin had acquainted him with the German attitude toward peace.
Most of his time was spent in conferences with Ambassador Sharp and
other American representatives and intimate friends, securing impartial
information on as many facets of opinion as possible regarding French
reactions to the general state of affairs, the feeling of the Ministry, industrialists and bankers, the newspapers and mass sentiment. He reached
Berlin, by way of Switzerland, on January 26.

Ambassador Gerard, with his usual efficiency, had made arrangements to expedite Mr. House's visit, so that the Texan was able to talk to the key men he chose to meet and depart from the German capital within four days, Mr. House having laid down the rule that, in order to avoid disagreeable or possibly embarrassing meetings—such as with Grand Admiral von Tirpitz—all interviews should be held in the Embassy. First, naturally, he went thoroughly over the situation with Gerard, who, it cannot be too often insisted, was the best-informed of American diplomats in Europe. Gerard was a good mixer. His burly, outspoken, almost rough-mannered personality concealed a deft capacity for social intercourse and a keen lawyer's mind. He was never under any illusions about the Germans and their intentions. He seemed to talk frankly with them, but they never knew what he really thought, unless he wished them to. It was a tribute to him that during years when hatred of the United States was growing steadily, he contrived to maintain the confidence and personal regard of an amazing number of prominent men of all shades of thought. The Kaiser, for instance, made confidences to him which must later have irked the memory of the hermit of Doorn House.

Gerard's pessimistic views, as to the future, were amply endorsed when Mr. House came to discuss matters with the five Germans he had chosen to be mouthpieces of their country's sentiments: Chancellor von Bethmann-Hollweg, Foreign Secretary von Jagow, Under Foreign Secretary Zimmermann, Solf, the Secretary for Colonies, and von Gwinner, head of the great Deutsche Bank.

The last two represented what passed for liberalism in the enemy-girt Empire. Solf, Mr. House thought, was as fair and broad-minded a German as lived—"I take it because he has lived a great part of his life out of Germany," Mr. House commented drily in his diary. He warned Mr. House, with injunction to strictest secrecy, that the resumption of unrestricted submarine warfare depended solely upon the issue of the current struggle for supremacy with the Kaiser between Bethmann-Hollweg on the one hand, and von Tirpitz on the other, with von Falkenhayn, the Chief of the General Staff, wobbling between the two, and showing an increasing tendency to yield to the Grand Admiral's assurances that the expanding fleet of larger U-boats could easily isolate the British Isles and do the Allies more military harm than would be risked by Germany through a break with the United States. Solf advised Mr. House to talk freely to the Chancellor, to stiffen the old Junker's back. Mr. House gathered that Solf was not inclined to belittle the dangers inherent in the hostility of the United States; and he, like most of the other members of the Civil Government, was jealous of the authority of the military leaders, and their disposition to ride roughshod over the Ministry.

Von Gwinner was not so outspoken as Solf, but, as an international financier, he was aware of what was happening to European civilization and asserted an anxiety for peace on practical terms. "Practical terms" furnished the nub of the problem. In Germany, as in Britain and France and the lesser belligerent countries, the statesmen and militarists had made such outrageous promises that acceptance of a peace based on reason would have precipitated a revolution against the governments responsible for it—or so they dreaded, at least. And Mr. House was inclined to agree with them; that is, unless the peace was coupled with a new world order insuring a vastly greater degree of economic security and political safety to all the countries involved.

This dilemma of the German Ministers was made plain to Mr. House when he conferred, separately, with the Chancellor and the Foreign Secretary after a dinner at the Embassy the following night, January 28. Bethmann-Hollweg, in Mr. House's opinion, was a truly pacific German, but a blundering, ineffectual old fellow. "The Chancellor drank copiously of beer," the Texan noted in his diary in one of those asides which make his record very human. "The beer did not apparently affect him, for his brain was as befuddled at the beginning as it was at the end." Bethmann-Hollweg consumed some minutes, as well as beer, trying to explain away his unfortunate plea to Sir Edward Goschen, the British Ambassador at Berlin, not to go to war over "a scrap of paper," the treaty guaranteeing Belgium's neutrality. The explanation struck Mr. House as pathetic rather than insincere, the attempt at self-justification of a man who had made a mistake, knew he had made a mistake, and was vaguely perturbed to have been "misunderstood."

But the point of their talk that night—so fateful, as history was to prove—was the inability of the two men, German and American, each swearing allegiance to peace, to bring their minds to a common meeting on the question how peace might be obtained. Bethmann-Hollweg insisted that the most generous terms his country could grant would be evacuation of the territories held by the German armies in return for an indemnity. Mr. House answered him that the Allies would never accept such terms, that the British, especially, would fight to their last man and their last guinea before they yielded. Bethmann-Hollweg, again with his characteristic ineffectualness, protested how much he admired the British. He thought little of the French, Russians or Italians; but the dream of his life had been to bring together "the white races," by which amazingly exclusive phrase he meant Germany, Britain, and the United States.

In the circumstances, Mr. House considered it useless to carry the discussion further, "indicating it by silence," he recorded pungently.*

With von Jagow, a few minutes later, he traversed the same general subject, and made just about as much headway. Most of their conversation dealt with under-sea warfare, and the ill-feeling it had aroused in the United States. Mr. House told the Foreign Secretary, as he had the British Ministers, that, far from weakening Allied morale, the German policy of merciless attack upon civilians, afloat or ashore, was steeling Germany's enemies to resistance and losing them the friendship of neutral countries. Von Jagow was politely noncommittal. As a Junker, Mr. House knew, he was really making money out of the war. All these men were working their estates with Russian prisoners, at six cents a day, instead of paying seventy-five or eighty cents to the sturdy Pomeranian peasants, whose bones were fertilizing battlefields from the Pripet Marshes to the Somme.

Zimmermann, the Under-Secretary for Foreign Affairs, came the next day. Mr. House considered him to be the subtlest and ablest of the German Ministers with whom he had acquaintance. They had been on excellent terms since Mr. House's visit to the Kaiser in 1914, and the Texan talked to him more earnestly, less suavely, than he had to Bethmann-Hollweg and Jagow, driving home the military uselessness of the acts of petty brutality with which the German military and naval people tried to frighten enemies and neutrals alike. Zimmermann gave him lip-service, but he more or less discouraged Mr. House by parroting the Chancellor's preposterous suggestion of a union against the world of the "white races," Germany, Britain, and America. Obviously, Herr Zimmermann was as yet unwilling to concede that proud title to the Latin-Indian strain of Mexico!

On January 30, Mr. House traveled from Berlin to Geneva, spied upon to the frontier, at least, by secret-service men, as he had been throughout

---

* "I have met few men I was more sorry for than Bethmann-Hollweg," Mr. House remarked, in discussing this meeting. "He was typical of the Junkers of his day, simple, honorable in purpose, intensely patriotic, but stupid and very ignorant and badly educated in a human sense. Imagine a German aristocrat, a German Chancellor—or such a man in any civilized country—who could restrict 'the white races' to those three countries! He was, like all his people, living in a dream world. He was a shadow of Bismarck. But that's the trouble with the Germans. They've always been 'ag'in' the world, just as some of our old unreconstructed rebels in Texas were always 'ag'in the government.' It's a pity. A great people, with a genius for local government, who keep on thinking they've still got to lick the Roman legions. A real League of Nations might have changed their attitude. I don't know, but I think so. It would have been worth trying."

his stay at the Embassy. Not until he was safe in Geneva did he dare to report by cable to the President. Everything he had heard confirmed Solf's story of a controversy between the Navy, backed tentatively by the Army High Command, and the Ministry, over the issue of unrestricted submarine warfare. The Ministry would be forced out of office if they admitted the technical illegality of such warfare, hence their hedging over the *Lusitania* case. Mr. House advised the President not to "insist upon that point. If you do, I believe war will follow." In a letter, written three days later, he made the prediction that "if the war goes against Germany, when the Army is disbanded trouble will surely come for the masters. If victory is theirs, the war lords will reign supreme, and democratic governments will be imperiled throughout the world."

He was, in a sense, discouraged by the results of his visit to Berlin; but he need not have been. His calmness, his gift for understatement, for conveying ideas by indirection, had made a weighty impression upon the civilian Government—had, indeed, stiffened the back of the old Junker, Bethmann-Hollweg. The Ministry were inspired to new efforts to retain the Kaiser's ear against the insidious urgings of von Tirpitz. On February 15, Gerard wrote to Mr. House, in London:

"Your visit did a great deal of good. You have the satisfaction of knowing you probably kept us out of war."

It would be a year, almost to a day, after Mr. House's departure from Berlin, before von Bernstorff reluctantly carried to Lansing Germany's announcement of what she was pleased to call "a submarine blockade" of the British Isles, which neutral ships must navigate "at their own risk." So long a respite had his efforts won. And though history teaches us that they were futile, the record of the intervening twelve months reveals that they might well have been otherwise. A little less egotism here, a little more wisdom there. After all, history is a chain of accidents. It might not have rained at Waterloo.

5

In Geneva, Mr. House met Ambassador Penfield, who came over from Vienna to report to him. Penfield's news confirmed all that Mr. House had learned in London, Paris and Berlin. The war was settling into a stalemate, with neither side nor any one belligerent sufficiently punished to be willing to talk peace. Austria-Hungary had become a dependency of Germany since the German Army had come to her aid, and driven the hard-fighting Serbs out of their little country and the invading Rus-

sians out of Galicia. The ruling class of the Dual Monarchy had regained confidence, and were quite content to let German technicians pull
the strings at the Bal Platz and Grand Headquarters. There was more
food than in Germany, which kept the townspeople and peasants reasonably content, although the Bohemians and Southern Slavs deserted by
battalions and regiments whenever an opportunity occurred. The Government was more bitter against the United States than the Allies because of the dismissal of Ambassador Dumba, the American munitions
trade with the enemy, and the State Department's brusque *Ancona* notes.
Austria-Hungary would do whatever Germany bade her to, despite occasional realization by the proud Austrian and still prouder Hungarian
aristocracies that even victory could not shake loose the chains which at
last had bound her to the Teutonic dream of Mitteleuropa; that dream
which, for centuries, has been the inspiration and the curse of German
leaders.

A letter from Thomas Nelson Page, in Rome—whom Mr. House had
hoped to visit—conveyed news as foreboding as Penfield's. Italy's military effort was getting nowhere, her troops pinned down in the moun-
tainous region on the Austrian frontier. She was nursing open wounds
to her pride as a consequence of British and French criticisms of her
failure to go to the assistance either of Serbia or of Montenegro, wounds
nonetheless sore because her Queen was a daughter of the ancient Monte-
negrin House of Petrovitch. Her parties and politicians were at odds.
Her people were unhappy. Her merchants complained of the prices they
were obliged to pay for necessary coal and iron from her Allies. Many
Italians remembered sadly how much better had been their business relations with Germany, and perhaps for this reason, as much as any other,
she delayed—and would delay for six months longer—declaring war upon
Germany—a fact which did not diminish the temper of her Allies' re-
criminations. Altogether, Italy, at the opening of 1916, was setting her
feet upon the road of suffering and disillusionment which was to provide the highway for Mussolini's march on Rome. Not that such an idea
had dawned, as yet, upon that bulletheaded pink Socialist, who was
serving a dubious apprenticeship in the trenches.

Mr. House was back in Paris, February 1. He remained a week, and
this time he made no attempt to preserve his seclusion. He had talks
with President Poincaré, Premier Briand, Jules Cambon, former Ambassador at Berlin; Pichon, editor of the *Petit Journal,* a former Minister of
State and afterwards in Clemenceau's Cabinet; his old friend, that stalwart and practical pacifist, Baron d'Estournelles de Constant; and many

others. Ambassador Willard traveled up from Madrid to inform him of the situation in Spain, the most powerful neutral after the United States, and a prey to both Allied and German propaganda. He spoke freely, however, only to Briand and Cambon, and after some hesitation decided to adopt a suggestion the President had made before he left America: to take the French into his confidence as to the Administration's real purposes, even to the extent of his discussions with the British statesmen. He was agreeably surprised by their receptivity.

They were not, it is true, willing to agree with his own conclusion that the ensuing campaign would fail to bring them a clinching victory, and they stood stubbornly for the recovery of Alsace-Lorraine as a primary consideration of peace—a striking change from the prevalent feeling Mr. House had noted in the Paris of June, 1914; but they were disposed to welcome the idea of intervention by Mr. Wilson as a means to terminate hostilities at the earliest possible moment. The decision tentatively reached at this conference was that, if the victories they anticipated did not materialize during the coming spring and summer, the President should initiate Mr. House's plan for a peace conference designed to reorganize Europe on a basis of justice, with disarmament the first clause in the projected treaty. If the Germans refused to enter such a conference, the United States would intervene by force of arms. Mr. House had no doubt of the Germans' refusal or of the fact that intervention would be costly to the United States; but, short of a miracle of conciliation or Allied victory, he could see no other alternative. And he was more than ever convinced, after his visit to Berlin, that a German triumph would be as dangerous to the United States, in the long view of history, as it would be to the European democracies.

Mr. House was led into making this confidence to Briand and Cambon, not so much because of the President's suggestion—with all his admiration for his friend, he never had much respect for Mr. Wilson's knowledge of European statesmen or affairs—but, rather, because of his growing impatience with the tedious caution and lack of initiative of his ministerial friends in London, and also through his admiration for Briand's breadth of mind. He had been told that Briand was notoriously lazy, and slack in his duties. He found reason not to dispute this criticism. On the other hand, the humanness of this Frenchman—who was to become the foremost apostle of peace in the tortured Europe of the postwar years—deeply impressed him; notably, Briand's assertion that, if Germany had not declared war, she must inevitably have achieved a peaceful economic conquest of the world by reason of the diligence and intelligence of her people, and the slothfulness of the wealth-fattened British and French democracies.*

One possible error of judgment, which might be charged against Mr. House's conduct of his conversations with French and British statesmen on this trip, hinged on his failure to offer any objections to their theories of "reasonable" terms of peace. His own explanation, given years later, was that it seemed futile to object to ideas which might never come to fruition. "You've got to rope your steer before you barbecue him," was his phrase. Perhaps a more concrete explanation is that he was thinking realistically, as he always did, according to the obvious facts of the moment, on the basis of what seemed essentially plausible to leaders of the Allied Governments. And the "reasonable" terms, which were demanded in Paris and London, were actually so in the main. There was no talk of indemnities from Germany, except to Belgium. On the contrary, there was a disposition, he gathered, to offer Germany compensation outside of Europe. The main stipulations were: restoration intact of Belgium and Serbia, return of Alsace-Lorraine, cession of Italia Irredenta by Austria, and possession of Constantinople by Russia, apparently as a bribe for the erection of an independent Poland. The weak points in this scheme were the inevitable menace to the future peace of Europe inherent in Russia's presence on the Dardanelles, which must have led to her embroilment with Britain, and the absence of any solution of the Austrian minorities question.†

* Mr. House believed that one of the unforeseen results of the war of 1914-18 was the rejuvenation it injected into the British and French peoples. They were shocked out of their supine acceptance of the benefits they had gained by easy colonial conquests. But he could not deny that in a few years they had lapsed again into the same self-satisfied attitude of the "have" nations. Perhaps there is an historical rhythm in such national phenomena. The immediate future may furnish the answer.

† I suggested to Mr. House, in Paris, in January, 1919, a permanent solution—if permanence there be in history—of the question of Constantinople and the Straits. The plan was to internationalize the city and a narrow belt of territory along the European shores of the Bosphorus, the Marmora and the Dardanelles, as the seat of the League of Nations. Communication between the Mediterranean and Black Seas would have been barred to all warships, free to commerce. The sanctity of this "District of Columbia" of the civilized world would have been guaranteed by all member nations of the League.

The advantages of the plan were: it offered a means of finally disposing of a source of conflict to three continents since the days of the Byzantine Empire; it conferred upon the League the dignity and prestige of sovereignty; it placed the seat of the League midway of the world's greater masses of population; it was bound to exert a restraining influence upon the troublesome Balkan cockpit; and none of the nations which had been interested in the city's disposition could offer

It is indicative of the extent of Mr. House's subsequent education in international politics that he hadn't, in February, 1916, thought seriously of the fate of the Czechs, Slovaks, Ruthenians, Croats and Slovenes. But he learned fast after he met Wickham Steed, of the London *Times,* and Thomas G. Masaryk, who was to become the first President of the Czecho-Slovak Republic. Mr. House and Dr. Masaryk first met at Mr. House's country home, at Magnolia, Mass., June 12, 1918. It was an historic day for the old Kingdom of Bohemia—and may yet prove to have had more significance than Neville Chamberlain conceded it at Munich.

6

Leaving Paris, February 8, Mr. House stopped off at La Panne, in response to an invitation from King Albert of Belgium. This was the beginning of a friendship which continued on a basis of personal affection until the King's tragic death in the Ardennes.* Mr. House reached London the following evening. The impatience with which British statesmen awaited his return was indicated by a call from Lord Reading, immediately after breakfast the next morning, with an urgent message from Lloyd George, who wished to confer with him at the earliest possible moment.† Mr. House, however, did not wish to talk to anyone

valid objection to it. Turkey would have been the gainer because, naturally, the city would have been a free port, and a help to her commerce; a well-behaved Russia would have been assured against naval attack; Britain would have been protected against a hostile Russia on the flank of her "lifeline"; Italy would have been contented to know that the city had not gone to Bulgaria or Greece; and Bulgaria and Greece, each, would have been satisfied in the knowledge that the other did not obtain the prize; France would have shared Britain's feeling.

Mr. House was interested in the idea, partial to it. But at the time he was looking forward to being the American representative on the Council of the League, and as has been made plain in these pages, he was always concerned for the climate in which he had to work. He made inquiries, and was told that the bleak Black Sea storms of the winter months were productive of much bronchial and pulmonary trouble. So he plumped for Geneva, where he had always been comfortable.

* King Albert's correspondence with Mr. House, like President Wilson's, was conducted by himself, never through the medium of a secretary, the letters, often running to three or four pages, written in English, in a small, beautifully legible script.

† Lord Reading, as Sir Rufus Isaacs, holding the office of Attorney-General, had been involved in the so-called Marconi scandal, which revolved around the issuance of a number of shares of stock to members of the Government and Commons. No peculation was ever proven, but it is significant of Mr. House's standards of political honor that he remarked to me, upon the occasion of Lord Reading's coming to this

before he had reported to Grey, upon whom he placed his chief reliance for cooperative action by the Cabinet. He spent the rest of that morning with the Foreign Secretary. Grey was disposed to dispute with him the theory that it would be better for the President not to make an issue of the stale *Lusitania* controversy, but instead, to intervene solely in the cause of the world's need for peace. Grey, perhaps not so much as his colleagues, was yet infected with the European's natural instinct to discourage American participation in a peace settlement under conditions which would allow the United States to influence its definite terms. He preferred to see us enter the war—and he agreed with Mr. House, then and always, that Germany would refuse to accept the President's interpretation of a just peace—on the grounds of a quarrel of our own, which would make us less likely to restrain the Allies' territorial demands. Mr. House persuaded the Foreign Secretary away from this stand at their first consultation, or at least thought he did. But it is likely that the pressure of other members of the Cabinet, the course of events and public opinion, sapped the potency of Mr. House's argument in later months. Grey was as honorable a man as ever lived, but he was an Englishman. For reasons which seemed good to him he didn't "stay put." *

The main satisfaction Mr. House derived from this discussion was that Grey agreed, with astonishing alacrity, that the President *should* demand a peace conference within a very short time—in Mr. House's words to the President, "perhaps soon after I returned." Grey said nothing, at this meeting, of awaiting the issue of the approaching campaign in France. And, above all things, Mr. House wanted to terminate the loss of life and property which was devastating the world economically and spiritually. Already he had discounted the cost to the United States of a belligerent policy. It had been manifest to him for the past year that Germany could not be impelled to abandon her military advantage, as she conceived it, except by force. It cannot be too often insisted, in justice to

country as Special Ambassador, that the incident illustrated the difference between the British and American extra-official codes governing the conduct of public men. "Any American politician who had been placed in Reading's position would have been driven from public life, whether justly or unjustly," he said. "I'm hanged if I know which country is right, but somehow I like the way our people feel."

* Dr. Seymour (*The Intimate Papers*) thought that Mr. House exaggerated the degree to which he had influenced Grey on the advisability of the United States' forgetting the *Lusitania* issue. Dr. Seymour made the point, and it was well taken, that Mr. House's gentle persuasiveness often convinced an opponent for the time being, but that, after the spell of Mr. House's personality had been dimmed by his absence, the subject relapsed to the original heresy. I know of a number of such instances.

Mr. House's memory, that, almost from the beginning of hostilities, he believed that the one circumstance which could save the United States from involvement would be a smashing Allied victory. This, if possible, was no longer probable for the Allies, unaided, although they continued to delude themselves throughout 1916.

The next day, February 11, Mr. House lunched at Grey's house with the Foreign Secretary, Balfour, and Premier Asquith, whom he met for the first time intimately. That evening he dined with Lloyd George and Lord Reading. On both these occasions he was at pains to drive home to the British statesmen the idea that they must not expect American help if they waited until they were in serious danger of defeat by Germany. In such a contingency, he said to them, the United States would be foolish, no matter what the future might hold for this country, to come in and assume the main burden of a war more than three thousand miles distant from American bases. Rather, the United States would adopt a policy of confining their interests to the Western Hemisphere, increasing their armed forces and the Navy to a point which would give pause to any aggressive policy by Germany. He quoted to them Mr. Wilson's theory: that the United States could never feel justified in fighting on the behalf of one nation or group of nations, but only for "the rights of mankind." He thought they understood him. All, except Grey, were most cautious in what they said, but he felt that he had made progress. So secret were these and other meetings of Mr. House with members of the Government, that the persons present always left the house separately and at wide intervals of time.

Mr. House made his final assault upon the inner group, which controlled the foreign policy of the Cabinet, at a dinner given by the Lord Chief Justice, February 14. Present were Lord Reading, Premier Asquith, Lloyd George, Balfour and Grey. Ambassador Page was supposed to attend this dinner, but he preferred to absent himself on the excuse that Mr. House's mission was unofficial, and hence should not be countenanced by the diplomatic representative of the United States. There was not, as might be thought, any personal pique or jealousy in his attitude. Page had his smallnesses, but not of this caliber. He was influenced solely by his distrust of President Wilson and the State Department, his passionate pro-Ally sentiments, and his stubborn unwillingness to lend himself to any move for peace which might permit Germany to emerge from the war unbroken. It is difficult to characterize Page's state of mind without being unfair to a man who, certainly, never intended to stoop to a dishonorable or unpatriotic motive; but his conduct, as a diplomatic representative of his President and country, was outrageous in the

extreme, even harmful. He wore himself out being wrong, and so hastened his end. He never knew that he would have lost his embassy but
for Mr. House's protection. His wrong-headedness is illustrated in an
entry in his journal at this time:

"House told me that we'd have a meeting on Monday—Asquith, Grey,
Reading, Lloyd George, he and I. No, we won't. No member of the
Government can afford to discuss any such subject; not one of them has
any confidence in the strength of the President for action. Therefore, on
Friday, 11th of February, I told House that I couldn't go with him to
any such conference, and I wouldn't." *

This is amusing as well as sad, because it is true that one of Mr.
House's difficulties was that all of these men, except Grey, were inspired
by a deep-seated distrust of the President's character and ultimate intentions; and this distrust they had absorbed, in the main, from Ambassador
Page, the President's official mouthpiece. It was largely because of Page's
complete misunderstanding of his own country's interests, and Mr. Wilson's habits of mind, that so many of the negotiations between the United
States and the British Government were conducted by Mr. House, who
could have saved himself much toilsome endeavor had he been able to
share his task with the Ambassador. Page, fortunately for his personal
feelings, seems not to have appreciated that his attitude relegated him to
the position of supervisor of a clearing-house for diplomatic detail. Looking back on those years, it seems remarkable that, with well-intentioned
but wrong-headed men like Page and Spring-Rice representing the two
countries, they never came to a break in relations. For this Mr. House
and Secretary Lansing deserve the credit.

The Lord Chief Justice's dinner was the crux of Mr. House's mission.
It was interesting, humanly no less than politically, for a number of reasons. Mr. House spread his cards on the table and invited free discussion, with results which would have delighted a student of psychology.
Asquith was ponderous and uncertain. Balfour unsheathed his rapier of
dialectic and let it flicker in and out, fencing cynically and impersonally,
as was his wont. Reading was the perfect Lord Chief Justice, witty, tolerant, beneficent toward all, drawing out one after another, fascinated by
the quiet shrewdness of the Texan and his aptness at debate. Lloyd
George was checked by Mr. House in his first impetuous attempt to
make a speech, and settled down to bring his really brilliant mind to bear
upon the salient issues under discussion. Grey was earnestly sympathetic
with Mr. House's arguments, considering Britain's future with a selfless
impartiality possessed by none of the other Ministers, apprehending better

* *Life and Letters of Walter H. Page,* Doubleday, Page & Co.

than his colleagues, too, the interests of the United States which were at stake.

Complaints were made of the inadequacy of the Russian and Italian efforts, and of the wastage of munitions Britain could ill-afford to spare; and Mr. House took advantage of the opening to point out that these sorely pressed and discontented Allies might be expected to accept favorable terms for an independent peace. He listened to boasts of the preparations in train for a spring drive, and gave it as his opinion that the Germans would strike in the West before the weather cleared, and probably in the neighborhood of Verdun. This was a remarkable prediction. Exactly one week from that evening, on February 21, the German drum-fire beat down upon the shallow trenches connecting Verdun's outlying chain of forts, and the Somme offensive necessarily was postponed for five months because of the absorption of French troops in resistance to the Crown Prince's thrust.*

Lloyd George and Balfour then brought up the subject of the terms of peace which would be acceptable to the several Allies, and the men around Reading's dinner table urbanely discussed the repartitioning of Europe, Asia Minor, Africa, and the islands of the South Seas—as a theoretical proposition, Mr. House understood; not a word was said of the Secret Treaties which already had allocated the unwon spoils. He thought afterwards—and he was seldom bitter—that this touched a high mark in hypocrisy, if not in diplomatic dishonesty. "Of course," he amended his judgment, "I wasn't there officially, strictly speaking, and those fellers thought the United States had no concern in what they were fighting for. But the English are close traders; don't fool yourself."

His triumph of the evening consisted in winning Lloyd George to acceptance of the principle of intervention by Mr. Wilson; but the Welshman would not commit himself to a definite time for intervention. And it was necessary for Mr. House, in turn, to pledge the attendance of the President at a conference to be held at The Hague. This is interesting, as an example of seeming inconsistency on Mr. House's part. In 1916 he had no hesitation in believing that the President should preside at a peace conference to be held in Holland. In the fall of 1918 he strongly disap-

---

* Mr. House was distressed when Lord Reading told him on February 22 that the Cabinet had decided, in consequence of his arguments, to make an early push on the Western Front. He need not have felt responsible. Ministers had not yet appreciated the seriousness of the day-old assault upon Verdun. But the incident is indicative of how lightly, despite their caution and ponderous procedure, British statesmen could reach drastic and far-reaching decisions. No wonder the generals were continually fuming against political pressure!

proved of the idea of the President's presence at a peace conference to be held in France. Why?

There are two obvious reasons for his change of mind. First, Mr. House, by October, 1918, had seen much more, at first-hand, of high-power diplomacy as played by the insiders. He knew more of the personalities in the game, and their supple adroitness, their gifts for intellectual chicanery, with which the President's direct, simple honesty, and sincere idealism, were ill-fitted to cope. Also the President, through his speeches and State papers, had acquired a position of world leadership which no statesman had possessed in centuries; and Mr. House sensed that this position must be jeopardized by personal contact with men who were politically unprincipled and actuated by selfish nationalistic motives. His second reason was that at the projected Hague conference the President was slated to preside, as was only right, considering that it would have been held in response to his summons, and upon neutral ground. The Paris conference, on the other hand, was held in the capital of a proud people, who were liquidating a victorious war, much of it fought on their own soil. The French would never have consented to acceptance of the chief of a foreign State in such circumstances. Indeed, Clemenceau stipulated against this as a condition to Mr. Wilson's presence in Paris.

The Lord Chief Justice's dinner is notable, historically, because it furnished an opportunity for shortening the war, which was missed by the British Government; but at the moment Mr. House had the temporary satisfaction of believing that he had carried his point, to the extent that the five Ministers—for Lord Reading was ex officio of the Cabinet's counsels—agreed during the following week in the principle that the President should call for a peace conference; with the proviso, however, that the call must be subject to their conception of the time most propitious to British interests. This was a half-victory for Mr. House, but a victory far beyond what Ambassador Page had prognosticated. The Texan even had dented Asquith's phlegmatic self-assurance, and won over Balfour's profoundly skeptical mind. But, of the five, Grey alone truly appreciated the scope of Mr. House's purpose.

In those weeks Mr. House came to love the tall, stoop-shouldered Englishman, whose coloring so aptly matched his name, whose life had been scarred by private griefs, and whose tired eyes were gifted with a spiritual sight far, far beyond their narrowing physical vision. He never forgot the afternoon Grey strode up and down the floor of his office, features working spasmodically in a rare burst of emotion, asserting the need for immediate action to save millions of lives—which were to be lost—no matter what the cost to the Government's prestige. There would be angry mobs in the street, no doubt. His windows would be broken. He might be driven from public life. His colleagues, too. But better this than that millions should perish or the world be held to postponement of a chance to work out a new order of civilization.

Grey's sincerity fructified in a Memorandum drawn up by himself and Mr. House, with the approval of the other Ministers. It is worth quoting here, if for no other reason, as a tragic commentary upon the mistakes of which well-intentioned statesmen are capable:

(*Confidential*)

Colonel House told me that President Wilson was ready, on hearing from France and England that the moment was opportune, to propose that a Conference should be summoned to put an end to the war. Should the Allies accept this proposal, and should Germany refuse it, the United States would probably enter the war against Germany.

Colonel House expressed the opinion that, if such a Conference met, it would secure peace on terms not unfavourable to the Allies; and, if it failed to secure peace, the United States would (probably) leave the Conference as a belligerent on the side of the Allies, if Germany was unreasonable. Colonel House expressed an opinion decidedly favourable to the restoration of Belgium, the transfer of Alsace and Lorraine to France, and the acquisition by Russia of an outlet to the sea,* though he thought that the loss of territory incurred by Germany in one place would have to be compensated to her by concessions to her in other places outside Europe. If the Allies delayed accepting the offer of President Wilson, and if, later on, the course of the war was so unfavourable to them that the intervention of the United States would not be effective, the United States would probably disinterest themselves in Europe and look to their own protection in their own way.

I said that I felt the statement, coming from the President of the United States, to be a matter of such importance that I must inform the Prime Minister and my colleagues; but that I could say nothing until it had received their consideration. The British Government could, under no circumstances, accept or make any proposal except in consultation and agreement with the Allies. I thought that the Cabinet would probably feel that the present situation would not justify them in approaching their Allies on this subject at the present moment; but, as Colonel House had had an intimate conversation with M. Briand and M. Jules Cambon in Paris, I should think it right to tell

---

* In fairness it should be noted that at the Reading dinner Mr. House urged the neutralization of Constantinople, a variation of the idea I suggested to him at the Peace Conference. Lloyd George and Balfour were against handing over this focal city to Russia. Grey and Asquith, strangely enough, thought that not to do so would insure another war. As if the control of the Straits by Russia could have been anything else but an incentive to war for Britain, France, and Italy!

M. Briand privately, through the French Ambassador in London,* what Colonel House had said to us; and I should, of course, whenever there was an opportunity, be ready to talk the matter over with M. Briand, if he desired it.

(*Intd.*) E. G.

Foreign Office
22 February 1916

This memorandum Mr. House confirmed by cable from New York, March 8, after conferring with the President, who altered it only by the insertion of the word "probably" in the second paragraph. The sole qualification in Mr. House's agreement, given for and in the President's name, consisted in the phrase: ". . . so far as he can speak for the future action of the United States." This phrase was dictated, not so much by fear of hostile sentiment in Congress, as by the possibility of Mr. Wilson's death in office or defeat for reelection if the summons for a conference were delayed so long.

It has been the fashion in recent years for a certain school of historians to deride President Wilson and Mr. House as puppets of British propaganda. Nothing could be farther from the truth. Neither of them had any illusions as to Britain's self-interest in the matter of our participation in the war. Or France's, either. When Grey showed Mr. House a transcript of House's conversation with Briand and Jules Cambon, furnished to the Foreign Secretary by Paul Cambon, which quoted House as stating that the United States would come to the rescue of France at her call, no matter how low were her fortunes, Mr. House was quick to brand this as an error. If France and Britain wished our assistance, they must say so while they were still able to defend themselves. The United States was not throwing its weight into the defense of nations which defeated themselves by their own arrogance and greed. The Grey memorandum is specific on this point.

The President and Mr. House were willing to intervene, if Germany proved recalcitrant in 1916, for one reason and only one reason: to serve the true interests of the United States. This was the reason for which the United States broke off relations with Germany and went to war in 1917. It may not be to our credit, idealistically, but the fact is that we used the European democracies and their Allies for our purposes; they did not use us, except incidentally. And if Mr. House were alive today, he would say that that is exactly what the United States has been doing since Britain and France declared war on Germany in September, 1939. President Wilson and Mr. House did not always see eye to eye, but they

---

* Paul Cambon, M. Jules Cambon's brother.

were agreed in the theory that, in the long run, the interests of the United States must harmonize with those of other democratic nations, and not with imperialistic, communistic or totalitarian governments. The chief difference between them was that Mr. House was inclined to translate this theory into instant action in the case of any threat to democracy in the Western World. He never quite forgave his friend for blundering into the phrase "too proud to fight."

"If this country ever gets to feel that way," he once said, "you might as well hang up a 'to rent' sign on the Capitol, and invite the Germans or the Japanese to move in. All countries have to fight to live, and the richer they are, the more often they'll be challenged. We wanted to outlaw war, make it as difficult as possible. That's what the League of Nations was intended to mean. But no intelligent man believes that you can abolish war altogether, any more than you can crime. Keep it from paying, that's the best you can do."

7

Mr. House sailed from Falmouth, February 25, and reached Washington, March 6. He made his preliminary report to the President during a two-hour automobile ride after lunch. Mrs. Wilson accompanied the friends, in accordance with her custom of being present at their conferences whenever possible. Afterwards the President and Mr. House talked together alone in the President's study until seven o'clock. The President warmly approved of all that Mr. House had done abroad. The cable confirming the Grey Memorandum was drafted by Mr. Wilson himself, in shorthand, and then typed on his portable machine; and at the conclusion of their discussion the President placed his hand on Mr. House's shoulder.

"It would be impossible to imagine a more difficult task than the one placed in your hands," he said, "but you have accomplished it in a way beyond my expectations." And when Mr. House replied, stressing his pride of achievement if the President were able to realize their plan of ending the war, Mr. Wilson retorted generously: "You should be proud of yourself and not of me, since you have done it all."

The link between the friends was still as strong as it had been when Ellen Axson Wilson died.

At this time, in March, 1916, when the President was willing to pledge the contingent intervention of the United States, not so much on the side of the Allies as on the side of humanity, he was being bitterly assailed for not doing so by the Republican press and personalities, hallooed on by ex-President Roosevelt. Naturally, his lips were sealed to defense of the course he had set for himself. He could only remain proudly silent, disdainful of the intemperate misinterpretations of his motives by partisan adversaries. But the iron entered his soul during those years. With all his eloquence, he was a strangely inarticulate man, in a personal sense. He hugged criticism to him, never flinching under the whips, exalting himself, like the son of the manse he was, in the secret knowledge of his rectitude. A sad thought. The experience did not sweeten or gentle his disposition for the sorrier days to come.

Mr. House returned to America to find himself confronted by a new complication, which threatened to undermine the confidence in Administration policy he had so carefully built up in London and Paris. On January 18, Secretary Lansing had addressed an informal note to the Allied Ambassadors, suggesting that all merchantmen be disarmed, in return for a pledge by Germany that they should not be attacked without warning, nor be fired upon, except in case of resistance or flight. On top of this, the German Government announced that, beginning March 1, all armed merchantmen would be treated as men-o'-war. In the Allied capitals, Lansing's well-intentioned move was taken to be a bribe offered to Germany to induce her to yield a flat disavowal of the *Lusitania* incident, and as such, another indication of President Wilson's pacifism and unwillingness to resist German aggression.

This was absurd, of course. The United States was demanding from Berlin an admission of the illegality of the attack upon the Cunarder, and Zimmermann had written Mr. House, January 29, and von Jagow had told Gerard, as reported by the Ambassador, February 8, that under no circumstances would Germany concede this point, inasmuch as it would have annulled her right, at some future date, to proclaim unrestricted warfare. Von Jagow stated explicitly that Germany had made no promises to us as to submarine warfare, nor would she; she had merely told us that certain orders had been issued to submarine commanders, and these orders were subject to change at any time. Zimmermann went so far as to write—and he meant it—that "if the United States Government insists on this wording, a break will be unavoidable." As has been made plain in these pages, Mr. House did not consider a break worth while on this issue—at the moment.

Mr. House had no difficulty in persuading the President—who, generously again, took the blame to himself and Lansing—to abandon the Lansing proposal. But in the meantime, and while Mr. House was at sea, a further complication had been injected into the situation through the introduction by Representative McLemore, of Texas, of a House

resolution warning American citizens not to travel on armed ships. The
President, against the advice of Speaker Champ Clark and Senator Stone,
of Missouri, Chairman of the Senate Foreign Relations Committee,
courageously fought this motion to defeat. But the very fact that it had
been introduced and received 135 votes to 275 when it was tabled, March
7, served to confirm the suspicions of French and British statesmen that
Mr. Wilson was a weak reed to lean on. And Mr. Wilson's prestige
was not enhanced by the fact that he was obliged to rely upon Republican votes to sustain his position.

On March 10 Mr. House wrote to Grey, elaborating the contents of
his cable of the 8th, which had been drafted by the President. "It is
now squarely up to you to make the next move," he said frankly, "and
a cable from you at any time will be sufficient." That is, Mr. Wilson
was ready to intervene on behalf of the Allies at a few hours' notice.

A week later, Mr. House derived a breath of optimism from von
Tirpitz's resignation from the Admiralty. He construed this as meaning the temporary triumph of the Civil Government in Berlin over the
advocates of unrestricted submarine warfare. What he seems not to
have appreciated was that it likewise constituted a monitory gesture by
the Grand Admiral, transferring responsibility for conduct of the submarine campaign to the pudgy shoulders of von Bethmann-Hollweg.
As Gerard indicated, if things went badly for Germany in the next few
months von Tirpitz's hand would be strengthened. He would have
a chance to make good on *his* promises. And then, on March 24, as if
to illustrate how little reliance could be placed upon any undertaking
by Germany, the unarmed Channel steamer *Sussex* was torpedoed without warning, and eighty passengers killed or wounded.

Mr. House, and von Bernstorff and Gerard, professed to be mystified
as to the motive for the *Sussex* attack. The answer is fairly obvious. It
was the Navy's way of expressing resentment for von Tirpitz's resignation, and contempt for the control of the Civil Government. Also, if you
take the point of view of the German Navy, the *Sussex* might have been
an unarmed passenger vessel, but, like all Channel steamers in wartime,
she carried British military personnel, and so might fairly be classed as
a transport. It is difficult to understand the indignation of the United
States Government over her torpedoing, except—and this is all-important
—that it was a complete exemplification of the essential inhumanity of
submarine warfare, which cannot, by its very nature, make any discrimi-
nation between civilian and service passengers, and contraband and non-
contraband. This is as true in 1940 as it was in 1916.

Mr. House felt, more strongly than ever, that the time had come to break with Germany, but he was baffled, when the President sent for him, March 30, to discover that his arguments of the past six months had been double-edged. Mr. Wilson's immediate reaction was, that if he broke with Germany, there would be no outstanding neutral nation to lead the way to peace, and the war might continue indefinitely—the precise phrases which Mr. House had been employing in urging upon his friend the advantages of early intervention by a neutral United States. But the Texan extricated himself from this situation, of his own creation, by suggesting that the President employ, in the note Lansing was preparing, no accusations against the German people—a forecast of the President's policy two years later—but, instead, confine himself to a denunciation of the German Government, making plain that, if the Imperial system of military aggression were abandoned, the United States would gladly resume friendly relations. If this were done, Mr. House thought, it would be possible for him, by midsummer, to open negotiations from Holland with Berlin, after securing the Allies' approval, and so bring about the international conference the President desired, under his leadership. Mr. Wilson expressed approval of the idea.

Reading over the entry of this discussion in his diary nine years afterwards, Mr. House noted that "my suggestion seems now like nonsense, and not even good nonsense." Dr. Seymour disagrees with this judgment, remarking that "he [Mr. House] appealed to the President's pacific instincts in order to arouse his belligerent will." But surely this is stretching charity too far. The program outlined by Mr. House was utterly impracticable. It would never have worked. It wasn't worthy of Mr. House, and he deserves credit for having realized so much. The truth was that he advanced the argument in a moment of disconcertion, when he realized the harm his own previous arguments had done in pinning the President's inelastic mind to a fixed idea.

Lansing was instructed to put teeth in the note and to prepare passports for Bernstorff, and the President asked Mr. House to warn the German Ambassador that the breaking point had been reached. It was due to Bernstorff that the break was averted. He told Mr. House that "a break must not occur," and begged for time to work on his Government, promising unreservedly that Germany was, and would be, sincere in her pledges. He impressed Mr. House very favorably. Bernstorff was often guilty of deception in the various phases of the tortuous policy he was compelled to pursue, but he never wavered from the conviction that the worst fate which could befall Germany would be the active hostility of the United States. On this ground, chiefly, Mr. House bent his influence to mitigating the harshness of the President's note.

The term "the President's note" is quite accurate, for the President discarded Lansing's draft and wrote his own version, eliminating finally a concluding paragraph, which, Mr. House contended, ended on a pitch of inconclusiveness, and laid bare his friend's closely coupled exposition of the whole theory of submarine warfare to one of those interminable arguments dear to the diplomatic mind. Much of the data Mr. Wilson obtained from material Mr. House had brought back from London. It is one of his greatest State papers, lofty, dignified, its humaneness never obscured by the legal acumen which made it practically unanswerable.

"Unless the Imperial Government," the President wrote, "should now immediately declare and effect an abandonment of its present methods of submarine warfare against passenger and freight-carrying vessels, the Government of the United States can have no choice but to sever diplomatic relations with the German Empire altogether."

Mr. House could not help but approve its tone. He was obliged to admit that it served the country's interests better than a break on the bare issue of the *Sussex's* sinking, in that it demonstrated patience and firmly placed Germany in a position from which there were only two ways of escape—and whichever way she took, her action must strengthen the position of the United States and the President. But he had ample cause for worry during the two weeks the German militarists and the Civil Government wrangled over the policy to be adopted. Mr. Wilson, in one of his sudden shifts of poise, swung over from his attitude of procrastination to an inclination to belligerence exceeding his friend's. "I evidently overdid it," Mr. House noted ruefully in his diary, May 3, "for I now find him unyielding and belligerent, and not caring as much as he ought to avert war."

Fortunately, von Bethmann-Hollweg and von Jagow carried the day in Berlin. The German response was ill-tempered and complaining as to the failure of the United States to compel the Allies to modify the food blockade—a ridiculous stand, in view of the fact that a year before Germany had refused to consider the suggestion of abandoning submarine warfare in return for such a modification—but it contained the two vital concessions for which the United States had contended. The German Government, it promised, "is prepared to do its utmost to confine the operations of war for the rest of its duration to the fighting forces of the belligerents," and no more merchant ships were to be sunk "without warning and without saving human lives, unless these ships attempt to escape or offer resistance." As a condition, however, to the execution of these pledges the note demanded, with veiled insolence, the cessation of trade restrictions by Britain, and stipulated: "Should the steps taken by the Government of the United States not attain the object it desires to have the laws of humanity followed by all belligerent nations, the German Government would then be facing a new situation, in which it must reserve itself complete liberty of decision."

This was the loophole of which Germany availed herself on January 31, 1917, and in so doing, started the chain of events which drew the United States into armed support of the Allies. But in May, 1916, Mr. House knew that Germany had gone as far as could reasonably have been expected of her, in light of her home problems, and he advised the President to accept the reply for its essentials. Mr. Lansing did not agree with this view; he thought the German reply unsatisfactory, perhaps because his legal mind detected the speciousness with which its pledges were hedged. The President was disposed to take a middle ground, agreeing with Mr. House that a break was no longer necessary, and with his Secretary of State that the legal quibbles in the note should be disowned in a reply. Mr. House thought a reply was unnecessary, might possibly lead to a succession of mutual harangues; he suggested that it would be sufficient if Lansing simply issued a statement of the same tenor to the press. He was wrong. The President and Lansing, thinking as lawyers, understood better than he the necessity of spiking, once and for all, any excuse Germany might seek to offer at some future date—as she did—for a resumption of illegal warfare. Together they concocted a reply which, Mr. House again had to admit, was "admirable." The last paragraph, written by Mr. Wilson, made the case of the United States clear beyond cavil.

The United States, it declared, "cannot for a moment entertain, much less discuss, a suggestion that respect by German naval authorities for the rights of the citizens of the United States upon the high seas should in any way or in the slightest degree be made contingent upon the conduct of any other Government affecting the rights of neutrals and noncombatants. Responsibility in such matters is single, not joint; absolute, not relative."

The *Sussex* notes, and indeed the whole chain of Mr. Wilson's State Papers dealing with illegal sea warfare, either by Germany or by the Allies, in the period 1915-17, are an exemplification of his creed, as President of the United States, that American citizens might travel and ship goods wherever they pleased, and had a right to, under the cloak of international law, and that it was the duty of their Government to protect them in doing so to the limits of its ability. Mr. House entirely agreed with him. So did Secretary Lansing. So did most Americans of that generation. They refused to admit the validity of a blockade, by submarines or any other means, which ignored the rules of cruiser warfare, and when it became apparent that a submarine blockade could not be conducted according to those rules, they became fiercely hostile to the use of submarines for other than strictly combat purposes. They believed that the United States could not and should not ever assent, directly or indirectly, to the use of the submarine against merchant shipping. It was the submarine which suggested to Mr. House his doctrine of the Freedom of the Seas, and if that adaptation of the Golden Rule to sea warfare is beyond the present spiritual stature of men, at least it is a conception of human dignity worth striving to attain.

8

While Mr. House was staying at the White House, during the height of the *Sussex* crisis, he and the President decided to send Grey a second cable, urging consultation amongst the Allies on the advisability of approving their plan for American intervention. Mr. House was responsible for this idea, but at the time he agreed with Mr. Wilson that the British Cabinet would most likely consider the suggestion an indication of American unwillingness to take drastic measures with Germany. There was a disposition in Allied and German circles to suspect that the approaching Presidential campaign inclined Mr. Wilson to reluctance toward adoption of a strong international policy. This was not true. But the fact remained that the situation undermined the President's influence abroad until after his reelection.

In after years Mr. House became convinced that their cable had been a mistake, for which he assumed the chief responsibility, in that it had strengthened the reluctance of the Allies to admit the United States to active participation in a peace. Perhaps, however, he failed to rationalize the principal factor in dictating the Allies' jealousy of American intervention: their fear that an unbiased United States would resist the application to Germany of such terms as were required by the Secret Treaties —of which he was ignorant in 1916—just as Germany was unwilling to accept our mediation through her knowledge that we would insist upon compensation for the invasion of France and Belgium, and denial of Balkan hegemony to Austria. Yet Mr. House, always more realistic than his friend, had perceived clearly, since the opening of hostilities, that only a strong Army and Navy could insure the power of the United States to enforce justice, and he thought, as has been said before in these pages, that if the President had acted a year before he did to build up the fighting services, our position would have been mightily enhanced in 1916.

And if he did not attach the requisite significance to the territorial ambitions of the Allies, he showed his understanding of the fundamental weakness of their scornful attitude toward the United States by an entry in his diary of April 30, a few weeks later: "It is the old story . . . What the Allies want is to dip their hands into our treasure chest. While the war has become a war of democracy against autocracy, not one of the democracies entered it to fight for democracy, but merely because of the necessity of self-preservation. If we go in, it will be because we believe in democracy and do not desire our institutions and the character of our civilization changed."

The cable to Grey of April 6, written by Mr. Wilson, signed by Mr. House, was sent simply as a desperate—and dubious—attempt to avert American hostilities against Germany, as well as in the belief that American intervention, as a neutral, would shorten the war, whether we ultimately became involved or not. It read:

"Since it seems probable that this country must break with Germany on the submarine question unless the unexpected happens, and since, if this country should once become a belligerent, the war would undoubtedly be prolonged, I beg to suggest that if you had any thought of acting at an early date on the plan we agreed upon, you might wish now to consult your allies with a view to acting immediately."

Nothing came of it for the reasons outlined above. Grey was in a difficult situation, himself. His own colleagues were divided in sentiment, and he felt obliged not to make suggestions for a peace conference to the French Government without an intimation from Briand that France was ready for a conference. There was, at the background of Anglo-French relations—and perhaps there always will be—the sinister fear of two peoples who speak different languages, and whose international policies are necessarily divergent in essentials, despite occasional coincidence, that one might or would betray the other. This may not be pleasant reading, but it is impossible for intelligent British and French statesmen to coöperate, unless they keep this trait forever in their minds. Grey was thinking of it when he wrote in his Memoirs: "I was afraid if I mentioned peace, the French would think we were going to *lacher* them."

Undiscouraged by Grey's lack of response, Mr. House cabled him a third time, May 10, with the President's approval, writing at greater length and in phrases tinged by a note of sternness, with the design of warning him that Germany's partial surrender in the *Sussex* case must serve to stimulate anti-British feeling in the United States and lead to a harsher attitude toward British trade restrictions. He said, in part: "The impression grows that the Allies are more determined upon the punishment of Germany than upon exacting terms that neutral opinion would consider just. . . . If the President is to serve humanity in a large way, steps should be taken now rather than wait until the opportunity becomes less favorable. . . . The convention should bind the signatory Powers to side against any nation refusing in case of dispute to adopt some other settlement than that of war. I am sure this is the psychological moment for this statement to be made."

In a letter of confirmation mailed the 11th, Mr. House elaborated this theme: "If we should get into the war, I feel sure it would not be a good thing for England. It would probably lead to the complete crushing of Germany and Austria; Italy and France would then be more concerned as to the division of the spoils than they would for any far-reaching agreement . . . looking to the maintenance of peace in the future and the amelioration of the horrors of war. . . . From my cable you will see how far the President has gone within the year. . . . Delay is dangerous and may defeat our ends. . . . All the things that you and I have wished to bring about seem ready now of accomplishment, and I earnestly hope that you may bring your Government to a realization of the opportunity that is seeking fulfillment."

But Sir Edward Grey's personal position had not been altered by the few days separating Mr. House's second and third cables. Weeks and months would not alter it. Inertia had paralyzed Allied diplomacy. Most statesmen were thinking in military, not diplomatic, formulas. The successful defense of Verdun had braced French official morale, its will to war. The British generals, and many Cabinet Ministers, were childishly eager to play with the new military weapons they had been creating. There was an equally childish feeling that the slovenly Russians at last would smash the Austrians, a feeling intensified by the anticipation that Rumania was coming in on the Allied side. Grey's answer, May 12, could be called insincere, if allowance were not made for the difficulties which beset him, the loneliness of his situation. Blaming the Allies' distrust of Germany's willingness for peace upon a bellicose speech to the Reichstag delivered by Bethmann-Hollweg, April 5, and ignoring completely the House-Wilson pledge, stated in the Grey Memorandum of February 22, to work for terms not "unfavorable to the Allies," the Foreign Secretary excused himself weakly for failure to consult the Allied Governments with the phrase: "The President's suggestion of summoning a peace conference, without any indication of a basis on which peace might be made, would be construed as instigated by Germany to secure peace on terms unfavorable to the Allies while her existing military situation is still satisfactory to her."

Mr. House was disappointed, the President irritated, by what they conceived to be the obtuseness of the Allied Governments, if not of Sir Edward Grey. And in order to justify the President and place his position beyond challenge, Mr. House launched two further strokes of policy. On May 19, once more with Mr. Wilson's approval, he cabled a fourth time to the British Foreign Secretary, and more firmly than in his third cable, so firmly, indeed, that the Cabinet in London were left without a shadow of an excuse for inability to realize the opportunity they were throwing away.

"My cables and letters of the past few days," he said, "have not been sent with any desire to force the hands of the Allies or to urge upon them something for which they are not ready, but rather to put before them a situation that arose immediately Germany agreed to discontinue her illegal submarine warfare. America has reached the crossroads, and if we cannot soon inaugurate some sort of peace discussion there will come a demand from our people, in which all neutrals will probably join, that we assert our undeniable rights against the Allies with the same insistence we have used toward the Central Powers. . . . There is a feeling here, which is said to exist in other neutral countries, that the war should end, and any nation that rejects peace discussions will bring upon themselves a heavy responsibility. If we push the Allies as hard as we needs must, friction is certain to arise. . . . I am speaking in all frankness, as I have always done with you. . . . The time is critical, and delay is dangerous. If England is indeed fighting for the emancipation of Europe, we are ready to join her in order that the nations of the earth, be they large or small, may live their lives as they may order them and be free from the shadow of autocracy and the specter of war."

Grey's answer was substantially a reiteration of his previous cables. He was unwilling to be an intermediary in carrying suggestions of peace to France. He seemed to feel that the President should negotiate direct with France, and it is possible that he knew exactly what he was talking about. Certainly, when Mr. House sounded out Ambassador Jusserand, he received no encouragement for a peace conference called upon any reason except unquestioned Allied victory. Mr. House gained the impression from the whole series of maneuvers in which he took part, that the British and the French, like the Germans, were scornful of the practical help the United States could contribute to the prosecution of the war. They were getting all the money and munitions they wanted, and they believed this was all they might expect, save for the moral prestige of our endorsement of their cause. They evidenced much the same feeling in 1917 and the early months of 1918. In Mr. House's opinion,

they were as surprised as the Germans—excluding a few like von Bernstorff—by the immensity of the military pressure the United States
brought to bear upon short notice.

"I have never ceased to be impressed," he said, not once, but many
times, "by the abysmal ignorance of the United States displayed by all
Europeans. An occasional individual like Lord Bryce, Sir Horace Plunkett or Bernstorff, had a glimmering of what we could do, knew something of our military prowess, but to the rest we were, literally, a nation
of mechanics and wasteful farmers. And I haven't any doubt that most
of them will soon forget what we did for them. The European is seldom
as well informed as the American of intelligence about affairs outside
his own country. Why, Clemenceau, with all his toughness of mind,
and despite the fact that he had lived here, really thought that American soldiers would be content to be brigaded with French or British
troops. They didn't even take into account the troubles which would
have come from differences in diet."

Without waiting for a final response from Grey, Mr. House dealt his
second stroke. He arranged with his friend, ex-President Taft, who was
President of the League to Enforce Peace, to invite Mr. Wilson to address a meeting of the League to be held in Washington, May 27. It was
his first thought that the President might employ this occasion to speak
out vigorously in demand for a conference to end the war, and make
more difficult the waging of all future wars. But the coldness of the
Allied Governments, and Bernstorff's blunt intimation that Germany
was not disposed to regard Mr. Wilson as a desirable mediator, led the
two friends to choose a loftier, more impartial and disinterested tone.
Mr. Wilson was to state, in general terms, the intention of the United
States to adopt its proper share of responsibility, jointly with other nations, for the maintenance of peace and justice in the world, resistance
to conquest and aggression. In its way, this speech, while more significant in its time and broader in application, really was an elaboration of
McKinley's last speech at Buffalo. After sixteen years, an American
President was thinking again in accordance with the true destiny of the
Republic—and not afraid to say so.

It was a great speech, in its fundamental concepts as much a product
of Mr. House's brain as Mr. Wilson's; for instance, in its stressing of the
need for "an universal association of the nations to maintain the inviolate
security of the highway of the seas," and "to prevent any war begun
either contrary to treaty covenants or without warning and full submission of the causes to the opinion of the world." Typical Wilsonian
phrases, which boom out of the past with a ghostly echo of mockery of

conditions prevailing since his death, in defiance of ideals which Americans once professed and later saw fit to repudiate, in the fanciful belief that the United States could shuck off their share of the world's burdens and retire behind a tariff barrier to live on funds hired out to less fortunate nations.

It is sad to have to add that the thundering roll of Wilsonian periods was marred by one of those infelicities into which the President was too often led by the temptation of the oratorical phrase, the tricky conjunction of words and ideas; of the war the President remarked, all too casually: "With its causes and objects we are not concerned." The Allies forgot the trenchant arguments for their cause, and on the excuse of these nine words dismissed the speech as lumping them with the Germans in blameworthiness for the struggle. Papers in London and Paris scolded more bitterly than ever. Ambassador Page reported gleefully that his friends were convinced anew that Mr. Wilson didn't understand the war, and was playing home politics to get himself reelected. So, for the time being, Mr. Wilson's effort of May 27 accomplished nothing for him abroad. It did him good at home, but that wasn't what he and Mr. House had planned to accomplish.*

Mr. Wilson would not have been human had he failed to be seriously irritated by the stupidity of British Ministers in ignoring his proffers of a peace conference and, failing a peace satisfactory to the Allies, an armed alliance with the United States. The Foreign Office, aside from its rejection of the President's repeated proffers of intervention, had chosen the moment of the *Sussex* crisis to deliver, six months after the issue had been raised by the United States, a most unsatisfactory reply to an American note protesting against arbitrary actions against our shipping, involving such diplomatic outrages as seizure of mails and removal of enemy subjects from American flag vessels. There was suspicion in the State Department that the Foreign Office had selected a time when the United States was in controversy with Germany to "slip over" a note which they knew must arouse American resentment. Yet, despite his feeling, the President yielded to a plea from Sir Edward Grey submitted through Mr. House, to cushion the sting of the American counter-reply by addressing it jointly to France.

---

* It may seem small to keep emphasizing President Wilson's weakness for the misunderstandable phrase; but Mr. House attached much importance to the harm done him, both at home and abroad, by these self-betrayals into over-elaboration of ideas. Such infelicities were unessential to the main themes of Mr. Wilson's addresses or State Papers. They were reflexes of the academic, not the political, mind; and the fact that they were honest in intent never saved them from being misconstrued and distorted.

Mr. Wilson's annoyance became more pronounced when the British Government, on July 18, published a "black list" of more than eighty American business firms, who were forbidden to trade internationally in retaliation for their relations with the business structure of the Central Powers. By July 23, he had decided to summon Page home for a visit to "Americanize" the Ambassador, and wrote Mr. House that he was planning to ask Congress for power to restrict loans and exports to the Allies, a step he actually took before Congress adjourned. Thanks to the unchallenged leadership he enjoyed—until he lost it by his own ill-advised policy two years later, after the war was won—Congress did grant him extraordinary discretionary powers, which would have given him a strangle-hold on the Allies had the Germans not thrown us into the arms of their enemies. Congress also passed the largest naval appropriation bill introduced up to that time, authorizing the construction of 137 fighting craft. It was Mr. Wilson's own fault that the bill had not been introduced, and passed, a year or more previously, when, as Mr. House thought, it might have had substantial influence upon both sides in the war.

The events of that fateful summer served to augment the President's irritation into occasional fits of petulance, another one of his traits due to an unnaturally cloistered life. In such moments, Mr. House was concerned for his judgment, although this did not mean, and never could have meant, that Mr. House was deficient in loyalty to, and admiration for, his friend and chief, whose nobility of soul and mind triumphed over defects of temperament until they were subverted by illness. For instance, Mr. House noted in his diary, September 24, that the President said to him that day: "Let us build a navy greater than hers [Great Britain's], and do what we please." Mr. House advised him seriously that such a policy, however justified, would almost certainly result in transferring to the United States from Germany the hostility of British sea power for any navy of challenging strength. The Texan had come to believe, in recent months, that the British Government's growing appreciation of our development, commercially and financially, was one of the elements underlying their unwillingness to grant us a chance to win prestige by leading in the initiative for peace.

Of this advice he said afterward, in one of those personal conversations in which he analyzed his own opinions and mistakes of judgment:

"I cheerfully admit that I did not see the full extent of the increase of our power through the war, or the exhaustion of the British Empire. After the peace, the British could not have challenged our purpose to rival or surpass their navy. They would have resented it; they might

have attempted to resist it. But they could not have stopped us. Nobody knew better than intelligent British statesmen, unless it was the
Japanese, the favor we did the other naval powers by negotiating the
Harding-Hughes limitation treaties. The truth was, we definitely took
the lead as the chief world power in those years. It is our own fault that
we have not taken reasonable advantage of our strength. I hope some
day we will, for the sake of our own people if not for humanity's."

But in 1916, and for some years afterwards, Mr. House conceived of
American international policy as best suited for the good of mankind if
it worked in cooperation with the British Empire's. He did not wish us
to yield unduly to British selfishness or to sink our national interests
without compensation; but he did think that American prosperity could
be most surely guaranteed by a recognition of the age-old principle of
the Monroe Doctrine: that a strong British fleet in being was the first
line of defense of the Americas against aggression by European imperialistic—or totalitarian—states, hungry for expansion. He would have held
the same opinion today. And he would have been as implacably opposed to British aggression as to German, Japanese, Italian or Russian.

It seemed to him, in the summer of 1916, that the British, equally with
the French and almost as stupidly as the Russians and Italians, had lost
completely their sense of perspective. He regarded as fallacious the military policy of attrition, which dictated the tactical—they scarcely deserve
to be called strategical—operations on the Western Front. He conceived
of war, *la grande guerre,* as a struggle of ideas, not a mass combat relying
upon brute strength. He was dismayed by the readiness with which the
British imitated, on the Somme, the same theories of wholesale slaughter which the Germans had demonstrated a failure at Verdun. He was
horrified by the blind ruthlessness of the measures by which British generals, backed by British statesmen, had suppressed the Easter Rebellion
in Ireland. He knew, all too well, the venomous effects British bigotry
and cruelty were achieving in the United States by proving simply that
they were more potent than Irish bigotry and cruelty.

And he did not excuse his friend, Grey—just raised to the peerage as
Viscount Grey of Fallodon—from joint responsibility for policies which
were losing Britain more friends in America than Germany was winning by propaganda. He had no patience with a Foreign Secretary who
could write him fretful letters, asking the United States not to be guided
in their objections to British violations of international law by "the un-
popularity of Great Britain or anti-British feeling that is the motive
force," and scolding that he was "unfavorably impressed by the action of
the Senate in having passed a resolution about the Irish prisoners,

though they have taken no notice of outrages in Belgium and massacres of Armenians." But if he did not excuse Grey as Foreign Secretary, he condoned him as a man, knowing that his friend's frail strength was being crushed by unnatural burdens, duties which were distasteful, and the pressing threat of blindness. The war of nerves, into which the disastrous struggle had lapsed, was crushing thousands of men besides Grey of Fallodon.

It was a bad summer. It was to sear and turn into a worse autumn, as bleak spiritually as it was physically.

9

Germany was marking time. The Civil Government was fighting to preserve its authority against the High Command, but the submarine flotillas were operating strictly in accordance with the rules of cruiser warfare. And the Foreign Office, for once taking Bernstorff's advice, gave over harrying the United States about the British blockade. It was the calm before the storm. The strangulating pressure of the blockade was curtailing food rations, withholding essential raw materials. By the use of shrewd propaganda, and registering German claims before the slow-moving British Admiralty had established the Grand Fleet's achievements, most of the peoples of the world had been led to accept Jutland as a German victory. Only the High Command in Berlin, and the sweating dockyard workers in the North Sea bases, knew how terribly the High Seas Fleet had been hammered, that never again might it venture abroad to risk the overpowering broadsides of Beatty's dreadnoughts and battle cruisers. On the several fronts the Army was meeting with more successes than minor defeats. The British were held to small gains on the Somme, won by bloody slaughter and restricted by imperfect staff work. Brusilov's offensive into Hungary was stopped. The work of demolishing a too-confident Rumania was well under way.

Yet, despite all this, sea power was justifying Mahan's claims for it. The temptation was growing to use the German Navy's only remaining effective weapon, which Berlin had conditionally suspended in the reply to Mr. Wilson's *Sussex* note. And one cardinal point of German policy was being maintained, with a sly persistence which never fooled either the President or Mr. House. This was a strict injunction to Bernstorff in Washington to obstruct every attempt by the President to mediate a peace. A Wilson peace could not be a victorious peace for Germany. So Bernstorff continued to write and talk of how urgently his Government desired peace, but skilfully avoided any commitment to definite or practical terms.

"I am happy to say," the German Ambassador wrote Mr. House, July 14, "the improvement in all American and German relations has continued. . . . Nevertheless, however, as you will have seen yourself by the newspapers, my Government is having a hard time, and has been strongly attacked for having given up the U-boat war at the request of the United States. You know the situation in Berlin so well that I need not discuss it at any length. I will only mention that there seems to be danger of the Chancellor being forced to retire on account of these attacks. That would, of course, mean the resumption of the U-boat war and the renewal of all our troubles."

On August 16, Gerard wrote Mr. House from Berlin: "The bitter attacks on the Chancellor continue."

The facts of the situation were that Germany, as bitterly torn by internal dissensions and intrigues as the Allies, was getting ready to veer around and accept a proffer, at least, of mediation from Mr. Wilson. The Army, knowing how badly the High Seas Fleet had been smashed at Jutland, and disturbed by the tremendous forces being organized by the Allies, was half-prepared to accept the Navy's premise that an unrestricted submarine blockade of the British Isles would bring Britain to her knees before putative American participation in the war could make itself efficient. But before adopting this last resort the Imperial General Staff was willing to encourage the Civil Government in an attempt to negotiate a peace on the basis of the *status quo*—in other words, a peace which would leave Germany victorious, and after a reasonable rest to heal her wounds, capable of renewing the struggle for world domination on far better terms than had prevailed in 1914.

Coincident with this, the Kaiser and the inside clique of the General Staff wanted to get rid of von Falkenhayn, partly in order to make him the scapegoat for the ill-omened Verdun offensive, partly because he lacked qualities necessary to win popular support behind the fronts in the tense days they saw ahead.* The man chosen to succeed him was the gigantic, close-mouthed idol of the German people, Paul von Hindenburg, conqueror—by proxy—of Tannenberg. The man the General Staff knew to be Hindenburg's brains, the saturnine, paganistic genius,

---

* Von Falkenhayn may have been an unsatisfactory Chief of Staff, but he went from Berlin to command—with the help of "the old *Ritter*," von Mackensen—the steamroller drive which put Rumania out of effective participation in the war. Even allowing for the inadequacy of Rumanian generals, equipment and personnel, it was a forecast of the *Blitzkrieg* which wrecked Poland in September, 1939.

Ludendorff, was simultaneously appointed Quartermaster-General, a post which has an entirely different significance in the German Army from what it holds in most others.

This step, which was taken August 30, was welcomed by Mr. House because he had been informed in Berlin that Hindenburg was friendly to the peaceful objectives of Chancellor von Bethmann-Hollweg, and was supposedly inclined to a treaty on terms less favorable to Germany than those desired by other Imperial advisors. Mr. House, at that time, apparently, was not aware of the symbolical greatness of Hindenburg, which strictly limited his qualities for leadership. Massive, imposing, patriotic, sincere and pious in disposition, Hindenburg, at bottom, was nothing more than an honorable old soldier, who was dependent for original ideas upon more intelligent men who obtained his ear. He was, for Germany's purposes at the end of the summer of 1916, the perfect figurehead for the General Staff and the Civil Government. To the people, to the rank and file of the Army, he loomed like the great wooden statue of him in Berlin into which patriots drove nails for the privilege of subscribing so many marks to the national defense funds. But he was then, and throughout his long life, a figurehead, a symbol for other men to use to mask their secret purposes, honorable or dishonorable, wise or unwise. He was as typical of Germany, under any rule, as the goose-step, arbitrary discipline, the Brandenburger Tor or the statue of Germania. And it was for these reasons that he became the uncrowned ruler of Germany, in August, 1916, and was made responsible for the course of events which drew the United States into arms against her and brought about the complete defeat of her ambitions.*

On September 3, von Bernstorff came up to Sunapee, New Hampshire, where Mr. House was "hiding out in the woods" to get some peace before plunging into the conduct of the crucial phases of the President's campaign for reelection. They had a long talk, which was notable chiefly for a hint from the German Ambassador that his Government thought it would be an excellent idea for the President to call Ambassador Gerard home, so that he might acquaint Mr. Wilson, Mr. House

---

* Mr. House was no more ignorant of von Hindenburg's limitations than other Allied and American statesmen. A year later, he had the Field Marshal's characteristics accurately in mind, and said frankly to intimates that one of the difficulties in estimating German policies consisted in figuring out how far an honorable, but intellectually negative, soldier like Hindenburg could be controlled by men who were spiritually his inferiors. He had a genuine feeling for Hindenburg, and never would lightly dismiss him from consideration, even after a man as unscrupulous as Franz von Papen succeeded in persuading him to raise Hitler to power.

and the State Department with the more intimate details of the situation in Berlin. Mr. House was not so naïve as to take this hint merely at face value. He suspected an unknown, ulterior motive behind it; but he thought there was merit in the suggestion. Berlin seemed to be temporarily quiet, Gerard certainly merited a vacation, and he could be of use in the political campaign in New York.

It was six weeks before Mr. House gauged the true motive behind the German desire to have the Ambassador available in Washington, midway of October. As a matter of fact, only good came of Gerard's trip. The Germans did not do us a disservice. He knew accurately the situation in Berlin, the counter-currents which were influencing the course of German policy, and he was able to disabuse Mr. House and the President of the scant lingering faith they retained in German protestations of a desire to make a reasonable peace. Gerard was convinced that resumption of unrestricted submarine warfare was only a question of time and German convenience. On the other hand, Mr. House and the State Department were able to acquaint Gerard with many circumstances of the international situation of which he knew nothing.*

The real meaning of the shift in the High Command in Germany was demonstrated with dramatic suddenness, some two and a half weeks after Hindenburg had taken over, in a Memorandum for Gerard from the German Foreign Office, transmitted to Bernstorff, and delivered by him, through the extraordinarily tortuous processes of the Teutonic mind, to Mr. House, either to be handed to the home-returned Ambassador or merely imparted verbally, whichever way Mr. House preferred.

---

* Gerard unwittingly made a diplomatic blunder on his arrival in this country. He crossed the Atlantic on the same steamer with a correspondent of the New York *World,* to whom he gave an interview, possibly in confidence, stating his belief that Germany would relapse into unrestricted submarine warfare. When Mr. House read this, and before he had seen Gerard, he sent me with orders to find the Ambassador and instruct him to deny the interview. This Gerard did, after verifying my message. The explanation was that Gerard, having been so long absent from the United States, had no conception of the earnestness with which the President was trying to avert our entanglement in the war, and the inevitableness of this happening, if Germany repudiated her conditional undertaking in the *Sussex* case.

As a secondary consideration, the sloganeers of the Democratic National Committee had wished on the President the questionable battle cry: "He kept us out of war!" And as a third consideration, Mr. House and the President were still honestly hoping to be able to force both groups of belligerents into a conference after the election had established the President's prestige at home. Mr. Wilson was more optimistic in this hope than Mr. House. Both were wrong. Gerard had a clearer conception of what was to happen than either of them. His one mistake was in talking to a newspaper correspondent before reporting to them.

In plain language, this Memorandum was a veiled threat, designed not so much for Gerard's information or the State Department's, as to plant in Mr. House's mind, and so in the President's, the intention of Germany to abandon cruiser warfare if the United States could not secure her the kind of peace terms she desired. It was diplomatic blackmail, and was so regarded, despite the German Ambassador's statement in his covering letter to Mr. House: "Of course the Memorandum is strictly confidential, and is not intended as a threat of more drastic U-boat warfare on our part."

The Memorandum, undated and unsigned, was brief. Its two essential sentences read:

"Your Excellency [Ambassador Gerard] hinted to His Majesty in your last conversation at Charleville [Imperial Grand Headquarters] in April that President Wilson possibly would try towards the end of summer to offer his good services to the belligerents for the promotion of peace. . . . Meanwhile the constellation of war has taken such a form that the German Government foresees the time at which it will be forced to regain the freedom of action that it has reserved to itself in the note of May 4th last and thus the President's steps may be jeopardized."

It is futilely interesting to speculate as to the possible effects upon the President's fortunes in the political campaign, then reaching its climax, had it been possible for the Administration to publish this suavely threatening communication, the text of which Bernstorff stipulated should be regarded as "strictly confidential"; indeed, three times, in his covering letter, he used the word "confidential" and once "confidentially." Mr. Wilson was profoundly discouraged by the course of the campaign and the inroads made by the Republican candidate, Mr. Hughes, in States he had been optimistic of winning. The country was ignorant of the great efforts he had made, through Mr. House, to check hostilities and minimize the possibility of the involvement of the United States. He had "kept us out of war," yes; but nobody, save Mr. House, knew better than he how nearly inevitable it was that, whoever was elected President on November 7, the future of the country would be increasingly perilous.

The story of the political struggle Mr. House waged for his friend must be the next chapter in this narrative. The sequence of international events, following Election Day, belongs properly to the story of the opening events of 1917, which frustrated all their hopes. The Memorandum of the German Foreign Office to Ambassador Gerard was the final episode in the diplomatic year, 1916. After November 7, the world lapsed rapidly into a chaos from which it was temporarily redeemed only by the gallantry of common men and the stumbling intelligence of their leaders.

10

Mr. House and his friends regarded his strategy in the campaign for Woodrow Wilson's reelection as the peak achievement of his career in partisan politics. It was boldly conceived; it took shrewd account of the psychology of the moment; and best of all, it made a really national party out of the Democrats. Mr. House, a Southerner himself, had long wished to see the party minimize the tyranny of the Solid South in its affairs; but he had not wished to see the dominant power transferred to the municipal machines of the northeastern industrial States. No, as he saw the future of the Democratic party, its strength should be founded upon a coalition of the South and the trans-Mississippi States. Such a coalition, he believed, would make for a spirit of liberal progressivism, which, in turn, might be expected to win votes in those northeastern States which had shown a desire to rid themselves of the shackles of political machines like Tammany Hall, and the nonpartisan industrial machines which worked with corrupt politicians and place men for their own selfish ends.

Idealistically, Mr. House's ambition would probably have been sufficient to induce him to attempt the conquest of the West. But there were ample sound, practical reasons for this particular strategy in 1916. The President had been obliged to identify himself with legislation and policies, national and international, which had made him exceedingly unpopular in the northeastern States. His domestic legislation had irritated bankers and manufacturers, brokers, factors and small business men to a degree which was as unfair as it was stupid. In foreign affairs, he had been obliged to irk the substantial group in favor of intervention in Mexico. In his dealings with Germany and Great Britain, again, he had offended large and important racial groups. Even the Irish were hostile to him—because they thought he was pro-British, although such prominent Republicans as Theodore Roosevelt accused him of being spinelessly afraid of the Kaiser. In New York, for instance, Mr. House anticipated that Tammany Hall would knife him, as was done, with the consequence that Hughes, the opposing candidate, carried the State's forty-five electoral votes—with controlled Democratic votes, corrupt votes, if you like.

It was a difficult situation for the Democratic National Committee, and the work of the Committee was handicapped further by the personality of McCombs, the National Chairman, who, it will be remembered, had nearly wrecked the 1912 campaign by his quarrels with McAdoo and his connections with Wall Street interests. McCombs, a

MRS. HOUSE—FROM A PORTRAIT BY LASZLO

sick man, was finally jockeyed into resigning, without insult to his feelings, through the diplomatic intervention of Bernard M. Baruch; and
Vance McCormick, of Harrisburg, Pa., was elected in his place, after
Frank Polk and several other men had declined what they knew would
be a figurehead's job. Mr. House also secured the choice of his son-in-
law, Gordon Auchincloss, as Treasurer. He knew there would be none
too ample funds for his purposes, and he was grimly determined to keep
a finger on the outgo. Money was everything in the plan he had formed.
Every dollar must count.*

It was an odd circumstance, by the way, and indicative of the differences in mental habit between the two friends, that, whereas Mr. House
wished to get away from the old-line professional wheelhorses of the
party in making important campaign appointments, the President was
deeply distrustful of such individuals as "highbrows." He thought the
party workers would lose heart, and the leading regulars desert. He
seems never quite to have understood Mr. House's response that the
regulars had nowhere to go, and that the point to be aimed at was not
so much the retention of the normal Democratic vote in the several
States, but the winning of Independent and Progressive votes from the
Republicans. Of course, it is only fair to say that Mr. House was by way
of being a wheelhorse at this sort of thing, and knew exactly how to
keep the safe party vote in hand. Mr. Wilson never had much appreciation of the mechanics of party politics. Why should he? He was
beyond middle age when he finally tried the game. And he was so fortunate as to have available as his lieutenant one of the ablest political
strategists and tacticians in American history. That he realized this,
himself, was proven by the fact that he wired Mr. House, just before
the Democratic Convention at St. Louis, begging the Texan personally
to take the National Chairmanship. Mr. House refused for reasons of
health, and because he knew from past experience that he could accomplish much more, in the strain and battering of a campaign, by holding
himself remote and carrying out his ideas through dependable assistants.

Mr. House's chief concern, in the tumultuous months preceding the
conventions, was lest the Republicans should nominate Colonel Roose-

---

* There is no intention here to reflect upon McCormick, who was a fine man
and a loyal friend to Mr. Wilson, and who, incidentally, gave of his best to the
campaign, as did his associates in the National Committee. But the facts are as
stated. The President wanted Mr. House to run the Committee, titularly as well as
practically, as has been said elsewhere. And Mr. House fully intended, and did,
run it practically. The plan of campaign was definitely his—and too much was at
stake. Mr. House always spoke appreciatively of McCormick's efforts. The President, regrettably and unfairly, was not appreciative.

velt, for Roosevelt's nomination would be a direct and positive menace to his underlying plan of winning blocks of Progressive Republicans and Independents, who had supported the Bull Moose candidate in the great schism of 1912. If the Republican Old Guard had accepted Roosevelt, their action would have been regarded as an endorsement of Progressive Republican principles, with incalculable effect. But the Old Guard were neither wise nor big enough to snatch the opportunity. They had the excuse of the Third Term—and it might have been as dangerous as they claimed. They found they could not foist Elihu Root, or any other of their members, on the Chicago Convention, and turned to Justice Charles E. Hughes, then, as now, on the Supreme Court bench, in the hope that his splendid record as a reform Governor of New York would satisfy Colonel Roosevelt. It did. Roosevelt threw overboard the ideas for which he had led his millions "to march to Armageddon to battle for the Lord," and Mr. House had his opportunity. Not such a good opportunity, at that. But he made it suffice.

Briefly, the House plan of campaign, as embodied in several memoranda, which should be in all political textbooks and which served as the basis for the Franklin D. Roosevelt campaign of 1932, was predicated on these considerations:

1. The candidates and stump speakers were to rest their case on the definite achievements of the Administration in domestic legislation, and an intelligent policy abroad to preserve American neutrality, help to work out a cooperative agreement for world peace, and maintain generous relations with Latin-American neighbors. "He kept us out of war" was the slogan, not a wise one, historically, but justified on the known facts when it was used. The domestic legislation enacted by the Democratic majority in Congress, under the President's leadership, was difficult to challenge, except on grounds of selfish interest and short-range thinking. It may be said of it that it has stood the tests of time.

2. In the tactical field, Mr. House divided the States into two groups. The major group consisted either of safe States or States in which it was not worth while to make a strong fight; and the second group—in three subdivisions—included the States in which he considered the party had chances of success. Subdivision one—Connecticut, New York, New Jersey, Maryland, West Virginia, Indiana, Missouri, Wyoming, Arizona and New Mexico—merited a maximum effort. Subdivision two—Maine, Massachusetts, Ohio, Illinois, Colorado, California, Oregon and Washington—merited less expenditure of effort. Subdivision three—Rhode Island, Wisconsin, Michigan, Minnesota and Iowa—merited still lower budgets.

3. The States in these three subdivisions were divided into units of not more than 100,000 votes, to be intrusted to supervisory committees, who were to work in cooperation with the precinct or voting district chairmen. The precinct chairmen were to furnish the unit committees lists of all voters, ranged in three classes: absolutely certain Democrats, absolutely certain Republicans, and those who were doubtful in party loyalty. Those definitely classed were to be ignored. The entire effort, all the available funds, were to be devoted to the doubtful voters. It was, of course, no more than an elaboration of Mr. House's well-tried plan in Texas. He figured—and believed he was borne out substantially in the result—that out of every unit of 100,000 votes roughly 80 per cent would be unchangeable. It was the 20 per cent who could be influenced by argument and propaganda. Money and time spent elsewhere were wasted. The main consideration was to obtain the necessary money, not to use in bribery, but to finance the right direct mental approach and propaganda material of high quality; Mr. House, for one thing, didn't believe in unsealed communications.

Having developed his plan and secured as good men as possible to run its machinery, Mr. House retired to the New Hampshire woods, and devoted himself as much as possible to the broad, general interests of the campaign. He knew from experience that the man who submerges himself in too many details never attains a great objective. It was a principle which he impressed upon all persons who received his trust.

His chief concern was over the President's capacity for handling the arduous task of Chief Executive and simultaneously acting as spokesman of his party. Mr. Wilson was not happy that summer. He didn't enjoy campaigning with the combative spirit of a Roosevelt. He was required to meet countless people whose minds and personalities were unsympathetic to him. He was subjected to abuse and misinterpretation, which his historian mind resented more than would have most men's. He had been compelled to assume almost incredible burdens of responsibility since coming into office. He was acutely aware that he was being betrayed by leaders of his own party.

Mr. House saw him bewildered, hurt and tense, under the strain. His tongue took on an edge. He showed bitterness and acrimony. Vexed over the obvious trend in New York, he was inclined to find fault with his lieutenants. He was almost childish in his feeling over the superior floods of money the Republicans were pouring into the fight. He told Mr. House that he and McCormick had "Newyorkitis" because they tried to convince him that he had friends there who were struggling for him. And in the same breath, he said he believed he could be reelected without New York. But, worst of all, Mr. House thought, was the tendency he was showing to ignore the European situation in favor of absorption in the campaign. A natural reaction, perhaps, from his resentment of the cavalier treatment his peace efforts had received in London, and the repeated violations of international law by the British blockaders. He seemed to feel that it would be just as well to let the European belligerents stew in their own juice, although it was only a question of time before the United States would be involved in another crisis with Germany.

Mr. House repeatedly assured him of victory in the campaign, but there was always the chance of plans going wrong. Hughes had not made the popular impression which had been anticipated for him; but he was pounding at every opening in the President's defenses; he had Big Business behind him; he had Theodore Roosevelt. And it is possible that Mr. House's confidence was shaken by the attitude of the President and several of the people around him. Stories passed back and forth. Already, there was more hostility toward the Texan in Washington than he was to understand fully for several years to come. At any rate, on October 20, the day after he received from Ambassador von Bernstorff the confidential Memorandum of the German Government previously cited, he took the grave step of suggesting to the President that, in the event of Hughes's election, he should ask Vice President Marshall and Secretary Lansing to resign, then appoint Hughes Secretary of State, and resign, himself, so establishing the Republican candidate as next in succession to the Presidency. In the ensuing two weeks, Mr. House took the advice on this point of Attorney-General Gregory, Secretary Lansing, and Assistant Secretary Polk. All three were startled by the boldness of the conception, but all agreed with Mr. House that it "would be the patriotic thing to do."

After the election, Mr. House asked the President what he would have done in this contingency. The President replied that he would have accepted his friend's advice, and resigned "immediately"; that he had taken the precaution to write Lansing before the election, so as to put himself on record and not be subject to the charge of having acted in pique.

This was an extraordinary incident, not for the greatness of soul of the Democratic statesmen involved, but as showing the mental confusion which had been engendered during the campaign. Mr. House, to those who knew him and were close to him in those days, showed complete confidence in the result of his efforts for the President. It is true that he had steel nerves, but his certainty was evidenced by quiet, reasoned firmness, open discussion of the facts of the situation, not by blustering or concealment of unknown bad news. He knew, for example, and spoke of it, that Hughes had played into his hands in offending Senator Hiram Johnson, of California. He never wavered in his confidence in the result of the full count of the California vote, not even on the night of November 7, Election Day. "I know how much work we did there," he said, "how much money we spent to reach every feller who might go with us."

And yet something had happened in those middle weeks of October to make him fear that he might be wrong. Perhaps it was only von Bernstorff's bombshell. That must have had some effect. But, aside from the threat of the German Government, he was seeing for the first time a side to his friend which vaguely worried him. He would never, otherwise, have given Mr. Wilson what amounted to a substantial warning of possible defeat. He would never, otherwise, on election night, after the searchlights had blazed out a victory for Hughes, have visited the Bar Association with his friend, Attorney-General Gregory, and looked up the legal procedure, required by the Constitution, for the surrendering of the Government to the Republican candidate.

The House strategy worked perfectly, thanks to California's 13 electoral votes, carried by a majority of 3806. Mr. Wilson received 277 electoral votes to Mr. Hughes's 254, and a popular plurality of 591,385 over the Republican. His share of the total vote was 49 per cent, which was 3 per cent more than Cleveland had received, the largest proportion of the popular vote received by a Democratic candidate up to that time. But even these figures do not indicate the actual impressiveness of the inroads made on Republican strongholds by Mr. House's strategy. Eight of the States carried by Hughes were won by a grand total of about 35,000 votes, so that a shift of some 18,000 votes in these States might have transferred any, or possibly all, of them to Mr. Wilson. Minnesota went Republican by 392 votes; Rhode Island by 4459; Indiana by 6942. By contrast, Mr. Wilson swept the rockbound Republican citadel of New Hampshire by a margin of 56 citizens. There was close figuring on both sides in other States.

Mr. Wilson and his family went to bed at Shadow Lawn, the summer White House in New Jersey, on election night, believing that he had been defeated. He was hurt, as any man would have been, who had given all he had to his fellow citizens; but he held his chin high, and took the bad news cheerfully. His daughters and staff were heartbroken, incredulous. His widow has written that she was secretly relieved that his burden had been lifted from him. They were not assured of his triumph until the morning of Thursday, the 9th, when the final vote in California's outlying counties was tabulated.

Mr. House, on the contrary, was placid and undisturbed. Friends, who stopped in to see him in the early evening, amused him with descriptions of the dolorous blanket of gloom which had descended upon the banquet given by the National Committee at the Biltmore Hotel in celebration of expected victory. Before he went to bed, at eleven o'clock, he had satisfied himself that, despite the Hughes sweep in the northeastern States, all the States which he had definitely promised Mr. Wilson, with an assured total of 230 electoral votes—only 36 votes short of a necessary majority of the Electoral College—were coming into the Democratic column with machine-like regularity. He had no doubt that the likely doubtful States would supply the votes lacking. By five o'clock in the morning, when he commenced to check by telephone from his bedside, it was evident, as the Far Western returns were reported, that the election had not been settled by the returns from the industrial States. His one fear, now, was that the wholesale concessions made by the Democratic newspapers in New York, except *The Evening Post,* the previous evening and that morning, would be turned to account to steal the election by default. Remember, as a youth he had seen, at close range, the miserable tragedy of the Hayes-Tilden election and contest. And he went to work energetically to bring pressure to bear in every quarter, directing extraordinary measures to be taken by State and County chairmen in the States which were still tabulating.

He was the least surprised man in the United States when the country awoke, the morning of November 9, to discover that, for the first time in our history, a solid block of Democratic States stretched across the continent from the Atlantic to the Pacific, from the Gulf to the Canadian border, with only two Republican States west of the Mississippi-Missouri watershed—South Dakota and Oregon. He had attained his dream. The agrarian and mining States, with all their undeveloped riches and pitiful lack of economic power, had been welded into a ring surrounding the powerful industrial States of the Lakes belt, the Ohio valley and the northeastern seaboard. At last these poorer sisters of the Union had a chance to offer organized opposition, defensively if not aggressively, to the densely populated centers, centers of banks, factories, blast furnaces, forges and avaricious politico-economic machines.*

* Mr. House had no illusions as to the varied composition of his own party. He didn't regard it as a band of crusaders pledged, one and all, for liberalism and good government. He thought many conservative Democratic members of Congress belonged in the ranks of the Republicans, and many progressive Republicans with

In the next four years, this fundamentally agrarian, thoroughly American block of States, so painfully erected, was wrenched apart, not so much by the impact of war as because two friends, without any selfish or inimical wishes of their own, found themselves prodded upon divergent roads, with consequences both considered disastrous for their country. The Democratic party lost, for a while, its proud position as the party of liberalism and progress, until another Democratic President, whom, as a young man, they had trained and fathered toward his destiny, re-created it after his own fashion.

the Democrats. "Oscar Underwood really wants the same kind of government as Cabot Lodge," he once said, when he was peeved by some cloakroom skulduggery. "I wish we had Borah in exchange for him. I could make a few more trades on the same terms."

Book 7

The War

I

THE smoke of the election bonfires scarcely had cleared from the skies before Mr. House concentrated his attention anew upon the threat to American interests so subtly conveyed in the German Government's Memorandum to Gerard. He was perturbed, as he had been for several months, by the President's drastic reaction against the Allies, and he was not made any happier by the discovery that Mr. Wilson's stern conscience took with extraordinary concern the moral obligation implicit in the campaign slogan: "He kept us out of war." The fact that he had been elected by such a slogan meant to Mr. Wilson that a majority of the American people expected him to continue his efforts to preserve neutrality. He was arbitrarily inclined to do so, and he was not disposed to consider the mental attitudes of the Allies in order to accomplish his purpose. He had given the Allies their chance of American support, and they had rejected it. He didn't feel at all responsible to them or civilization for what happened to them. He wanted one thing: peace for the American people. And he was willing, at least at the moment, to initiate any peace—a victorious peace for Germany—to gain his end. Perhaps he wasn't thinking straight, but certainly he was thinking honestly, if shortsightedly.

Mr. House, with much keener perception of the psychologies of the different nations, took an opposite stand. He saw that the Germans were preparing to employ their threat of abandonment of cruiser warfare as a lever to compel the President to intervene with a bid for peace, which they would accept only on their own terms, but which they hoped would place the Allies in the wrong, if the Allies rejected it—as the Germans knew their enemies must. That would leave the way open for unrestricted U-boat warfare, and would, the Germans hoped, drive a wedge between the United States and the European democracies. Whether this latter contingency eventuated or not, the Allies would be embittered by the fact that the President had played Germany's game. For Mr. House knew, as well as the members of the German Government, that the Allies would regard acceptance of a conference, to which Germany assented, as tantamount to a surrender of all for which they had been fighting, at the very moment when their armies were making a dent in the German position in France. In Mr. House's opinion, the President would get precisely nowhere by intervening under existing circumstances.

It boiled down to this: Mr. Wilson thought he could force a peace conference on the basis of the prestige of the United States. Mr. House thought he knew that Mr. Wilson could not. For there was the rhythm of Fate in the ugly situation. The United States were caught in the meshes of the net which had entangled civilization. The Germans didn't care what course was taken by the United States, although Berlin was perfectly willing to use American influence to attain its own imperialistic purposes. The Germans were confident that they could handle the United States, whatever Mr. Wilson did. The Allies, less egotistical, more tolerant of facts, objectively cynical, if you like, foresaw that the United States must be dragged into the war, no matter what immediate policy Mr. Wilson pursued, or else abandon their position as a great power. Hence it was not to their interest to treat Mr. Wilson's sensibilities with more than frigid courtesy. The situation, as Mr. House saw it, was governed by inexorable laws of logic. The future of the United States was bound up with the democracies, not with the imperialisms. But he sympathized with his friend's dilemma, and was determined to be patient. He was sure that the current of events would carry the day with Mr. Wilson's conscience.

On November 14, the President summoned him to Washington. Mr. Wilson had decided to address a note to all the belligerents, demanding cessation of hostilities in the name of humanity. Unless he did so, he argued, the country, in the words of Mr. House's diary, "must inevitably drift into war with Germany upon the submarine issue." He conceded that Germany, in the sinking of the *Marina,* October 28, already had violated her promise of May 4. If we were to maintain the position we had assumed in the *Lusitania* and *Sussex* cases, we must break off relations with her. He shrank from doing so. In a desperate effort to avert this last recourse, he would make this bid for peace, hoping there was enough favorable sentiment in the Allied countries to obtain their consent. Mr. House replied to him, gently, that his note would infallibly be considered an unfriendly act, now that after two years of war the Allies' successes on the Somme and at Verdun had given them a breath of victory. They would regard his gesture as a purely selfish move by the United States, blaming him personally for it, to avoid a crisis with Germany. More, they would accuse him of wanting to reward Germany for breaking her promises to us.

"He was much worried over my position, and asked me to think it over at length," Mr. House recorded. The President suggested that his objective might be assisted, if Mr. House went to Europe to elucidate his position. Mr. House replied that he would do so, if the President wished, but that he did not believe it would do any good, and added: "I should prefer Hades for the moment rather than those countries when such a proposal was put to them." He contended "again and again that we should not pull Germany's chestnuts out of the fire merely because she desired it, was unruly, and was gradually forcing us into war." The two friends argued until late into the night without reaching an agreement, one of the rare occasions when this occurred, the Texan adopting a more uncompromising stand than ever before. When they parted the following morning, the President said that he would draft the note he had in mind, as soon as he had completed his message to Congress, and send for Mr. House again to go over it with him.

On the 27th, Mr. House was called back to Washington, and the President read to him the first draft of the note. Mr. House thought the document "wonderfully well-written," but once more Mr. Wilson had committed the political error of incorporating a phrase which would —and in a revised form, later did—"make the Allies frantic with rage." This was the statement: "The causes and objects of the war are obscure." The President agreed to take this and several other criticisms into consideration, and alter the tone of the note. But he was just as determined to send it, and Mr. House returned to New York in a mood of discouragement.

A conversation with Jusserand, the French Ambassador, December 3, confirmed him in his pessimism. In London, he knew, the note could not possibly receive even as understanding a reception as might once have been granted it, however coolly; for Asquith and his friend, Lord Grey, had resigned, and the Cabinet had been reorganized with Lloyd George as Prime Minister. The most belligerent factionaries in England were in control, their announced policy to fight the war through to "a knock-out blow." True, Grey's successor was Balfour, an admirer of Mr. House's, and the new Foreign Secretary had retained Lord Grey's private secretary, Sir Eric Drummond. Balfour, Grey cabled Mr. House, would expect to preserve the intimate relations previously existing between the head of the Foreign Office and the Texan; and Balfour, too, sent a friendly message, expressing his desire for reciprocity and cooperation. But Balfour was committed to the "die-hard" principles of the new Cabinet. Mr. House shook his head sorrowfully. His friend was in for a bad time.

"It just couldn't be helped," he said afterward. "The President had a good idea. The trouble was that nobody else shared it with him. And it hurt him."

While the President hesitated to launch his note, his self-confidence jarred by his friend's persistent disapproval, the German Government, on December 12, put forth, with dramatic suddenness, the peace-offensive Mr. House had been confidently awaiting. It was one of the few subtle documents to emanate from the Berlin Foreign Office, skilfully phrased in vague, unspecific terms, its design palpably to trick the Allies into an uncompromising refusal, which might serve to prejudice them in the eyes of the United States and other neutrals, and so build up a justification for the resumption of ruthless U-boat warfare. Another motive behind it may well have been the discovery by Bernstorff that the President was contemplating a stroke for peace. Little went on in Washington which escaped the vigilant spies of the German Ambassador. So perhaps he had advised his Government to force the President's hand, which was precisely the effect of their note, whatever their intentions.

But before this happened, by a margin of hours, the British Ministry blundered again—or, if blundered be too strong a word, they showed the same old inability to comprehend that the President and Mr. House were trying to help them. Sir Cecil Spring-Rice, in Washington, wiser than his Government this time, sent a messenger to Mr. House, December 17, to ask if the Texan could ascertain unofficially, through Bernstorff, the nature of Germany's terms, and volunteered to cable the Foreign Office to delay the Allies' answer to permit Mr. House time for the attempt. Mr. House thought it an excellent idea. There was a faint possibility that the Germans were in a mood of reason. It could not hurt to try them, but before he asked Bernstorff to act for him he must know positively that the Allies would wait for the information.

The Foreign Office cabled Spring-Rice the following day that it would be impossible for the Prime Minister to postpone a public statement in Commons. For this, it would seem, the responsibility rested partially upon Ambassador Page. Lord Robert Cecil, who was then Secretary for Blockade, wrote Spring-Rice, December 19, that Page had called upon him that afternoon, and in response to a question as to why his Government were anxious to have confidential information about the British response to Germany, replied that he thought it was in connection with the President's projected note. He added that he thought the

American Government would "fully anticipate" an Allied response to the effect that the German note had been an offer "to buy a pig in a poke." Neither Page nor Lord Robert seems to have understood that Mr. House had asked, not for information as to the British attitude, but for delay, in order to give the Allies time to reply to Germany more intelligently. Another illustration of how poorly Page served his own Government, notwithstanding his recent trip home for "Americanization"; although Mr. House suspected that the prime reason for the bland refusal of the Foreign Office to understand his message might have been the fear of the Ministry that Bernstorff would produce terms capable of saving Germany from complete defeat.

While this maneuver was in process of frustration, the President was stampeded into action by his fear, wholly justified, that the Allied responses would be of such a character as to bar all chance of peace. For the first time in their partnership in foreign affairs, he did not consult his friend upon a step of prime importance, writing an affectionate apology from Washington that events had moved so fast—which was the truth—that there had not been time for Mr. House to be called to examine the revised draft of the note they had gone over together. It is easy to read too much significance into such an incident, knowing what happened afterward. But it was the first, and for nearly two years the only, incident of the kind. Mr. House never took it seriously. He realized that time was pressing, if Mr. Wilson were to make the move he believed to be right. Also, there was the fact to be considered that Mr. Wilson knew his friend disapproved of the step. Further argument would have been fruitless, so long as the President was set upon the course he had plotted. And not merely fruitless, painful. The President salved the sting, had there been any, by enclosing to Mr. House the original draft of his revised version.*

The note, sent to all neutrals as well as belligerents, met with the reception Mr. House had predicted for it, perhaps, so far as the latter

---

* It may be that the significance of this incident is exaggerated. But there were already influences inimical to Mr. House, working upon the President by suggestion rather than by direct innuendo. And the fact cannot be escaped that this was the first of four occasions on which Mr. Wilson rejected Mr. House's advice on policies of supreme importance. History proved him wrong this time, as it did each of the three succeeding times. This first time he seems to have appreciated his mistake, for he promptly showed a disposition to lean more heavily than ever upon his friend, although his personal correspondence indicates a steady weakening in personal affection, as verbally expressed. But it was not until October, 1918, that he was moved again to depart from the course Mr. House most urgently recommended to him, with consequences disastrous to his health and his ambitions.

were concerned, because the President perpetrated another of his unhappy pedagogical phrases: "The objects which the statesmen of the
belligerents on both sides have in mind in this war are virtually the
same, as stated in general terms to their own people and to the world."
The Allied capitals fumed with indignation at the implication that their
war aims were identical with those of the Central Empires and the
"unspeakable" Turk, the rapers of Belgium, Serbia and the Armenians.
British liberals, who had been sworn admirers of Mr. Wilson, who had
stood by his policy against the criticisms of their own people, men like
Lord Bryce and Sir Horace Plunkett, were as bitter as Northcliffe and
Lord Curzon. Page wrote that King George had wept in discussing it
at a Buckingham Palace luncheon. The French were savagely, the
Germans amusedly, contemptuous. Gerard showed what he thought
of it by writing Mr. House that the Germans' conception of a peace
conference was to secure an opportunity to rig separate treaties with
France and Russia. And finally, the Allies sent curt replies, disputing
the President's assertion of a similarity of war aims amongst the several
belligerents, and refusing negotiations as being hopeless, so long as it
was notorious that neither reparation, restitution nor guarantees against
future offenses could be expected from the Central Empires. Their
terms of peace must be based upon such a formula.

So Mr. Wilson, two months after his reelection, found himself drastically reduced in reputation and prestige abroad, and likewise with a
considerable section of his own people, who wrote editorials and went
about saying: "Ha, we told you so! There's the unregenerate schoolmaster for you. No judgment, no sense, no courage. But you *would*
reelect him. Now, if Hughes were coming in—" And Mr. Wilson
sulked in the White House, sore and as yet unrepentant. "There will
be no war," he told his friend dogmatically, January 3, 1917, according
to an entry in Mr. House's diary. "This country does not intend to
become involved in this war." He knew, as his conduct evinced a few
weeks later, that war was as inevitable as anything human could be;
but he refused to take the advice of his Cabinet officers and Mr. House
to augment military and naval preparations. Mr. House understood
the psychology of his attitude, if no one else did. Woodrow Wilson
hated the very thought of war. He did not want war. And he did his
best to avert it by willing that there should not be war. He was mistaken, he deceived himself; but he was sincere. And here again, the
appalling idea suggests itself that, if enough other men in Europe and
America had bent their wills to the same purpose, there might not have

been war. There might have been peace for all the world on terms acceptable to every nation.

Mr. House was deeply grieved over his friend's disappointment, and, notwithstanding his own pessimism, encouraged Mr. Wilson to make another attempt to stem the tide which was running so strongly against them. At their conference of January 3, the President brought forward as his idea—as he frequently did—an idea which Mr. House had conveyed to him in a letter of December 27: that he should make a public statement of the general terms of a settlement which might have some chance of giving a reasonable degree of satisfaction to all concerned. They decided that it would be best to keep to an impersonal tone, and ignore territorial adjustments, except for the stipulation of a free, united Poland, to which principle both Russia and Germany had pledged themselves independently. The President was enthusiastic over the idea, and Mr. House thought that if the speech accomplished no more, at least it would establish beyond refutation Mr. Wilson's eagerness to serve all the belligerents. It would be a last dyke to withstay the rising flood.

The first draft of the speech was completed a week later, and the two friends went over it, January 11. The President made two changes in his text on Mr. House's advice. He struck out a sentence: "This war was brought on by distrust of one another." And he dropped the word "humiliate" from a sentence: "Both sides say they have no desire to humiliate or destroy the other." But Mr. House overlooked the phrase which was to frustrate much of the good the speech might otherwise have accomplished: "It must be a peace without victory." Therefore he was equally responsible with the President for the unfortunate reaction to the speech in the Allied countries, after Mr. Wilson delivered it before the Senate, January 22.

Aside from this one trespass of the honest, academic mind into the crotchety, warped and distorted field of politics, it was one of the best speeches of Mr. Wilson's career. It committed him, consciously or unconsciously, still further to the road he was to travel in lofty splendor to a cruel and lonely end. It restored him to the good graces of international liberals like Lord Bryce. It was a clarion call to intelligent men and women all over the world, who still believed in the brotherhood of man. And it carried forward, with defter, bolder touch, the lesson McKinley had tried to teach the American people at Buffalo: that their interests could not be confined to their own sub-continental borders. It was a complete answer, in logic, to those timorous ones who think that a statesman and man of affairs like Washington would have preached against the acceptance of world power by a nation which *was* a world power, whether or not it found satisfaction in the responsibilities of such an onerous stature.

"I am proposing, as it were," declared the President, "that the nations should with one accord adopt the doctrine of President Monroe as the doctrine of the world: that no nation should seek to extend its polity over any other nation or people. . . . There is no entangling alliance in a concert of power. When all unite in the same sense and with the same purpose, all act in the common interest and are free to live their lives under a common protection."

But Germany had made up her mind before Mr. Wilson mounted the Senate rostrum. The Kaiser had yielded to the promises of Admiral Holtzendorff, Chief of the Navy General Staff, backed by Hindenburg and Ludendorff. Von Bernstorff, who had kept the cables hot, urging and reurging upon his Government the necessity for conciliation of the United States, had received definite word on January 19 that the decision was irrevocable. He wrote Mr. House from Washington, the next day, canceling an appointment. "All I have to say, I told you over the phone, and I repeat it now, viz., that I am afraid the situation in Berlin is getting out of our hands." Six days later, he did call upon Mr. House, and told him dejectedly that "the military have complete control in Germany." But he agreed to cable once more a plea for a statement of terms acceptable to his Government. He received them, apparently, at the same time as the notification to the President of Germany's contempt for the United States.

Bernstorff's letter, dated in Washington, January 31, reached Mr. House the same day. It was outwardly temperate and courteous in tone, but the contents would have told the story, even had he not been dispatching simultaneously a more drastic dose of poison to Secretary Lansing: ". . . to show President Wilson our confidence," he concluded the introduction, "my Government through me desires to inform him *personally* of the terms under which we would have been prepared to enter into negotiations, if our enemies had accepted our offer of December 12th." The terms, briefly, would have placated France by allowing her to retain the few miles of Upper Alsace occupied by her troops; stipulated for a new frontier with Russia and Poland; restitution, and apparently, augmentation of the German colonies; restitution of the occupied area of France, but with stipulations for "strategical and economic changes of the frontier and financial compensations"; restoration of Belgium, "under special guaranty for the safety of Germany"; "economic and financial mutual compensation on the basis of the exchange of territories conquered and to be restituted"—an indirect demand for indemnities;

compensation for the losses of German business firms and individuals; and—the Freedom of the Seas! *

So far as I know, Mr. House never replied to this letter, except possibly a brief acknowledgment of receipt. He received presently, by telephone from Washington, the news that Secretary Lansing had been apprised by Bernstorff that the next day, February 1, Germany would proclaim a barred zone around the British Isles and in the Mediterrannean, in which "all sea traffic will be stopped with every available weapon and without further notice." One American passenger steamer, properly identified and carrying no contraband, might traverse the zone in each direction once a week.

It would be inaccurate to say that Mr. House was surprised. It was what he had anticipated. "It looks as though we were going to get this business out in the open," he said at the time. "I can't say I'm sorry. Anything's better than waiting in the dark. But be careful what you write. This is a time we must all keep our heads. Germany's like a mad dog, cornered, and that's when you must watch out for yourself."

He took the midnight train for Washington, after making arrangements with the police and local military authorities to see that the city should be protected in any unforeseen emergency, and warning Dudley Field Malone, the Collector of the Port, to investigate unusual activity aboard the interned German merchant fleet, of which he had been apprised by the British Secret Service.

2

Mr. House found his friend "sad and depressed," disappointed and bewildered by a turn of events he had refused to permit himself to anticipate. The President was awaiting the preparation of a note by Secretary Lansing in response to the German announcement; but he had not yet made up his mind to send von Bernstorff home, although the insolent hypocrisy of the German Ambassador's letter to Mr. House, which he read, served to arouse him to greater indignation. Mr. House

* It may seem strange to the reader that so many foreign governments and representatives communicated directly on matters of importance with Mr. House, instead of the State Department. There were two reasons for this. One was that he had acquired a unique reputation for discretion and sagacity. The other was that the State Department, as organized at that time—thanks largely to Bryan— was susceptible to leaks. Secretary Lansing and Under-Secretary Polk, who did much to lay the foundations for the present Foreign Service, were not responsible. They had inherited a system which they lacked time to cobble adequately. Such a situation could not happen today, with the Department staffed by career men.

was amazed to hear him say that, even if Bernstorff were given his passports, it did not necessarily mean war. The President was as stubbornly convinced, this morning of February 1, as he had been on January 3, that it would be a crime for him to allow this country to enter the war. "He spoke of Germany as 'a madman that should be curbed,'" Mr. House recorded in his diary. "I asked if he thought it fair to the Allies to ask them to do the curbing without doing our share. He noticeably winced at this, but still held to his determination not to become involved if it were humanly possible to do otherwise."

Mr. House, himself, had no doubt of the eventual issue of a diplomatic break, considering the frame of mind prevailing in Germany. Twice before, after the *Lusitania* and *Sussex* crises, he had thought the best policy would have been a break in relations, and on these occasions he had believed, not too optimistically, that Germany might have been brought to her senses. Now, he was sure, it was too late. Germany had received an impression of American timidity, which would steel her to whatever measures suited the policy of the High Command. All the President had gained by his well-meant hesitation was a prolongation of the war and a consequent exaggeration of the future drain upon the American effort.

Lansing came over from the State Department at half-past eleven with the note he had written, which was approved by both the friends. There was a discussion, then, as to whether it would be best to give von Bernstorff his passports at once or await the committing of what the diplomats call an "overt act." Mr. House and the Secretary of State were agreed on that point. If the United States adopted the latter alternative, it would be equivalent to acceptance of Germany's ultimatum. Mr. House also brought forward the argument that the country would be in a better position with the Allies, when the issue of war was finally presented, if decisive action were taken promptly. Mr. Wilson, however, had one cogent reason for a slight delay, in that he had given his word to Senator Stone, Chairman of the Foreign Relations Committee—who, up to this time, had given him loyal, if reluctant, support—not to hand Bernstorff his passports without notification to the Missourian. Stone was in St. Louis, and was telegraphed to be in Washington for the session of Congress, on the 3rd, at which the President announced the step he had taken.

It is indicative of how strongly Mr. Wilson felt that in his address he persisted in clinging to his delusion that war could be avoided. "I refuse to believe that it is the intention of the German authorities to do in fact what they have warned us they will feel at liberty to do," he said. "Only overt acts on their part can make me believe it even now."

Despite Mr. House's conviction that war was inevitable, he did not abandon his efforts for peace, nor, for that matter, did von Bernstorff, during the two weeks before he sailed from New York. Mr. House had no doubt that it was the German Ambassador who was responsible for a call paid by the Dutch Minister, February 10, with a proposition that the President should summon a conference of neutrals at Washington, a scheme too fantastic to be practicable at the moment. Its only possible result, Mr. House knew, would be to arouse the ire of the Allies at a time when the United States needed their friendship and confidence almost as much as they did this country's. And, of course, anything which emanated from Bernstorff was suspect in the circumstances.*

The only possible corridor to peace, as Mr. House saw it, lay through Austria. The old Emperor Franz Josef had died on November 21, and with him had perished the one cohesive personal force which had united the disjointed segments of his crazy Empire, tied together more by economic reasons, by the need of mutual trade of the Danube Valley states, than by the dynastic principle. Franz Josef, as a lad, had survived the storm of 1848. Dull, narrow-minded, an autocrat of autocrats, he was actuated by a stupendous conception of responsibility, which led him to devote painstaking care to every detail of his bureaucratic government. By means of a certain blind arrogance of personality he had wooed the Hungarians back to loyalty. He had won sympathy through the tragedies of the Empress Elizabeth's death and Mayerling (his sensations must have been too numbed to feel overmuch the assassinations at Serajevo). More, in his old age he had become a legendary character, and the lighthearted Viennese, at any rate, called him *gemütlich* for his primly discreet liaison with their beloved Frau Schratt. He

---

* Bernstorff left this country broken-hearted, for all his cynical exterior. He never forgave his Government for their indifference to his reiterated advice against antagonizing the United States, and their refusals to see that what Mr. House and the President called a "reasonable and just" peace would advantage Germany in the long run (see his book, *My Three Years in America*). He seems to have made the mistake, with his superiors at the Foreign Office, of trying to give them the impression that he could control Mr. House, and through him, the President. Why he did so is difficult to say. He certainly didn't underrate Mr. House, and from personal acquaintance he was an unusually intelligent man, and as honest as his position allowed him to be. He was a much abler man than his French and British contemporaries in Washington, and had a far keener perception than either of them of the latent power of the United States.

was a symbol. When he died, something of the breath of life went out of the Austro-Hungarian monarchy, which could not be replaced by the smart German technicians who swarmed at Grand Headquarters and in the Bal Platz.

Conditions were very different in Austria in February, 1917, from what they had been in February, 1916, when Mr. House had been last in Europe. The people were unhappy, discontented, war-weary. So, too, were the old Emperor's successor, Karl, and his wife Zita, who had been a Princess of Bourbon-Palma. One of her brothers was serving in the Belgian Army, and was engaged in intrigues with the French, of which Mr. House knew nothing, to secure a separate peace for Austria. Mr. House's plan was to work through the new Austrian Ambassador at Washington, Count Tarnowski, who had not yet been allowed to present his credentials. He was strengthened in this desire by a brilliant young diplomatist, Sir William Wiseman, who had joined the British Embassy in December, really to serve as a connection, independent of the Embassy, between Mr. House and Downing Street. For this reason the President, Secretary Lansing and Mr. House decided not to dismiss Tarnowski with Bernstorff. If he could be made use of, well and good. The answer would be furnished by the Austrian response to a note of February 18, demanding Austria's position on unrestricted submarine warfare. Austria replied, March 6, in a note evasive in tone, but indicating the extent to which she was under German influence by insisting that neutrals aboard the ships of belligerents traversed the barred zone at their peril. Relations with Austria were broken, and Count Tarnowski was sent home without ever having entered the State Department. The last corridor to peace was closed.

But before this happened Germany perpetrated a blunder so offensive that it would probably have pushed any man, except one as sincerely peace-loving as Woodrow Wilson, into war. The British Embassy turned over to the State Department, on February 26, the text of a telegram from Mr. House's friend Zimmermann, in Berlin, to von Eckhardt, the German Minister at Mexico City, which had been acquired by the British Naval Intelligence—as Eckhardt afterwards testified, from the safe in his Legation—and deciphered. It was dated January 16, and warned Eckhardt, three days before Bernstorff was told as much, of the imminent declaration of unrestricted submarine warfare. He was advised, if the United States declared war, to approach Carranza, then in power, with an offer of an alliance, Germany pledging her assistance in the reconquest by Mexico of the States of Texas, New Mexico and Arizona; California was excluded, probably as a bait to Japan, with whom, Zimmermann also suggested, Carranza should conclude a similar alliance.*

Mr. Wilson actually was loath to authorize the publication of this cable. The State Department, through Assistant Secretary Polk, called on Mr. House to use his influence to persuade the President of the wisdom of acquainting the country with the lengths to which Germany was prepared to go in attempting to harm a people whose only offense was that they had refused to assent to illegal repression of their rights at sea. The President finally agreed, with the sad realization that, in doing so, he was flogging national resentment beyond the danger point. For a mighty wave of passion rolled from coast to coast, sweeping States which, up to then, had paid scarcely any attention to the progress of the war and, by reason of their interior situation, had little interest in the problems of the Atlantic seaboard or the munitions profits being acquired by industrial communities.

Mr. Wilson was driven on, despite himself, in the course against which he had so valiantly set his face. On the very day that the State Department received the Zimmermann cable, he had been obliged to appear before Congress to request powers to arm merchant vessels and protect, by whatever means necessary, American citizens and property on the seas. He stressed the fact that, as yet, Germany had not committed an overt act, but did not attempt to conceal that the measure he advocated amounted to the declaration of a state of armed neutrality, which in itself would be separated by a hairline from a condition of outright hostilities. The House, March 1, gave him a thumping majority of 403 to 13. In the Senate, however, passage was held up by a filibuster led by Senator Stone and Senator La Follette, of Wisconsin, one of the most execrable examples on record of this peculiar Senatorial form of parliamentary obstruction—in this case, in clear defiance of almost the entire membership of the Senate, who were balked in their will simply because the session expired automatically at noon, March 4, Inauguration Day. It was not a feat to the credit of so great a liberal statesman as Senator La Follette, Mr. House thought, an American who professed to believe

---

* This, perhaps the most dramatic piece of secret-service work of the war, was an exploit of the redoubtable Admiral Reginald ("Blinky" was his service nickname) Hall. The British had complete control over German code messages, whenever intercepted, for the reason that, early in the war, Russian divers had obtained from a sunken submarine in the Baltic her lead-bound signal books. Later, British divers obtained a second set from a submarine which went down off the southeastern coast of England. No matter how the Germans changed code, with these two fundamental samples to work on, the experts of the Black Chamber in Whitehall had little difficulty in deciphering the messages sent to them for solution.

in majority rule, no matter what were his personal convictions as to this particular legislation. The Senate majority rebuked the two recalcitrant Senators by adopting a manifesto for the record, with seventy-five signatures, asserting that the measure would have passed had it been possible to procure a vote.

It was at Mr. House's suggestion that the President immediately issued a public statement, in which he branded Stone and La Follette and their handful of followers as "a little group of wilful men, representing no opinion but their own" . . . who . . . "have rendered the great Government of the United States helpless and contemptible." The response of the people was spontaneous and nationwide, and justified Mr. Wilson, he felt, in ordering the Navy Department to proceed with the duty of placing armed guards on all vessels traversing the barred zone. But shipping companies were reluctant to risk their property without the added protection of convoys, and this drastic step the President was not yet prepared to take. He had the issue placed squarely before him, however, eight days after his inauguration, when the *Algonquin* was *spurlos versenkt,* in the German phrase, off the Scillys. On March 19, three American steamers were sunk in the zone, the *Vigilancia* with the loss of fifteen lives.

Mr. Wilson still recoiled from what he conceived to be the horrible expedient of committing the country to war. At the Cabinet meeting, March 20, all the members brought pressure upon him to summon Congress at the earliest possible moment. He spoke tentatively of April 16 as the date, but the Cabinet persuaded him to advance it to April 2. Mr. House's old friend, Postmaster-General Burleson, son and nephew of Texans who had fought with Sam Houston, told him bluntly that "the people wished this country to go into the war actively." To which Mr. Wilson made the extraordinary reply that "it did not make so much difference what the people wished as what was right."

The President issued the call the next morning, but even then his Cabinet advisors had no idea of his intentions. A mood that might justly be called frantic possessed official Washington. There was a unanimous sentiment in the Cabinet that the President must cease vacillating, must decide one way or the other, with the certainty in the members' minds that if he persisted in attempting to compromise, after Congress met, there would be a most unfavorable reaction in the country, which was becoming more bellicose every day. Secretary Lansing came to New York, March 24, to beg Mr. House to write his friend whatever he thought best, Lansing being confident that his advice would parallel the Cabinet's. There was a fear that otherwise Congress "would run away with the situation," take it out of the President's hands, with possibly disastrous consequences to his leadership. But the Cabinet had worried unduly. When Mr. House reached Washington, March 27, no arguments were necessary. Painfully, slowly, after his habit, Woodrow Wilson had made up his mind for war. "What else can I do?" he asked his friend, piteously. "Is there anything else I can do?"

And having put his hand to the plow, Mr. Wilson set himself to driving a straight furrow, which was another of his habits. He was nervous and overwrought, racked by one of the headaches which were his bane; but he was no longer fretful and petulant. At last, he knew what he must do. He didn't want to do it, but his conscience had told him he should. That was enough.

Mr. House's first concern was to ease his agony of soul, telling him gently that while it was not really as difficult a situation he faced as others over which he had triumphed, it was one for which he was ill-fitted by temperament. Every emergency he must handle had been handled before, not only in this, but in other countries. War was a routine affair. This was merely a bigger war than others. His task would not be so difficult as the job he had done in "taking a more or less ignorant, disorganized party in Congress and forcing it to pass the Federal Reserve Act, the Tariff Act, the Panama Tolls Act, and such other legislation as he had gotten through. He had taken a gamble that there would be no war, and lost; and the country would hold it to his discredit unless he prosecuted the war successfully. . . . I made him feel, as Mrs. Wilson told me later, that he was not up against so difficult a proposition as he had imagined."

Here, again, you have the secret of Mr. House's hold upon Woodrow Wilson. He never argued a point, once he saw that the President's view of it could not be altered. But he kept on throwing ideas into the grasping, knife-edged mind of a man who was sensitive to facts, honestly presented. If the facts were on Mr. House's side, he was confident that in time his friend would weigh them and adopt them. Neither man was egotistical about his own beliefs. Either was capable of being wrong, and admitting it. And it was for this reason that, during the trying weeks after Bernstorff was dismissed, Mr. House refused the pleas of people who wanted him to press the President toward war. He knew Woodrow Wilson better than anyone. He knew how much the man was suffering. And he knew the Calvinistic honesty of purpose which animated his friend's intellect. Mr. Wilson was a scholar, before everything. He could not resist the reiterated impact of facts. And thanks to his prolonged deliberation, Mr. House thought, he had one tremendous advantage on his side. No man, in this country or abroad, could claim that he had rushed the United States into war.

"If a country and a President ever went to war with clean hands, it was the United States and Woodrow Wilson in 1917," Mr. House once phrased his feeling. "They say the bankers and industrialists pushed us into the war. You know how ridiculous that is. Wall Street and Big Business had no use for the Administration, and no power over it. I don't suppose any Administration was ever more unpopular in Wall Street, and those people were still sore over Hughes's defeat. They'd poured money out to support him. The truth is, that the Morgans, the Du Ponts and people like that had backed the Allies because they were afraid to see Germany win, and naturally, they took a good chance to make money. The country went into the war for much the same reasons. We had learned that we couldn't exist safely in the same hemisphere with a Germany that was governed by an imperialistic military clique that was hell-bent for world domination. Forget the submarine warfare, and remember the Zimmermann note. That was enough to show us how the wind was blowing. If Germany had won, she would have taken over the British fleet, Bermuda, the West Indies—and where would we have been? How safe would the Canal have been? We hadn't any choice, and I don't see how we ever will have a different choice, if the same situation arises again with Germany or any nation." *

Mr. Wilson went before Congress the evening of April 2 to deliver his address, requesting the two houses to declare the existence of a state of war with Germany. In following this course, he disregarded the advice of Mr. House, who had thought he should say forthrightly that a state of war actually existed, and ask for the means to wage it. Mr. House feared that, in leaving the decision to Congress, the President might precipitate a time-wasting and acrimonious debate. Mr. Wilson preferred to follow the strict course of Constitutional procedure, which makes Congress the department of government possessing the power of declaring war. He would seem to have been right, and Mr. House wrong. Mr.

---

* There is an obvious similarity between the placative policies of Premiers Chamberlain and Daladier in 1938-39, and those of Mr. House and President Wilson in 1914-17, toward Germany. In both instances, the democratic statesmen went to the limit of accepting national humiliation and probable domination of Europe by Germany. In both instances, the reward of their exhibitions of tolerance was the conviction of their own peoples, and the neutrals, that the responsibility for war could not be placed upon their shoulders. And in both instances, Italy played the same spoils-mongering game, delaying action in order to pick the winner in the conflict. She lost out by these tactics in 1919, whether unfairly or not. It will be interesting to see the result of Mussolini's present policy.

House was no respecter of precedents or legalisms, and he was privately inclined to regard the Constitution as an anachronistic document.

But the Texan need not have concerned himself. Mr. Wilson, his horizon cleared of doubts and misgivings, was at his best. He stampeded men who, several months previously, would have listened in sullen silence to the matchless peroration of his address:

"It is a fearful thing to lead this great peaceful people into war, into the most terrible and disastrous of all wars, civilization itself seeming to be in the balance. But the right is more precious than peace, and we shall fight for the things which we have always carried nearest to our hearts—for democracy, for the right of those who submit to authority to have a voice in their own governments, for the rights and liberties of small nations, for a universal dominion of right by such a concert of free peoples as shall bring peace and safety to all nations and make the world at last free. To such a task we can dedicate our lives and our fortunes, everything that we are and everything that we have, with the pride of those who know that the day has come when America is privileged to spend her blood and her might for the principles that gave her birth and happiness and the peace which she has treasured. God helping her, she can do no other!"

Four days later, April 6, after the shortest possible deliberation compatible with legislative dignity and the gravity of its decision, Congress declared that a state of war existed between the United States and the German Empire. "We shall fight . . . for democracy. . . . This is a war for democracy." Many people, a catholic group—liberals, conservatives, radicals, American Legionnaires, pundits, men of brains, men of brawn—have laughed at Mr. Wilson's slogans, which came straight from a heart quivering with anguish. It is easy to mock them in the light of some of the misdeeds perpetrated since by men of every nation. They savor a little, perhaps, of that academic preciousness which is the curse of the phrase-maker, who cannot always strike the golden note. But there was nothing shoddy about them at the time Mr. Wilson uttered them nor is there, in reality, today, although it may be true that he erred in seeking to simplify the diverse motives and ambitions of the scores of races involved in the conflict, the complex idealisms of himself, Clemenceau, Lloyd George and other statesmen, each sincere according to his vision.

Mr. House had no illusions on the subject.

"Men never attain the ideal," he said, after Hindenburg had installed Hitler as Chancellor. "Probably, it is better so. Men must have something to work for. But I wonder how many of the men and women, who criticize us so lightly, really knew the world we had to work with. It was a sick world. It had been sicker than we knew before the war. It had reached one of those crises of development which come to civilization every so often. We made it better for a time. We made people try to make something better than they had known. Do you think Russia or Germany or Italy will ever be the same again? They are in evolution, and where they are headed I don't know, and nobody else does. But they are that much better off than they were before the war. The new nations we made are certainly better off than they were, I don't care how much men's greed and intolerance have distorted the ideal. Can we blame Poland or Jugo-Slavia for not attaining true democracy when we, the great traditional democracies, let them down by placing our national interests before the world's? The way to democracy was through the League. America repudiated the League. But then I don't blame our people too much for that. They needed leadership, and they didn't get it. You know, a democracy needs leadership as much as any other form of government. It has to be fought for. It is a privilege, and you don't get privileges at a cheap price. We fought for it, and we shall have to fight for it again, if we prize it as we should. But remember this: we fought for it in the war, first of all, to preserve it for ourselves, after that for other peoples who might want it or think they wanted it. It would cease to be democracy, if we fought to force it upon others. Democracy is like real religion. You take it, if you want it. If you don't, you leave it alone."

3

Mr. House's contribution to the war was his service as coordinator, not only of the American effort, but of the joint operations of the Allies associated with the United States. He early reached the conclusion, which was strengthened a few months later after his visit to Europe at the head of the American War Mission, that the principal advantage possessed by Germany was not superior military efficiency, but the concentration of energy permitted by her dominance of her own allies. This, with the interior position she occupied, enabled her to make decisions with speed and execute them with a minimum wastage of men and materials. It was, in the final analysis, the advantage always possessed by an imperialistic or totalitarian government over democracies, in which, whatever the exigencies of war, the theory of free will, of individualism, struggled energetically to justify itself. In Washington, as in Paris or London, the national Legislature debated interminably, bureau and department chiefs wrangled over preferences; the public must be told at least something of what was going on, and business men must be conciliated. In Berlin, the Reichstag did what the Chancellor bade it to do, and the Chancellor took his orders from the Great General Staff. So it was in all branches of life.

Within a week after Congress confirmed the President's request, Mr. House's small apartment, at 115 East Fifty-third Street, became one of the nerve centers of the world's attempt to check Germany's last convulsive bid for supremacy. A telephone on the desk in his tiny study connected directly with the switchboard in the Department of State and the White House. He had only to lift the receiver off the hook and ask the operator for Lansing or Polk or the President. Presently his friend, Sir William Wiseman—who now, in addition to his duties as liaison officer between the Foreign Office and Mr. House, had become chief of the British Intelligence in the United States—rented the apartment immediately overhead, and established direct cable communication with Downing Street. Mr. House seldom left his home except for his invariable walks, morning and afternoon, unless it was to respond to an appeal from his friend in Washington. An endless stream of callers poured in and out of his doors, often on a headway of five or ten minutes: the leaders of politics, business, finance, agriculture, and labor. Often, in the months to come, you might call on him and find bankers and Standard Oil men sitting in the hall, industrialists in the dining-room and dollar-a-year men and labor leaders in the living-room, besides distinguished citizens from out-of-town, dazed by the quiet, orderly confusion. And, more often than not, these gentry would have to wait while Mr. House saw a journalist whose opinion he valued for its impartiality, or admitted first a War Department courier with a pouchful of dispatches from the capital. Others were flurried, worried, nervous, impatient. He was always calm, low-voiced, unhurried. Yet he never permitted the most important of his callers to stay an unnecessary minute. And he was uniformly courteous to the bores he was obliged to see because they happened to be influential in their communities.

"Tired?" he responded to a question after an unusually hard day. "A little, but I'll have a nap before supper. Some of these fellers do beat the devil, though. A man from Boston—you'd know his name—wired for an appointment about the Liberty Loan. It took all of five minutes to tell him what he ought to have known, to put his thoughts in a memorandum I could send to McAdoo. He might just as well have spared himself the trip, but he was like a lot of other fellers. He had an idea he couldn't make his point unless he talked to me face to face.

You don't need to talk to a man, if you have a good idea. It should read as easy as it talks."

His task, as frequently in the past, would have staggered a man of superior vitality, let alone one so frail in seeming as himself. The answer was complete nervous control, spontaneous economy of effort, the ability to consider the most harassing problems without succumbing to worry. "You can try just so hard," he would say. "You can't try any harder. You can accomplish just so much, with a mite of luck, maybe. You can't accomplish any more, so long as you know you have put your best into it."

Nobody knew so well as he the plight of the Allies that rainy April, 1917. The United States had entered the war in the bare nick of time to save them. The flaccid Czar had abdicated, March 15, and the Kerensky Government was beginning its brief, wobbly tenure of existence. Russia was slipping gradually out of the Allies' orbit. In France, General Nivelle had met with crushing defeat in his Champagne offensive, an attempt to exploit an insufficiently developed tactic: the surprise attack *en masse,* without exhaustive artillery preparation. The French Army was on the verge of mutiny. Regiments were being decimated as punishment for wholesale refusals to enter the lines. The disgusted British canceled their agreement to a temporary unified command by the French generalissimo, and so postponed for an expensive year the coordination of military effort essential to success on the Western Front. Worse, so far as Great Britain was concerned, the $400,000,000 Morgan loan was coming due July 1, and British money chests were empty. Without the help of the United States, they could have discharged the loan only by selling securities at ruinous prices, which would have had repercussions on the whole range of the American market as well as their own. And on top of that, the German submarine campaign was justifying the wildest claims von Tirpitz had made for it. In two weeks of April, one hundred and twenty-two ocean-steamers were sunk. In the first six months, sinkings would total 2,500,000 tons of British and 1,500,000 tons of Allied and neutral shipping.

Mr. House could not understand the supine inefficiency with which the Lords of the Admiralty met this situation, of which they must have had ample warning in advance from their unexcelled Secret Service. They had made no adequate preparations for it. Weeks were spent in arguing over the establishment of a convoy system, which, to the younger line officers, remembering the century-old lessons of the Napoleonic wars, was the obvious answer to the U-boat terror. But conservative seniors protested that there were not enough escort vessels available; it would mean

stripping the fleet, releasing Britain's far-flung grip on the seven seas—as
if the war at sea could be won in the South Atlantic or the Pacific. It
was not until Mr. House introduced Admiral Willard Benson to their
councils that they were persuaded of the practicability of blocking the
Straits of Dover and laying the North Sea mine barrage, which made
the sea lanes of the North Atlantic all but inaccessible to the U-boats.
Their minds seemed to be bent on compensatory, not preventive, measures. The Ministry pleaded hysterically for American building aid. The
United States must launch 4,000,000, 6,000,000, 9,000,000 tons of merchant
shipping a year. We must abandon our capital ship construction, which
would have given us the most powerful battle fleet in the world, and concentrate upon destroyers and submarine chasers. Actually, we built and
completed 267 of 285 destroyers contracted for, several hundred of which
were tied up in reserve for twenty years, until the outbreak of hostilities
in Europe in September, 1939, and Japan's increasingly menacing attitude in Asia procured funds from Congress for their recommissioning.
And we sacrificed, with unappreciated generosity, the splendid fleet of
dreadnoughts and battle cruisers we had on the ways.

The pleas of the Allies in these early months of our association with
them were not for soldiers, but for ships, food, and above all, money;
but so confused, so conflicting were their demands, as to bewilder the
Government agencies responsible in Washington. On Mr. House's
urgence, a procession of Allied missions steamed across the Atlantic to
straighten out their problems with the American executives charged with
supervision of domestic production. Balfour, at his own suggestion,
cabled over the day before Congress declared a state of war, headed the
first British Mission; Marshal Joffre and René Viviani led the way for
France. On the heels of these trail-breakers came technical missions, the
British commanded by Lord Northcliffe, whose capable, hustling brain
and spirit of camaraderie made him the ideal man to get along with
Americans; the French by André Tardieu, whose broadmindedness and
journalistic training lifted him far above the level of his country's statesmen. Later, in September, again on Mr. House's advice, Lord Reading
was sent over to iron out the details of financing the Allies' requirements,
which ultimately reached advances of $500,000,000 a month.*

It is another indication of Mr. House's uncanny gift of prevision that

* This was not Lord Reading's first visit to America. He had come over in 1915,
with Sir Basil Blackett, of the Bank of England, to arrange the Morgan loan. Although he had never been connected with the Treasury, he was regarded in London
as the keenest member of the Government in financial matters. And he was a
master of the delicate art of negotiation. His career rivaled Disraeli's. He never

on August 10 he wrote the President a letter forecasting the maleficent influence of the enormous loans the United States was placing at the disposition of the Allies: "I cautioned McAdoo to give, when he had to give, with a glad hand, for in any other way we will lose both money and good will. As long as we have money to lend, those wishing to borrow will be agreeable, but when the bottom of the barrel is reached, it may be a different story. It is their turn now to be pleasant; later it will be ours in order to collect what they owe."

And, incidentally, it is significant both of Mr. House's power and of the value attached to his time, that Northcliffe cabled Lloyd George, with a touch of awe, in reassurance that a month's advance would be provided the British Treasury: "He [McAdoo] was five hours with House last week."

While Mr. House was helping the statesmen of the Allies to decide and coordinate their most pressing needs, he was equally assiduous in assisting the President to organize the executive direction of the home front, upon which the Allies must rely for the supplies for which they clamored. He was aided materially in this latter task by Mr. Wilson's sound grasp of the American theory of government, and the President's courageous readiness to utilize to the full the latent—and to Mr. House's mind, the dangerous—powers inherent in the Presidency. Here, once more, you have an illustration of Mr. Wilson's single-mindedness, his absorption in any undertaking to which he addressed himself, his willingness to bury his personal prejudices to carry through to completion what he conceived to be just and necessary. For instance, Mr. Wilson hated as much as Mr. House the idea of censorship, but he was willing to grant to the Committee on Public Information, set up in Washington, authority which Mr. House thought unwise. He knew no half-measures; he hated compromise.

Otherwise, the two friends agreed perfectly on the measures essential to raising funds and speeding up production, as they did likewise on the military effort and its handling. They picked General George Goethals, builder of the Panama Canal, to head the Emergency Fleet Corporation as the best man in the country to produce ships fast enough to overcome the ravages of the U-boats. They agreed on Bernard M. Baruch as Chairman of the War Industries Board, heedless of Wall Street complaints that he was "a stock-market gambler." "Most of those complaints

attained the Premiership, as Disraeli did, but he could match this with the achievement of having been the first Jew to become Viceroy of India. His handling of the financial negotiations in the United States might fairly be set off against Disraeli's puissance in purchasing the Suez Canal shares.

came from men who *were* gamblers in the market," Mr. House commented on this appointment. "I always had the feeling they were fellers Baruch had trimmed one time or other." Mr. House procured for Herbert Hoover the appointment of Food Commissioner, afterwards changed to Food Administrator, upon his return from Belgium. This was Hoover's introduction to the American political world, of which at the time he knew nothing. And when the question of fuel rationing became imperative, the two friends lured Dr. Harry A. Garfield from Williams College to be Coal Administrator. The Red Cross they placed under Henry P. Davison, who resigned his partnership in J. P. Morgan & Company to accept the post.

"Never in any of our previous wars was the country put into action so rapidly and efficiently," Mr. House said. "Oh, we made mistakes, many of them, but we learned from each one, and without loss of time. There was wastage. There had to be. But we put the pressure wherever it was needed. You can't give the President too much credit for what he did. Theodore Roosevelt and his friends sneered at him. They said he was a pacifist, and he wouldn't know how to fight a war. He fought that war better than Lincoln fought the Civil War, and it is quite true that he was just as much of a pacifist at heart as Lincoln."

Nothing could more graphically illustrate this statement than the shaping and conduct of the Administration's military policy. Mr. Wilson, as a historian, was intimately acquainted with the sorry attempts of Lincoln to dictate the strategy of his armies. In the President's thought, it was immaterial whether Lincoln had been right or wrong in his conceptions. The fact was that he had interfered with his field commanders, demoted them and shifted them when they failed, until he had learned his lesson and pinned his faith to Grant, even after the holocaust of Cold Harbor and the Wilderness. Mr. House had the same theory of military policy, and so did Newton D. Baker, Secretary of War, as pronounced a pacifist in inclination as the President. The three made the decision, at the opening of hostilities, that the war should be fought by the men whose function it was to conduct it, the men who were trained for this purpose. The General Staff would have general supervision, but the Commander-in-Chief in France would be given free rein. It would be his to win or lose. He would be supported, unquestioningly, given all he asked for, in so far as it was available.

The General Staff, asked to select a Commander-in-Chief, nominated Major-General John J. Pershing, who recently had commanded the punitive column sent into Mexico after Villa. He was a junior in the list of major-generals, and he was selected solely on the basis of his record, his efficiency rating. It meant nothing to the President that he was a son-in-law of Senator Warren, of Wyoming, one of the Republican leaders in Congress, or that he owed his rank to ex-President Roosevelt's promotion of him from Captain to Brigadier-General for his conduct of the Mount Dajo expedition in the Philippines. The General Staff said he was the best man for the post. That was all Mr. Wilson wanted to know. And Pershing was sent off to France, with a small staff, to lay his plans for an expeditionary force with the Allied commanders, and map out the part the American Army would play in the next year's campaign.

The General Staff also advised that this war was on too vast a scale to permit the country to rely upon its traditional system of recruiting troops by the volunteer method. The United States must raise and train men by the million, and in a hurry, and to do this it would be necessary to institute the draft system, plans for which were ready for execution in the files of the War Department. We had resorted to a half-hearted attempt at drafting in 1863, and it had been a source of trouble, rather than benefit, to the prosecution of the Civil War—among other things having precipitated the Draft Riots in New York City in the crucial week of Gettysburg, the only real attempt ever made to overthrow the Government of the United States by revolution. But Mr. Wilson cheerfully assented to the recommendations of his military advisors, and was rewarded by a national response as patriotic as it was unselfish.

It is interesting, at this point, to note that Mr. House, in the first weeks after the United States entered the war, failed to see the need for a major American military contribution, an instance of shortsightedness which, perhaps, should be attributed to the feeling of overconfidence prevalent amongst Allied statesmen, who told him repeatedly that what was needed mostly from this country was food, munitions and shipping. The Allied Governments and their military chiefs did not believe that the United States could improvise, in the time they deemed available, field armies of a size commensurate with the scope of operations in France. Nor, indeed, had they any conception of the quality of troops American initiative could supply at short notice; it is a commentary upon British Staff Officers, brought up on Henderson's *Life of Stonewall Jackson,* that they forgot entirely the impressive showing made by American Armies, North and South, in the Civil War. Both the French and the British were trying continuously throughout the American campaign in France and Flanders to instil their own tactical ideas in American officers, who knew, much better than they did, that the more cautious European tactics, saving of casualties as they were, were ill-adapted to the nervous, impetuous energy or American troops. The Americans had much to learn of modern trench warfare, but they had to learn it in their own way and at their own expense.

The Administration's military policy was misunderstood by its political opponents at home, an unavoidable misfortune, for military policy to be effective must be cloaked in secrecy. Criticisms of lack of purpose were furthered, too, by Republican excitement over the rejection of Colonel Roosevelt's offer to raise a division for service in France, the passing over of Major-General Leonard Wood for Commander-in-Chief, and finally, the realization that General Wood would not be sent to France at the head of the division he had trained. No explanation of these circumstances was vouchsafed during the war, although since then some light has been shed upon them in the memoirs of individuals concerned. The fact was that the Administration—and specifically President Wilson, Mr. House, and Secretary Baker—had nothing to do with the rejection of these two distinguished men. They were barred from foreign service on the stipulation of General Pershing, who was supported in his views by the General Staff. Mr. House, at my request, went out of his way to secure Colonel Roosevelt and General Wood the interest of the President in their desire to fight for their country.

In order to clarify this controversial incident, it is necessary to delve into past history. Colonel Roosevelt and General Wood had been patrons of General Pershing. He had climbed to eminent success, under Wood's command, while Roosevelt was President, and the latter had taken the unprecedented step of jumping him, as has been said, from Captain to Brigadier-General over the heads of thousands of officers, with consequent heartburnings in the service. It is to Roosevelt's credit, by the way, that he publicly announced he was "promoting Captain Pershing, despite the fact that he is the son-in-law of the Chairman of the Senate Military Affairs Committee." Roosevelt and Wood, subconsciously, at any rate, considered that Pershing was under obligations to them. So he was, personally. But Pershing knew that the two were inimical to the Wilson Administration, and that Wood was as much of a politician as Roosevelt, frequently mentioned for the Republican Presidential nomination. He could see only trouble ahead for himself, potential harm for the army under his command, and influences disruptive to discipline, if either or both came to France for duty with troops.

Other considerations were that Roosevelt, in 1917, was thinking of service in the terms of 1898; he wanted to lead a division of volunteers, and there were to be no volunteers outside the Regular Army and the National Guard; he knew nothing of the technique of modern warfare, nor, for that matter, did Wood, who had never commanded large bodies of troops in the field, and had no General Staff or War College training. It is perfectly true, also, that none of the officers under Pershing had commanded large bodies of troops, except during the recent mobilization on the border, and that Wood had an excellent record as an organizer and administrator; had, as a young contract surgeon, been instrumental in capturing Geronimo, the famous Apache chief, and had placed the country in his debt by his organization, despite the Administration's frowns, of the Plattsburg camps for training civilian officers. But this didn't get by the fact that Pershing, and a majority of the General Staff, considered him unfitted for duty in France.

Wood's state of mind is shown by his handling of his interview with Mr. House, and Colonel Roosevelt, if more diplomatic, was almost as ill-advised in what he said to the President.

"Well, I saw Wood," Mr. House said afterward. "He wasted my time talking against the President, instead of giving me reasons for suggesting that we go after Pershing again. And his friend, I understand, was politely poisonous when the President saw him. They make me understand why Pershing doesn't want either of them. I think he's right. This is no time for politics in fighting. If we're going to win this war, it won't be by making Presidential candidates. I'll bet you they never get Pershing after a nomination. He's got too much sense."

4

The Balfour Mission came to Washington, ostensibly, to offer the fruit of the British Government's experience in waging modern war on an intercontinental scale, but actually to attempt to "sell" the British Empire to the American people. It was the fashion in after years to represent the United States as having been bamboozled into the war by clever British intrigue and propaganda. Mr. House and the President were innocent, stay-at-home Americans, ignorant of world affairs and the wicked ways of European diplomacy. They were tricked into committing the country to participation in a "war for democracy," which wrought nothing for democracy, cost a third of a million casualties, billions of dollars for our own expenditure, and more billions in repudiated loans. That always has been an easy way for certain Americans to evade the country's responsibility for having dodged acceptance of membership in the League of Nations, and cooperation with the associated powers in implementing the impromptu measures of the Treaty of Versailles.

The truth is that the British propaganda in the United States had been so inept that there was a general feeling amongst Americans that Great Britain was not doing her share of fighting in the war. It was not until Mr. House dropped the idea for an organized campaign of propaganda in Northcliffe's mind that the Government in London really took hold of this problem, and worked it out with typical British thoroughness. "I do not know how far House speaks for the President in this matter of propaganda," Northcliffe cabled Lloyd George, August 15, "but in the course of our interviews he referred to it again and again. He said the war was being fought without imagination." The result of this was the establishment in London of a department of propaganda under the immediate supervision of John Buchan, the Scots novelist and historian, afterwards Lord Tweedsmuir, late Governor-General of Canada. But Northcliffe's was the guiding brain which dictated the strategy of the campaign; and behind Northcliffe, remote in the shadows, might be traced the subtle influence of Mr. House. It would be more truthful to say, in this and other matters, that Mr. House—and through him the President—suggested British policy, than that the Ministry in London dictated ours, save only as Mr. House's opinion coincided with theirs.

This is practically illustrated by the two most important subjects of discussion which arose during Balfour's visit to Washington. These were the questions of the Secret Treaties between the European Allies and Japan, and the character of American naval construction. And it should be stated before describing either of them that Mr. House was fully alive to the essential selfishness of Britain's international policies. It must be remembered that he knew more of the inside of British statesmanship, objectively and subjectively, than any American of his time— probably more than any Frenchman. At least Clemenceau came to think so, and no shrewder judge of men and their motives ever lived than "The Tiger."

Balfour reached Washington from Halifax, April 22. He passed through New York without leaving his special train, but Mr. House, at Wiseman's suggestion, prompted by Spring-Rice, had a brief conference with him at the Pennsylvania Station. Mr. House's purpose was to advise the Foreign Minister to minimize the importance of his mission, to make it seem more in the nature of a visit of courtesy, so as to discredit the suspicion which was prevalent in liberal circles that he had come to America to negotiate a secret alliance. Mr. House also advised him to avoid discussions of peace terms at this time, lest he start a chain of arguments and claims which might arouse Allied jealousies and divert attention from the all-important end of defeating Germany. Balfour concurred with him.

Balfour's first meeting with the President was unsatisfactory. There were too many people present, and Mr. Wilson was never at his ease in a large group. He telephoned Mr. House to come to Washington, and asked his friend to arrange "a family dinner" at the White House, with just Mrs. Wilson and the two of them present to sound out the Foreign Minister on the subject of war aims, a point which rightly bothered Mr. Wilson in his search for means to cooperate sympathetically with the Allies, without, however, committing the United States to fighting for other countries' selfish or unjust objectives. This involved the question of the Secret Treaties, and on April 28, when Mr. House conveyed the President's invitation to Balfour, he sat down and discussed them with the Foreign Secretary, for the first time, on a basis of mutual confidence. Balfour apparently was frank in his admissions, so far as they went. He produced a map with the Secret Treaties' readjustments of boundaries traced on it, and gave it to Mr. House. In a large, spacious way, he described the allocations of booty involved. Alsace-Lorraine, of course, was to be restored to France; Belgium and Serbia were to be restored; Austria was to yield Bosnia and Herzegovina to Serbia, and Serbia was to give up to Bulgaria the section of Macedonia allotted to the Bulgars in the settlement of the First Balkan War; Rumania was to have Bessarabia—this is important, in view of later accusations that Rumania arbitrarily annexed this Russian province in defiance of the Western Powers —and the Banat of Temesvar, afterwards divided between her and Serbia, and the forelands of Transylvania from Hungary.

Poland was to be free, and Mr. House and Balfour embarked upon a detailed discussion of the Danzig problem, the difficulties inherent in which were plain to both of them. "At the moment, I do not look upon this with favor," Mr. House noted in his diary that evening, "particularly since the Germans and the Poles would be antagonistic and ready upon the slightest provocation to find grievances against one another." It is strange that at no time, in the discussions of Poland's future and her need of access to the Baltic, neither before the Peace Conference nor during its deliberations, did the statesmen of the Allies and the United States ever canvass the possibility of seeking to establish some kind of federation of Poland and Lithuania, which would have provided Poland with the maritime facilities Danzig afforded, and have left Western Germany her connection with East Prussia.

It is true that there was a fierce animosity between the Lithuanians and the Poles, complicated by the Lithuanians' numerical inferiority and the overbearing attitude of the Poles, which resulted in the seizure of the Vilna district, about one-third of the country's area; but the two countries had been more or less united in the days of the old Polish kingdom, and in the seventeenth century the Sapiehas, Grand Dukes of Lithuania, had been bidders for the Polish throne. (As a matter of fact, their descendants were pretenders to the non-existent throne in the confused period following the war.) The two people were racially akin. Their valid interests were common. They would have been stronger together than they were separate, as is evidenced by the destruction of Poland in the fall of 1939, and the surrender of Lithuania to dependency upon Russia. So it would seem that intelligent pressure by the Great Powers in 1919, insistence upon a joint constitution which would have insured to Lithuania her integrity in a federal union, might have made for the advantage of both countries, and simultaneously have banished the specter of Danzig from European politics. It was not done, as so many other things either were not done or were ill-done, simply because the Peace Conference lacked the time to give adequate attention to the host of vexed problems inseparable from the colossal task of reconstructing Europe. A contingency which would have been avoided, as will be shown, had Mr. Wilson been willing to accept Mr. House's plan for negotiating primarily a tentative, instead of a conclusive, peace.

As to the Dual Monarchy, Mr. House agreed with Balfour that it should be reduced to the three states of Austria proper, Hungary, less the cessions cited above—and Bohemia. This is significant as evidence that Mr. House, like the British and French Ministers, had not at this time conceived the Republic of Czecho-Slovakia, despite the fact that Czechs were intriguing for it in this country and Europe and that Czech Legions already had been formed in France and Russia. The answer was that Mr. House had yet to encounter the dynamic personality of Masaryk, and the keen perception of Western Slav problems possessed by Wickham Steed. He shared, with most Americans, an abysmal ignorance of the racial setups in Eastern and Southeastern Europe, a defect which he was very soon to remedy.

Italy, Balfour told him, claimed the port of Trieste, Italia Irredenta and Dalmatia. Mr. House was willing that she should have Italia Irredenta, but he thought it unwise to deprive Austria of her only port, and he foresaw trouble if she were to be allotted the wholly Slav province of Dalmatia, despite its link with the Republic of Venice in the remote past. Turning, next, to Asia Minor, Balfour outlined roughly the projected division of Anatolia, Syria, Palestine, and the Arab lands. Italy and France were to split Anatolia and Syria, from the border of Palestine to the Straits, into "spheres of influence." "It is all bad, and I told Balfour so," Mr. House recorded. "They are making a breeding place for future war." Another instance of his prescience. Her impending defeat at Caporetto was to deprive Italy of even a semblance of the rights she had been promised, and the resurgence of Turkey, under Kemal Ataturk, was to expel the Greeks who supplanted her, the whole sequence of events kindling a resentment which Mussolini has been assiduous to keep smoldering.

The other arrangements embraced in the Sykes-Picot Treaty were equally disturbing to Mr. House.* Britain was to have Palestine (this was prior to the Balfour Declaration for a mandated Jewish State), Mesopotamia, and a vague region "contiguous to Egypt" and including what are now the States of Transjordania and Iraq. T. E. Lawrence had not emerged, at this date, from the obscurity of desert warfare, and if Balfour knew anything of the promises to the Arabs, which the extraordinary little Englishman had been authorized to make, he kept his silence. It is probable he was ignorant of them. The permanent staff of the Foreign Office always have had a way of secreting minor details from their political chiefs.

Nothing was said about the German colonies or about Japan's share of the spoils, but Balfour had a conference with Lansing about this time in which he did mention that the Caroline and Marshall Islands were to go to the Far Eastern ally. He conspicuously withheld mention of Shantung, which was to bring on one of the major crises of the Peace Conference.

It is unpleasant to seem to impute double-dealing to a great man, but one finds difficulty in understanding how Balfour came to forget one important promise he made to Mr. House at this interview. "I asked him," Mr. House noted, "if he did not think it proper for the Allies to give copies of these treaties to the President for his confidential information. He thought such a request entirely reasonable and said he would have copies made for that purpose. He was not certain they had brought them over, but if not, he would send for them." There is no record that he ever did so, and certainly neither Mr. House nor the President saw the Secret Treaties until they were spread on the Board at the Peace Conference. Two evenings later, April 30, when Balfour came to dinner at the White House, Mr. House "asked Balfour again about the

* It might be said that the Sykes-Picot Treaty, although it outraged the Arab States, has since justified itself practically by the advantageous position in which it placed Britain and France in the Near East in the present war. They are assured of control of the Canal and the oil fields, and their armies in Syria, Palestine and Iraq are perfectly situated to frustrate Russo-German thrusts through Iran, the Caucasus, and into the Balkans.

Allies' treaties with each other, and the desirability of his giving copies to the President. He again agreed to do so."

On this occasion, Balfour substantially recapitulated the information he had given Mr. House. Mr. Wilson listened to him with complete detachment, making no comments or criticisms of moment; but afterwards he indicated to Mr. House that he shared the same misgivings. It may be asked why, then, neither of them took steps before the Peace Conference, either at this time or later, to attempt to mitigate arrangements which they judged to be unwise, and incompatible with the motives which had brought the United States into the war. Mr. House frequently discussed their joint reaction to the Secret Treaties. He had the same feeling, in 1917, that he had had when Grey first touched lightly upon the Allies' tentative division of the spoils they anticipated.

"What could we have done?" he argued. "We had just entered the war. We had done nothing to justify us in having a voice as to treaties, which had been concluded before we were a belligerent. If we had attacked the principles of the treaties then, we would only have created hostility to us amongst the Allies. And suppose, as is possible, that we might have been able to persuade the British to take our view. The French, the Italians, and so far as we knew, the Russians, would almost certainly have refused to relinquish their ambitions. We should have divided the powers fighting Germany into two groups, and by that much have reduced our offensive strength. We couldn't very well have said to the Allies: 'All right, you fight your war against Germany, and we'll fight ours.' That wouldn't have gotten us anywhere. The main thing was to beat Germany, and fuss about other problems afterwards. It was a bad situation, but I don't see what else we could have done, except to let Balfour know—and I told other Englishmen and Frenchmen the same thing—that we didn't like what they were fixing to do. At the Peace Conference—well, you know what it was like there. The way we had to work, the only thing to do was to get some settlements, any settlements almost, before the rest of Europe smashed up like Russia. It's easy for people, after an emergency, to sit back and say: 'Now, you should have done this or you should have done that.' But the fellers who are working there in the heat and confusion, they can see just so much, and time is pretty close to their shoulders."

Balfour's admissions about the Secret Treaties are doubly important historically, in that they bear upon Mr. Wilson's unfortunate statement, August 19, 1919, in his testimony before the Senate Foreign Relations Committee, that he had not been informed of their provisions before going to Paris. "The whole series of understandings were disclosed to

me for the first time then." I saw Mr. Wilson several times before he
left Washington on his fateful tour of the country in the interest of the
League of Nations. His utter weariness, mental and physical, the haggard pallor of his face, were silent testimony to his state of health. He
was a sick man, then. Many others noticed this—Sir William Wiseman,
for one. There is no doubt in my mind, and Mr. House had the same
feeling, that the President had forgotten, in the course of the endless
sequence of problems which had beset him, the whole circumstance of
the interview with Balfour, and the supplementary information his
friend had given him.

"The man just forgot," Mr. House put it. "If I hadn't had Miss Fanny
to keep my papers in order and prod my mind once in a while, I would
have forgotten a lot, too. It is ridiculous to suppose that the President
would have told an untruth. It wasn't in him to lie. And why should
he have lied? He had nothing to gain from it. The Secret Treaties
weren't his fault. He was guided in the way he thought about them by
what I've told you."

It was during the presence of the Balfour Mission in Washington that
the British brought up the question of the suspension of work on the
American capital-ship program in favor of destroyers, the most efficient
weapon to use against the submarine. This program would have made
the American battle fleet relatively, if not positively, superior to the
British, in that the vessels building and contemplated would have been
more modern, more heavily armored and armed, and speedier. Mr.
House frankly suspected an ulterior motive in the British suggestion,
notwithstanding his appreciation of the pressing need for destroyers, for
he was keenly aware of the touchiness of the Admiralty over the bare
idea that there could be in existence a fleet capable of challenging British
sea power. He was not so much concerned with danger from Britain
or any other European power, supposing Germany was defeated, as he
was with Japan, whose disposition to profit from the worldwide chaos
he had perceived with that sixth sense which guided him in politics. So
he advanced a counter-proposition to Balfour and Sir Eric Drummond,
the Foreign Secretary's confidential secretary. To concentrate upon
building destroyers would leave the United States, after the war, much
less powerful than Britain. In return for this sacrifice in the common
interest, let the British Government agree to give the United States an
indefinite option on a specified number of her capital ships, the option
not to be exercised except in the event of trouble.

This proposition fairly took the wind out of the Britishers' sails. They
didn't know how to reply to it, so they stalled for time. The subject was

of great importance. The Prime Minister must be consulted. "A reply within the next day or two." But no reply came, and no answer was made until after Balfour's return to London, when he cabled, early in July, suggesting as an alternative "that the six major powers at war with Germany all enter into a naval agreement providing for mutual assistance against any maritime attack for a period of four years after the conclusion of the present war." This, however, didn't suit Mr. House's book at all. He suspected, again, that it was a roundabout way of persuading the United States into what might fairly be termed "an entangling alliance." On the other hand, in later years, he was inclined to attribute to the chain of ideas he had started, the inception of the Harding-Hughes Naval Limitation Treaties of 1922.*

His plan to put the screws on Great Britain, in return for postponing capital-ship construction, came to nothing in the end, because Mr. Wilson had become convinced that the capital ship had ceased to be of "much value" with the development of the submarine, an opinion which has been disproved by naval experience. Also, Mr. Wilson was not particularly interested in the future economic stake in Asia. He could not envision anything beyond a defensive war against Japan, and such a war, he held, quite rightly, would be all to her disadvantage, in light of the distance at which it would have to be waged from her bases. In addition, he made the more practical objection that any such arrangement as Mr. House contemplated, or Balfour's alternative proposition of a treaty, would have to be submitted to the Senate; and he could not imagine the Senate approving any kind of treaty which would tie us so closely to Great Britain.

5

The summer campaign on the Western Front was a reiteration of the bloody, slogging tactics of the two previous years. Germans and Allies traded casualties and bits of shell-torn trenches. That was all. What advantage was gained, on balance, went to the Germans, who, to win, had only to hang on to their positions. There was a brief ray of hope for the Allies in the autumn, when Byng breached the German lines at Cambrai, in the battle of November 20-December 4, by the first

* It is interesting to speculate as to the possible influence upon Japan's policy in continental Asia of the American capital-ship program had we pushed ahead with construction of the six battle cruisers and ten dreadnaughts for which Congress had appropriated. These units were so far behind at the end of the war that the country was not shocked by the agreement, in the 1922 treaties, to junk all except the two battle cruisers which were remodeled into the giant aircraft carriers, *Lexington* and *Saratoga*.

massed use of tanks; but the British Staff muffed the opportunity. They hadn't the reserve troops at hand to exploit their first success. The stalemate was resumed. The main Allied success of the year was in Palestine, where Allenby wrecked the Turkish armies in the great battle of Ascalon and entered Jerusalem, December 9. But Cambrai, Ascalon and Jerusalem were discounted by the Italian disaster of Caporetto, October 24, which threatened for a while to put Italy out of the war. And on November 8, Lenin overturned the Kerensky Government in Petrograd, and Russia ceased to be a factor in the war, although it took the Western Democracies some time to realize as much. The Bolshevist Revolution was to be a worse defeat for them than Caporetto, for its after-effect was to release some forty German divisions from the Eastern Front for duty in the West.

But until Kerensky fell, internal conditions in Germany, and more especially in Austria, were as unsatisfactory as in the Allied countries. Perhaps more so. At Mr. House's urgence, the President, in his Flag Day speech, June 14, made the first of the series of public utterances in which he differentiated, with telling effect, between the blameworthiness of the German people and their masters. His words bore fruit in the revolt of the German Reichstag, July 19, which compelled von Beth-mann-Hollweg's resignation by the adoption of a resolution for "a peace of understanding and the permanent reconciliation of the peoples." In Austria, peace sentiment was still more pronounced; Bohemia and the Southern Slav provinces seethed with unrest; at last, there was a food shortage; casualties, almost as large as Russia's, had broken the heart of the Army; the aristocracy were disgusted with the insolence of their German tutors. So Mr. House had little doubt that Count Czernin, the Austrian Foreign Minister, if not the peace party in Germany, was partially responsible for the appeal addressed to all the belligerents by the Pope on August 11.

Mr. House thought that the President should reply to the Pope on a constructive note, both to hearten the German liberals and to bolster Kerensky's attempt to improvise a democracy upon the ruins of Czarism; but Mr. Wilson, in one of his more bellicose moods, was inclined to ignore the Vatican's bid for a peace of compromise. In the course of the next two weeks, he came around to Mr. House's opinion, and dispatched a very able reply along the lines of his Flag Day speech. "We cannot take the word of the present rulers of Germany as a guarantee of anything that is to endure, unless explicitly supported by such conclusive evidence of the will and purpose of the German people themselves as the other peoples of the world would be justified in accepting." The speech accomplished what Mr. House had hoped for it. It did not close the door to peace; it stimulated the resentment of the liberals in the Central Empires against their Governments; and it emphasized the independent purpose of the United States in fighting Germany, not for spoils, but for justice.

6

Before the end of this summer of 1917, with the frustration of their own offensives on the Western Front and the lapse of Russia to the status of an inactive partner, the Allies had revised their estimates of the American man-power needed to win the war. They wanted Americans, now, in hundreds of thousands. They said openly that without such assistance the war would be lost in 1918. But their idea of how American troops should be used in France was very different from Pershing's. They were skeptical of the possibility of Americans being trained in the technique of modern warfare in time to be useful in the crisis looming ahead. They wanted Pershing to release his men by battalions and regiments for incorporation with French and British units. And Pershing squared that paving-block of a jaw of his, and replied coldly that he would resort to this step in a dire emergency, but otherwise he would insist upon the preservation of its identity by the American Army. The Allied commanders, balked, turned to their statesmen, who, in turn, resorted to a calculated policy of sniping at the American Commander-in-Chief in Washington. It was the natural course for them to take. Intrigues were rife in the High Commands of both the French and British Armies, and parallel intrigues played back and forth between the two Armies.

Consider, for a moment, the politico-military picture of what was happening behind the scenes in London and Paris, and at the Headquarters of the French and British Army Groups, in September, when Lloyd George—egged on by General Sir Henry Wilson and his group of Irish-baiting, ultra-conservative Brass Hats of the old tradition—made his effort to compromise the French demand for unity of command by suggesting the establishment of a Supreme War Council, to be preceded by an Interallied War Conference at Paris for coordination of the Allies' endeavors with the Godsent American aid. Lloyd George was reasonably safe in the saddle, so long as he resisted the French insistence upon the necessity of a French generalissimo; the British public needed to face absolute disaster before they would be willing to see British troops entrusted to an alien commander. To this extent, Lloyd George was not personally responsible for what happened afterwards. But the British

High Command was sharply divided in conception of strategic policies.
There were the Westerners, who maintained that the war could be won
only in France, and Sir Henry Wilson's school, who believed, in Lloyd
George's phrase, in "knocking the props" from under the Germans
wherever the enemy was weakest. They insisted upon diverting troops
to the Palestine campaign—with notable results, it must be admitted.
They said, and rightly, that one-half the men who had been casualties
on the Western Front that summer would have sufficed to enable the
Saloniki force to sever Germany's communications with Turkey. Haig,
Commander-in-Chief in France, and Sir William Robertson, Chief of
the Imperial General Staff—General Wilson's friends held him in contempt because he had been a ranker—were honestly persuaded that the
Germans must be defeated and driven out of France and Belgium if
victory were to be attained. The Near Eastern ventures they referred
to as "side-shows." The disagreement was embittered by the corollary
fact that General Wilson, with Lloyd George's support, seems to have
been gunning for Robertson's job.

In Paris, the Painlevé Cabinet was about to fall, under the onus of
tremendous casualties, scant accomplishments and universal dissatisfaction. Clemenceau would come in, with his tigerish, steel-tipped energy
and his crisp slogan: "Je fais la guerre!" Pétain, the defender of Verdun,
was Commander-in-Chief, but the darling of the more advanced French
professional soldiers was Foch, miscalled "the rock of the Marne."
Pétain was a thorough, competent soldier, cursed perhaps with an un-
imaginative streak and the caution of a Norman. He was a splendid
defensive fighter. Foch was more the offensive type, one of the most
brilliant strategists of modern times, coolly daring, resolute, an individu-
alist. But his brother was a Jesuit priest, and to many Frenchmen the
Jesuits are anathema. There was a suspicion in French radical circles
that he was also a Royalist, and it should be remembered, in this connection—as has been demonstrated in recent years through the activities
of the Croix de Feu—that there is a surprising amount of Royalist and
Imperialist sentiment in France. It would be much stronger if the
Orleans or Bonaparte families ever produced an outstanding personality.
In any case, in 1917, after Nivelle's defeat, there was as sharp a division
between the two schools of thought in the French General Staff as in
the British. The one point on which the dissidents agreed completely
was the necessity for an Allied Commander-in-Chief, and their joint
disgust with the parochialism of the British, in being unwilling to yield
the honor to the country on whose soil the struggle was being fought
and whose soldiers had displayed a sounder grasp of strategy than the

British cavalry generals, whose background had been the limited field of petty Colonial wars.

To sum it up, and show yet more clearly how dangerously the Allied effort was being hamstrung by mutual jealousies, in the two services and between the two services, the British thought the French expected too much from them, and the French thought the British were not carrying their fair share of the load. Both, of course, were partially justified, just as there was much to be said for each of the factions in the two General Staffs—and in the Ministries, too, for that matter.

This was the situation when the British and French Governments appealed to President Wilson to send a Mission to London and Paris, headed by Mr. House, to assist in the work of coordinating plans for the next—and crucial—year's campaigns. Mr. House did not want to go. He was more concerned with the organization of the American campaign of industrial production, and he likewise believed that it would be preferable to send the two Cabinet officers whose work was most closely linked with the conduct of the war, Baker and McAdoo. But the British and French Ministers replied explicitly that they wanted Mr. House, whom they knew and with whom they were used to working harmoniously, and whose knowledge of the general situation necessarily was more intimate than any other American's.

The President's first thought, to Mr. House's dismay, was that the American War Mission should be constituted as a permanent body in Paris, and that his friend should remain abroad at the head of it. Mr. Wilson's "single-track mind," as he himself called it, had grasped the essential problems of the war with the decisive clarity which distinguished it whenever he concentrated upon a given subject. He was dissatisfied with the way the war was being fought, and he felt that it was for the Americans to show the way to more efficient procedure. He knew, as well as anyone, the American as a type, even if he knew comparatively few Americans individually. "The American people would not be willing to continue an indefinite trench warfare," he told Mr. House at a luncheon on the *Mayflower,* September 16. But Wiseman scotched the President's idea of stationing Mr. House permanently abroad by pointing out, in a letter to the Texan, of October 10, that this would mean "no less than shifting the center of gravity of the war from Washington to London and Paris," the last thing the President sought to do.

The American War Mission sailed from Halifax, October 29, aboard the cruisers *Huntington* and *St. Louis.* It included General Tasker H. Bliss, Chief of the General Staff, and Admiral Willard S. Benson, Chief of Naval Operations, and a number of other experts representing the Treasury and the bureaus in charge of munitions, food, shipping, etc. Mr. House carried a "letter of marque," a power of attorney to act for the President, which Mr. Wilson had typed on White House stationery. It was typical of Mr. Wilson that he did not see any reason for furnishing the State Department with a copy or keeping so much as a carbon for the Executive files; and it was equally typical of Mr. House's status abroad that he never had occasion to present this document to the statesmen with whom he deliberated.

Mr. House reached Plymouth, November 7, the day before Lenin seized power in Petrograd and while the Italians, after losing 750,000 men, were trying desperately to stabilize a line of defense which would secure Venice. This same day, at Rapallo, Lloyd George, Painlevé and Sonnino, Foreign Minister of Italy, and their military advisors, were creating the Supreme War Council as an expedient for coordination of military effort, short of the essential objective of unity of command, Lloyd George stubbornly refusing also to include the Chiefs of Staff in its composition because of his dislike of his own Chief of Staff, Robertson. To such depths of pettiness were responsible statesmen committed in those dreary, fear-ridden days. Well might Mr. House remember, as he contemplated the confusion and undercurrents of intrigue in the Allied capitals, the words of his English friend, Wiseman: "The best asset that Germany has today is the 3000 miles that separate London from Washington." The war-waging structure taking shape in Washington was far from being as efficient as it was to become a year later, but it did not labor under the handicaps that snagged so many of the spasmodic efforts which wearied London and Paris.

"There was a funny thing about Lloyd George," Mr. House once commented. "Almost anybody he took a fancy to could influence him, and sometimes not so well as when he thought for himself. He thought straight when he thought Welsh."

The members of the House Mission plunged immediately into their several tasks. Mr. House occupied himself with probing the fundamental aspects of the general situation. He was impressed by a talk with Lord Lansdowne, who had been Foreign Minister in Balfour's Conservative Cabinet a dozen years past. He was one Englishman of position who perceived the need for reason and justice—those two symbolical words to which Mr. House and Mr. Wilson clung consistently—in dealing with Germany, and believed that a statement of moderate war aims for the Allies would strengthen the influence of liberal opinion in Germany. Mr. House also met, for the first time, General Jan Christian

Smuts, the South African soldier-statesman, and noted admiringly that "he is one of the few men I have met in the Government who do not seem tired." They were to be associated closely, in the future, in the drafting of the Covenant of the League. He listened with interest to M. Paul Cambon's prediction, the only one of its kind to reach his ears, that the Allies would win the war by the next autumn; privately, Mr. House was beginning to think that if they didn't win by then, they would lose it, and that only American aid in abundance could procure victory for them.

Lloyd George returned from Rapallo on the 13th, and Mr. House dined alone with him that evening. The Prime Minister was faced by a revolt in Commons over the meager concessions he had made to the French at this conference, he said, and asked for some word of approval from the President, which he might use to support his case. It is instructive, too, to take note that at this date, five days after Bolshevism had triumphed in the Russian capital, neither he nor Mr. House—nor, for that matter, Cambon—had comprehended the full significance of this epochal event. Lloyd George, for instance, spoke of the urgent need of American aid "until Russia can recover sufficiently to make a drive on the Eastern Front," and Mr. House evidently accepted this as a possible contingency when he cabled Mr. Wilson that night to the same effect. Cambon, earlier that day, had referred casually to the fact that no Russian delegate was expected to attend the impending Interallied Conference in Paris, and merely remarked upon this that "Russia desired from the Allies a new declaration of the objects of the war," which he deemed unnecessary. His implication was that Russia was still, however sullenly, on the Allied side.

The President replied to Mr. House's cable with the bold vigor he sometimes assumed, which perturbed his friend's more political mind. It was the genesis of a strange and unexplained misunderstanding, which is worth describing here as a possible link in the tenuous chain of events leading up to the breach in their friendship two years later. As a prelude to explanation of the incident, it should be said that this cable, like all those they interchanged, was in their personal cipher, which had been devised by Miss Denton. Mr. House always supposed that it was known only to the three of them. He never knew that Mrs. Wilson was intrusted by the President with coding and decoding their messages, transmission of which was handled by the State Department.

Mr. Wilson's cable designated Bliss to be military member of the Supreme War Council, asked Mr. House to sit in the first session, and opened with the blunt statement: "Please take the position that we not only approve a continuance of the plan for a war council but insist on it. We can no more take part in the war successfully without such a council than we can lend money without the board Crosby * went over to join." Mr. House hesitated to hand this dispatch, as framed, to Lloyd George for use in Commons, because he feared it might be distorted by the Prime Minister's opponents into a seeming advocacy by the President of one particular plan for achieving Allied unity of command. Instead, he issued a public statement, paraphrasing the President's words, the essential portion of which reads: "Colonel House . . . has received a cable from the President stating emphatically that the Government of the United States considers unity of plan and control between the Allies and the United States is essential in order to achieve a just and permanent peace."

He was surprised when the following day, November 19, brought a Reuter's dispatch from Washington to the British newspapers: "President Wilson denies that he sent a cablegram to Colonel House stating that the United States considers that a united plan and control between the Allies and the United States is essential to a lasting peace. This denial was issued through Mr. Joseph Tumulty, the President's private secretary." This cold repudiation all but cut the feet from under Mr. House's position in London. It must have done so with an envoy less well known to the members of the British Government and newspaper editors. And even so, it created a situation most dangerous, not only to Mr. House, but to Lloyd George, who was being savagely attacked for the Rapallo Agreement by the Opposition in Commons, led by ex-Premier Asquith. In the circumstances, Mr. House had no recourse but to show Lloyd George the text of the President's original cable, with its forthright commitment of Mr. Wilson to a military policy, which, Mr. House knew, had been dictated by the Prime Minister's personal prejudices.

This incident has never been explained. So far as is known, a cable of Mr. House's, November 20, mildly protesting by indirection the humiliation inflicted upon himself and frankly outlining the harm he had averted from the British Ministry—by sheer force of personal prestige, incidentally—was never answered. It would seem that a conspiracy of silence was invoked to hush up a disagreeable episode. The President certainly had not been aware of the harm which might have been done, and he was not so small as to have resented Mr. House's precaution in safeguarding him from involvement in British domestic politics. As choice as he was about the phrasing of his public utterances, there are

* Oscar T. Crosby, Assistant Secretary of the Treasury.

innumerable instances, at this time and later, of his yielding to Mr. House's criticisms. He was as loyal to Mr. House during the ensuing eleven months as Mr. House was to him. But in some way or other he was induced to lend himself to the one rebuke he ever administered to his friend, with consequences, it is fair to assume from the record, which he afterwards regretted and preferred to ignore. The incident's most important aspect, after all, was that it did not harm the cordial relations which continued to exist between them.

The House Mission crossed to Paris, November 22. Clemenceau had been Premier since the 16th, and Mr. House was delighted to find in him a practical statesman after his own heart. "I can't think of a European statesman, except Grey," he remarked at the time of "The Tiger's" death, "that I liked better to work with. He was a practical realist. He confined his idealism to France, that's true, but he was always willing to listen to your case. I tell you, my friend, he was a great man. He knew what he wanted, and he didn't waste time. He felt the same way I did about speech-making."

As to Mr. House's last observation, thanks to a plot engineered by himself and Clemenceau, the opening session of the Interallied Conference was concluded in exactly eight minutes, the various delegates being dispersed to their several committees to work in peace and seclusion upon their problems. The friendship between the slight Texan and the stocky, Mongoloid Breton, in his black skullcap and cotton gloves, lasted as long as Clemenceau lived. "He is a smart man, that Colonel," was Clemenceau's tribute. "He thinks first what he wishes to do. Then he does it. He speaks soft, but there is steel in his backbone. He is no talker—but how he talks when he must!"

Mr. House and General Bliss had a conference with Clemenceau and General Pétain, November 25, when the Americans' worst suspicions of the Allies' military plight were statistically confirmed. Pétain said that the French losses, as of that date and of finality—that is, of men abolished from the rosters through death, permanent incapacity by wounds and capture—had reached the appalling total of 2,600,000. He saw no reason to anticipate that casualties would not be maintained at the same proportionate rate during 1918. He had 108 combat divisions, in the line and in reserve, and of these eight were scheduled for transfer to Italy. These divisions averaged 11,000 men, which meant, he said, that he must hold the 500 kilometers of the French front with 1,100,000 men. The British, he added, had sixty divisions in France and Flanders, with a strength of 1,200,000 men, holding a front of 150 kilometers, which the French thought an unfair distribution of the burden. They forgot that much of the French front lay on positions of such natural strength, in Alsace, say, that it could be held with a minimum of troops, and those not of the first class. The positions of the five British Armies were much more vulnerable, as was to be demonstrated after the first meeting of the Supreme War Council resulted in the extension of the front of Gough's Fifth Army to the left bank of the Oise in January. Pétain also estimated that the German strength on the Western Front was roughly equivalent to the combined French and British strengths, and he believed that, if the Russian front became inactive, they would be able to bring forty divisions from the East, which they did, without waiting for the conclusion of the Treaty of Brest-Litovsk, so confident were they of the acquiescence of their Bolshevik tools.

If Pétain's purpose was to disturb the Americans, he achieved it; but he was not entirely candid in his presentation of the situation. He ignored the presence of corps and army troops, which would have brought his total of effectives up to double the number he enumerated. Yet the fact remained that in November, 1918, the American Army in France, fit for battle, exceeded the British effectives, a situation which was largely due to the efficiency of British transport arrangements, conducted over a distance of 3000 miles, which, as Wiseman had indicated, was the principal margin between victory and defeat for the Allies. Pétain made the stipulation, at this conference, that the United States must have a million men in France by the spring of 1918, with another million behind them for replacements and reinforcements. The United States had them ready when the time came.

Clemenceau and Lloyd George reacted upon each other like a pair of tomcats disputing a fence-top promenade. Clemenceau was furious over the limitation of powers and functions of the Supreme War Council, which had been left in his lap by his predecessor. He wanted, at least, to have the senior military members the Allied Chiefs of Staff; but Lloyd George refused this concession because it would have meant sharing authority in the council with Robertson, and he was, as a matter of fact, building up a situation in London and France which would result in Robertson's resignation in February, and the advancement of George's pet military man, Wilson. He had, likewise, the much more valid excuse for his conduct that the British people were still unalterably opposed to unity of command. He believed, and Mr. House thought with reason, that if he yielded more than he had at Rapallo his Government would be overthrown in Commons. The most he could be persuaded eventually to concede the French was an extension of the British front by the Fifth Army in January, with the consequence of so weak-

ening Gough's position in the Somme valley as to make possible Ludendorff's thrust of March 21 following. It was only after this catastrophe
that he could be induced to send to France several hundreds of thousands
of reserve troops, apparently retained at home to guard against the farci-
cal menace of a German invasion.

In the state of mutual suspicion and antagonism prevailing between
Clemenceau and Lloyd George, it was necessary for Mr. House to
assume his favorite role of conciliator—"to make the wheels go 'round,"
as he liked to say. For example, when the French Premier learned that
Lloyd George could not be induced to nominate his Chief of Staff to
the Council, he said angrily that in that case he would nominate a
"second- or third-rate man"; but after Mr. House had talked to him he
abandoned this idea, and nominated Foch's Chief of Staff, General
Maxime Weygand, perhaps the ablest of the younger French commanders, the man who afterwards turned back the Red Army at the gates of
Warsaw, and who, in 1939, was placed in command of the Allied Armies
in the Near East. Clemenceau, Mr. House considered, was a much
more reasonable man than his British colleague. He was constrained
to see the difficulties of Lloyd George's position, and rallied up to aid
him as much as possible. The two chief objectives, he agreed with Mr.
House, were to fight the Germans, not one another, and to achieve the
maximum degree of coordination of effort with a minimum wastage of
time.

The Interallied Conference met in the Salon de l'Horloge at the Foreign Office, November 29. The Supreme War Council held its first
meeting in the Trianon Hotel at Versailles, December 1. It canvassed
loosely the whole field of Allied military activities, and their subsidiary
problems of supply and transportation. Mr. House was not impressed
by the potential efficiency of so large and varied a body. There was
much talk, very little action. The contrary had been true of the Interallied Conference, which Clemenceau had promptly dissolved into committees of experts, each charged with specific tasks. In the Supreme
War Council, the statesmen were inclined to think in terms of politics,
the soldiers as strategists. They wandered around the map from the
new training camps in America to Flanders, Italy, Palestine, and Saloniki.
Mr. House found himself more than ever convinced that he and the
President were right in their feeling that the one path to victory for the
Allies lay through a centralized command. Victory was a one-man, one-
staff job. But he realized more clearly than he had before he came
abroad how impossible it was, for the present, to expect the British
Cabinet to counter the stubborn prejudice of their nationals against

placing British Armies under a Frenchman. He was most uncomfortable as to the future. It simply boiled down to the fact that the British people needed a stiff jolt to awaken them to the peril of the situation. "They had to have the fear of God put into them," he remarked grimly.

Naval problems, he noticed, were handled much more expeditiously than those dealing with land warfare. The French, with typical logic, had recognized the claims of the British to take the lead at sea, just as they held they should have the command ashore. Admiral Benson and his technical assistants were similarly imbued with a desire to assume whatever burdens the British Admiralty asked of them. It was arranged to send over immediately a division of dreadnoughts to augment the Grand Fleet, and a tentative undertaking was made to send the whole Battle Fleet in the spring, if the British margin of superiority was threatened. Otherwise, the American naval effort would be concentrated upon building destroyers and submarine chasers, and mines for the projected North Sea and Channel barrages. These latter projects were essentially American in their originality of conception. Benson even devised for the British an anchor-block which might be expected to hold mines in position on the slime-covered, chalky bottom of the Channel.

Throughout these weeks of tedious negotiations in London and Paris, the Germans were taking advantage of Russia's collapse to launch undercover peace feelers, which would strengthen the pacifist groups in the Allied countries and the United States. The Vatican was used repeatedly, and the Spanish Court. In December, the British Cabinet sent General Smuts to Switzerland to hold conversations with Count Mensdorff, who had been Ambassador at London. Baron Lancken, the German Civil Governor in Belgium, also made overtures to Briand for direct conversations on neutral ground. But the British, French and Italian Governments were wary of all such propositions, seeing in them an attempt to disrupt the Allies' relations and to secure for Germany a victorious peace on the basis of the *status quo*. Mr. House, however, thought that the Allies owed it to their peoples to make a statement of the terms they desired through the Interallied Conference. This suggestion the President heartily approved in a cable of December 1, which, by the way, indicated beyond challenge that he had a definite knowledge, and an equally definite detestation, for the terms of the Secret Treaties. But Lloyd George, Clemenceau and Sonnino were as loath as the Germans to commit themselves to repudiations of the spoils of war. Mr. House's struggle in Paris would have been fruitless if it had not inspired a few weeks later the President's address on the Fourteen Points.

He was profoundly disturbed by the lack of unity between the three Western Allies, the jealousies which racked their own internal organizations and vitiated their sporadic attempts to cooperate in the common interest. He noted, as of December 1: "She [Germany] has no superior ability, but she has superior organization and method. Nothing is buttoned up with the Allies; it is all talk, and no concerted action." And in his confidential report to the President, he wrote: "If this war is to be won, better team work between the Allies must be effected. As now conducted there is great loss of energy and resources. . . . Unless a change for the better comes, the Allies cannot win, and Germany may. For six months or more the ground has been steadily slipping away from the Allies."

The second and concluding meeting of the Interallied Conference, December 3, was as colorless as the first. The fact was, Mr. House believed with Clemenceau that it would have been better if the work of coordination had been done under cover, instead of in the midst of pomp and ceremony, which seemed to promise results in excess of what could be gained within the short time available. Progress had been made in reorganizing the technical services, but a more satisfactory job could have been achieved without the elaborate gatherings of statesmen and military commanders. In the same way, he thought that the Supreme War Council would function better when it became accepted as a division of the routine of war mechanism. He conceived more of a distaste for conversation as a medium of action than he had yet possessed, which is saying a great deal; and he was inclined to laugh at the speech he was induced to make at the second session, the first speech of his career, complimenting his associates on the work they had done. "I wish I could say what I would really like to say, but I do not dare to do so," he jotted in his diary.

He was not to forget this experience, which guided him in his conduct, so far as was possible, at later international conferences.

7

The House Mission sailed from Brest on the *Mount Vernon,* December 7. Mr. House reached Washington, the 17th. He was most anxious to persuade the President of the necessity of making a complete statement of the principles for which the United States was fighting, and which would exculpate the country and himself from responsibility for the more selfish territorial ambitions of the Allied Powers. And once more he was relieved to discover that his friend had been thinking along the same line, as he read Mr. House's cabled reports from Paris, and was eager to work out a program sufficiently wide and elastic to give confidence to the liberal elements in all the belligerent countries. With the help of information obtained from The Inquiry—the fact-finding body set up by Mr. House to compile information for the anticipated Peace Conference—and material he had brought home with him, the two spent a considerable part of the next three weeks in constructing the President's Address to Congress of January 8, 1918, in which he laid down and analyzed the Fourteen Points to be considered in reorganizing the tortured fabric of civilization.

It was easily the most vital and impressive of Mr. Wilson's State Papers, and perhaps had as much to do with breaking down German will to victory—if Herr Hitler and his supporters are to be believed—as the sledge-hammer blows of the fresh American troops in the summer and fall of the year. It was the first great Allied victory of the war, the first psychological disaster for Germany, and not the less so because official sentiment in Allied countries was inclined to sneer at its lofty idealism, its inevitable Wilsonian phraseology, its occasional resort to vague and sounding figures of speech—"open covenants, openly arrived at," for instance. But it served its major purpose in solidifying American sentiment, and in establishing the unselfishness of the ends for which the United States was fighting.

The influence of its ideas increased amongst the Allied masses from month to month. It is doubtful if any State Paper in history ever achieved more fully its purpose. Only in Bolshevist Russia was it repudiated as being a cloak of liberal ideology put forth to mask the sinister intentions of the capitalistic system. Its effect would have been even more instantaneous had not Lloyd George, in wangling a cagey deal with Labor, felt constrained to make a speech before the British Trades Union Congress, January 5, which followed parallel lines, although by no means so concretely. We have the testimony of Mr. House, and of Balfour, that Lloyd George had not seen the text of Mr. Wilson's speech, and that the President substantially had finished his speech before the cables carried the Prime Minister's, and made no alterations in his text after reading what Lloyd George had said. The Fourteen Points were a perfect example of the minds of the two friends working harmoniously together.

Looking backward over twenty years and more, it is baffling to observe how often the most intelligent statesmen of the Western world were either wrong in their interpretations of national and international political phenomena or else saw but a distorted fragment of the pictures that were shaping out of the chaos of the war. This was especially true of their judgments regarding the weaker countries. Outside of a handful of intellectuals and newspapermen, who had been following with sympathy the Russian revolutionary movement since the Japanese War—men like Lincoln Steffens—nobody in Western Europe or America adequately appreciated the immensity of the overturn in Russia. It was incredible to Mr. House and most of the men he worked with, that a mighty, if sodden, empire could be so rapidly hurled from one end of the social scheme to the other. They involuntarily thought back to the French Revolution, and expected that sooner or later a strong man would appear and re-create a more intelligent Government than Czarism, founded upon the same pillars of capitalism. They failed wholly to appreciate that in Russia you had a semi-Asiatic people, and no middle class sufficiently large to play the part of the French bourgeoisie in stabilizing revolutionary movements. They were bewildered and aghast by what was taking place before their eyes. They did not know how to meet the situation. And this psychological attitude must be kept in mind in estimating the mental components which entered into the ultimate drafting of the post-war treaties.

Similarly, they regarded Italy and her ambitions with a stingy and ill-humored tolerance. Italy had come into the war as a huckster, buying into what she believed would be the victorious side. Then she had not pulled her weight in the boat. She had been a troublesome, expensive Ally. So they were not inclined to stretch their patience to granting her such really outrageous demands as the Dalmatian coast, and they deliberately squeezed her out of the share of Anatolia she had been promised, and yet allowed Greece to start another war in an unsuccessful bid for the same kind of plunder in much the same area. They failed to take into account the possible after-effects of such humiliation, heaped on top of Italy's war sacrifices. And the results were incipient Communism, Fascism bred to check it—and Mussolini, plus an Italy resentful of having been treated, as she thought, as a second-class power. For this, of course, British and French statesmen were chiefly to blame, but if you go over the records of the subsequent Peace Conference and the drafting of the several treaties, you will find that the American delegates were equally disposed not to consider Italy's problems of the future with the understanding they might have shown. Italy was treated like a poor relation, and she hasn't forgotten it.

But the worst failure to foresee the political and economic problems of the future was in the handling of the disintegration of the Austro-Hungarian Empire. All during the last two years of the war and the

Armistice and after, there was deliberate sapping at the integrity of this top-heavy agglomeration of peoples, races, religions, cultures and languages. The one theory of responsible statesmen seemed to be to split it apart, tear it down and never mind what happened later. Once again, intellectuals and newspapermen tried to make the statesmen comprehend the basic excuse of the Dual Monarchy: the necessity for a Danubian Economic Federation. But in the Propaganda Ministries, and at the Conference tables, the one idea was to liberate the subject peoples and start them off on the new road of nationalism, without a cautionary word or a treaty provision against the rearing of tariff and exchange barriers. Self-determination was a great catch-phrase. It would have been a sturdier phrase to build new nations on if they had been taught, at the same time, the wisdom of maintaining sensible trade relations with neighbors upon whom they had reckoned for many generations to buy and sell their joint products of pigs, cattle, lumber, tobacco, oil, horses, coal, wheat, iron, and manufactured goods. It was the failure to see the economic interdependence of the Danube Valley and Balkan peoples, which laid bare Southeastern Europe to Hitler's thrusts, and preserves it today as the cockpit and trouble center of a Europe which doesn't yet know whither it is headed or how it will get to a peaceful destination when at last it finds a plausible path.

The fact is unescapable that the plight of the Danube peoples rests upon the responsibility of statesmen who could see only the military tinsel, the aristocratic glamor, of a decadent and outworn system of bureaucratic government. They did not see, those statesmen, that beneath the glitter and the glamor there were functions without the preservation of which the peoples of the Danube Valley could never know permanent peace or prosperity. And, to a degree, this criticism lies as aptly against Woodrow Wilson and Edward M. House as it does against their European colleagues. The Fourteen Points constituted a weighty argument for redrawing the map of Europe. They were not, in themselves, conclusive or detailed enough to be a complete guide to the task of rehabilitation of subject nations. Much more was needed. It is sad to think that the wisest of men are never infallible in vision. And it is only fair to add that Mr. House and the President, at this time and afterwards, were constricted in their endeavors by the differing viewpoints of the statesmen with whom they were obliged to work. There is no doubt that one important disadvantage, inseparable from any attempt by the United States to cooperate with foreign nations in any cause, no matter how worthy or honorable, always must be the unavoidable differences in national and racial ambitions and ideals.

"I've never been able to figure it out entirely," Mr. House said of this problem. "You can't have all you want, as a rule. Life is give and take. If we have to join in an intercontinental war again, I suppose the same troubles will arise. It boils down to this: you just can't fight your allies and your enemies at the same time. You've got to side with one or the other of them, and the best of allies can do the things you wouldn't care to do, yourself, perhaps just for selfish reasons."

These factors suggest themselves automatically in surveying the diplomatic history of the opening months of 1918, when the issue of the war was hanging in the balance. The entry of the United States had been offset temporarily by the withdrawal of Russia, which signed the Treaty of Brest-Litovsk under military compulsion and after prolonged wranglings and hysterical attempts to bluff the delegates of the Central Powers. Italy was bled white. The achievements of the British Armies in Palestine and Arabia were discounted by the immobilization of the Saloniki troops. The German withdrawal in the Somme area to the new Hindenburg Line had dislocated the British plans for a crushing summer offensive, which had produced the one partial success at Cambrai. The stalemate in the West was unbroken. Against it could be charged only the war-weariness of the Dual Monarchy, and a portentous outburst of industrial disorder in Germany, the contemporary significance of which the Allies were disposed to exaggerate. But the strikes were easily suppressed, and week by week German combat divisions were shifting from the Eastern Front to lend an overwhelming weight of veteran troops to the concentrations fronting the overextended British Fifth Army.

It is not surprising, then, that the Central Powers seized this opportunity to try another peace offensive.* They had been successful in seducing Russia out of the war. They were almost as optimistic about Italy, and they did not, as yet, realize how competently Clemenceau was restoring the morale of France. Another consideration with the enemy Civil Governments was that President Wilson's incisive presentation of the Fourteen Points of peace had placed them on the defensive with their industrial and liberal groups. This was so true that Chancellor Hertling of Germany and Czernin, the Austrian Foreign Minister, felt compelled to answer the President in speeches delivered simultaneously before their Parliaments, January 24. Both speeches were inconclusive, although Czernin's, by the eagerness with which it grasped at the possibility of a suspension of hostilities, confirmed the reports Mr. House was receiving from his agents in neutral countries of the exhaustion of the

---

* Congress had declared war against Austria, December 7, 1917.

civilian populations. The truth was that the peoples of the Central Empires were being kept in the war by the failures of their enemies to register knock-out blows, and the promises of Ludendorff to smash the Western Front and separate the French and British Armies. If Ludendorff failed, the heart would go out of them.

So Mr. House encouraged the President to resume his psychological attack upon the enemy. The result was Mr. Wilson's address to Congress, February 11, in which he stated with the increasing boldness which had come to dominate his mind in the past year: "The method the German Chancellor proposes is the method of the Congress of Vienna. We cannot and will not return to that. What is at stake now is the peace of the world." This speech achieved exactly what the two friends had looked for in "building a fire back of Ludendorff," as Mr. House put it; but the subtlety of its appeal passed over the heads of Congress and the American public. Perhaps it seemed anticlimactic after the clarion call of the Fourteen Points address. An immediate response to it, however, was an offer of peace "secretly" telegraphed by the new Emperor Karl to the King of Spain, which was picked up in transit by the ubiquitous British Secret Service. This was passed on to the President, February 26, by the Spanish Ambassador at Washington. Again, it was inconclusive, indefinite, a bargaining lead, obviously intended to preserve most of the Eastern European gains of the Central Powers. It could not very well have been otherwise, considering that the Berlin Government, at the moment, was bringing pressure to bear on Vienna to accept a new treaty of alliance, which placed the Dual Monarchy irrevocably under the tutelage of Germany, and specifically, of the General Staff. But it showed to Mr. House how strongly the tide of civil unrest and discontent was running behind the military fronts of the Central Empires. Hold the German Army in the West a few months longer, and the break would come with a suddenness he was among the few to foresee and lay plans to exploit in the interests of all the nations.

Another complication in the relations of the Western Democracies, in the opening months of 1918, was the growing insistence of the French and British Governments upon American participation in intervention in Russia. Mr. House always had been opposed to the intrusion of the Western Powers in Russia's affairs. He was in touch with newspapermen and Red Cross workers in Petrograd and Moscow, whose reports of the instability of the efforts of White Russian factions to beat down the Bolshevists were supported by the judgment of many of their British comrades. He could see nothing but wasted effort in the proposition of intervention, as urged notably by the French. He had more than a suspicion that the French were animated principally by the desire to safeguard their vast capital investments in Russia. He was also disturbed by the eagerness of the Japanese to occupy Eastern Siberia and the Pacific provinces. He was beginning to grasp the full implications of the opportunities the war had given Japan to "fish in troubled waters." Mr. Wilson agreed with him in a general way. But the arguments brought to bear on them were difficult to resist, and for reasons of policy, such as a plea from Clemenceau that intervention would stiffen French morale, the President ultimately felt obliged to yield against his own and Mr. House's judgment and the advice of the State Department. The summer of 1918 saw small American Expeditionary Forces in Siberia and at Archangel on the Arctic coast of European Russia. The Archangel column accomplished nothing, except to build up pension cases; the Siberian force may have had some effect in restraining the attempts of the Japanese to drive a wedge, which, as one of their generals said, would permit the Mikado's cavalry "to water their horses in Lake Baikal." Twenty years ago Japan herself was unwilling to credit the extent to which white civilization had dissipated the achievements of a century of industrialism.

Mr. House never saw any reason to take pride in his share in the Russian policy of the United States. He was, on the contrary, inclined to wish he had paid more attention to the Russian scene in earlier years. The only source of satisfaction to him was that British and French statesmen, including diplomats who had served in Petrograd, seemed to be as ignorant of the subterranean forces seething beneath the structure of Czarism as the Americans who had never studied Russia at firsthand. Indeed, as has been said, American engineers, newspapermen and business representatives had much keener perceptions of what was going on than all except a handful of Europeans in similar positions. As, later, Mr. House came to understand.

8

Ludendorff loosed the most destructive and swift-paced offensive of the war against the British, March 21, using an elaboration of a tactic developed by the Germans on the Eastern Front. It consisted of a comparatively brief but overwhelming barrage, backed by gas and smoke shells, and the rapid advance of divisions, hauling light artillery with them, the support divisions leapfrogging those in the front waves as soon as specified objectives had been attained. Fresh German divisions were hurled in series at tired and battered British divisions. Gough's Army was all but obliterated. Within a week, British losses had amounted to 120,000 men, with the capture of several thousand guns. One hundred German divisions were pounding thirty-five British and fifteen French divisions. Amiens was threatened. Before a new front could be improvised, at the end of the first week of April, it looked as though the enemy might make good their intention of shoving between the Allied armies and crushing the British against the Channel coast. And having been stopped, at terrible cost, in the battle of the Somme, Ludendorff attacked again in Flanders; on the Aisne, May 27-June 5; and finally put all his dwindling resources into the second battle of the Marne, in which American troops first showed their offensive qualities, and the German thrusts were stayed with an effectiveness the enemy appreciated weeks before the Allied commanders understood that the initiative had passed definitely into their hands.

Few, if any, of the Allied statesmen or soldiers had as vivid a perception as Mr. House of the significance of Ludendorff's desperate attempt to win the war by storm tactics. He was as calm as usual the morning after the first intelligence of the destruction of the British Fifth Army reached New York. Destruction was not too strong a word, as he admitted. Such opposition as the Germans were meeting came from fragments of battalions, military police, bits of supply details and cavalry. Strictly speaking, there was no front, nothing more than groups of men dying splendidly to hold back the gray-green waves. It is no reflection upon the British to say that, despite their heroism, the Germans were stopped as much by exhaustion as by enemy resistance. There is a limit to what the best troops can accomplish, and that limit is governed by men's ability to withstand fatigue and to obtain supplies of food and ammunition.

Mr. House pointed this out that morning. I find myself tempted to emphasize his calm poise because his apartment was crowded with the agitated leaders of American finance and industry. I doubt if there was an outstanding man in Wall Street who did not find his way to East Fifty-third Street at some hour that day. Those who remained in their offices kept the telephone ringing. A panic gripped the city, the like of which it was not to know again until the Black Week of October, 1929, and the period of the Bank Holiday immediately after F. D. Roosevelt's inauguration. To business men and bankers—to many newspaper editors, also—it seemed as though the bottom had collapsed from under Allied resistance. Americans had taken for granted that the entrance of the United States into the war had secured victory for the Allies beyond possibility of challenge. In London, too, the population of the

City had been living in a fool's paradise, compounded of dependence upon American aid and the soporific effect of a censorship which had concealed the danger to the Western Front produced by the British public's opposition to unity of command, and Lloyd George's policy of retaining in England, Scotland and Ireland hundreds of thousands of trained and partially trained troops, who should have been bulwarking Gough's dozen or fifteen under-strength divisions. The British people did not even know, nor the American, that in January an attempt of the French to form a pool of reserve divisions, to reinforce any threatened spot, had been thwarted by Haig's admission that he had only sufficient divisions to maintain precariously his actual front.

I cannot better picture the feeling of dismay which prevailed all over the United States, and was centralized in New York as the country's nerve center, than by saying that men as practical and unemotional as the late Charles M. Schwab, Thomas W. Lamont, John D. Rockefeller, jr., Elihu Root, Thomas N. Perkins, Benjamin Strong and many others were among those who called on Mr. House, tight-lipped and pallid with anxiety, for words of guidance in their tasks of nursing along the towering business structure which had been expanded to help the war effort. And I have sometimes thought that it was his cool honesty, his recitation of the controlling facts of the situation, which did most to stabilize the War Front in America as the Battle Front in France was being rebuilt by the common sense and iron nerve of Foch.

"It looks bad," Mr. House said that morning. "And I'll tell you one thing: it means that the war is going to be over this year. Ludendorff is putting in all he has. If he makes a clean break through, he'll take Paris and drive the British into the Channel. And the war will be over mighty soon. But if we stop him now, he's finished. There'll be hard fighting. But we'll have won the war before winter. It's a question of what they do in France. The main thing is for people not to get panicky. That's what I'm telling those men out there"—he waved his hand out the study door—"not to get panicky, just to keep their shirts on. It's a bad situation, so bad I don't think it can get worse. And that's good for us. We have time, if we can hold out. The Germans have got to win *now*. You know how we're raising men. Well, this puts the ball in our hands. And if the Allies can hold on, we'll win for them. Before winter. So quickly it will surprise people."

He reiterated the same sentiments, even more strongly, several days later, after the Germans had frightened the Allies still worse by bombarding Paris with new long-range guns from a distance of seventy-five miles. "It sounds sensational," he said. "It's ingenious. But I don't believe you can win a war by firing guns at a target you can't see, even from an observation-balloon. I'm putting my trust in Clemenceau and Foch. The French are pretty practical people. They don't stampede easy."

The Ludendorff offensive had two immediate results of great benefit to the Allies. It dramatized the need for unity of command, and it spurred the French and British to a colossal effort to rush American troops to France. At a conference at Doullens, five days after the offensive began, British and French leaders agreed to give Foch powers to coordinate the action of the Allied Armies. This was a compromise, but it worked so well that a week later, April 3, at a second conference, in Beauvais, his authority was increased by its extension to "the strategic direction of military operations"; and finally, with the President pushing hard for unity of command—which Mr. House and General Bliss consistently had recommended—the British surrendered, April 24, and the generalissimo was yielded the absolute authority of Commander-in-Chief of the Allied Armies. It was high time. Without this measure, the Allies might not have been able to create the pool of reserve divisions essential to plugging gaps in the front, and the Germans might profitably have exploited their initial success in the subsequent battles of the Aisne and the Marne.

The willingness of the Allies to divert ocean tonnage to the transportation of American troops was motivated, in part, by a secondary policy which they sought to impose on the United States at the risk of precipitating a controversy, which, if it had not been handled diplomatically by Mr. House and the President, might have alienated the sympathy of the United States, and would certainly have curtailed the efficiency of the American Army in France. Ever since they had decided that they required heavy reinforcements of American troops for the 1918 campaign, it will be remembered, the Allied Cabinets and High Commands had clung to the idea that the best way to use Americans would be as minor units incorporated into British and French brigades and divisions. A memorandum submitted to Mr. House by General Pétain in Paris, December 6, had expressed this view; and continuous pressure was exerted upon Pershing to secure his assent. (See his own Memoirs, and those of his principal subordinates.) Pershing was doggedly opposed to such a scheme, which, he knew, would make impossible the formation of an integrated group of American armies in France, and would also—as was grasped, perhaps, more definitely by General Bliss's political mind—tend to undermine the prestige and influence of the United States in shaping questions of major strategy and the formulation of peace terms. Indeed, it would almost seem, in studying the various proposals and counter-arguments of the Allies, that they were pointing deliberately toward this latter objective. The British and French Governments were fearful of the idealism, the determination to forge an unselfish peace, which animated Mr. House and the President. If they were more fearful of the President's opposition than of Mr. House's, it was because he remained to them, until he came to Paris, a figure of mystery, clothed in the mantle of the world's most powerful sovereignty, and speaking, as it were, from behind the temple veil.

After the March offensive, they deluged Mr. House, the President and the War Department—Secretary Baker was in France at the moment, about to return home, and he did not escape personal importunities, either—with cables and spokesmen primed to gain their purpose. They employed every resource of intrigue. On the slightest excuse they would have endeavored to obtain Pershing's recall and the appointment of a more pliant commander in France. But while Mr. House and the Administration advised Pershing to compromise with his persecutors in the interests of the new-won Allied unity, and to make good the deficiencies in the Allies' ranks, all representatives of the American Government insisted that the incorporation of American troops with Allied units must be understood as only temporary. The instant the emergency created by the German offensive had been terminated, all Americans were to be returned to their own divisional and corps organizations.

So insistent was Mr. House upon doing nothing to weaken Pershing's position that he bluntly advised the President, May 20, while the controversy was still raging, to refuse a request that he should be sent to France to resume his place upon the Supreme War Council. "What Lloyd George wants is someone to overrule Pershing," he wrote. "They probably intend to bring up the same old question." As a matter of fact, all Pershing needed was to be safeguarded against sharpshooting in his rear. He handled his problem with unusual aplomb for a fighting soldier, showing excellent temper and a reasonable desire to sacrifice everything short of the dissolution of his army into the Allied ranks. At a meeting with Foch and Lord Milner, the British Secretary of State for War, June 5, the three worked out the compromise Mr. House originally had passed on to all concerned. Priority was to be given to 410,000 infantry and machine-gunners in June and July, and these troops could be available for use by the Allies—but temporarily. Otherwise, other free shipping was to bring over complete divisional organizations to be placed in the line with the American Army, under the American flag. The American Government had promised, in March, to send 480,000 men during April, May, June and July. Actually, thanks to generous British provision of tonnage, 949,601 men were transported in these months. By the end of October, on the eve of the Armistice, there were approximately 2,000,000 American soldiers in France, about 200,000 more than the numbers of Haig's armies, and if the war had lasted several months longer the strength of American combat divisions in the line would have exceeded the French total. It was these hastily trained divisions, armed mainly from the resources of the Allies, that held Château-Thierry on the Marne, were instrumental in squeezing out the great German salient menacing Paris, then pinched out the St. Mihiel salient, were only deterred by French business politics from smashing through to Metz, which was under their railroad artillery, and finally breached the Argonne *massif,* regardless of casualties, and were on the point of severing one of the two main lines of the German retreat from France when Ludendorff surrendered.

You will have to dig deep in the memoirs of Allied commanders and statesmen to find a few sparse references to the contributions made by the American Army to victory in its relatively brief experience of battle. But Mr. House had no doubt as to why the war ended in the fall of 1918 in an Allied victory. Without the Americans, it was lost. Mr. Wilson's trenchant, closely reasoned State Papers; the subtle trend of Mr. House's diplomacy; the strategical conceptions of Pershing, which led him to pick for his troops a position threatening the German jugular vein leading through Metz; the courage of American doughboys and raw volunteer officers; the daring originality with which the Navy attacked the submarine problem, lifting the British Service out of a traditional lethargy which had irked its own junior officers; the soaring vision shared by American bankers, industrialists and labor leaders and their followers, even in States where the war remained a faint and scarcely heard echo of events beyond men's understanding—all these elements combined with many others in creating a psychology in the tired, discouraged Allied peoples, which checked the trend of events and turned defeat into victory.

"I don't like to call names," Mr. House said in his old age. "It is cheap. Men don't get anywhere by doing that. But I wish our friends abroad had shown a different spirit. They had fought alone as long as they could. We were fresh and strong. It was for the well-being of all of us. It's too bad we didn't do a better job with the opportunity we had. But let it go at that. The world looked good to us November 11, 1918. I hope it will look as good to other men some day."

But there were Allied leaders who saw clearly through the murk of jealousies and conflicting ambitions. Tardieu, the Frenchman, lived to write: "Without means of payment in dollars the Allies would have been beaten before the end of 1917. America's entry into the war saved them. Before the American soldier, the American dollar turned the tide." And July 27, 1917, the hardheaded Northcliffe cabled Churchill from New York: "I have long believed the war can only be won from here." There is a prevision of future animosities, however, in a line in a cable Wiseman sent Mr. House from London, August 12, the same year: "The British Government understands, though it is reluctant to admit, the most powerful position of the United States."

This is something that the British Government is still "reluctant to admit"—except that "Uncle Shylock" has been replaced as pet devil by the figure of Herr Hitler. I remember once saying to Mr. House that it was not unnatural for the British, and especially the English, to resent the development of the United States into a position of what amounted to world supremacy. "After all," I added, "they think of us as one of their pups." He laughed. "Where did you get that phrase?" he asked. "Yes, I think you've hit it off right. It is a mistake to say that they think of us as Colonials. They feel differently about us than about the Canadians or Australians. The Canadians and Australians still belong. But we turned out to be a pup that left the old breed and struck off by itself. They won't forgive us for that. But they make a mistake in letting it influence their attitude. They're going to need us more than we need them. It's a pity."

Book 8

Planning for Peace

In the course of his missions abroad, Mr. House had become impressed with the need of planning ahead for the peace which ultimately must terminate hostilities, and seek to establish a world order with a chance of permanence. He discussed the idea with a number of his friends at home and in Europe, and discovered that, whereas the Foreign Offices of the Allies were provided with archives, records and statistics bearing upon past European settlements and international points of controversy, the State Department in Washington was bare of practically all such important information. In the rush of improvising an organization for war, nothing was done in this matter, until the President, in connection with his reply to the Pope's appeal to the nations, had brought home to him the value of facts and figures dealing with the war aims of the Allies and the counter-claims of the Central Empires. The result was a suggestion from Mr. Wilson that his friend should undertake the formation of a group of experts—historians, geographers, anthropologists, economists— to be charged with the collection of the required material. Secretary Lansing gave the idea his approval, the State Department and the Intelligence Bureaus of the General Staff and the Navy offered to cooperate as needed, and so—in an atmosphere of secrecy, which, perhaps, was not as worthy as the motives of the project—the body known as The Inquiry was constituted.

Mr. House's brother-in-law, Dr. Sidney Mezes, president of the College of the City of New York, was made director. Walter Lippmann, at the time on the staff of *The New Republic,* was secretary. Dr. Isaiah Bowman, director of the American Geographical Society, offered the use of the Society's building, map collections and library, in New York, and also gave The Inquiry the benefit of his personal advice and assistance. The most distinguished scholars in America cooperated with a keen satisfaction in the Administration's recognition of their capacity to advise in the formulation of treaty terms, for it was the first time the Government of the United States had invited the assistance of the men who might be considered the best theoretical experts on the subjects at issue. Charles H. Haskins, J. T. Shotwell, David Hunter Miller, George Louis Beer, Douglas Johnson and Clive Day were among the chiefs of the several divisions of studies established. They divided amongst themselves and their associates, equally well-fitted, the whole field of European, African, Asiatic and oceanographic interests to be considered by the future Peace Conference. Their reports, exhaustively prepared, frequently amended and redrafted, especially after the Peace Conference convened, were models of precision, tolerance and commonsense. It may honestly be said that, whatever were the mistakes and distortions of the peace, whatever the errors in policy of the American Commissioners, not a particle of blame attached to their advisers of The Inquiry, who frequently, as Mr. House has testified, showed a more statesmanlike grasp of problems than the Allied Chiefs of State and Foreign Offices.

The President, Mr. House and their associate commissioners had access to all the available facts, yes, and to the counter-facts, bearing upon the problems before them. It is sad, then, as sad as it is unescapable, to reflect that, despite this prodigious work of organization in advance of the Conference, the deliberations of the dominant figures remained subject to the whims, human failings, accidents of temperament, individual and national greeds, which would seem to be inseparable from the efforts of men to bring wisdom and justice to the solution of questions entangled with human ambitions. None of the experts, practically, was satisfied with the peace as finally drafted. This was true, not only of the American representatives at Paris, but of many of their confrères of the delegations of experts attached to the British and French Commissions, as well as of natives of smaller nations. The peace was not an experts' peace. But that statement brings up the challenge: Could it have been? Can any peace embrace perfect justice?

2

About the time The Inquiry was launched—and working in collaboration with several of its experts on international law—Mr. House began to devote more attention to the mooted subject of a League or Association of Nations, which might be developed as an instrument to avert war. Many men, including his friends, Mr. Wilson, Lord Grey, Lord Robert Cecil, Lord Phillimore, Balfour, Dr. Lawrence Lowell, of Harvard; Dr. Nicholas Murray Butler, of Columbia; ex-President Taft and ex-Senator Elihu Root, were thinking deeply and broadly along the same lines. In France, too, Léon Bourgeois and other liberals were drafting tentative plans, which, in the main, varied from the conceptions of the Anglo-Americans in emphasizing the creation of a military super-State, with the obvious purpose of restraining Germany. These men probably gave no more attention to the subject of a Society of Nations, as it was sometimes called, than many others—men, for instance, like David Hunter Miller, of The Inquiry—but their names were better known and carried more weight. Still, it would be manifestly as untrue of the Covenant of the League, as drafted in the tumultuous period, 1917-19, as of the Constitution of the United States, to say that it had any one or several authors. It represented a painful, harassed synthesis of scores of minds. It was born of the pangs of a frightened and perplexed civilization.*

But, allowing for this, the salient characteristics of the Covenant grew, as reflections of many intellects, in the brains of Mr. House, Cecil, Lord Phillimore—whose draft plan was forwarded to the President by the British Government, in July, 1918, and reforwarded by him, unread, to Mr. House, Dr. Butler, Dr. Lowell, and Mr. Root. All of these men had been exchanging ideas for months and years, and each influenced the thoughts of the others—and was influenced, in turn, by men and women remote from this group. Mr. House drafted the first American version of "a Convention" for a League at Magnolia, Mass., July 13 and 14, 1918. Hastily thrown together, with Professor Miller's assistance, its twenty-three articles formed the structural and philosophical basis for the President's tentative draft, which used all but five of its articles, and was the

---

* General Smuts is not included in this list because he came into the picture after the Armistice. Dr. Seymour disputes the usual theory that Smuts was sole author of the idea of Mandates as a compromise disposition of the German colonies, and that the President adopted the idea from a pamphlet Smuts published in London, December 16, 1918. Dr. Seymour's argument is that the President was discussing League administration of conquered colonies aboard the *George Washington,* six days previously. It is true, too, that Smuts' original conception was applied only to European and Near Eastern conquests. But it is quite probable that the President had advance information of the Smuts pamphlet, and it should be remembered that the South African—as Baruch shrewdly has said—was very much of a sophist. He wanted German Southwest Africa as a reward for the Union's war efforts, and very likely had hopes of picking up the administration of German East Africa into the bargain. His pamphlet was a "teaser" designed to open up the field of colonial conquests to his idea. He was too intelligent to have believed that the Slavs and Rumanians would accept Mandates for territories to which they laid claim by right of race.

Sir Eric Drummond contributed valuable suggestions to the League discussions in Paris, and before that, such British liberals as Noel Buxton, H. N. Brailsford, and Philip Snowden had counseled with Mr. House, Cecil and the other original sponsors of the League. It is really invidious to single out individuals for credit in the creation of this most grandiose of man's social conceptions.

first official American plan, incorporated with the final preliminary British version for presentation to the League of Nations Commission of the Conference in Paris. Out of this document the Covenant of the League was hewn, for better or worse, the mistrust the French entertained for its lack of sovereign authority having been freely employed by them as a bargaining lever with the President to procure his acceptance of their more onerous demands upon Germany.

Mr. Wilson was not, and never pretended to be, the author of the Covenant. He served as its editor, first, afterwards as its chief advocate, and finally as its destroyer as an efficient tool in international affairs. It might be added that, of all those whose names have been enumerated here, he, and he alone, thought that the usefulness of the League in the immediate future would be circumscribed by acceptance of the amendments attached to the Covenant by the Republican majority in the Senate. None of the League's authors or supporters accepted the Covenant as Bible writ. Its compromises were innumerable, and had to be, in the circumstances. Consequently, some thought it should be stronger, some weaker, some mistrusted the implications of the Mandates system, some thought the Mandated territories should be administered directly by the League, some thought the small Powers had been given too much authority, some thought the contrary. And, of course, there was always the dissent between those who believed in the possibility of a new world order, and those who could not conceive of man's ability to control the Old Adam in himself. If the Covenant was a compromise and a jumble, so was the Constitution, as Mr. House and others have thought, pointing to its twenty-one Amendments and the fact that several of its provisions are dead letters.

Secretary of State Lansing is not included in the list of "stepfathers" of the Covenant because, while he gave loyal and intelligent support to the President and Mr. House, his attitude seems to have been governed by a skepticism which evolved into serious doubts of the document's value after he perceived, in Paris, the extent to which the President was disposed to compromise other elements tending to a lasting peace, in order to secure the adoption by the Conference of the plan he had come to consider his own. These doubts were transformed into more or less secret disapproval when he saw, later, how the President was determined to antagonize the Senate and the public opinion which rallied to the support of Congress. But Lansing did have one lightning-clear vision of the Covenant's chief weakness, perhaps a fundamental reason for the League's failure to exert the moral influence men expected from it.

In a letter to Mr. House, April 8, 1918—three months prior to the

Texan's writing of "the Magnolia draft"—he stressed in detail the question whether it would ever be possible for a League to function, if it consisted of both democracies and autocratic governments: ". . . I have reached the conclusion that the only certain guarantor of international peace is a League of Democracies, since they alone possess the trustworthy character which makes their word inviolate. A League, on the other hand, which numbers among its members autocratic governments, possesses the elements of personal ambition, of intrigue and discord, which are the seeds of future wars. A League composed of democratic and autocratic governments and pledged to maintain peace by force, would be unreliable; but a League, composed solely of democracies, would by reason of the character of its membership be an efficient surety of peace. To my mind it comes down to this, that the acceptance of the principle of democracy by all the chief powers of the world and the maintenance of genuine democratic governments would result in permanent peace. . . . We must crush Prussianism so completely that it can never rise again, and we must end autocracy in every other nation as well."

There is a prophetic ring to Lansing's statements, which must be more impressive to those who reread them today than they were to Mr. House, and to Root, Taft and Lowell, to whom, among others, he read them. It was by no means certain, then, or even anticipated, for that matter, that the Hohenzollerns would be expelled from Germany. The inward decay of the Habsburg Empire, before the vicious thrusts of Allied and American propaganda, was not appreciated so much by the men who were provoking it as by the Austro-Hungarian statesmen who were seeing it happen beneath their eyes. All that was happening in Russia was convincing Mr. House, at any rate, that that unhappy country was a long way from any true democracy. And what of Japan, whose cautious advance toward her present bid for the hegemony of Asia was slowly taking shape from opportunities of worldwide confusion which seemed to her statesmen too good to be safe? No, Mr. House thought in 1918 that Lansing's view was narrow, unrealistic, and colored by a legalistic mentality. What he would have thought in 1940 is entirely a question of speculation. He would, however, almost certainly have ascribed the condition of the post-Munich world to the failure of the League to function, and the blame for that he would have laid to the refusal of the United States to assume the obligations imposed upon them by their ruthless acceptance of the economic, and hence material, power which had been thrown to them by the collapse of Europe. And he would, with equal likelihood, have granted Lansing a human appreciation of mankind's congenital weakness, which previously he had denied.*

He believed implicitly that no League of Nations was practicable which differentiated between nations. All must join, however governed. All must accept responsibility for the machinery designed to check wars. All must be willing to demonstrate a love of peace, a will to cooperation and a readiness to offer reasonable economic cooperation. Without such a universal disposition, he could not foresee anything more than a world divided into continental areas, each mutually jealous, and each area, by reason of the widespread distribution of the territorial interests of the Great Powers, disposed to interfere in another's regional concerns. It was not for such a settlement that he struck off, at Magnolia, in two days, one of the embryos of an instrument, which surely deserves to be bracketed with the other noble efforts by Americans to curb the baser instincts of men for the common good. He did not think the Covenant, to which he, as much as anyone, gave form, was a perfect document or correct in all its principles. He hoped to see it amended, as the unwritten British Constitution, the American Constitution, have been amended and revised. But he did believe that the Covenant contained the germs of a system which could balk covetous and predatory nations and dynasties, and lead gradually to a more just distribution of the world's wealth by compromise, instead of by war and revolution. And he did not believe that the United States could prosper, as they should, if they persisted in retiring behind tariff barriers and expensive fleets, leaving the rest of the world to simmer in poverty and festering antagonism.

"This world is getting small," he put his thought. "It's going to get smaller. We've all got to live with each other, if we want to live decently. I want a big Navy, the way things are, but you and I know how to spend that money in ways that would make men and women better and more intelligent."

3

It is amusing to recall, now, how few people appreciated, in midsummer of 1918, the dramatic imminence of the German defeat. This had been apparent to Mr. House and a few others by the middle of July, when Ludendorff was pinched out of the huge Marne salient; but they were chary of expressing their confidence, lest over-optimism should

* It is interesting that the Lansing conception of a League of Democracies is the theme of Clarence Streit's book, *Union Now,* published in 1939, which has aroused more interest in the theory of organized international cooperation against war, military and economic, than any other publication of the past twenty years.

weaken the public concern in the war effort and perhaps produce a set-back. And while the reports of the military commanders in France indicated a loss of offensive spirit in the German ranks, and a passage of the initiative to the Allies and Americans, there was still the possibility that, by shortening their lines, the Germans might be able to cling to positions well within the French frontier. This would mean another winter of trench warfare and enforced inaction, with harmful effects to civilian morale. It seemed best to confine the emphasis of public statements to the limited truth that the Germans were everywhere on the defensive.

August 8 was described by Ludendorff in his Memoirs as "the Black Day for the German Army." On August 14, a conference of dignitaries of the Central Empires was hastily convened at Great Headquarters at Spa. The two Kaisers, their Foreign Ministers and Chancellor Hertling were given the crushing news by Hindenburg and Ludendorff that the German Armies would be compelled henceforth to remain on the defensive. There was no talk, as yet, of surrendering; but the military commanders advised an immediate bid for peace through one of the neutral powers. There seems to have been temporizing in undertaking this disagreeable task. Hertling probably was loath to accept the historical role of admitting Germany's frustration, if not defeat—and there was a hope that the Allies and Americans might become exhausted. But "Black Days" were becoming more frequent for the Germans, and Hindenburg began to press the Berlin Government for "immediate" peace proposals. Yet two days afterwards Reading, in London, was so uncertain of the future that he cabled that the commanders in France were expecting a "great effort" would be necessary to insure peace in 1919. Within the week, the Bulgarian front collapsed north of Saloniki, justifying technically the claim of the "Easterners," in the British War Office and Imperial General Staff, that the war would be won in Turkey and the Balkans. Bulgaria was the weakest link of the Central Empires. She was out of the war by unconditional surrender, September 30; Austria's plight became desperate, and even the doubters in London began to see victory as a question of weeks rather than months.

On September 27, while the Bulgarian crisis was boiling to a climax, Mr. Wilson made his Liberty Loan speech at a rally in the Metropolitan Opera House, in New York, a reiterated simplification of the general terms for peace he had laid down in the Fourteen Points, but in this instance aimed more directly at the military masters of Germany, with veiled warning to the Allies not to commit themselves to a similar policy of imperialism. It was a knife-blow at the self-confidence of the German people, disruptive of discipline at the front, stirring discontent amongst civilians, one of those masterly demonstrations of simple psychological appeal, at which the President seems to have excelled all other orators who addressed diverse and alien races.

". . . It will be necessary," he said, "that all who sit down at the peace table shall come ready and willing to pay the price, the only price that will procure it. . . . That price is impartial justice in every item of the settlement, no matter whose interest is crossed; and not only impartial justice, but also the satisfaction of the several peoples whose fortunes are dealt with. That indispensable instrumentality is a League of Nations formed under Covenants that will be efficacious. . . . I believe that the leaders of the Governments with which we are associated will speak as they have occasion, as plainly as I have tried to speak. . . . Unity of purpose and of counsel are as imperatively necessary in this war as was unity of command in the battlefield."

Perhaps Mr. Wilson touched the zenith of his fame and satisfaction that night. A distinguished audience, an audience representative of all sections of the country and all shades of political opinion, applauded him continuously, even though, as Mr. House considered, the more subtle passages of his speech evaded the understanding of men and women of intelligence, who were swept off their feet by the war hysteria of the moment. But nothing could take from Woodrow Wilson the satisfaction—if he cared for it—that that night he was lifted up, as never before, to the perilous heights of an idolatry which was to continue unabated, until in Paris he set his convictions against those of men less scrupulous than himself, and afterwards compromised ideals in which he had professed to have conviction. Mr. House was always sorry for him for that reason. Idolatry and hero worship are the most dangerous manifestations of war hysteria, the Texan believed—as he believed that Abraham Lincoln had been more kindly treated by fate than his friend.

The Metropolitan Opera House speech had been suggested by Mr. House, in a letter of September 3, as a maneuver to commit the Allies "to some of the things for which we are fighting." He foresaw, more accurately than his friend, the accentuation of reactionary sentiment which would be produced in the Allied countries by a decisive victory; and he was fearful of the continued support of Labor and liberal sentiment for American principles of peace. He was also influenced by a letter from his friend, Sir William Tyrrell, urging the formation of a League of Nations as a preliminary to the end of hostilities for the sake of its effect upon the deliberations of the Peace Conference. "To agree with France, England, Italy and Japan," Mr. House wrote, "upon the Covenant for a League of Nations would not prevent its incorporation

MR. HOUSE AT THE TIME OF THE PEACE CONFERENCE—FROM A PORTRAIT
BY LASZLO

into the peace treaty. It would rather make it the more certain. . . . If such a document as we have in mind should be accepted and made public, it could not have any but a good effect in the Central Powers and should shorten the war."

The President accepted the idea of making such a speech for the general purpose outlined by Mr. House—that is, to confirm the Allies' support of the principles embodied in the Fourteen Points; but he rejected, as he had all along, with typical consistency, the suggestion to proceed with creating the League in the conditions which must prevail so long as the fighting continued. Both friends, it might be said, were consistently inconsistent in this disagreement. The President thought, probably rightly, that an atmosphere drenched with the poisonous hatred of war would be inimical to the attainment of an ideal Covenant. Did he secure a better atmosphere in which to work in the Paris of 1919, still shaken by four years of terror, convulsively trying to reassure itself by an implacable desire to humiliate its foes? And as for Mr. House, several months later, he was favoring postponement of the Treaty, as well as the Covenant, in favor of a purely tentative settlement of military questions and boundaries, pending a leisurely redrawing of the world's map. There was much to be said for both of them in their attitudes. The situations confronting them were fluid, charged with perils as unpredictable as impossible of complete avoidance, and frequently defying solution, save by compromises for the purpose of securing temporarily the political life of some leader, whose removal would have slowed up or frustrated the work of the Conference.

The Metropolitan Opera House speech produced results eight days later. Prince Max, of Baden, a liberal dilettante, whose aristocratic connections, it was hoped, would enable him to bind closer the jarring fabric of the Empire, became Chancellor, in succession to Hertling, October 4, with the approval of the Reichstag. He had been under pressure to move instantly for peace while the negotiations leading to his acceptance of the post were in progress. Ludendorff was still opposed to any policy resembling surrender; but Hindenburg, a much more human character than the Quartermaster-General, was becoming unwilling to continue the sacrifice of German lives to stave off a decision, the hopelessness of which was daily reported to him by subordinates at the front. On October 5, Prince Max addressed Mr. Wilson through the Swiss Government, requesting him to invite the Allies to grant an armistice on behalf of Germany and Austria, and to inaugurate negotiations for peace on the basis of the Fourteen Points.

The President was impressed by this evidence that Germany was installing a semblance of parliamentary government, and showing simultaneously a disposition to abandon her previous recalcitrance. In Paris and London, and at the French and British headquarters, there was a disposition to look upon the offer as a trap, designed to afford time to extricate the German troops and combat trains from the pincer jaws of the Allied armies—which, indeed, was exactly its intention. Mr. House, too, feared that his friend might be tempted into a premature response, which would, if it did nothing worse, create dissension with the Allied Powers. He telegraphed and wrote the President, urging him not to reply directly, but to issue a statement that he was sending Mr. House abroad to confer with the Allies "regarding the communication received from the German Government." He suspected, correctly, that the Allies would seize any opportunity which arose, in case the German spirit of resistance was stiffened by hard terms, to throw the responsibility upon the President's shoulders. He insisted that delay was to the advantage of the Allies and the United States, but that it would be unwise to give Germany a harsh refusal.

Mr. House was better-informed than his friend as to the extent to which the war hysteria had gripped the United States. Therefore he was not so surprised and shocked as Mr. Wilson by the immediate clamor in Congress and the newspapers for uncompromising rejection of the German note, a clamor markedly more strident on the Republican side of the fence. If ever a man, reputed to be a statesman and historian, revealed how lamentably he was lacking in such qualities, it was Henry Cabot Lodge, of Massachusetts,* who demonstrated, in debate on the floor of the Senate, that he had no perception of the significance of recent military events, no comprehension of the tremendous changes which were impending in Central Europe. He seems, for instance, to have been quite unimpressed by the abdication of Czar Ferdinand of Bulgaria, October 5, the day on which Prince Max had sent his note, although it was plain to students of European politics—the experts of The Inquiry and newspapermen with a knowledge of contemporary problems, say— that what was happening on so drastic a scale in the weakest of the Central Empires must be a forecast of what would happen, at any moment, in Germany and Austria. But allowing for Senator Lodge's lack of statesmanship, he was spokesman for millions of Americans of his party, and Mr. House did not care to see the President, by some mischance, play into the hands of his opponents, particularly with a Congressional election impending in November, some four weeks off.

* The grandfather of the present Senator of the same name.

Mr. Wilson summoned his friend to Washington, Monday, October 7. Mr. House reached the White House at nine o'clock that evening, and the President lost no time in reading him the reply he had prepared to Prince Max's note. It confirmed Mr. House's misgivings, in that it "did not emphasize the need of guarantees providing for thoroughgoing acceptance of Wilson's peace conditions." The President, Mr. House noted in his diary, October 9, "seemed much disturbed when I expressed a decided disapproval of it. I did not believe the country would approve of what he had written." Lansing came in presently, and apparently did not disagree with Mr. House's objection. The President argued for half an hour, persisting his inability to redraft the reply, and suggesting that his friend might be able to "embody what I had in mind." But he worked on amendments to his own draft until one o'clock Monday night, and the next day returned to the task. Mr. House remarked that he had had a change of heart overnight, and realized at last "the nearly unanimous sentiment in this country against anything but unconditional surrender." This was the difficulty confronting him, in Mr. House's estimation: how to leave the door open to the Germans for a real surrender, and yet not drive them to desperation, while conciliating the furious demand for victory which came from the United States and the Allied countries.

The President did an excellent job in his final draft, Mr. House thought. Without rejecting the German proposal, the reply stated simply and briefly that the United States could not consider such a request, unless the Central Empires first furnished definite guarantees of good faith, positive agreement to accept the Fourteen Points as the basis of peace, assurance that the new Chancellor spoke, in fact, for the German people and not for their masters, and gave an undertaking to evacuate occupied territories.

It accomplished its purpose. Mr. Wilson's political opponents at home could not very well cavil at its reasonable willingness to negotiate with a Germany properly humble, and able to convince of the honesty of her intentions. The Allied Premiers and commanders, while privately resentful that the German Government had addressed the President of the United States and not themselves or Marshal Foch, were likewise held to silence until they discovered the character of Prince Max's next communication. In Germany, the Civil Government, fumbling for means to curb the military chieftains, were encouraged to try to meet the President's stipulations, although they felt constrained to yield to Ludendorff's insistence that their reply should contain another trap to permit the extrication of the Army, so that it could be used to influence the future peace negotiations. This second note, of October 12, accepted the President's major conditions, but demanded that the German evacuation should be arranged and supervised by a mixed commission, thus affording Ludendorff the time he sought to withdraw his troops, as occasion served, either to a defensible line within the French and Belgian frontiers, or, intact with arms and equipment, into Germany, prepared to resist peace terms requiring uncomfortable concessions.

Mr. Wilson, now, was perfectly able to see the ulterior motive in this stipulation. He and Mr. House spent most of October 14 in writing what amounted to an ultimatum, which, within the space of a page, demanded sternly an unequivocal response. Again, it avoided the urgences of the war mongers and super-patriots of all countries, who clamored to "hang the Kaiser," "bust the Boche," "smash the Huns." But it left all details of the Armistice to "the judgment and advice of the military advisers of the Government of the United States and the Allied Governments." It warned that no armistice would be granted while Germany continued "illegal and inhuman practices," and until "absolutely satisfactory safeguards and guarantees" had been furnished for the supremacy of the armies arrayed against Germany. The terms of peace would depend upon the kind of German Government with which the Allied and Associated Powers must treat.

Prince Max and the other members of the Government perceived that Ludendorff had been deluded in thinking that they could cozen Mr. Wilson or sow dissent between the United States and the Allies. They took heart and asserted themselves. Ludendorff was summoned to Berlin, where he gabbled of "national honor"—the enemy should be made to fight for such terms. He demanded reinforcements. There were none. The morale of the populations of the larger manufacturing cities, the seaports, the capital, was crumbling. The situation was developing, which, within three weeks, would bring revolutionary movements in Kiel and Hamburg, November 7, the proclamation of a republic in Bavaria, November 8, and send the Kaiser fleeing to Holland, November 10, after formally abdicating the preceding day. And these great and far-reaching events—of which we are still feeling the consequences today, twenty-two years afterwards—would have been caused as much by the subtle mind of Mr. House and the dialectic skill of Mr. Wilson as by the hammering guns of the armies fighting in France, on the Isonzo front in Italy, in the Balkans and in Palestine. The two friends had proved, even as had two Russians they were beginning to take stock of, that words, ideas, could be as explosive as trinitrotoluol, as asphyxiating as poison gas.*

The German Government replied to the President, October 20, accepting all his conditions, adding that submarines had been instructed not to sink passenger ships—actually, submarines were being wirelessed to return to port as fast as they could be reached—and that the retreating German troops had been ordered to respect private property, this last a pledge the Government were not very well capable of enforcing. On October 23, Mr. Wilson turned over his correspondence with Prince Max to the Allied Governments and commanders for implementation.

Mr. House already was at sea, delegated to represent his friend in the elaborate inter-governmental negotiations which must lead up to the suspension of hostilities, and the next stage of erecting a structure for formulating the terms of peace. He was happy as he sailed. He would be disturbed, before he landed, with misgivings for Mr. Wilson's future. But, so far as he knew, the friendship which had lasted so many years was still intact, despite several foreboding incidents. His parting with Mr. Wilson had been affectionate on both sides, and marked by the last expression of complete personal confidence which he was to receive. "As I was leaving," Mr. House recorded, "he said, 'I have not given you any instructions because I feel you will know what to do.'" And to confirm these words, Mr. House carried, besides a formal commission as "Special Representative of the Government of the United States of America," a letter, written in Mr. Wilson's tall, sloping, accurate script, appointing him "my personal representative," and reciting further that: "I have asked him to take part as such in the conferences of the Supreme War Council and in any other conferences in which it may be serviceable for him to represent me. I commend him to the confidence of the representatives of the Governments with which the Government of the United States is associated in the war."

It was the most remarkable authorization ever given by a President of the United States to any citizen, amounting, in truth, to a blanket power of attorney.

---

* The Wilson-House psychology of pounding home the difference between the German people and their Government has been followed by the Allied leaders in the present war. The Birmingham speech of Prime Minister Chamberlain, February 24, 1940, was a case in point. It developed frankly the Wilsonian idea that the Allies had nothing against the German people, but would refuse to make peace with a Nazi Government. The difficulty today, however, is that Hitler's censorship of the press and the air neutralizes much of the effect of such an appeal. It is questionable, as yet, how effective is the Allies' counter-effort of scattering propaganda from aeroplanes.

4

The incidents about to be described are interesting, in so far as I was concerned with them, only because of their significance as possible connecting links in the chain of events leading up to the separation, a year later, of Mr. House and his friend in the great work they had wrought together, and were to continue, futilely, apart. It is scarcely necessary to say that Mr. House was not, consciously, in any way responsible for this separation; it cannot be called a "break" or a "rupture" or a "breach," for it came about gradually, imperceptibly, and on the volition of Mr. Wilson. Or if not entirely on his volition, at least with his tacit acceptance of what was done in his name. Mr. House made three separate attempts, tentatively, after their separation had lasted a year, to indicate to the President his continued friendship and affection. The second of these, a letter dated June 10, 1920, I wrote myself, at his request. "You're farther away from this than I am," he said. "I want to be sure it's phrased right. I simply want him to know that I'm not going abroad this summer to trade on my past connection with him." This letter, like its predecessor of March 11, and the third, of November 1, both of 1920, was answered by Mr. Wilson in a tone of friendly, but detached, cordiality.

In the spring of 1918, a chain of newspapers published a series of articles by me under the general title "The Real Colonel House." The material was obtained from Mr. House or friends or sources indicated by him, and was endorsed by him to the extent that he read and personally corrected the proofs, making many alterations, in fact. The President was referred to continually in terms which, personally, I considered savoring of effusiveness. Certainly, he and the work he had done were neither belittled nor minimized. The idea of the series was to destroy the "whispering campaign" which was conducted against Mr. House in both political parties, as well as by business men and financiers who disliked his policies. He agreed with me that he had best abandon his pose of anonymity in the interests of the country and the Administration. This pose, in any case, had ceased to have a purpose after the publicity which had been focused upon his trips abroad during the war; and there was a possibility that its continuance would cripple the work he hoped to do in negotiating peace and setting up the League of Nations.

In May, 1918, my articles were issued as a book, under the same title, by the George H. Doran Company, of New York. Proofs were read again, by Mr. House himself and by a committee of his friends, which included, for The Inquiry, his brother-in-law, Dr. Mezes, and Lippmann.

Many more changes and elisions were made, most of them tending once more to draw a dubious veil of secrecy over Mr. House. I had no objections to what was done. My one desire was to insure him against any embarrassment and discomfort; for this reason, I refused an offer for motion-picture rights from Warner Brothers, then an infant producing company, which had risen from the stage of proprietors of a chain of nickelodeon theaters by filming a grotesque version of Gerard's book of memoirs with the title, "The Kaiser, Beast of Berlin."

"Don't let me in for anything like that," Mr. House said with a shudder. "Poor Gerard!"

I told him that, of course, I wouldn't think of doing so; that, in the first place, I disagreed as cordially as I knew he did with that form of propaganda, which served only to stimulate excessively the war hysteria of the American people.

The book aroused much attention, despite the fact that its newspaper version had been read by several million people. It brought home to the American public, for one thing, the real meaning of the House doctrine of the Freedom of the Seas. In England, where several hundred copies got out, various statesmen offered five pounds for it. It was withdrawn in England, and its advertising in the United States was canceled, because the publisher received a suggestion from George Creel, Chairman of the Committee on Public Information—as the Administration called the body charged with censorship—that its sale was regarded as harmful to the national interest. The publisher was justly outraged. Anybody could secure copies of files of the newspapers in which a more extended version had appeared. But this was in the early summer of 1918, with the public all but insane over the issue between victory and defeat in France. The tide had not yet turned. The power of the Administration amounted theoretically to that of a dictatorship. Any man who strove to thwart that power risked ruin.

The publisher telegraphed the White House, stating Creel's suggestion and asking for confirmation of it. He received a wire in reply from Tumulty, agreeing that it was thought best, in the national interest, that the book should be withdrawn. "I'll be damned if I withdraw," snapped Doran. "But I will suspend advertising. And that's all I will do!"

And the reader can find whatever amusement he pleases—or any lesson—in the fact that the one country in which *The Real Colonel House* was published without restriction, was Japan, where many editions in the idiom were sold, and where, for some years, it was the textbook of the liberal movement.

Mr. House was neither diverted nor amused by the incident. He agreed with me that, as a manifestation of the spirit of censorship, inimical to American institutions, it was to be deplored. "But I knew things like this would happen if the President gave Creel such powers," he said; "Creel or anybody." He also said that the President had mentioned the book to him in a good-natured manner, which, however, indicated that Mr. Wilson had been advised that it was not doing him any good. "I am sure you couldn't help it, House," he said. "We all have this kind of thing happen to us." Mr. House was quite certain that Mr. Wilson, himself, never had read the book; but that he had been told by people of whom he was fond—and who must certainly not have been fond of Mr. House—that it had been intended to undermine his prestige. Perhaps he thought that his retiring friend had become intoxicated with reflected authority, and was embarking upon an active political career. That is one way such careers are started in this country, although nothing was farther removed from Mr. House's plans. He was looking forward to serving the United States in the League of Nations.

It is a strange incident, and one not at all in keeping with Mr. Wilson's character. Friendships with men of equal intellect and similar tastes he seems seldom to have maintained. But he was not, by nature, a jealous man. After he was dead, and Ray Stannard Baker, in the authorized biography, *Woodrow Wilson and World Settlement,* had endeavored to pin on Mr. House responsibility for having betrayed the President during his absence from Paris, Mr. House referred again to this subject, which we often discussed. He was willing to admit, by this time, that in retrospect he could detect a loosening in the bonds linking him with his friend after the appearance of my book.

"But I didn't see it then," he said, "nor for a long time afterward. Perhaps I didn't want to. It was so difficult to credit of the President. He was never small. And you didn't write anything to hurt him or make me seem more important than I was."

The second incident with which this chapter deals has to do with Mr. Wilson's statement to the country in October, 1918, asking the people to elect a Democratic Congress to support him in his war aims. This statement marked the turning point in his career. Up to the time of its issuance, he had the warm support of many independents and progressive Republicans. Indeed, it was their votes which had reelected him in 1916. These men were prejudiced against him by an action they regarded as partisan and un-American, a deliberate attempt to capitalize the nonpartisan loyalty which had been yielded to him after the country entered the war. It aroused the Republican politicians to fury, and gave them an argument for votes of which they would otherwise have been deprived. It procured the bitter resentment to his policies of the Republican majority elected to the Senate, and the consequent attachment to the Treaty of Versailles of the Lodge Reservations, which were acceptable to all the friends of the League—and to the Governments of the Allied Powers, if Lord Grey may be believed—except the President, and we may suppose, the small group of politically irresponsible intimates upon whom he relied for advice during his illness.

Thus Mr. Wilson's October manifesto to the country deprived the League, from its foundation, of the influence of the United States, which Mr. House and its liberal friends had relied upon to mitigate the rigors of the post-war treaties and ameliorate the enmities of victors and vanquished. They saw the United States acting as the gyroscope of a new world order. But the antagonistic force the President set in motion produced the economic chaos of the succeeding decade, the each-one-for-himself policy of the Great Powers, culminating in the failure of the Kreditanstalt Bank of Vienna, and the worldwide depression, of which it was the first symptom, and which reached the United States in October, 1929. The direct results of this depression in the last decade were the suspension of debt payments between the nations, the collapse of Republican Germany, the reckless intransigeance of the totalitarian Governments and an armaments race, which has produced a series of wars rapidly assuming the proportions of a second World War. Nor is this the whole story of the disastrous consequences of Mr. Wilson's action. A League of Nations, of which the United States was a member, could easily have curbed Mussolini and Japan—Hitler would probably still be ranting in Munich beer halls. Ethiopia and Albania would be free nations today, along with Czecho-Slovakia, Poland and Austria, supposing the last-named had declined *Anschluss,* and China would be working out her own destiny, however painfully.*

It is difficult to find in history a parallel record of evils on so vast a scale, which may be traced to one man's momentary surrender to an egotism scarcely typical of his character. And Mr. Wilson made this tragic mistake without the approval of Mr. House, and, as shall be shown, actually against his advice and constructive counter-suggestion.

The record of *The Intimate Papers* is incomplete on this most important episode in the relations between the two men. It appears in two quotations from Mr. House's diary, the first of September 24, 1918, reciting a conversation in the White House several days previously:

* This was written before Hitler had overrun Denmark and two-thirds of Norway, and hurled his Armies across the Dutch, Belgian and Luxembourg frontiers in the early morning hours of May 10, 1940.

"The President spoke of politics in general and expressed an earnest desire that a Democratic Congress should be elected. He said he intended making a speech or writing a letter about two weeks before the elections, asking the people to return a Democratic House. I did not express any opinion as to the wisdom of this."

To this quotation is appended a note by Dr. Seymour: "When House advised with the President, silence invariably expressed dissent. Nothing more was said to House about this, and he was on the Atlantic when the appeal was issued. On October 25"—this was at sea, after he had heard by wireless of the appeal—"he wrote in his diary: 'I have been greatly disturbed by the President's appeal for a Democratic Congress. All he says is true, but it is a political error to appeal for a partisan Congress. If he had asked the voters to support members of Congress and the Senate who had supported the American war aims, regardless of party, he would be in a safe position. . . . It seems to me a needless venture, and if I had been at home I should have counseled against it. He mentioned, the last time I was in Washington, that he thought of making an appeal. I made no reply, which always indicates to him my disapproval. As a matter of fact, we were so absorbed in the German notes that I brushed the question aside and gave it but little attention. I am sorry now that I did not discuss it with him to a finish.'"

Mr. House forgot that he *had* expressed his disapproval. He forgot, too, that it was not on the occasion of his last meeting with the President in Washington—he stopped at the White House twice during the first two weeks of October, the second time October 14, when he helped draft the President's ultimatum to Germany—that this conversation occurred. His diary is explicit as to the date, as cited above. And the entry is definite in its fixing of the time of the conversation because it includes a *précis,* several hundred words long, of other subjects discussed, notably the content of the Metropolitan Opera House speech, and where it should be delivered, the President having suggested the Economic Club, and Mr. House arguing successfully for a more representative body.

The fact is that Mr. House advised the President strongly against the issuance of such a statement over the direct telephone from his study to the State Department, several days before his sudden departure for France to resume his seat on the Supreme War Council. He did it at my suggestion. He may have forgotten this incident because of the rush of affairs which beset him at the moment—I dragged him out of a conference to talk to him—and because Miss Denton, his secretary and remembrancer, knew nothing about it. And then, again, he may have "forgotten" it, with his usual generosity of heart, because he did not wish to place the President too much in the wrong in his testament, as embodied in *The Intimate Papers*. This feeling appears again and again in Dr. Seymour's book. Mr. House was always most loath to say or write anything which placed his friend in the wrong. He preferred, and perhaps wrongly from the angle of history, to let history discover the facts impartially and from the open record.

I went uptown to see him that day because *The Evening Post* had received a dispatch from its Washington correspondent, David Lawrence, who was unusually well-informed about what went on at the White House—Lawrence had been Mr. Wilson's private secretary at Princeton —stating flatly the President's intention to issue an appeal to the country for a Democratic Congress. I knew enough of Mr. House's political philosophy to be certain that he could not have advised such a step, and in all probability knew nothing about it. We had an understanding that I could go to him at any time, day or night, with intelligence I deemed of sufficient importance. So I had no hesitation in interrupting him, although I knew how occupied was his time, and, indeed, had not expected to see him again until, as he had said at our last parting, "we meet in Paris."

He listened to my report with open disapproval.

"No, I didn't advise that," he said. "Of course, it's bad politics."

"Could it have been Burleson?" I asked.

"No, I don't think so," he answered slowly. "I think he would have let me know. I'll talk to the President, now."

I followed him to the study. He asked a couple of men there to excuse us, and closed the door behind him, picked up the direct telephone, and asked for the President. I heard what he said. After repeating my information, he said earnestly, in his slow drawl:

"Now, I wouldn't do that, if I were you, Governor. I believe you'd get just the same result if you asked the people to vote for men who'd support you, regardless of party. The people believe in you. They'll see the point."

There was conversation, back and forth—I could hear, but not understand, the President's clipped, precise voice—elaborating on this theme. Then he said "Good-by" and hung up the receiver. "I think it will be all right, my friend," he said. "He agreed with us. And I want to thank you for coming up. You were quite right."

Years later, after *The Intimate Papers* were ready for publication, he asked me to read the proofs of the last two volumes. I remarked to him about the version of the incident given by Dr. Seymour, and reminded him of our talk, and the telephone conversation with the President. He stared at me with the peculiar blank expression he adopted whenever he didn't want you to read his thoughts—his poker face.

"I know," he said. And after a pause, repeated: "I know."

That was sufficient to tell me that he did not wish to go further into the matter.*

5

The nine days following Mr. House's arrival in Paris, October 26, were probably the busiest, if not the most momentous, of his life. The Allied statesmen and military commanders were in the throes of drafting armistice terms, and they were floundering badly in a maze of the conflicting national interests which continually beset them. Almost the sole object the French, British and Italians shared in common was a blind, haphazard desire to extricate themselves from the obligations involved in acceptance of Mr. Wilson's Fourteen Points as a basis for those terms, and inferentially, of the future treaty. It was Mr. House who fused them to a common purpose, at the same time binding them to acknowledgment of their acceptance of the general principles the President had enunciated, and to which they had given lip service.

The day before his arrival, Foch had summoned the several commanders-in-chief to a conference at Senlis to submit his draft of the military terms of the Armistice. Haig and his advisers thought Foch's terms too severe; Pétain thought they were not severe enough; Pershing approved them, but five days afterward veered around to Pétain's point of view; Diaz, the Italian, was concerned only about Austria, of which stricken country his Government remained as fearful as they had been since Caporetto—they were astonished when the Austrians offered to surrender on the 30th. With Pershing's last-minute objections to Foch's terms Mr. House had scant patience. The principal difficulty, in the way of military approval of Foch's terms, came from Haig, who was obsessed with the idea that Germany would refuse to accept them. The British palpably wanted to quit fighting, probably because their lines of advance were more disrupted than those of the French and Americans and they would have the farthest distance to advance against opposition, as the German right wing swung back through Belgium. Haig, also, was impressed by the fact that he continued to meet organized resistance, and was making comparatively few captures of *matériel*. Foch, Pétain,

---

* Incidentally, any newspaperman will understand how popular I was in my office when, after assuring the editors that the appeal to the country would not be issued, it appeared a week or so later.

Pershing and Bliss—who, it will be remembered, was the American military member of the Supreme War Council and agreed with Pétain—knew, better than Haig, the ominous danger confronting the Germans from the thrust to encircle Metz, which was to be started November 14 by the newly formed American Second Army and a French army already mobilized in Lorraine. This British reluctance to weaken the powers of the German commanders to make trouble later was based, not on the quantity of armaments to be surrendered—Haig agreed with Foch's specifications—but on the Generalissimo's requirement for occupation, not only of the left bank of the Rhine, but of four bridgeheads on the right bank, which the British thought would rekindle the embers of Germany's national pride.

The question of military terms was not the only source of division in Allied circles. Foch, on his part, resisted the demands of the British Admiralty, supported by the French naval commanders, for the surrender by the Germans, in addition to 150 submarines, of ten battleships, six battle-cruisers and a number of light cruisers and destroyers. He was contemptuous of the value to the Germans of their surface fleet, and of all people, it was Lloyd George who agreed with him. One gains the idea from the deliberations of the Supreme War Council, which was now called the Allied Council, that the British Government and their Army commanders were anxious to terminate hostilities on any terms which would get the Germans out of Allied territory without additional loss of man power.

It was Mr. House's principle, in this situation, to adopt the opinions, as to military matters, of Foch as Generalissimo, and as to naval matters, of the British Admiralty. And mainly through his mediation, Foch's terms were accepted, and a compromise reached on the naval terms by which the British and French Admiralties were conciliated with a stipulation for the internment of the number of ships specified "in neutral ports to be designated by the Allies and the United States of America *or failing them, Allied ports.*" This convenient phrase was inserted at the last minute when it was found difficult to select a satisfactory neutral port, neutrals, naturally, not wishing to be charged with the responsibility either of offending Germany in her plight or of safeguarding so formidable an armada. The result was the last cruise of the core of the High Seas Fleet to Scapa Flow, and the scuttling of these first-line units of the Imperial German Navy.

Another controversial point, which was to vex the peace negotiations and to prove a sore spot for years afterwards, was introduced by Clemenceau at the meeting of the Council, November 1. This was for the in-

clusion of a clause providing for "reparation for damages," which, he
said, was "all I am asking." It was rejected, but he returned to it the
next day, and the Council finally accepted a clause in the financial section, written by Klotz, French Finance Minister: "With the reservation
that any future claims or demands on the part of the Allies remain un-
affected." Mr. House took for granted from the text of the debate that
this referred solely to Clemenceau's demand for "reparation for damages." He was reinforced in his conviction by a debate at the session,
November 3, between Lloyd George and Hymans, the Belgian Foreign
Minister, who wanted "a more ample phrase than merely 'damages to
the civilian population.'"

"It is then for indirect compensation that you ask?" said Lloyd George.

"I do not ask for it now, but I should like to have a phrase referring
to it," replied Hymans.

"I think it will be a mistake to put into the armistice terms anything
that will lead Germany to suppose that we want a war indemnity,"
insisted Lloyd George.

Hymans agreed. It never entered Mr. House's head, at that time, that
this seemingly harmless phrase would be employed at the Peace Conference as an excuse for the extortion of such punitive indemnities as were
involved in the cost of the war and pensions resulting from it. And
yet, a few weeks later, in the "khaki election" by which he intrenched
himself in power, the British Prime Minister was promising that he
would make the Germans pay for all they had cost Britain. But that
was after the Armistice had been signed, and the Sparticide Revolts had
demonstrated Germany's helplessness.

There was a controversy at the first session even as to the method by
which the Germans should be notified that the armistice terms were
ready for their consideration. The French, with understandable pride,
insisted that the Germans must request the terms; and Mr. House suggested that they should be communicated to President Wilson, and that
after he had endorsed them, he should inform the Germans their request
for an armistice would be granted. But this, objected Clemenceau,
would be the same as inviting the Germans to a conference, which he
was sure Foch would refuse to do—"and I would never permit him to
do it." Lloyd George settled the issue sensibly by amending Mr. House's
idea with a formula providing that the President should advise the
Germans to send a flag of truce to the French lines. This was October
29, before the Italians had heard of the Austrian offer of surrender, and
they protested that, if the Germans stayed hostilities and the Austrians
did not, this would leave them to carry on the war alone. Mr. House

occasionally found a sense of humor of great assistance to him in such
deliberations. As a matter of fact, the armistice terms for Austria were
settled before those for Germany, and the Dual Monarchy was out of
the war, November 4, seven days prior to her ally, a contributing factor
to Germany's willingness to accept the drastic terms imposed upon her.

For Mr. House, however, the most difficult aspect of his negotiations
in the period, October 26-November 4, was the sinister undercurrent of
opposition to formal and specific approval of the Fourteen Points, without which, he knew, the President would refuse to continue operations
with the Allies, an attitude of which he entirely approved. The hostility
of the Allies to the Fourteen Points, as binding on themselves, broke
out actively at the first session of the Council, October 29. The British
objected bitterly to Point II, the Freedom of the Seas; at one time or
another in the next few days, Lloyd George protested that, if he accepted
it, "it would only mean that in a week's time a new Prime Minister
would be here, who would say that he could not accept the principle";
and that "Britain would spend her last guinea to keep a navy superior
to that of the United States or any other power." He was also one with
the other Allies in wanting to make certain that Point VIII, dealing
with evacuation of occupied territories, be interpreted to include reparations for damage done.* The Italians didn't want to be bound by any
of the Points, and objected especially to IX, dealing with the readjustment of their frontiers. As for Clemenceau, he began by disliking the
whole Fourteen, but was frightened off when he realized that continued
discussion might imperil the inclusion of the United States in the Armistice. "It would amount to a separate peace between the United States
and the Central Powers?" he said interrogatively. And Mr. House re-
joined grimly: "It might."

His position was strengthened morally by a cable from the President,
on October 30, sent at his request and confirming him in the threat he
had made to Clemenceau. At that day's session, Clemenceau said that
he was having "an elaborate brief" prepared, "setting forth France's objections" to the entire program of the Fourteen Points. Mr. House
checkmated The Tiger by promptly suggesting that this undoubtedly
would incite the Italians to write a similar memorandum, with the certainty of intruding complications about their territorial ambitions, which,
he knew, Clemenceau wished to minimize. He added suavely: "If the
Allied Governments felt constrained to submit an elaborate answer to
the President containing many objections to his program, it would

---

* Another reason why Mr. House accepted the Klotz reservation.

doubtless be necessary for the President to go to Congress and to place before that body exactly what Italy, France and Great Britain were fighting for, and to place the responsibility upon Congress for the further continuation of the war by the United States in behalf of the aims of the Allies."

Clemenceau was visibly disturbed, and Mr. House proceeded to capitalize his advantage by showing the Premier a document which Lloyd George had handed him a few minutes before, the draft of an answer from the British Government to the President, explaining their position on the Fourteen Points. The first paragraph declared that "clause two, relating to what is usually described as the Freedom of the Seas, is open to various interpretations, some of which they"—the Government—"could not accept. They must therefore reserve to themselves complete freedom on this subject when they enter the Peace Conference." The second paragraph stated the feeling of the Allied Governments that Point VIII, as to restoration of German-occupied territories, should be understood to imply "that compensation will be made by Germany for all damage done to the civilian population of the Allies and their property, by the forces of Germany."

Mr. House was amused by the rapidity with which Clemenceau clutched at this excuse to avoid an *impasse*. He renounced his intention to draft objections, and adopted the limited exceptions of the British as his own, which was in line with Mr. House's aim to narrow the argument within bounds so strait as to restrict the Allies' opportunities for captiousness—in other words, jockeying for bargaining power at the Peace Conference. Of course, Mr. House knew that the last thing wanted by Clemenceau or Lloyd George was to have the United States withdraw from their support, and then be obliged to go before their peoples and explain how it happened.

The first benefit Mr. House derived from the consolidation of the British and French objections was to gain their support in resisting the demands of the Italians and Belgians. The Italians, who were against all the Fourteen Points simply because of the bargaining advantage this attitude gave them in arguing for repudiation of Point IX, were thrown out of court. The Belgians were satisfied with the recognition of rights of civilian populations for damages contained in the interpretation of Point VIII. But Mr. House was a long way from being finished with his battle, which raged intermittently throughout the following four days, for the acceptance by the British of the principle of the Freedom of the Seas. The British were genuinely concerned over the application of this new, vague, and never-resolved doctrine to the right of blockade, which they regarded as the keystone of their sea power. We have had an illustration, within the past year, of how important it is to the preservation of their Empire.

Mr. House was not disposed to resist their claim in this regard, and he secured an expression of opinion from Mr. Wilson that, while the law of blockade required altering—this had to do with the use of submarines (sic)—"there is no danger, however, that it will be abolished." And still Lloyd George shied away from it, with the invincible insularity of the sea-bound Briton. The only concession Mr. House could get from him was a letter, dated November 3, confirming a verbal statement "that we were quite willing to discuss the Freedom of the Seas in the light of the new conditions which have arisen in the course of the present war."

This, as all the statesmen concerned understood, meant that it was to be thoroughly threshed out at the Peace Conference, but Mr. Wilson never made use of the opportunity—as Mr. House thought, because of the President's faith that, with the establishment of the League of Nations, the Freedom of the Seas ceased to be a doctrine concerning any one or two or more nations. The seas *were* free, and guaranteed to be so by the League's machinery. A misplaced confidence for which the world is paying dearly today.

On November 4, Mr. House was able to forward to his friend an Allied memorandum, definitely endorsing the Fourteen Points, defining the meaning of "reparation," as has been described above, and reserving free discussion on Point II. With it went a note stating that the Germans would receive terms for an armistice if they addressed Marshal Foch. Mr. Wilson made no criticism of the wording of the memorandum, and forwarded it, together with a copy of the note on Armistice terms, to the German Government. Evidently, he was satisfied with the arrangement Mr. House had concluded. Mr. House himself thought the exceptions taken by the Allies tended to strengthen the President's, and weaken the Allied statesmen's, positions in the Peace Conference. Certainly the Germans took no account of the two exceptions to the Fourteen Points. They signed the Armistice at 5:30 o'clock in the morning of November 11, without reservations. Whether there was justification for the complaint of their delegates to Versailles, that the Treaty was not fairly based on the Fourteen Points, is a question which will probably be debated as long as men remember the document and its after-effects. But nobody can dispute the fact that, without this widespread belief in Germany, Hitler could never have created the Third Reich or warped the German people into tolerance of the cruel, rapacious and intolerant practices of his Nazi followers.*

6

The undercurrents of antagonism to American ideals, as much as the crossplay of conflicting ambitions between the Allies, which Mr. House had detected in the Armistice negotiations, inspired him with misgivings for the impending Peace Conference. And these misgivings were strengthened by the President's personal defeat in the Congressional elections, which, he knew, had undermined Mr. Wilson's prestige with British and French statesmen. He foresaw endless wrangling and delay in the deliberations of the Conference, and hungry, war-torn, socially embittered Europe could not afford postponement of a return to something approaching normal living conditions. Bolshevism was spilling over the frontiers of Russia, which was being tormented anew by the brutal grapplings of Red and White armies. Anarchy prevailed in Finland and the Baltic States. In Austria-Hungary, the King-Emperor Karl abdicated, November 13, and Republican governments were proclaimed. Bolshevist agents were working in Budapest, preparing the way for Bela Kun's brief Soviet. Nobody knew what was going to happen in Germany, except that the reports of French Secret Service agents led Foch to exclaim with satisfaction that she was "flat." Starvation reigned from the Rhine to the Baltic, and east of Switzerland to the extremities of Russia. The Balkans were a waste. In the Allied countries the people were only less cold and hungry than in the other lands, where old people and children were dying by hundreds of thousands, and typhus took a hideous toll, and soon, with the tightening of winter, the worst epidemic of influenza the world had ever known would reap a richer harvest from weakened populations than man had been able to obtain by abuse of his own inventions.

It seemed to Mr. House, in this ghastly situation—which grew ghastlier, week by week—that the best way to salvage Europe from her woes would be by the adoption of a quick preliminary treaty of peace, an elaboration of the terms of the Armistice, supplemented by a tentative

* A sorry commentary on human nature was contained in a speech by the President of the American Club of Paris at a Washington's Birthday Dinner, February 22, 1940. He characterized the twenty-one years between November 11, 1918, and September 3, 1939, as one long Armistice. The "new war," he added, was simply a continuation of the old. Of course, he was right.

delineation of German frontiers and an acknowledgment of reparations
—these last, remember, in his mind, to be limited to damages done in
the occupied territories, and possibly at sea. The acceptance of the principle of the League of Nations could be included in the terms of the
temporary treaty, binding upon all signatories. This procedure, he believed, would permit early disarmament, and readjustment of the nations'
economies to peacetime conditions. It would afford the delegates to the
Conference ample leisure to sit down and frame deliberately, in an
atmosphere of decreasing hatred, a thoughtful reorganization of world
society.

The idea was so sound that there was practically no opposition to it.
Clemenceau, who remarked practically that it would take a year to draft
a definitive treaty, accepted it finally when Foch assured him the military terms could be drawn up in forty-eight hours. He had been unwilling, otherwise, to agree to demobilization until after a definitive treaty
had been accepted by Germany. Lloyd George, Balfour and the other
Britishers were more favorable towards the plan than the French
Premier. *But this was in the first half of February.* A preliminary
treaty, even then, would have been to the advantage of all concerned.
It would have staved off much suffering, and in all probability have
permitted the drafting of a definitive treaty which would have been
less harmful in its consequences than the Treaty of Versailles, with
equal advantages accruing to the treaties imposed upon the other enemy
powers.

Mr. House's original idea, however, had been to proceed with the
drafting of the temporary treaty as soon as the Armistice was signed
by Germany. He was thwarted in this, in the first place, by Mr. Wilson's
insistence upon attending the Conference, and his delay in coming to
Paris, occasioned by his desire to deliver his annual message to Congress,
December 2. This made impossible the procedure Mr. House desired,
and was not one of the least harmful results of the President's determination to steer the peace negotiations in person. On the other hand, it
would be unfair to place the full responsibility upon Mr. Wilson's shoulders. All the Allied Premiers wanted to delay the Conference. All, and
especially Lloyd George, had political fences to mend; they felt the need
of consolidating their positions at home. And perhaps it was no more
than human that they hesitated at the idea of a Preliminary Peace, sus-
pecting they would lose, in a less bellicose world mood—as must have
been the case, with the passage of time—some of the profits of war they
had been promising their peoples. Yet it is indicative of the validity of
Mr. House's plan that discussion of a Preliminary Treaty persisted in

the Conference until after the President's return to Paris on his second trip abroad. Balfour points out, in a special memorandum contained in *The Intimate Papers,* that as late as April 25, 1918, a report to the Council of Four from the Naval experts was headed: "Draft articles concerning the Kiel Canal for insertion in the *Preliminary Treaty of Peace with Germany."* And he proceeds to remark: "It has not been found possible to trace when the idea of a Preliminary Peace was dropped. No formal decision seems to have been taken on the subject." If there was a particular reason, at this late date, it was probably the delay of more than two months in preparing the Military Terms, which Foch had casually promised to deliver in "forty-eight hours." Foch thought like a soldier; he had no comprehension of the tediousness of diplomatic procedure.*

Whatever the reasons for the failure of his plan, Mr. House always thought that, had it been possible or practicable to draft a Preliminary Treaty immediately after the Armistice, or even within the first six weeks of the Conference, the result would have been to stabilize the European situation so as to curtail the revolutionary movement in Germany, and give business a chance to get on its feet in time to avert the wave of currency inflation, which later swept the Continent with incalculable loss to all peoples. It would certainly have given the German Republic of the Second Reich a better chance to survive. As it was, Europe and the rest of the world were maintained in a state of suspension and fearful anticipation for almost eight months, from November 11 up to the signing of the Treaty of Versailles, June 28, by Germany's resentful delegates.

In the meantime, nationalism was running rampant in the victor countries, and serious statesmen like Clemenceau and Lloyd George were talking largely of "trying" and "hanging" the Kaiser. It is humorous to reflect that while the menaces of these leaders of great nations came to nothing, a real attempt to seize his person, and spirit him off to condign

---

* Mr. Wilson seems to have been suspicious of the original idea of a Preliminary Treaty because it included no more than a pledge by the belligerents to accept the principle of a League of Nations. He was willing to accept a strictly Military and Naval Treaty, but his discovery, after his return to Paris in March, 1919, that the Council of Four—on which Mr. House had sat for him—had been trying to expedite the territorial and financial terms, inspired him and his biographer, Baker, with the belief that an attempt was being made to smother his ideals for a just peace. He never realized that the time for a Preliminary Treaty had passed. Too much time had been consumed over the League. But he was no foggier in mind, by now, than his associates, including Mr. House. The truth was that all these men were attempting a task beyond human capacity, within the time limits allowed them by the pressure of events over which they had no control.

punishment, was made by a little band of Tennesseeans from the American Army, apparently in a mood compounded of Armistice boredom and hilarity. They succeeded in reaching Count Bentinck's chateau, and were apprehended by the Dutch authorities—through the presence of mind of the Kaiser's entourage. It was a harebrained, graceless exploit, but if it did nothing else it frightened the British and French statesmen into realization of the foolish illegality they were threatening to undertake. What a commentary! That America's own Judge Lynch and his noose-law should have to teach a lesson to Clemenceau and Lloyd George.*

7

President Wilson's decision to head the American Commission to Negotiate Peace, and the policy he adopted in selecting the three Commissioners to serve with himself and Mr. House, had a profound effect upon his own future, upon the attitude of the Allied chiefs of state, and upon the whole course of the Conference. As has been shown, his decision to go to Paris, and the delay in his departure from Washington, frustrated Mr. House's ambitious plan for a temporary treaty to be concluded as soon as possible after the Armistice, and conversely encouraged the Allied statesmen in their disposition to string out the proceedings so as to give them more time in which to maneuver for position and bolster their claims for nationalistic advantages—in plain words, to reckon just how much they could take from Germany and her allies.

Mr. House thought his friend was making a mistake in coming to Paris. The subject had been broached several times by Mr. Wilson during the months preceding Mr. House's departure in October. Whether he was right or not, Mr. House deduced from the way the President talked that he was not asking for an opinion; indeed, that he would not welcome an opinion on the wisdom or lack of wisdom in his decision. Mr. Wilson simply stated that when the Peace Conference was held he intended to head the American delegation. There was no precedent for such a mission for a President, he owned, but he considered that the circumstances, the extraordinary devastation of this greatest of wars in history, the hazards to future civilization, the necessity of reconstructing the world's scheme of international relations, all these justified him in the departure from tradition. Mr. House, himself no re-

---

* This performance was hushed up at the time, but it was common gossip in the A.E.F., and the Allied Governments heard of it after the Dutch filed a vigorous protest with the United States. The "hang the Kaiser" talk continued, but there was no heart in it.

specter of precedent and tradition in politics, was still disposed to doubt
that it would be a good thing for Woodrow Wilson or the Peace Conference. But his lips were sealed. It would have been sufficiently difficult for him to counsel against the President's wish, even had he been
asked for an opinion. He contented himself with remaining silent when
the subject was discussed, except in so far as he was asked about details
of arrangements.

"What could a man in my position have said?" he asked, in discussing
it. "If the President hadn't gone to Paris, I should have headed the
delegation. It would have looked to him or to anyone as if I resented
being deprived of the honor, if I advised him not to go. I hoped I was
wrong, but I wasn't."

That Mr. House was not wrong in his forebodings became evident as
soon as the Allied Governments were apprised that the President was
coming. Mr. House was placed, despite himself, in the embarrassing
position of having to advise his friend that he could not expect to be
presiding officer of a Peace Conference held in the capital of a belligerent
state, which considered itself the chief sufferer of the war and entertained
peculiar ambitions for avenging former slights received at the hands of
Germany. Also, that the Allied Chiefs of State resented the idea that he,
a sovereign, and their superior by European standards, should sit in the
Conference with them. He would place them at a disadvantage, urged
Clemenceau, and Reading, for Lloyd George, spoke as directly to the
same effect. Clemenceau began by being very tart about it. He was
planning to dominate the Conference, and he didn't want anyone to
share the spotlight with him. He suggested that he and the other Chiefs
of State should visit the President at his residence and arrange programs
informally with him, the decisions taken at these meetings to be formally
adopted by sessions at the Quai d'Orsay.

The feeling of the Europeans was so strong, and was shared by so
many of the American friends of the President in Paris, London and
Washington, that Mr. House was compelled to cable his friend, November 14: "Clemenceau has just told me that he hopes you will not sit in
the Congress because no head of a state should sit there. The same
feeling prevails in England. . . . Everyone wants you to come over to
take part in the preliminary conference. . . . It is of vital importance, I
think, for you to come as soon as possible, for everything is being held
in abeyance. . . . In announcing your departure, I think, it is important
that you should not state that you will sit at the Peace Conference."

The President was angered by this message, which, indeed, may have
served to widen a little further the crevasse between the two friends.

He responded in a tone to which Mr. House was not accustomed, although its sharpness was intended primarily for Clemenceau and the English marplots, as Mr. Wilson considered them: "I infer that the French and British leaders desire to exclude me from the Conference for fear I might lead the weaker nations against them. . . . I play the same part in our Government as the Prime Ministers play in theirs. The fact that I am head of the state is of no practical importance. . . . It is universally expected and generally desired here that I should attend the Conference, but I believe that no one would wish me to sit by and try to steer from the outside."

That settled the matter. Mr. Wilson heeded Mr. House's advice to the extent of confining his announcement of his trip to the ambiguous phrase that he was sailing "for the purpose of taking part in the discussions and the settlement of the main features of the Treaty of Peace. It is not likely that it will be possible for him to remain throughout the sessions of the formal Peace Conference." But it was impossible, after Mr. Wilson had gone so far in making known his determination to participate in the active negotiations, for Mr. House to permit his friend to be "pocketed"—Mr. Wilson's own expression—by the jealousies and suspicions of Lloyd George, Clemenceau, Sonnino, and the statesmen of the smaller countries who took color from them. To have done so would have been to undermine the prestige of the United States, let alone the President's. So Mr. House let it be known quietly that the President, as a man of sense, would decide after his arrival the question of his sitting in the Conference; but in such a way that the opponents of Mr. Wilson resigned themselves to the inevitable. By the time of the President's arrival, Clemenceau was expressing approval of his intention, and the British had tacitly accepted it. Mr. House had a suspicion that Clemenceau's change of mind was due to his having reasoned out the probable consequences to the President of vulgar contiguity. "It might be that he believes it will pull Wilson down from his high pedestal," the Texan jotted, with rare cynicism, in his diary.

He could never understand how his friend, a student of Constitutional history and of the theory and practice of government, had failed to appreciate the two factors which must work against him in this self-appointed mission. To Mr. House one of the idiosyncrasies of the American system was the combination in one man of the positions of sovereign, chief of state and party leader. The objections of the European statesmen were well founded. There was no sovereign in the Western world who possessed the powers of the American President. Mr. Wilson, in Paris, either had to hold himself a notch above his associates of the Council of Four or yield something of his authority. Furthermore, in coming to Paris he surrendered the unique supremacy he had won in the world crisis through his assumption, under his friend's advisement, of the role of prophet, oracle and lawgiver. Such a role, as has been said before, required the spell of mystery, of aloofness. It was imposing only at a distance. In Paris, Mr. Wilson became just another statesman, wearing the same kind of clothes, eating food like common men, occasionally losing his temper in a very human way. The common people, during his first two months in Europe, regarded him with awe as a superhuman being, burnt candles before his picture, crossed themselves when he passed in the street, named babies after him; but the moment he resisted the demands of their leaders they turned upon him with a revulsion of hatred which knew no reason. Streets named after him were renamed. Sullen crowds reviled him. It was necessary for Mr. House to speak stiffly to Clemenceau about the unbridled license of denunciation in the Paris press. Clemenceau changed that overnight. He couldn't get on so well without Mr. Wilson in Paris, now. He had discovered that the President was concerned primarily with the League. And then, too, the President was an asset in taking the brunt of checking the pestiferous Italians. So Clemenceau played him against Orlando, and Lloyd George played him against Clemenceau, and the three played him against the Japanese and the small fry, at need.

The President's policy of ignoring the Republican party, in naming the three additional Peace Commissioners, was likewise to prove a source of fatal embarrassment to his plans for world reorganization. Mr. House, on frequent occasions, advised him, with an insistence the Texan seldom permitted himself, to nominate one or two Republicans who were congenial to these plans. Both Taft and Root, Mr. House pointed out, could be relied upon to work harmoniously with the delegation. They were among the staunchest advocates of the kind of League his friend wanted, and they had given utterance to valuable nonpartisan support of Mr. Wilson's expressions of war aims, notably the Fourteen Points. Their presence on the Commission would lend weight to its suggestions in the eyes of Europeans, and would add to its prestige at home. Mr. House thought, too, that, as a representative of the Cabinet, McAdoo would be a better choice than Lansing, although he did not belittle the Secretary of State. His contention, without assuming any vanity, was that he had a more intimate acquaintance than Lansing with the personalities at the Conference and the general diplomatic problems to be covered. It was futile, then, to have two diplomatic Commissioners. McAdoo, however, had a first-hand knowledge of the finan-

cial problems, and could have waded into the thorny questions of reparations and economic readjustments with an authority not possessed by
the Commission's advisers from private life, wise and efficient as they
were. Lansing's position in Paris was further complicated by his dissension to the President's purely idealistic concepts. Lansing was a thoroughly practical lawyer, with an analytical, legalistic mind. His criticisms and objections got under the President's hide, and paved the way
for his arbitrary and unjust dismissal after Mr. Wilson's judgment had
been warped by illness and enforced solitude.*

"Why, after the November elections," Mr. House said, in a long-
subsequent conversation on this subject, "I would have named Lodge.
He was going to be Chairman of the Foreign Relations Committee, and
he was showing a disposition to be nasty. But if the President had fed
him a lump of sugar he'd have been the most pleased old feller in
Massachusetts. It would have been a nice gesture to the Senate, and
would have taken the sting out of the President's manifesto for a Democratic Congress. The country would have liked it. But you could never
make the President see that sometimes the best way to handle an opponent is to take him into camp with you."

Of the other Commissioners, besides Lansing, General Bliss was one
of the agreeable surprises of the Conference. With a splendid record as
a soldier, he reinforced by his work the reputation for statesmanlike
qualities he had begun to accumulate as a member of the Supreme War
Council. The one objection to him was that, as a soldier, he had no
political connection, and hence was of no value to the President in winning friends at home, either in the Democratic or Republican ranks.
The fifth Commissioner, Henry White, was an amiable gentleman, of
unimpeachable ancestry, who had married a Vanderbilt and was nomi-

---

* Lansing was in a most difficult situation in Paris. The Secretary of State found
himself intrusted with secondary duties. The Allied statesmen took most of their
problems to Mr. House, if they did not go to the President. It must have seemed
to him occasionally that Mr. House was Secretary of State, and he a mere member
of the American Commission. He would not have been human if this had failed
to irk him. In Washington, it was one thing to know that the Ambassadors
accredited to him, and the belligerents' Foreign Offices, were in more intimate contact with the Texan than with himself. Mr. House was in New York. But in
Paris, the same situation developed under his nose, in the Hotel Crillon, where both
he and Mr. House lived and worked. The fact that the President showed a marked
preference for Mr. House's counsel did not help matters. It was apparent to all
who saw him that he was under a continuous strain, despite his unfailing courtesy
of demeanor. If, in the end, he came to nourish a certain resentment against his
situation, Mr. House was the last man to blame him for it. Their relations were
outwardly cordial, at least, and so far as Mr. House was concerned, genuinely so.

nally a Republican. He had never been a worker for the party, and
the Republican politicians resented his selection as much as though he
had been a Democrat. He brought to his work a fluent knowledge
of French, Italian and German, which none of the other Commissioners
could boast, and admirable connections with European aristocrats gained
in the Diplomatic Service. His services to the Commission were routine,
and were exceeded in value by those of many of the experts—for example,
Arthur Hugh Frazier, of the Paris Embassy, and Colonel Stephen Bonsal
(in the diplomatic field), and Baruch and Lamont (in the complicated
sphere of economics). This is said despite a statement by Mr. House,
quoted in *The Intimate Papers:* "White's lifelong diplomatic career and
wide European acquaintance smoothed over many a difficult situation.
If there was ever the need of a peacemaker it was at Paris, and White
proved himself time and again master of that craft." One of Mr.
House's failings was an unwillingness to find fault when nothing could
be gained by fault-finding; but he was under no illusions about White,
who was anything but a peacemaker.*

It is indicative of that widening crevasse between Mr. House and
Mr. Wilson, that the President did not see fit to consult him as to these
three appointments, none of which was determined upon until after the
election. It may be said, with reason, that the President was under no
obligation to consult his friend as to the men with whom both of them
would have to work during the trying months ahead. There was none.
But the fact that Mr. Wilson failed to do so was in striking contrast with
the course he had followed, up to this time, throughout his Administration. It meant that he was aware his selections would not meet with
Mr. House's approval, and that he did not care that this was so. He
was determined to snub the Republican party, and to demonstrate to
the country that he was superior to the political code of courtesy, which
hitherto had prevailed in selecting delegations to international conferences.

This was a new Woodrow Wilson. Mr. House was not happy, as he
set about the task of organizing the elaborate preparations for the Conference.

* See, for his troublemaking propensities, Mrs. Wilson's book.

Book 9

The Peace That Was No Peace

I

PRESIDENT WILSON landed at Brest on Friday, December 13. Sailors and newspapermen wagged their heads solemnly, and predicted a jinx on his future; but the President believed the date a good omen, since he regarded thirteen as his lucky number, and Friday could only accentuate its beneficence. An odd superstition for a man of his mentality. He had gone so far in early life as to drop his first name, Thomas, not so much for conciseness as because the letters of Woodrow Wilson numbered thirteen. He came to France in the best of spirits, apparently not yet having realized the blow to his prestige he had sustained in the November elections, the significance of which had registered with politicians as adroit as Clemenceau and Lloyd George. And the plain truth is that, if he had entertained misgivings, they must have been banished by the ovations accorded him in Paris, London and Rome. He seemed to Europeans in this dark, dreary December, 1918, like a figure of almost supernatural portent, literally a new saviour of mankind, or, perhaps, a Jove sprung from the loins of the fabulous New World. But instead of thunderbolts his admirers pictured him as armed with the promise of a happiness and security which they craved with a hunger doomed never to be satisfied. It was a role beyond the capacity of any human being. It was to be a curse to the man called upon to assume it.

This Europe to which he came was very weary, frightened, either sullenly resentful or revengeful. The Chiefs of State, with whom he would be obliged to dicker on a plane to which he was unaccustomed, were all men of great nervous vitality, much more so than himself; but each mirrored the psychic neuroticism of the mass of the population. They were weary, too. The ecstasy of victory was losing its stimulus. Already a month had elapsed since the Armistice, which had been renewed—as it must be, again and again—as a reluctant creditor extends a note for a debtor he is determined to bleed to the last penny. Men's thoughts, now, were concerned with the division of the spoils. How much could the enemy pay? Not with comfort, but under the muzzles

291

of cannon. Their perceptions blunted by the strain of four and a half years of agony, by the very magnitude of the responsibilities and sensations they had been compelled to suffer, the Chiefs of State were in no mood for an idealistic settlement of the issues at stake. They wanted security and profit, not the brotherhood of man, working in common for the common good, which was Woodrow Wilson's ambition. They had, as Clemenceau revealed in his satirical comment to the Chamber, December 29, little use for the *"noble candeur"* of Monsieur Wilson. But of this Mr. Wilson took less account than Mr. House. He had the peoples with him, hadn't he? After a decade of public office, his faith was unshaken in the mass instinct of the people. Deal fairly with them, tell them the truth—and they would follow you. So he believed, not understanding, apparently, that the people have a parallel mass instinct: they recognize the mistakes of their leaders, occurring from incognate thinking.

Mr. House received his friend in Paris with mingled feelings. The Texan had been ill for several weeks, would resume his labors too soon, and succumb again, in mid-January, to the prevalent influenza, with consequences which may well have contributed materially to the frustration of the ambitions he entertained jointly with Mr. Wilson. But throughout his illness Mr. House had kept in touch with what was going on, had endeavored to steer the course of events in his friend's favor. And he did not like the ideas he sensed to be developing beneath the surface of the complex situation, which shifted back and forth from Paris to London and the other capitals. Men's emotions were getting out of hand. Thinking was becoming confused. With the increasing realization of Germany's helplessness, a predatory feeling was being fanned to flame in the Allied countries. Lloyd George and his military "yes man," Sir Henry Wilson, who had been fearful the Armistice terms were too stiff, were becoming as virulently determined as Clemenceau to wring from Germany every *pfennig* she could pay, short of a starvation worse than was currently destroying her old people and children.

As a matter of fact, the Allies needed the President's intellectual guidance more than ever, but Mr. House suspected uncomfortably that speeches and addresses, which would have echoed across the world when delivered in Washington, would be muffled and dissonant in the fetid atmosphere of Paris. He hoped not. Everything depended upon how Mr. Wilson handled himself in an unfamiliar and more or less unpleasant *milieu,* how well he adjusted himself to meeting jealous or hostile personalities. This was no occasion for the "single-track" mind, of which his friend liked to boast deprecatingly. It demanded flexibility, toler-

ance, farsightedness, iron control of temper and prejudice. Every quality, indeed, which Mr. Wilson had failed to reveal in the past. The one
circumstance which encouraged Mr. House was that his friend's affection and confidence in him seemed as strong as ever. If they could continue to work together, harmoniously, complementarily, they ought to be
able to frustrate the forces of selfishness which were bent upon turning
the peace into an engine of persecution, a breeding-ground for future
wars. The League was everything, as Mr. House saw it. Upon it, if it
was created in the image they had conceived, they might rely for correction of the injustices inseparable from any peace.

He was pleased to find Mr. Wilson even more disposed than himself
to place the League first in the task confronting them. And he was also
pleased to be able to retire from the center of the stage, which he had
occupied against his inclination. He was always most at ease when working in the shadows. It was typical of him that he failed to understand
the position he had acquired with European statesmen during the war
years and the brief post-armistice period. Nobody—not even Woodrow
Wilson, legendary figure though he was—could take from him that position, despite his inclination to yield it. For it was founded upon a conviction, shared by all schools of European political thought, of his probity,
fairness and wisdom. He had managed, in the last five years, to wind
his way in and out of the toils of diplomacy without making an enemy
of importance. Men who were not his friends believed in him; his intimates placed his counsel above that of their colleagues. He was easy to
talk to. He did not assert his dignity. He was familiar with all the
major problems to be discussed, and when he lacked knowledge of a specific subject, he knew where to go for it. Hence, whatever his wish, it
was impossible for him to step off-stage. He had to share the spot-light
with Mr. Wilson, Clemenceau and Lloyd George. And this was to
make for trouble. He was to be cast in the part of trouble-shooter of the
Conference, which meant that he would be constantly in the foreground,
a shining mark for everyone who had an ax to grind with the President.
It meant, too, that whenever someone stupidly or maleficently resuscitated a problem he had solved for a less apt solution, the final blame
would be his in the eyes of those who were intent upon shielding Mr.
Wilson from all blame.

He was to be the victim of his own friends almost as much as of the
little group of intimates who dinned suspicions of him into Mr. Wilson's ear.

2

While the President went off on his tour of the Allied capitals, Mr. House continued to devote himself to the thankless job of organizing, as thoroughly as possible, the machinery for the Peace Conference. He adopted, as a primary objective, the rule he had formulated for the Armistice conferences: "As soon as you get more than ten men in a room everyone wants to make a speech." His theory was to split up the problems amongst committees of experts, working under subcommittees of the several Commissions of plenipotentiaries. He devised, for instance, the Council of Ten—composed of Mr. Wilson and Secretary Lansing or himself, and the Premiers and Foreign Ministers of France, Britain, Italy and Japan—which, ultimately, was reduced for efficiency's sake to the Council of Four: Wilson, Clemenceau, Lloyd George and Orlando. The Japanese took small interest in the Councils of Ten and Four until near the end of the Conference, when, naturally irritated by refusal of their request for a racial equality clause in the League Covenant, and the suspicions cast upon their good faith as to the Shantung recession, they demanded a seat on the smaller Council. It was theirs of right, and they were accorded it.

One reason for Mr. House's return to importance in Paris was the President's absorption, during the early weeks of the Conference, in the subject of the League. This threw upon Mr. House the responsibility of the infinitely laborious, personal negotiations with the other Chiefs of State and Foreign Ministers, dealing with problems equally important— in the eyes of the Europeans, more so. Roughly, the Conference was confronted by seven major problems: the League Covenant; Germany's eastern and western boundaries, and security measures for France's satisfaction; the amount of Reparations, and measures for collecting them; Italy's claims upon Austria, and the allocation of the Slav lands of the Dual Monarchy to Serbia, Rumania, Czecho-Slovakia and Poland; Japan's claims; the territorial limits of the new nations; and Russia.

As to the Covenant, Mr. House was in substantial agreement with his friend. His chief contribution to what was done in Paris consisted in harmonizing conflicting points of view between the President and the Allied delegations. The most serious difficulty, at first, was the insistence by France upon the constitution of the League as a super-military State, either with an international army or an international general staff, its objective being to curb Germany. Both the Americans and the British were unalterably opposed to such an idea. And probably no one but Mr. House could have persuaded Clemenceau to abandon it, over the objections of his own advisers. "'You are right,' Mr. House quotes the French Premier in his diary, January 7, 1919. 'I am for the League of Nations as you have it in mind and you may count upon me to work with you. . . . I think of you as a brother . . . and we will work together just as if we were parts of the same Government.'"

One must have known something of Clemenceau to appreciate what this implied, especially since the doughty, egoistic, irascible old Tiger regarded Mr. Wilson with a blend of dislike, apprehension and veiled contempt—not too veiled, sometimes. He sneered at the President for being "Christlike," and the two quarreled more than once. At a session over the disposition of the Saar, one of the thorny points upon which Mr. Wilson was compelled to compromise, on March 28, they came to an open breach. The President demanded whether Clemenceau wished him "to return home." "I do not wish you to go home," snapped Clemenceau, "but I intend to do so myself." Which he did. The honors were with Mr. Wilson, on this occasion, but he showed that he was worried when he told his advisers the next morning: "I do not know whether the Peace Conference will continue. M. Clemenceau called me a pro-German and abruptly left the room."

This incident dramatized an embarrassing situation of Mr. Wilson's own creation. He had insisted upon sitting in at the Conference. In order to do so, he had foregone his superiority as a sovereign. He was not used to dealing on equal terms with men who were his equals, and when he did so he often irritated them profoundly by his bearing and manner of speech. So reserved and reasonable a person as Lord Robert Cecil once refused to have further intercourse with him, and was only persuaded to resume their meetings by Mr. House's tact and a change in Mr. Wilson's attitude. Lloyd George, who had a very pretty temper and an arrogance beyond most sovereigns', was known to throw up his hands, with a sputter of sulphurous language, after emerging from an hour with the President. It might be added that the President was most objectionable to his European associates when he was right in his arguments. Another one of his difficulties. He had never learned from Mr. House that the more right a man is, the more he can afford to help his opponent to feel that the value of the idea came from mutual effort.

The question of Mandates for the disposition of the German colonies and the Arab sections of the Turkish Empire was likewise a source of prolonged dissensions, too complicated for narration here, over the terms upon which the Mandates were to be distributed, held and administered. Much that was done was done hastily, and the injustices of the Sykes-Picot Treaty and the Balfour Declaration on Palestine were to plague the British for years to come. With these matters, however, Mr. House and the President had little to do. They were the products of the Secret Treaties entered into before the United States became a belligerent. All the Americans sought was to see to it that the idea of conquest was relinquished for the principle of administration of these lands under the supervision of the League, and on conditions—which Japan has since made a dead letter—contingent upon the League's satisfaction. There was a hint of future developments, by the way, in the fact that Japan, the least contentious of the Allies, was forced, against her will, to precipitate one of the meanest problems of the Conference by the domineering policy of Premier Hughes of Australia in refusing to countenance a racial equality clause in the Covenant.

The Covenant, resulting from weeks of hectic debate, was a reasonably efficient instrument, all the more so because it failed to satisfy the extremists, who wanted either a super-State over all States or an impotent central bureau for the collection of statistics. The Europeans, who began by being skeptical of the utility of the idea, accepted it finally with enthusiasm. The greatest strain upon its structure was imposed by the preliminary demands of the Senate, which were a direct consequence of Mr. Wilson's personal errors of judgment and lack of political tact. It says much for the work done on the fundamentals in Paris that the other nations were perfectly willing to accept the Senate's demands of March, 1919. But the Allied Statesmen would scarcely have been human had they not taken advantage of the President, when he returned to Paris from Washington with a demand for the protection of the Monroe Doctrine, to pry from him concessions on such items as the Saar Basin, Reparations and the Austro-Italian frontier. There was never any serious objection on their part to inclusion of the Covenant in the Treaty, which was still another obsession of his. The objections came from the Republican majority of the Senate, but even the Senate was willing to tolerate this device to bind the League more firmly into the international structure, after its criticisms were accepted. Looking backward, one is inclined to wonder whether Mr. House and the President were not wrong in emphasizing this point. As a part of the Treaty of Versailles, the Covenant was burdened with a share of the ignominy heaped upon the master document. If it had been negotiated and signed separately, it could have stood on its own feet for what it was worth.

The problem of German boundaries on the west—with France—precipitated one of the bitterest controversies of those turgid, stormy months. Mr. Wilson stood like a rock against Clemenceau's demands for the creation of a buffer State, the Rhenish Republic, and yielded on the temporary allocation of the Saar Basin to France only because it was understood that the product of the coal mines should be charged against the destruction of mines in German-occupied territory, and the future of the region was to be decided by a plebiscite, under the jurisdiction of the League, after the French had obtained a quantity of coal sufficient to indemnify them. He resisted all suggestions for a buffer State, including Mr. House's well-meant, but ill-advised, plan for one similarly based upon the right of ultimate disposition by plebiscite. The farthest he would go was to agree to demilitarization of the Rhineland, and for the termination of that status by Hitler France has herself to blame. It is difficult to see why he was afterwards so pilloried for these settlements of a most vexed and perplexing question. His great mistake, in which Mr. House and the other Commissioners had almost equal share, was in yielding, against the unanimous advice of his financial experts, to the fantastical, utterly uneconomic Reparations clauses. But that is a subject for later and more elaborate discussion.

He erred, too, in yielding to Italy's demands upon Austria, but it is quite true that he frustrated her most outrageous claims. He certainly played cheap American politics in withholding endorsement of Japan's request for an expression of racial equality in the Covenant, to which all races were invited to subscribe; and he seems to have displayed his usual diplomatic awkwardness in negotiation in the conduct of the deliberations on the method of disposing of the German territorial rights and economic claims in Shantung. But here, again, Mr. House must share superficial responsibility with him, although Mr. House would appear to have taken the long-range view of problems which were involved with the feelings and prejudices of other countries. The Japanese were in a strong position in Paris. They managed their affairs intelligently and reasonably. They asked for comparatively little, and most of what they desired they should have been granted. As a matter of prestige, alone, they demanded the transfer to them of Germany's title to Shantung, as conquerors of the peninsula, pledging a recession of all save the economic rights to China. They kept their pledge. What they have done since in Shantung and other parts of China has nothing to do with their claims under the Treaty of Versailles, except that the confusion resulting from the Treaty, and the breakdown of the League, undoubtedly encouraged them in the formulation of their China policy of the past decade.

Mr. House was in closer touch than Mr. Wilson with the organization of the new nations which were formed out of the wreckage of Russia and the Central Empires. The President did little in these matters, beyond giving voice to the opinions of the Commission's experts; but Mr. House, through his connections with Paderewski, Masaryk, Beneš and the Balkan statesmen, exerted a personal influence which did much to smooth the first steps of these infant or enlarged States. It was one of his essential characteristics, however, that all he did he did in the name of his friend. "When you write about the Czechs," he would say, "don't mention me. Talk of the President. They couldn't get anywhere without him."

Russia was the insuperable problem of the Peace Conference, which, strictly speaking, could or would have nothing to do with her unless the Bolshevists were willing to cooperate with the United States and the Allies. This they declined to do by rejecting an invitation to a conference on Prinkipo Island, in the Sea of Marmora, with the Western powers and representatives of the other Russian factions. To make the situation more difficult, the United States and the Allies were at odds over it, and the Allies were hopelessly divided amongst themselves. Mr. Wilson and his colleagues were firmly set against any participation in acts of intervention. Their one desire was to get the American Siberian column home as soon as possible. The British military men wanted to put an army into the Crimea—on American money; but the Cabinet were split on the question. The Italians saw no profit to themselves in Russian adventures. Only the French were eager to extend a hand to the White Armies, and they, too, must have American backing if they were to be successful. There was a general failure by all the Allies to grasp the facts as to what was happening in the vast area spanning a continent and a half. Their diplomats disagreed, their soldiers disagreed, their business men disagreed. So there was a deal of talk, and nothing done, except later the dispatch to Poland of a few hundred French staff officers, who improvised an organization capable of turning back Budenny's Red Armies in front of Warsaw. Really, stray bands and columns of adventurous Germans had more to do with salving the Baltic peoples from Bolshevism. If the French hadn't been afraid of reviving the spirit of German nationalism, they would probably have raised an expeditionary force from their former enemies; but the danger of such a course was too obvious for Clemenceau and Foch to tolerate the solicitations of their hotheaded followers. The bare truth was that Europe was too exhausted to undertake the suppression of Bolshevism.

3

The Peace Conference was convened informally, January 12, 1919, coincident with the second renewal of the Armistice, and its first plenary session was held six days later. Two months had been lost. Germany's blanket note to the Allies and the United States must be renewed a second time, without any information for her as to the terms upon which it would be transformed into a mortgage upon her resources. All that the world had to show for this passage of time was the return of Lloyd George to power, Clemenceau's confirmation in office by a vote of confidence in the Chamber, the deaths of hundreds of thousands of men, women and children—and the presence of Woodrow Wilson in Paris, which millions of people hoped would justify the sufferings entailed by the delays it had caused. And Mr. Wilson, as has been said, was sincerely concerned, after his own habit of mind, with the parlous state to which the world had been reduced. He was devoting himself to the drafting of a Covenant for the League, which, he believed fanatically, would make impossible the recurrence of such conditions as were reported to him, but of which, personally, he saw very little. He would continue to devote himself to this task until after his visit home, making vague gestures of interest in the other ponderable questions which challenged the best minds the nations had assembled in Paris. As a consequence, the concrete work of the Conference, the compilation of terms, punitive and corrective, for presentation to Germany and her allies, drifted aimlessly in a back-water of muddled purposes.

The Conference was leaderless. It was leaderless at this crucial moment because Mr. House was ill again, very ill, and as it happened, his was the single mind amongst the dominant personalities which combined the qualities of statesmanship and political craft requisite to the coherence of so many opposing forces. Clemenceau was a leader, bred in the narrow tradition of *revanche,* not an administrator or creator. His Ministers were bureaucrats. Tardieu alone was creative, and Tardieu had limited initiative previous to February 19, when Clemenceau was shot in the shoulder by a Communist assassin, another hindrance to progress. Similarly, Lloyd George was a dynamo of energy, but he relied upon assistants for ideas. Of the men close to him, Balfour and Cecil were first-rate thinkers and administrators, but sorry politicians, as Balfour had proven in his one essay as Prime Minister early in the century. Smuts had the best mind of the Britishers, but Smuts was a Colonial, who could speak only for South Africa. The Italians, Sonnino and Orlando, were routine politicians, products of their country's hidebound, multi-party system, which was presently to collapse under the blows of Fascism.

There was just the one man in Paris who possessed the skill, the intellectual equipment, the personality and the prestige to fuse a synthesis of orderly endeavor out of the tangle of conflicting interests. It is true that as soon as he could sit up Mr. House defied his family and physicians, and tried to pick up the reins he had been obliged to drop. Nobody resisted his resumption of them, but he lacked the physical strength to do the job of which he would otherwise have been capable. And by this time the Conference definitely had assumed the tendency it was to follow to the last episode at Versailles. Power was concentrated in the hands of the President, Clemenceau and Lloyd George. The British and French Premiers had adopted the policy of playing off their war aims against Mr. Wilson's demands for his conception of a League Covenant, and whether he realized it or not, Mr. Wilson was committed to an endless series of wrangling bargains and compromises to attain the end he sought. All hope of a Preliminary Treaty had gone by the board, although that fact was not realized by any of the leaders, including Mr. House himself. Lying on his couch, flushed with fever, he refused to admit discouragement to his callers, despite a record in his diary, January 22: "The President came to see me today to tell of what was going on in the meeting at the Quai d'Orsay. As far as I can see, they are not getting anywhere, largely because of the lack of organization." The best he could do was to advise the President to have international committees of experts constituted to thresh out the details of the various settlements —the old House theory of delegating authority under a supervisory body —in this case, the cumbersome Council of Ten. This device helped materially, but the pattern of the Conference was set too stiffly to be radically altered.

It would be a mistake, however, to give the impression that Mr. House, during his illness, achieved nothing of value to the tedious progress toward peace. He was a vital factor in procuring the agreement of the Conference, January 25, to the inclusion of the Covenant in the Treaty, a primary objective with his friend, about which Mr. Wilson worried so much and needlessly, since it was a matter of indifference to Lloyd George and Clemenceau—to Lloyd George because Lord Robert Cecil felt as strongly about it as Mr. Wilson, to Clemenceau because he attached little importance to the League in his fiery determination to safeguard France's future, and to the pair jointly because they intended to use their "concessions" to facilitate the President's approval of their nationalistic ambitions. Mr. House likewise lent his influence to the British in securing the assent of the President to the admission of the Dominions and India as independent members of the League. "I never had patience with the alarmists who claimed we were giving the British Empire six votes," he said, in discussing his action. "I thought, and I still think, that, as time goes on, the Dominions—and especially, those with Pacific interests—will be inclined to adopt our policies rather than England's. They are really much closer to us than to England in questions of international policy. As a matter of fact, I was amazed that the British didn't see that allowing the Dominions and India the status of independent powers in the League would loosen the fabric of the Empire. It will encourage them to think for themselves, for their own interests.* And as for the Empire's six votes, supposing they can be held together on occasion, we could always have brought against them in counter-balance many more from the Pan-American Republics. The British and other Powers didn't realize this until after the Covenant was drafted. It would have given us preponderant authority in the Assembly."

A third enterprise which took shape under Mr. House's direction was the organization of the Supreme Economic Council to handle problems of food, finance, blockade, shipping and the supply of raw materials. The great contribution of the United States to Europe, in the period immediately succeeding the war, was the furnishing of emergency food and sanitary services to the devastated countries, and Mr. House saw to it that this was intrusted to the expert guidance of Hoover, who had been brought to Europe for the purpose at the end of November, and had spent the intervening weeks mostly in waiting upon the reluctance of the Allies to permit any amelioration of their enemies' condition. Hoover's work in this field was a classic performance of its kind, surpassing in scope his achievements in Belgium, and to Mr. House a more valid claim to immortality than his term in the White House.

Sick or well, Mr. House was kept continuously at the job he did best: conciliation of opposing personalities. He preached this doctrine tirelessly to the President, made peace, January 30, after the President had had "a first-class row" with Clemenceau, Lloyd George, Hughes of Aus-

---

* Mr. House made this statement before Ireland had acquired Dominion status and later assumed her somewhat hypothetical claim—in absence of Empire acceptance—to freedom. He would have been interested to see how his predictions came out in 1939. Ireland proclaimed, and has maintained, neutrality, yet is bound hand-and-foot economically to Britain, so that her position is entirely dependent upon the conception of British interests which prevails in London. Australia, Canada, New Zealand and even South Africa threw themselves into war behind the Mother Country with the same enthusiasm as in 1914. India has given tremendous military aid, despite Congress threats of civil disobedience and Gandhi's equivocal stand— this latter factor the result of Gandhi's own dread of Communism and appreciation of the eagerness with which Japan would exploit an India undefended by Britain. Otherwise, no doubt, there would be nothing equivocal about his demands—as Mr. House anticipated.

tralia, and Massey of New Zealand. "The President was angry," he noted. "Lloyd George was angry, and so was Clemenceau. It is the first time the President has shown any temper in his dealings with them." Hughes was the most perniciously difficult figure at the Conference, stubbornly determined, at any price, to wring from the British representatives the rewards he believed had been won by the matchless Anzac divisions in the Near East and France. Again, when the President wanted to substitute a purely American draft of the League Covenant for one written by Miller and Hurst, the English economist, making Cecil so indignant that he refused to meet the President or discuss it with him, Mr. House induced his friend to see the unreasonableness of his stand. This had the makings of an inherently nasty situation, a breach in the Anglo-American League front, which was the liberal, constructive front. It was an indication of Mr. Wilson's growing ego, his intellectual intoxication by the adulation with which he had been received in Europe. As the future was to reveal, this did not make for emotional stability.

There is significance in the fact that about this time, the end of January, Mr. House encouraged his friend not to entertain misgivings regarding his concentration upon the Covenant, to the exclusion of practically all other phases of the peace. This was typical of Mr. House. He saw that there could be only waste of energy in an attempt by Mr. Wilson to divide his interest. It would be better for all, if he settled the drafting of the Covenant to his satisfaction and then returned to Paris, after submission of it to the Senate, with his mind clear for the conclusion of the complicated military, naval, territorial and reparations terms. For Mr. House, more vividly than any of his colleagues, felt upon his shoulder in those days the urgent press of time. He saw Europe crumbling while the Conference talked and intrigued, its sentient thoughts upon the future rather than the present. As a realist, he accepted this state of mind, which had developed during his illness. The best policy in the circumstances, he believed, was to settle the future as rapidly as possible, and return men's worries to concentration upon the world's prevailing problems. And, unconsciously, his alertness of perception colored his own mental processes, inclining him more and more to compromise the issues at stake, in the belief that almost any peace, even a peace of glaring injustices, would be preferable to the uncertainties of the moment, which kept millions of men under arms and hindered the revival of industry, agriculture and transportation.

He was relieved when the first official draft of the Covenant was completed, February 13, humorously reminding his friend that it satisfied his pet superstition, in that it was connected with the thirteenth day of the month, and the number of clauses, twenty-six, represented twice that number; there would have been twenty-seven, if the President had not been obliged to drop a declaration for religious freedom because of his unwillingness to fight for the racial equality clause the Japanese had requested as a natural corollary of his suggestion. Mr. House seems to have felt more strongly about this injustice than Mr. Wilson, who revealed an unaccountable lack of appreciation that one of the mightiest powers in history was rising across the Pacific, a power with which the United States must find a community of sympathy and ambitions or else be prepared, sooner or later, for a struggle more taxing than any they had known.

The Covenant was read by the President to a plenary session of the Conference on the afternoon of February 14. There was discussion of the document, all extremely favorable, by Cecil, Orlando, and Venizelos of Greece. Stout old Léon Bourgeois raised the sole dissenting voice, providing an illustration of the breadth of definition required for the word "liberal" by staging a last-minute defense of the French conception of a military League. But this was simply a gesture, tolerated by Clemenceau because it gave him yet another bargaining point in the struggle to come over frontiers and reparations. The President had no ground of complaint. The League, which he had made his own, received the endorsement of the Allied and Associated nations. Europe, North and South America, Asia, Africa and Oceania gave it their benediction, eagerly hopeful for the future of this first attempt by men to curb their periodic lapses into barbarism.

Several hours later, Mr. Wilson rode through streets lined by cheering throngs to take the train for Brest. The President of the Republic and Madame Poincaré, Clemenceau and his Cabinet, and most of the members of the Conference were at the station to bid him farewell and godspeed. And he enjoyed the plaudits, a light almost of gaiety upon his craggy features as he bowed right and left. It was just as well, for this was to be the last time he would be taken to their hearts by the Paris crowds.

"The President bade me a fervent good-by," Mr. House recorded in his diary that evening, "clasping my hand and placing his arm around me. The entire occasion was a fitting tribute to him and was an appropriate ending to a very memorable visit. He looked happy, as well indeed he should."

Those were memorable words, for that was the last time Woodrow Wilson demonstrated affection for Edward M. House.

4

Mr. Wilson was absent from Paris for twenty-eight days, from February 14 to March 14. It was during this period, according to Baker, his official biographer—whose charges were published during his lifetime—that Mr. House betrayed the trust confided to him as the President's representative on the Council of Ten and Acting Chief of the American Peace Commission. Baker charged that Mr. House participated in an intrigue engineered by Balfour—whose surface cynicism really concealed a singularly impersonal and generous philosophy of life—with the design of abandoning the plan for a Preliminary (Military) Treaty, forcing through, in the President's absence, the territorial and financial terms desired by Britain and France, and thus killing the League. How the League could have been killed, even supposing the accompanying assertions to be true, it is difficult to comprehend. The Covenant had been tied into the Treaty, the President's draft approved by the Allies, and all that remained for him to do was to secure approval of his work by the Senate. But Baker's charges are dogmatic. "Thus while it is too much to say that there was a direct plot, while Wilson was away, to kill the League or even cut it out of the Treaty, one can affirm with certainty that there was an intrigue against his plan of a preliminary military and naval peace—which would have indirectly produced the same results."

The truth is, that the idea of a Preliminary Treaty was Mr. House's, not Mr. Wilson's. It was he who had led, was leading, the fight for it. Had he been allowed his way, work on it would have been begun November 12, before the burial of the bodies of Corporals Beaufils and Durocq and Gunner Seyler, the last men to die as the buglers were starting to blow the "Cease fire." It would have been finished before Christmas. Similarly, the League meant more to him, practically, than it did to his friend. He had written the first American draft, remember. The bright finger of his mind was on every one of the clauses the President had read to the last Plenary Session of the Conference, and he had a much clearer perception of the uses to which the League machinery could be put than Mr. Wilson. He stayed in the background because he wanted Mr. Wilson to have the credit for whatever was accomplished.

Baker also charged that the British had brought Winston Churchill over from London, after the President left, to lend more emphasis to the militaristic—i.e., reparations—claims of his Government. And he complained that the League "was scarcely mentioned in the conferences until just before the President returned." The truth is, that Churchill,

THE STATUE OF MR. HOUSE ERECTED IN WARSAW DURING HIS LIFETIME

It is not known whether this statue was demolished by the Germans, as was
President Wilson's.

as Secretary for War, came over to decide, once and for all, what was to
be done about Russia, that he was at great pains and some inconvenience
to arrive before Mr. Wilson left, and attended the last meeting of the
Council of Ten at which Mr. Wilson was present before sailing, February 14. He returned to London the following Monday, the 17th, and
had nothing more to do with the abortive attempt to hasten the Treaty.
As to the failure to discuss the League in Mr. Wilson's absence, that was
a matter of courtesy to the President. One can imagine his anger had
revisions or amendments been taken up behind his back. Furthermore,
there was nothing to be done with the Covenant, pending his return
with intelligence of its reception in Washington. But this did not imply
that Mr. House was letting the League be ignored. He cabled his friend,
February 27, a suggestion, endorsed by Balfour and Cecil, that an immediate effort should be made to start the League functioning, with the
members of the League Committee of the Conference as a provisional
Council under the Covenant. His idea was that the Council of Ten
could refer certain problems to the League for disposition, and so gain
prestige for it. Mr. Wilson replied to him, March 4, objecting very
sensibly that such a step would give "some advantage . . . to the critics
on this side of the water if they thought we were trying in that way to
forestall action by the Senate and commit the country in some practical
way from which it would be impossible to withdraw."

Baker read sinister implications into other of Mr. House's activities.
For example, he charged that the introduction by Secretary Lansing of
the words *"inter alia"* into a resolution proposed by Balfour, February 22,
for study of general treaty terms, while the Ten were awaiting a report
from the military experts, had laid the foundation for wholesale *sabotage*
of the President's policy, and specifically had opened the way for the
Japanese demands—reasonable, face-saving demands, as has been said—
as to Shantung. The fact was that the Japanese claims had been made
weeks previously. But Baker would have been much more positive that
"inter alia" covered an iniquitous purpose had he known that Lansing's
amendment had been prompted by Mr. House, whose purpose was to
make certain technically that the League Covenant should be eligible to
insertion in the Preliminary as well as the Definitive Treaty. The
Americans resorted to this legal device to broaden the scope of a Preliminary Treaty for two reasons: it had become increasingly apparent in
the past week that Foch's military experts were bogged down in their
work, presenting the possibility that the Preliminary Treaty could be
made to include approximate definitions of the territorial and financial
clauses; and they wished to avoid interminable arguments with Clemen-

ceau and Bourgeois, who resisted every American suggestion to implement the Covenant in order to build up their bargaining advantage.

Finally, Baker did not scruple in his book to suppress from the President's parting statement to the Council of Ten, nominating Mr. House as his substitute, the all-important sentence, inclusion of which destroyed Mr. Wilson's case against his friend: "But he"—the transcript of the *procès-verbal* is in the third person—"did not wish that, during his unavoidable absence, such questions as the territorial question and questions of compensation should be held up." This sentence was accepted by Mr. House, Secretary Lansing and their associates of the Ten as an authorization for them to proceed tentatively with the settlement of the details as to frontiers and reparations. Surely, they were correct. The President was a master of English, and had a trick of saying precisely what he meant. Furthermore, Mr. House advised him of this intention in a talk they had the morning of the day Mr. Wilson left Paris. The entry in Mr. House's diary, February 14, includes this report of what he said and the President's reaction:

"I outlined my plan of procedure during his absence; we could button up everything during the next four weeks. He seemed startled and even alarmed at this statement. I therefore explained that the plan was not to actually bring these matters to a final conclusion but to have them ready for him to do so when he returned." Mr. House then proceeded to outline the program to be followed in preparing for a preliminary peace, as including reduction of the German Army and Navy to a peace footing, delineation of German boundaries and arrangements for disposition of the enemy's colonies, the amount of reparations and time in which they should be paid, and agreement as to the future economic attitude toward Germany. "I asked him if he had anything else to suggest in addition to these four articles. He thought they were sufficient. I asked him to bear in mind while he was gone that it was sometimes necessary to compromise in order to get things through; not a compromise of principle but a compromise of detail; he had made many since he had been here. I did not wish him to leave expecting the impossible in all things."

Nothing could have been more candid than Mr. House's outline of intentions, which "startled and even alarmed" the President for the simple reason that he had been so absorbed in the drafting of the Covenant that he had paid scant attention to the obstacles accumulating in the path of the project to confine the Preliminary Treaty to military, naval and air terms. It is true that these obstacles should have been foreseen; for instance, determination of the size of Germany's peacetime army. But they were not foreseen, in part because the soldiers and sailors were so scornfully confident of the job assigned to them, and had to be checked and corrected again and again; in part, because Germany's prostration incited the Allies to augmentation of their demands upon her with the passage of every week. The terms they would have accepted in November seemed weak to them in December, and ridiculous in February.

Within two weeks after the President's departure, Mr. House realized that it would be as easy to include a general summary of territorial and financial claims in the Preliminary Treaty as to await the tedious procedure of the military experts. Likewise, his realistic cast of mind warned him that the moment had passed for a peace of justice, such as he had planned. He noted in his diary, March 3: "It is now evident that the peace will not be such a peace as I had hoped, or one which this terrible upheaval should have brought about. . . . The American Delegation are not in a position to act freely. The elections of last November in the United States have been a deterrent to free action by our delegates. The British elections, and the vote of confidence Clemenceau received in the French Chamber of Deputies, put the finishing touches to a situation already bad. If the President should exert his influence among the liberals and laboring classes, he might possibly overthrow the Governments in Great Britain, France and Italy; but if he did, he would still have to reckon with our own people and he might bring the whole world into chaos. . . . It would be a grave responsibility for any man to take at this time."

It is to be doubted, in view of occurrences in the ensuing two months, whether Mr. Wilson, in fact, could have overthrown one or more of the Allied Governments. Certainly, when he appealed to the Italian people over the heads of their Government, in his manifesto of April 23, the result was the removal of his picture from the household altars of the peasantry. The situation, indeed, was worse than Mr. House envisioned it, and it was not to be improved by Mr. Wilson's trip home, which emphasized the increasing disaffection in opposition circles, not with his theories of a League—to which the American people, regardless of party, were extremely partial—but with his own personal conduct and obvious intention to ignore the rightful share of the Republican party, as the majority party in Congress, in the Government, of which he was the executive head.*

* The situation in Congress in the years 1919-20 confirmed Mr. House's doubts as to the wisdom of the American system of Government, which makes possible— it has often happened in the last two years of a President's second term—a division of responsibility between a President of one party and a Congress in which one or

What, then, did Mr. House do during the four weeks of the President's absence from Paris? Unquestionably, he made several mistakes of policy much more deserving of criticism than the straw man of intrigue Baker set up to demolish. But these mistakes were merely expressions of a tentative willingness to discuss certain arrangements put forward by the French, and his motive in each case was to hasten the conclusion of peace. He may have been wrong in attaching as much importance as he did to the need for the earliest possible peace, even a peace of limited injustice, with the confident expectation that wrongs inflicted upon the defeated enemy could be righted through the machinery of the League, as the poison of fear and hatred gradually evaporated from the European atmosphere. The answer to this is that Mr. House had as strong a predilection for justice as Mr. Wilson, but his political experience had taught him that occasionally the longest way around was the shortest way home. And he did not, while Mr. Wilson was away, commit his friend and chief to any policy, righteous or unrighteous. All that was done in Paris, without the President, was undertaken subject to his approval. Mr. Wilson was forced to compromise his ideals, not because of mistakes of Mr. House, but because of errors of judgment for which he, himself, was responsible. Mr. Wilson was not betrayed in Paris by anyone but Woodrow Wilson, who permitted himself to succumb to an egoism which, as cannot too often be insisted, was an exaggeration of his lifelong self-sufficiency.

It has been said that Mr. House made several mistakes. His partisans could dispute the assertion. But they are worth discussion for the sake of an open record. One has been referred to: his suggestion to set the League to functioning before its acceptance by the Senate, a suggestion made in good faith, and actually rescinded by himself before the President negatived it, investigation having convinced him of the impracticability of the idea. His judgment was more at fault when he showed an inclination, in a cable of February 24, to accept a French proposition for the establishment of a Rhenish Republic, with the proviso that after a limited term of years it should be permitted to decide its future by plebiscite. Mr. Wilson very properly replied, March 10: "I hope you will not even provisionally consent to the separation of the Rhenish provinces from Germany under any arrangement, but will reserve the whole matter until my arrival." But here, again, Mr. House was actuated by the exigencies of the situation, although this does not alter the fact that the President's unfaltering determination compelled the French to yield their

both Houses are controlled by the opposition party, with the effect of hindering efficient government, destroying business confidence and thwarting the popular will as expressed in the elections.

demands—at the cost of a further delay in completion of the Treaty, and the frustration of the last faint hope for a Preliminary Treaty. It should be added, at this point, that Mr. House was thinking ahead of his friend regarding the ultimate objectives of the Conference, and as he said afterwards, in discussing his "mistakes," it is difficult to decide whether they were "mistakes" for the reason that they were not put to trial.

An entry in his diary, February 9, illustrates his motive in being willing to tolerate temporary injustice for the purpose of reestablishing a sound economic basis in Europe. It is particularly interesting because it forecasts the creation of the Rome-Berlin-Tokyo Axis, and the subsequent international alignment of nations which prevailed in the opening months of 1940. This entry is a digest of a talk with Balfour, whose skeptical, exploring mind was a source of delight to Mr. House, and quite baffling to Mr. Wilson:

"We talked at great length of the French proposal of setting up a 'Rhenish Republic' as a buffer state between Germany and France. The French have but one idea and that is military protection. They do not seem to know that to establish a Rhenish Republic against the will of the people would be contrary to the spirit of self-determination, and that if we should establish it, the people could at any time become federated with the other German States. If we did such a thing, we would be treating Germany in one way and the balance of the world in another. We would run the danger of having everything from the Rhine to the Pacific, perhaps including Japan, against the Western Powers. The Germans would at once begin to intrigue to bring about such a combination against England, France and the United States. Their propaganda would be that England and the United States were undertaking to form an Anglo-Saxon supremacy of the world, and that we were using France as a pawn for the establishment of our purpose. . . . Yet we both have a profound sympathy for France and for the unhappy situation in which she finds herself—a situation which is serious because there are practically two Germans to one Frenchman. The only hope France has for the future is the League of Nations and the spirit we hope to bring about through it. If, after establishing the League, we are so stupid as to let Germany train and arm a large army and again become a menace to the world, we would deserve the fate which such folly would bring upon us."

Mr. House's most serious mistake—and one for which Mr. Wilson was even more to blame—was his acceptance of the Reparations terms, anchored in the Treaty by the insistence of the Allies, in flat contradiction to their pledges contained in the Armistice. In flat contradiction, that is, if the Armistice terms meant what they did to the Americans. But Mr. House was under no delusions as to the preposterous inequity of the British and French demands for compensation. He regarded them as so absurd, so unworkable, that they could be relied upon to demonstrate their own impracticability. He was content to let the Allies demonstrate the character of their demands by attempting to apply them in practice, confident that the machinery of the League, in which he expected the United States to exercise an influence for sanity, would supply the means for adequate revision after Europe had regained a more normal mental attitude. He did not, like Mr. Wilson, succumb to the blandishments of Smuts, and assent to the reasonableness of including pensions in the bill Germany was to be handed. It simply didn't make sense to him, he said at the time—and afterwards—that the French should coolly discuss the possibility of extracting $200,000,000,000, and the British, more moderately, a slight $140,000,000,000, from a Germany which had been bled white in the past five years.

Baruch, who was as much of a realist as any of the American financial experts, was more dogmatic than Mr. House about the Allied demands. "There isn't that much money in the world," he said, after emerging from a meeting of the Committee on Reparations. "The most we can figure getting out of the Germans is $20,000,000,000, and I think we'll be lucky to get $12,000,000,000. It doesn't make sense." *

In light of what happened afterwards, it is obvious that Mr. House would have been on sounder ground if he had offered more resistance to terms in which he didn't believe. It is always dangerous to try to anticipate the course of history, and this is nonetheless true as to German reparations because the average American, in 1919, saw no reason why the Germans shouldn't be made to pay. There can be scant comfort in the realization that our people were as unreasonable as the Allies in their desire to inflict punishment upon the defeated enemy. And conversely, there should be slim satisfaction for Mr. Wilson's apologists in the reflection that in March, 1919, a poll conducted by a chain of newspapers, spanning the country from coast to coast, resulted in a vote of two to one in favor of membership in the League. It was the President who

---

* An exhaustive economic survey of Germany, recently completed by American economists, estimates that $100,000,000,000 of her national wealth was consumed, directly and indirectly, during the period 1914-18. What this meant as a reduction of her capacity to pay even the more moderate reparations, calculated by the American experts in Paris, may be gauged from the fact that a report of the National Industrial Conference Board fixed the wealth of the United States, in 1937, at $321,791,722,000. There can be no comparison between the national wealth of Germany and the United States.

annihilated this feeling for international cooperation by his stubborn refusal to compromise with men whose egotism, it is true, was as arbitrary
as his own.

Both Mr. House and Mr. Wilson must share the blame for having
assented to the enforcement upon Germany of admission of war guilt,
in connection with her acceptance of the obligation of reparations. No
clause in the Treaty stung Germans of all classes more than this one
upon which Clemenceau staked his political life. In retrospect, it seems
unfair, if not unjust, if for no other reason than because it was imposed
by *force majeure*. The men who drafted the Versailles Treaty believed
that it was based on justice, that the war could, indeed, have been averted
had Germany been willing to use her influence to check the Austrian
attack upon Serbia. But here you run the danger of complicating the
legalistic frame of mind with the metaphysical. When a man or a nation
has been wrong, what earthly use does it serve to bludgeon an admission
of sin out of one or the other? This, at least, was Mr. House's considered verdict upon his state of mind in 1919. He never thought the admission would amount to more than a salve to France's pride of rightness, a nasty prick to Germany's self-respect as a great nation. He
wished he had stood out against it, but the bare truth is that most of the
men at the Peace Conference accepted it as a hedge against future violations of the world's peace. A fallacious idea, as the world knows today.
And suppose Mr. House and Mr. Wilson had stood out against it? If
Clemenceau meant what he said—and he habitually did—it would have
resulted in the dissolution of the Conference, a relapse of Europe into a
tangle of international complications. Remember, no course was easy for
the men of 1919. They had sown the whirlwind.*

As to Italy's demands upon Austria-Hungary, Mr. House, Clemenceau
and Lloyd George were disposed to be less sympathetic than Mr. Wilson,
whose ineptness in negotiation did as much to precipitate a nasty situation
as the recalcitrance of the Italians, Orlando and Sonnino, under constant
pressure from Rome. It was Mr. Wilson who yielded the Tyrol to Italy
against the inclination of his associates, who were more impressed by the
President's principle of self-determination than by the real purpose which

---

* Dr. James T. Shotwell, of Columbia University—who was one of the experts
of the American Peace Commission—disputes this view in his *What Germany Forgot* (Macmillan, New York, 1940). He holds that Germany's economic distress in
the post-war years was the result of her wartime expenditures, not of reparations,
and that the war guilt clause was simply a legal phrase to insure her technical responsibility for reparations. This strikes me as a very legalistic argument, and with
all respect to its author, I cannot subscribe to it.

was accomplished by the protection Italy gained from a strategic frontier and control of the Brenner Pass. From a practical point of view it would seem that Mr. Wilson was right and the other three wrong. Three hundred thousand German Austrians were sacrificed to provide a barrier against future wars, but surely this was one of the few essentially practical compromises Mr. Wilson permitted himself. Like the allocation of the Sudetenland to Czecho-Slovakia, it was a compromise between irreconcilable differences in theory, which had to be adjusted if nations were to be given a reasonable security to maintain independent existences. Mr. House and the President were in agreement that Fiume should be internationalized under the jurisdiction of the League, the only sane disposition for a port which was of significance to a hinterland controlled by three nations, Italy not being one of them. Its ultimate annexation, through d'Annunzio's hysterical campaign, was a product of the confusion in world affairs produced by Mr. Wilson's quarrel with the Republican majority of the Senate.

It is impossible to discern, in a factual analysis of what went on in Paris during the President's absence, a serious ground for assertion that he was "betrayed" by anyone. Mistakes were made, yes—and more mistakes would be made or exaggerated after the President's return. But only a hostile intellect could read into the mistakes of the American representatives at the Conference a disposition to intrigue or a weakening of the American purpose to secure the best possible peace in the circumstances. On the other hand, it is true that progress was more rapid in the President's absence than while he was present. There were two reasons for this: his absorption in the League, and his lack of experience in working with men who were his intellectual equals, and whose policies were frequently at variance with his. And it should always be considered, in this respect, that Clemenceau and Lloyd George and the other Chiefs of State in Paris were as convinced of the rightness of their motives as was Mr. Wilson. A fact which Mr. House never lost sight of, but which was frequently obscured to Mr. Wilson by his crusading zeal.

When Mr. House cabled his friend, March 1, that the Preliminary Treaty could be ready for the Germans' scrutiny by April 2, he meant that it could be ready if the President approved it. Mr. Wilson was not committed to anything. Certain principles had been tentatively discussed and tentatively adopted. If Mr. Wilson could suggest other compromises or terminology, satisfactory to Powers which considered themselves on a par with the United States, then those alternatives would be adopted. It is a commentary upon Mr. Wilson that, in the main, he could not provide alternatives. It would be May 7 before the Treaty, which, by then, was a Definitive Treaty, would be ready for the German delegates to weep over. Those weeks were consumed in Mr. Wilson's desperate efforts to escape the consequences of his own acts of omission or commission—his partisan appeal for the election of a Democratic Congress, his insistence upon heading the American Peace Commission, his determination to place the Covenant before the military, territorial and economic clauses, without which Europe could not be started upon the long and tedious road to reconstruction. Perhaps he was right in this last determination, but while he was enjoying the luxury of virtue the fires of hatred and vengeance were flaming higher. When February had passed without the negotiation of a Preliminary Treaty, Europe had missed its last chance for a peace to be forged in a mood of deliberation and charity. Perhaps, too, there never was such a chance. We shall never know because the chance was missed.

5

Mr. Wilson returned to France in a much less friendly and conciliatory mood than had animated him when he left amidst plaudits and cheers. The reception of his addresses in Boston and New York had not been too enthusiastic. Newspaper comment had become increasingly unfavorable since the election. Republican editors, politicians and business men no longer considered themselves obligated to offer nonpartisan support to a President who had proclaimed himself a most ungracious partisan. Anyway, the war was over for Americans. They were still willing to do their share, and more, in liquidating it. They wanted a League of Nations, regardless of whether they were Republicans or Democrats. And they wanted the Germans punished. But they were beginning to think about the Presidential elections in 1920, and so far as the Republicans were concerned, they were determined to capitalize every advantage Mr. Wilson presented to them.

Mr. House journeyed to Brest to meet the President and report on his stewardship. He wanted to impress his friend with the necessity of securing an early peace, and yielding compromises to secure such a peace. Personally, he felt—and always felt—in no way apologetic for the compromises he had discussed with the British and French Ministers. He was, accordingly, surprised to find the President antagonistic to any thought of compromise, and suspicious of the arrangements which had been considered in his absence. Mr. House did not know, then, and probably never knew, how bitterly resentful was his friend of the steps the Texan had taken in his absence. But Mr. Wilson did give a hint of his dissatisfaction in the acerbity with which he spoke of the dinner to the members of the Senate Foreign Relations Committee, which he had tendered them at Mr. House's insistence before he left Paris.

"He said," Mr. House noted in his diary, March 14, "'Your dinner for the Senate Foreign Relations Committee was a failure as far as getting together was concerned.' He spoke with considerable bitterness of the manner in which he was treated by some of the Senators. Knox and Lodge remained perfectly silent, refusing to ask any questions or to act in the spirit in which the dinner was given." Mr. House wondered in just what spirit the dinner was given. Mr. Wilson, he knew, detested the two men he singled out for special mention, and was capable of a scorching courtesy which might well have been resented by them. Neither was a man lightly to be dismissed in politics. They controlled the two great States of Pennsylvania and Massachusetts; they were amongst the half-dozen senior statesmen who dominated the new Republican majority in Congress; they were sticklers for personal dignity; and they considered that their party had been rudely flouted by Mr. Wilson. They were leaders of the cabal which would break the President a few months hence, and prostrate him, physically and mentally.

Mr. Wilson's irascibility and lack of perspective were demonstrated to Mr. House by his sudden announcement, the evening of his arrival off Brest, that he would insist that peace should be made simultaneously with Austria-Hungary, Bulgaria and Turkey at the same time as with Germany. This procedure, it was evident to Mr. House, would delay the peace indefinitely, and he undertook to consult the American legal experts, with a view to the drafting of a special clause in the German Treaty, binding the Germans to accept the terms of the Treaties with their allies. But nothing ever came of the President's demand, the preposterousness of which must have become apparent to him after he cooled down. Similarly, he talked a great deal, after his arrival, of tying the League Covenant into the Treaty so that they could not be separated. He and his apologists, afterwards, gave the impression that this was done in order to avert the "plot" or "intrigue," supposedly prevalent in his absence from Paris and designed to *sabotage* the League. Nothing could have been more untruthful. The Europeans had accepted the idea of the League. They wanted it, as a means to peace and to insure the continuing assistance of the United States in curbing Germany's military strength. The President was so insistent upon tying the Covenant into the Treaty because there was a growing inclination in the Senate to ask for its divorcement, as a measure so important that it deserved to stand alone as an international instrument. There was a good deal of sense and justice in this view. As has been said, the League's prestige would have been greater had it not been insolubly linked with a Treaty of punishment and denunciation.

The interview between Mr. House and the President, in the Presidential suite on the *George Washington* that night of March 13, takes on special importance because of Mrs. Wilson's description of her husband's reaction to it, as contained in her reminiscences. This is the most forthright expression of Mr. Wilson's apparent drift away from his friend's influence of which we have anything approaching authentic record. Much which happened later becomes more understandable through her record, which suggests that in recent months he had been listening to a flood of gossip and criticism of the role played by Mr. House. From whose lips it came, of course, there is little, if any, doubt. Mrs. Wilson reveals herself as hostile to the friendship which had preceded her influence. Elsewhere in her book, she quotes Mr. Wilson's physician, Rear Admiral Cary T. Grayson, as equally hostile. The attitude of Baker—the President's press liaison representative during the Conference—is manifested in his authorized biography of Mr. Wilson, previously noted. Creel, who, as head of the Committee on Public Information, had the favor of the White House group, was notoriously critical of Mr. House's extra-official position in the Administration.* There were others, not so important in the public eye, but with easy access to the President, who lent their voices to the chorus, which painted Mr. House as self-seeking, pliant, a tool of the foreign statesmen and opponents at home. None of the President's own relatives, his daughters or their husbands, seems to have joined what became, in future months, an anti-House cabal, working on lines parallel to and as destructive as the Senate Republican cabal.

Mrs. Wilson is explicit in her several statements, which, it must be admitted, are the stuff of which history is made. For history is as much compounded of misconceptions as of truths, and sometimes the misconceptions are the more potent and lasting in their effects upon the lives of humanity's incoherent masses. This anecdote, which follows, was certainly a factor in preventing the membership of the United States in

---

* See Creel's *The War, the World and Wilson*. Mr. House asked me, on one occasion, to attend a lecture of Creel's at Town Hall in New York, and challenge him if he made certain statements. He made them, but before I could rise from my seat that grand old gentlewoman, Mrs. Theodore Douglas Robinson, sister of ex-President Theodore Roosevelt, had gained her feet, and Republican though she was, had checked him far more effectively than I could have done. It sometimes seemed as though Mr. House had as many friends on the Republican side as on the Democratic. They admired him, as Mrs. Robinson said, because they respected him despite the fact that he was a Democrat.

the League of Nations. To that extent, perhaps, it was as important to mankind as the President's error in asking his countrymen to give him partisan support, in a moment when Republicans and Democrats were sinking loyally their party feelings to help him lead them to victory:

"My husband and Colonel House talked on while I waited in my adjoining stateroom. It was after midnight, and very still aboard, when I heard my husband's door open and the Colonel take his leave. I opened the door connecting our rooms. Woodrow was standing. The change in his appearance shocked me. He seemed to have aged ten years, and his jaw was set in that way it had when he was making superhuman effort to control himself. Silently he held out his hand, which I grasped, crying: 'What is the matter? What has happened?'

"He smiled bitterly. 'House has given away everything I had won before we left Paris. He has compromised on every side, and so I have to start all over again and this time it will be harder, as he has given the impression that my delegates are not in sympathy with me. His own explanation of his compromises is that, with a hostile press in the United States expressing disapproval of the League of Nations as a part of the Treaty, he thought it best to yield some other points lest the Conference withdraw its approval altogether. So he has yielded until there is nothing left.' " *

Now, the facts are that Mr. Wilson had won substantially nothing, except a League generally in the image his creative workers had envisioned for him, before he left Paris; the Great Powers at the Conference had accepted this League and its Covenant, but were intending to wring from him further concessions to their interests, as a return for granting him such concessions as recognition of the Monroe Doctrine; he had no one but himself to thank for the growing Republican hostility and suspicion at home; he did not have to win back any concessions made by Mr. House in his absence—on the contrary, he yielded rather more of consequence than Mr. House had considered tentatively, such as the Tyrol, the *impasse* which made possible d'Annunzio's seizure of Fiume, and the acceptance of blanket reparations, including Smuts' theory of passing on war pensions to a Germany which was literally starving.

A few pages farther on in her reminiscences, Mrs. Wilson narrates how she discovered—what was unfortunately, for Mr. House's sake, entirely true—that a number of newspaper correspondents, American and British, in Paris, were representing him as "the brains of the Conference," and asserting that "the only constructive work of the American delegation had been done while President Wilson was away." This was a

* Op. cit., pp. 245, 246.

most regrettable lapse in the obligations of friendship on the part of the guilty correspondents. Every newspaperman who had Mr. House's confidence knew that he loathed and detested such tributes. His whole career in politics was a record of different feeling and inclination. He was continually warning correspondents to play down his own part in affairs. The trouble was that he did such a transcendent job in Paris, that the newspapermen, who were aware of the extent of his contribution of ideas, were determined to see that he got credit for it, and went overboard in their expressions of appreciation. But they received no thanks from the victim of their misspent kindness. He wanted the credit to go to Mr. Wilson.

Mrs. Wilson quotes Grayson as having discovered Mr. House posing for a photograph with one of these correspondents. She also says that she read one of the articles to Mr. House, who was embarrassed and asked her to give it to him. Mr. House would certainly have been embarrassed in such a situation, but mostly by the realization that the wife of the man he regarded as his best friend believed him capable of inspiring reports unfavorable to that man. She says that she repeated an expurgated report of the incident to the President, who exclaimed: "Oh, I am sorry you hurt House. I would as soon doubt your loyalty as his." "I think he is a perfect jellyfish," Mrs. Wilson quotes herself as replying. And the President's answer is a commentary upon the state of mind to which he had been reduced, in seeking to escape conviction of his own responsibility for his mistakes: "Well, God made jellyfish, so, as Shakespeare said about a man, therefore let him pass and don't be too hard on House. It takes a pretty stiff spinal column to stand against the elements centered here."

It is not strange that Mrs. Wilson comments after this: "The conversation of the afternoon when he fled my drawing-room proved to be my last with Colonel House. He did not come to our house again except for business meetings at which others were present; and on these occasions I did not see him."

So the crevasse was widening until very soon it would become a breach. The wedges had been driven in slowly, but effectively. Yet it is a further commentary upon Mr. Wilson's attitude, his mental processes, that he continued to lean heavily upon his friend in the last weeks of the Conference, when Clemenceau and Lloyd George were reaping the delayed fruits of the bargaining advantages they had acquired through relatively unimportant concessions they had made, with every parade of reluctance, in the course of the drafting of the League Covenant. He, for instance, adopted enthusiastically Mr. House's scheme for accelerating negotiations by the reduction of the Council of Ten to a Council of Four —more often, in the Italians' absence, a Council of Three. He made use of Mr. House's painstaking jockeying for position, in the weeks of his absence, to keep down the concessions he must have made in any case. It was Mr. House's initiative which spiked the reiterated—and causeless— rumors that the Covenant would be excluded from the Treaty, by outlining a policy committing the President's associates of the Four to it, brushing aside their huckstering exploitation of the opposition at home by a counter-threat of the withdrawal of the United States from the Conference, a counter-threat which had been useful in the Armistice negotiations. The final revision of the Covenant, which was accepted by the Conference, April 28, was the product of his supervision, and was, in itself, a notable diplomatic victory for the United States in its recognition of the Monroe Doctrine. When Mr. Wilson became ill, April 3, it was Mr. House who took over his friend's burdens, in addition to the weight of detail on his own shoulders. Mr. Wilson entertained no misgivings of treachery at that moment.

Mr. House seems not to have known of the President's cable for the return of the *George Washington,* which was sent by Admiral Benson, April 7; but it was the vigorous policy of adjusting the conflicting interests of the Powers, pressed by Mr. House during this period, which saved the Conference, despite the fact that it was about to be disturbed by the Italian crisis over Fiume and the Japanese demands in Shantung. Dr. Seymour has correlated the circumstances surrounding the cable for the *George Washington,* and proven conclusively that Baker and Creel erred in assigning it any importance in what happened in Paris. If Clemenceau, Lloyd George or Orlando were aware of it, it left them undisturbed. Most positively, he did not threaten them, as a group or singly, with his departure unless they abandoned their conceptions of reparations and territorial readjustments. They would have regarded it—and did, if they learned of it, as was possible—as the gesture of a sick man, a gesture of weakness.

"He wasn't feeling well at the time," Mr. House remarked, speaking of the incident after it came to light. "I recall he was very discouraged. These fellers who try to make out that he bluffed George and Clemenceau don't know what they are talking about. You couldn't bluff those fellers that way. And anyway, the terms we were whittling on, along about that time, were already taking the shape they did take finally; they were the only terms possible by then. We'd postponed things too long to get what we wanted or what we could have gotten earlier. As a matter of fact, the President was in a better frame of mind, so far as I could see, after his illness. There was trouble enough, but good Lord, he began to see that he had to be satisfied with what was possible, not what we could have gotten two or three months before."

In the Italian crisis, the President took definite action on his own responsibility, after consultation and advice. He had only his personal impatience and intemperateness of the moment—an excess of the irascibility which characterized his stay in Paris—to blame for the impossible position into which he was maneuvered by Clemenceau and Lloyd George. Or perhaps it would be more accurate to say that they permitted him to maneuver himself into this position. It is difficult to weave a fair picture out of the testimony available, because no one involved told the whole story, even from an isolated point of view. But as a premise to start from we may take it for granted that Mr. Wilson exaggerated the helplessness of the Italians to resist the decisions of the Conference, while Orlando and Sonnino believed that, because the President had made concessions to the French and British, they could fight him with equal success into granting their demand for Fiume and a slice of Dalmatia. Mr. House thought, too, that Orlando had an idea that Mr. Wilson did not have the support of his delegation in opposing Italy. This is very possible. Supporters of the President were going around Paris asserting, "in confidence," that Mr. House had given away valuable principles, and several of Mr. House's entourage were not less forward in decrying the President's blunders in a field of negotiation with which he was unfamiliar.

By the end of the third week in April, the Italians were disposed to take a firm stand on what they conceived to be their rights, all the stronger because anyone, surveying the history of the Conference with the advantage of "hindsight," must admit that the Italians throughout the deliberations were treated as orphans by the French and British. "Orlando has ceased to attend the meetings of the Council of Four, and relations are very strained," Mr. House noted in his diary, April 22, on the eve of the crisis the President invoked. Previous to this, on the 19th, Mr. House had advised his friend, in a compact but detailed memorandum, to suggest a disposition of "Fiume and all the territory in dispute south of Fiume"—that is, the strictly Slav province of Dalmatia—"to be held by the Five Powers as trustees for the League of Nations, the actual disposition to be made at some time in the future when, in the judgment of the League of Nations, it will be wise to do so. This will give the Italians a chance to educate their public to what they know will be the final decision."

Italian officials of secondary rank were saying that their chiefs "must go home," that their dignity had been insulted. Mr. House thought that they were bluffing, that Orlando and Sonnino might return to Rome, leaving the rest of their delegation behind them—as they did—but that they would surely return to sign the Treaty for the sake of national prestige. In the circumstances, he believed, it was advisable to force a showdown, the United States working toward this purpose with France and Britain. He had no objection when the President, at a meeting of the American Commissioners at the Crillon, April 21, read aloud the text of a statement, by no means so definite as Mr. House had proposed, but endeavoring to remind the people of Italy of the American position and its impartial aim to deal justly with all the peoples whose interests were at stake. He contented himself with advising the President to discuss the statement with Clemenceau and Lloyd George, and he reiterated this advice at an interview with the President, the morning of the 23rd. The President did so, later that morning, at a meeting of the Council of Four —really Three, in Orlando's continued absence.

Clemenceau and Lloyd George could not have been satisfied with Mr. Wilson's statement of the case, for they suggested the substitution of a statement which Balfour had drafted, and which was stronger in tone than Mr. Wilson's. It is uncertain what considerations governed the President's psychology at this moment, but at any rate the notes of the *procès-verbal* record him as declaring his intention of publishing his statement that evening. The Wilson statement was in the name of the American people; the Balfour statement, on a loftier, more impartial plane, spoke in the name of all three Powers associated with Italy in the Council of Four. Clemenceau and Lloyd George, apparently, made no attempt to dissuade the President from his contemplated action. Whether out of craft or impatience with his strong-headedness or a mere sense of pique, they permitted him to proceed alone in his intention, with the consequence that the anger of the Italian nation, regardless of party, was focused upon Mr. Wilson's head. For in proceeding alone, he had placed himself publicly in the impossible position of appealing to the Italian people over the heads of their Constitutional leaders, and he spoke, not in the name of the Conference, but simply as the sovereign representative of the United States. Idealistically, logically, he was in the right in what he said, but he betrayed a naïve lack of comprehension of the fundamental principles of international political relations, and of the psychology of a proud and hurt people.

Why did he do this? Why did not Mr. House intervene, at the last moment, to attempt to halt his action? Was he tricked into a false move? Were Clemenceau and Lloyd George glad to avail themselves of it to undermine his prestige? Did his manner to them, and to Mr. House, indicate that criticism of the wording of his statement would not be welcome?

Whatever the answers to these questions, the result of his statement was to postpone the conclusion of the Austrian Treaty, to save the Orlando Ministry from defeat in the Italian Chamber, to secure the Americans the active hostility of Italy, and to weaken the American power of resistance to the claims Japan was advancing, with sudden urgency, as to the disposition of the spoils she had won for the Allies in the Pacific.

The Japanese, as has been explained previously, were in a much stronger position than the Italians—or, indeed, than any of the European victors. For this Mr. House and Mr. Wilson must share responsibility, along with the marplots of the Conference—the British Dominions, led by Hughes of Australia—whose native populations or territorial contiguity to Asia inspired them with fear of the racial equality clause the Japanese had demanded should be coupled in the Covenant with the President's declaration for religious freedom. This definite injustice to Japan, as one of the Five Great Powers signatory to the Covenant and the Treaty, cannot be overemphasized, no matter what reasons actuated the statesmen who had humiliated her as few Great Powers ever have been humiliated. Mr. House and his friend were fearful of disrupting the League, and frustrating their ambitions for it as an influence for sanity in the world, if they alienated the British Dominions and the British Home Government, which was in a position of embarrassment its liberal members did not seek to conceal. At the same time, they were obliged to conciliate Japan by acceding to her not unreasonable demands for "face-saving" in Shantung, even at the cost of China's refusal to sign the Treaty, and her more debatable demands for the Caroline and Marshall Islands, thus providing her with a chain of maritime pill-boxes flanking the American route to Asia. Mr. Wilson showed his parochialism by attaching less importance to the Northern Pacific Islands, a distinct menace to the influence of the United States in the Western Pacific, than he did to the estrangement of China. The day Orlando returned to Rome, April 24, the chief Japanese plenipotentiary, Viscount Chinda, forced the issue with a curt announcement that Japan would refuse to sign the Treaty unless the Conference accepted her pledge to return the Shantung Peninsula to China, after Germany's economic privileges were assigned to her.

Once more, the Americans were in an impossible position. What else could they have done but yield? Japan had gone to the extreme of accepting the inclusion of the Monroe Doctrine in the Covenant, without, as she had vaguely threatened, demanding an equivalent clause to protect her paramount interests in Asia. She had been patient. She had been of great assistance to the Americans in the formulation of the Covenant. She had asked for nothing outside the actual sphere of her more or less legitimate interests. And so, after suffering what her people regarded as a slap in the face, she succeeded at the end in obtaining her material demands, but in such a way as to leave her sore in spirit and contemptuous of the much-vaunted idealistic principles of the League. She had seen, at first hand, the lamentable rivalries of the European Powers and the Americas, and she left Paris in the mood to embark upon the imperialistic designs in Asia which have created a plague-spot scarcely less dangerous to world peace, and especially to the future of the United States, than the identical situation created in Europe by France's insensate desire to cripple Germany.

6

Whatever may be said of the mistakes and mishaps of the Peace Conference, it maintained a standard of suspenseful melodrama to the end of its deliberations, which Hollywood at its violent best has never rivaled. When Tardieu, for Clemenceau, read an abstract of the Treaty at a plenary session held at the Quai d'Orsay, May 6, most of what fell from his lips was news—and news of great moment—to the vast majority of the delegates present. Up to the last, there was speculation as to whether Italy and Belgium would sign. "Brave little Belgium" was as keen for the spoils of war as the nations that had liberated her. She was irked and recalcitrant over the refusal of the Conference to compel the Netherlands to cede a frontier strip to her, complained because she had not been represented on the Council of Ten, had objected to the occupation of Luxembourg by French troops, and demanded priority in reparations. She was consoled by the granting of the last of these demands in recognition of her sufferings during the German occupation. Italy signed because, not only did she want the prestige of being a signatory to a treaty which humbled Germany, but she hoped that by doing so she might win belated support in the Council of Four against the Jugo-Slavs.

The Germans appeared the next day, the anniversary of the sinking of the *Lusitania,* in the Hall of Mirrors at Versailles, where Bismarck had proclaimed the German Empire of the Hohenzollerns. Clemenceau, curtly, peremptorily, the venom of 1871 vibrant in his voice, addressed them briefly. They were handed the bulky document, with its itemized list of cessions and penalties imposed upon them, terms ranging from the sublime to the ridiculous—surrender of Alsace-Lorraine and their colonies, relinquishment of their choicest coal and iron mines, return of captured French battle flags, virtual disarmament, loss of most of their war and merchant fleets and the pick of their livestock, restitution of the skull of a petty African chief. Worst of all, this ruthless instrument of vengeance required them to sign an admission of their guilt for the war they had lost. It is small wonder that Count von Brockdorff-Rantzau, head of their delegation, shaken and ill—and typifying in his own mind, at least, the victims of his ruined caste—should have spoken bitterly against this excess of humiliation inflicted upon a proud nation: "We are far from declining any responsibility that this great war of the world has come to pass. But we deny that Germany and its people were alone guilty."

His words are still a blot upon the escutcheons of the nations which exacted them, including the United States. We have to thank them, in part, and the agony of resentment which wrung them from the spokesman of the German people, for the plight in which the world finds itself more than two decades afterwards. It is not enough to recall the puerile threat of the Kaiser to Gerard, the bombastic assertions of other German leaders, of what Germany would do, the terms she would inflict, in victory. Mr. House and Mr. Wilson, and the American and European liberals who endorsed their ideals, were not aiming at a German peace. All that can be said for them, by way of excuse, is that they trusted to the League to right the wrongs they accepted—as they thought, temporarily —and that their high ambitions were frustrated by the human frailty of one whom they admired most. Why should it have been so? Was the air on those heights of idealism too rarefied for the lungs of an apostle of world brotherhood and democracy? It is not pleasant to remember the raucous laughter which mocked that failure in dirty, plague-ridden Moscow.

The Treaty was a trouble-maker from the beginning of the attempt to execute it. Even after the Germans had retired to digest its details, there was no certainty that they would sign. Within three days they began a series of protests, which had an immediate effect upon that prince of sophists, Smuts, who, by the 16th, was telling Mr. House that he and his South African colleague, Louis Botha, were considering refusal to sign, unless the Conference revised the terms to meet some of the German objections. Smuts, who had inspired the leveling against the Germans of pensions for Allied soldiers, in order to bolster his political machine in the faraway Union! Mr. House had his hands full, striving to resist the demands for tinkering with the Treaty, which, he believed—and probably rightfully—having been faultily drawn, should be left to the League for gradual correction in application. Only confusion could have come from hasty, controversial amendments. He tried to bring the Italians and the Jugo-Slavs to a compromise of their claims, and found the Italians now reasonable, the Jugo-Slavs uncooperative because they believed that if they gave in to Italy the Conference would be inclined to favor Austria-Hungary in Croatia, Carinthia and the Banat. He failed, principally, through lack of interest on all sides. It was as much as he could do to curb the French in delaying the proposed measures for bludgeoning Germany into submission if she persisted in refusing to sign. And Lloyd George and his military "yes-men" were having another fit of the blues, fearful of what would happen if Germany did withhold signature, anxious to yield anything the Germans demanded—at the expense of France, of course.

One thing, which seriously concerned Mr. House in these weeks of confused debate and garbled counter-purpose, was the insistence of the President in upholding the Council of Four in their refusal to make public the text of the Treaty. The Germans printed and sold copies for public distribution as soon as it was available to them, and it is a fact that the first "bootlegged" texts available to members of the Senate were translations from the German reprints. This, naturally, accomplished nothing in mitigating the wrath of the Republican majority over the President's "highhanded ways." Many Senators who were not extremists, including members of his own party, were provoked by what they considered an additional indignity inflicted upon the Legislative branch of the Government by the Executive. As Mr. House anticipated, it made more thorny the President's path after he returned home. "The Germans are giving us an example of open diplomacy," Mr. House entered in his diary, May 31.

He did, however, support Mr. Wilson in resisting the demands for alterations in the text. The principal concession to the Germans was in providing for a plebiscite to settle the disposition of Upper Silesia, a concession which Mr. House was disposed to question because he doubted whether a plebiscite could be held fairly or honestly in the existing circumstances. Certainly, remembering what happened in this area in 1938-39, it is evident that the plebiscite wrought no lasting, useful purpose. The time had long since passed in May-June, 1919, for concessions, amendments, redrafting. The Treaty was there, for good or ill, struck off in intolerance and accumulating hatred. The objective to concentrate upon, in Mr. House's judgment, was the creation of an international spirit which would come to believe increasingly in the amelioration of its faults and the enhancement of its recognizable good points.

So the weeks passed until June was drawing to a close. The Germans fumed and blustered. Foch methodically made his arrangements for extending his invasion of the right bank of the Rhine. The Allies squabbled and called names behind each other's backs. The American troops continued to sail home, very thankfully, at the rate of 300,000 a month. The Allied reply to the German protests was delivered, June 16. The Germans became angrier. They burned the French battle flags they were obligated to surrender. They would send only one plenipotentiary to represent them. The German crews scuttled the Scapa Flow fleet, to the intense indignation of the British, who tried to blame the Americans for these ships having been technically interned instead of surrendered.* The French blamed it on British "sloppiness." Clemenceau was persuaded by Mr. House not to occupy Essen as a punitive measure, to ignore the German acts as unworthy of notice. And on June 23 the Germans gave in, and sent word they would sign.

Five days later, June 28, to the accompaniment of booming guns and fanfares of trumpets, the representatives of the Weimar Republic filed slowly into the Hall of Mirrors and affixed their signatures to the Treaty, which was to make almost impossible their sturdy effort to erect a democratic Second Reich upon the ruins deserted by the Hohenzollerns. Impossible, that is, unless the newborn League of Nations employed its shadowy powers, conditioned on men's instinct for goodwill, to moderate the Treaty's harshness. German liberal statesmen wrought their best to create a partner of the democracies. No names shine brighter in the post-war decade than those of Friedrich Ebert, the saddler President; Gustav Stresemann, who collaborated faithfully with Briand and Barthou to ward off the gathering storm; and Walter Rathenau, whose brilliance was quenched by a Nazi assassin.

What did Mr. House and Mr. Wilson think of the Treaty which they had striven to make a testimony to tolerance? Mr. Wilson, after several years of illness and frustration, a helpless cripple, shut off from all con-

---

* Lloyd George, of course, was mainly responsible for the policy of internment rather than surrender. As a matter of fact, when the balance of the High Seas Fleet was surrendered after the signing of the Treaty, the British officers who inspected the capital ships pronounced them unfitted for British crews. They had been built for short North Sea cruises, with an emphasis upon shell-resistant qualities, divided up into small, dark compartments, cold, clammy, ill-ventilated. They were useless for British or American naval policies.

tact with reality, saw fit to permit an attempt by his lieutenant, Baker, to shift the burden for what had not been done to Mr. House, his friend. But there is a better and more honorable clue to how he felt in an address he made to the assembled members of the American delegation to the Peace Conference, June 3, while Paris awaited the Germans' decision. The meeting was called to canvass the possibility of amendments to meet the German protests. Its sense was that, while desirable, such amendments were hardly practicable.

"The great problem of the moment," the President said, "is the problem of agreement, because the most fatal thing that could happen, I should say, in the world, would be that sharp lines of division should be drawn among the Allied and Associated Powers. . . . What is necessary is to get out of this atmosphere of war. . . . I don't want to seem unreasonable, but my feeling is this: that we ought not, with the object of getting it signed, make changes in the Treaty, if we think that it embodies what we were contending for; that the time to consider all these questions was when we were writing the Treaty, and it makes me a little tired for people to come and say now that they are afraid the Germans won't sign, and their fear is based upon things that they insisted upon at the time of the writing of the Treaty. . . . Though we did not keep them from putting irrational things in the Treaty, we got very serious modifications out of them. If we had written the Treaty the way they wanted it, the Germans would have gone home the minute they read it. Well, the Lord be with us."

On June 29, the day after the Treaty was signed, Mr. House wrote in his diary a statement of his feelings, which, as the years passed, he did not essentially alter, although he was a man who was capable of changing his mind as new conditions arose and facts previously unrealized became perceptible to him:

"I am leaving Paris, after eight fateful months, with conflicting emotions. Looking at the Conference in retrospect there is much to approve and much to regret. It is easy to say what should have been done, but more difficult to have found a way for doing it. . . . How splendid it would have been had we blazed a new and better trail! However, it is to be doubted whether this could have been done, even if those in authority had so decreed, for the peoples back of them had to be reckoned with. It may be that Wilson might have had the power and influence if he had remained in Washington and kept clear of the Conference. When he stepped from his lofty pedestal and wrangled with representatives of other States upon equal terms, he became as common clay.

"To those who are saying that the Treaty is bad and should never have been made, and that it will involve Europe in infinite difficulties in its enforcement, I feel like admitting it. But I would also say in reply that empires cannot be shattered and new States raised upon their ruins without disturbance. To create new boundaries is always to create new troubles. The one follows the other. While I should have preferred a different peace, I doubt whether it could have been made, for the ingredients for such a peace as I would have had were lacking at Paris. . . . The same forces that have been at work in the making of this peace would be at work to hinder the enforcement of a different kind of peace, and no one can say with certitude that anything better than has been done could be done at this time. . . . And yet I wish we had taken the other road, even if it were less smooth, both now and afterward, than the one we took."

The only major change which Mr. House made with the passing years, in this contemporary estimate, was a strengthening of his conviction that the chief element in the failure of American policy in Paris was the presence of Mr. Wilson. "You mustn't blame him," he said, again and again. "He believed he was doing right. But it was the sort of situation he wasn't used to or fitted to handle. Up to then I had gone out and wrestled with the trouble-makers, the kind of men he didn't like or know how to handle. He didn't know how to handle men like Clemenceau and Lloyd George. Damned good men, my friend, good politicians, who had spent their lives struggling for power or to get in power and keep there. It hurt him to do that sort of thing. It hurt something in him deep down, something very fine. And when that was hurt he wasn't at his best. He got mad. And he could get mad faster and better than any man I know. Why, I remember that just before he was to leave Paris, after the Treaty was signed, one of the Frenchmen who was friendly to us came to me and said that he had given no answer to an invitation from Poincaré to a state dinner the night of his departure. The French were all upset about it.

"I went to ask him about it. He said: 'No, I'm not going. I'll be damned if I do. I'd choke if I had to sit beside Poincaré again.' 'But you can't refuse, Governor,' I told him. 'It isn't you, alone, who are involved. This is a compliment from the President of the French Republic to you as President of the United States, as the representative of the American people. You would be insulting the French people in the name of the American people.' Well, he went, but he sat beside Poincaré glowering, and he hardly said a word all evening, and left as early as he could."

7

These concluding days in Paris afforded the last opportunities for personal intercourse between the two men whose friendship had meant so much to their country and the world. In after years, Mr. House insisted that he had detected no lessening in the trust the President imposed in him, and at the time, no diminution in friendliness, although as he looked back, he said, he was regretfully aware of an all but imperceptible coolness, which he had set down to Mr. Wilson's perturbation by the trend the negotiations had taken. Of course, by this time, Mr. House was aware of Mrs. Wilson's active hostility to him, but he admitted that he had not been disposed to attach any importance to her feeling. It was incredible to him, always, that she could have vitiated in any degree the friendship which had united him with the President, the mutual confidence and interdependability.

There is a striking thumbnail sketch of Mr. Wilson in an entry in his diary of June 10. Both he and his friend were sitting for portraits by Sir William Orpen, which had been ordered by the British Government for the war archives. Orpen showed him that day the unfinished portrait of the President. Mr. House remarked on it: "It is an entirely different-looking gentleman from Sargent's esthetic scholar and has more of the 'rough and tumble' look. I have seen him look as Sargent sees him one time in twenty, but I have seen him nineteen times out of twenty look as Orpen sees him. I think I never knew a man whose general appearance changed so much from hour to hour. . . . It is not the President's face alone that changes. He is one of the most difficult and complex characters I have ever known. He is so contradictory that it is hard to pass judgment upon him. . . . When one gets access to him, there is no more charming man in all the world than Woodrow Wilson. I have never seen anyone who did not leave his presence impressed. He could use this charm to enormous personal and public advantage if he would."

On the 11th, Mr. House had his last extended interview with his friend. He was leaving for a week's holiday in England, and their talk was in the nature of a cleaning-up of matters to be left in Mr. House's discretion after Mr. Wilson sailed for home. There was no disagreement between them, the President, for example, assenting to Mr. House's suggestion that he should name Root to represent the United States on the bench of the International Court provided in the Covenant. The President told Mr. House that he had decided to endorse the proposition for amending the Treaty to provide for an Upper Silesian plebiscite, but Mr.

House made no reference to his own feeling that such a measure could not be conducted honestly and would only kindle fresh resentment between Germany and Poland. After Mr. House's return to Paris, the President accepted the wording by him of a statement for publication in the London *Daily Mail*. The single concrete indication that their relations had deteriorated is contained in Mr. House's diary, the entry of June 29:

"My last conversation with the President yesterday was not reassuring. I urged him to meet the Senate in a conciliatory spirit; if he treated them with the same consideration he had used with his foreign colleagues here, all would be well. In reply, he said: 'House, I have found one can never get anything in this life that is worth while without fighting for it.' I combated this, and reminded him that Anglo-Saxon civilization was built up on compromise."

There you had the issue between them finally joined. They never met again, although they continued in active correspondence until August 29, several days prior to Mr. Wilson's departure from Washington on his speaking trip for the League of Nations, which destroyed his health. The President, throughout this period while Mr. House continued to represent him in Paris, signed his messages "affectionately yours" and expressed warm personal interest in his friend and the members of the House family. In a message of August 15, the last signed personally by Mr. Wilson, he showed no loss of confidence in the ultimate success of his fight for the Treaty and the League Covenant. "We are going through a tremendous storm of all sorts of difficulties here, but the ship is steady and the officers not dismayed. We unite in the warmest messages."

The concluding message, of August 29, was occasioned, ironically, by the annual publication in the newspapers—as stated previously, it had occurred toward the end of every summer of Mr. Wilson's Administration—of reports of a break in their personal relationship. Mr. House cabled the President, August 26, from London: "Our annual falling out seems to have occurred. The Foreign Office received a cable the other day saying that we were no longer on good terms and asking that the Prime Minister and Balfour be informed. The Press Representatives also told me that they had the same news. I am wondering where this particular story originated and why they wanted the Prime Minister and Balfour to be informed. Tyrrell said it came from one of their men in New York and not from Washington. Affectionately yours, E. M. House." The President promptly cabled back, through the State Department, to the American Embassy: "Am deeply distressed by malicious story about break between us and thank you for the whole message about it. The best way to treat it is with silent contempt."

And there you have the record. The curtain descended, obviously not in enmity at the moment. Whatever feelings Mr. Wilson had cherished against his friend, during the trying months in Paris, must have been moderated temporarily in the perspective of time. A few days before he left for the West, September 2, Mr. House's English friend, Wiseman, lunched with him. They had some conversation about the absent Texan. Wiseman remarked that Colonel House "is trusted by all the statesmen in Europe." "And rightly," said the President, "for he is trustworthy." *

Mr. Wilson was not, perhaps, as buoyant in spirits as his message to Mr. House, quoted above, might suggest. For to one who saw him in those blistering, anxious days in Washington, when the temperature of partisan heat in the Senate Chamber outran the records of the pavement thermometers, he was a worn, haggard, sleepless and tormented man, living on his nerves and poised on the brink of collapse. It is a tribute to his courage that he continued, for three grueling weeks, his fight for the recovery of the ideals he had mortgaged in Paris. But the collapse was inevitable when it came in the night of September 25-26, as the Presidential train was running between Pueblo, Colorado, and Wichita, Kansas. Say this for Woodrow Wilson. He went down, like the soldiers whose deaths in battle had agonized him, fighting in the last ditch for what he believed to be right and just.

8

A considerable majority of the Senators to whom Mr. Wilson presented the Treaty of Versailles, July 10, 1919, were either dourly hostile or lethargic in their reception of him, and this applied to many members of his own party, who felt that he had slighted them in the past or else resented his misstep of last October, which had cost them the control of Congress and the flow of patronage and appropriations to which they had been accustomed. But many more than two-thirds of the Senate, including Republicans, restricted whatever hostility they entertained to the President himself. They had no fundamental criticisms of the Treaty or the League Covenant, except that they objected to the neglect of their Chamber's opinions on the tremendous issues involved. They felt that the President had treated them, as Senators, with a scornful contempt which they had not merited by past conduct, and which was tantamount

* Statement by Wiseman to Dr. Seymour, *Intimate Papers*. Last recorded comment by Mr. Wilson upon Mr. House.

to an attempt to belittle the prerogatives of the Legislative branch of the Government, under the Constitution, in its right of supervision of the treaty-making powers of the Executive. It would not be inaccurate to say that many, if not all, who felt this way, simply wanted to hurt and embarrass the President, individually. They did not, as a body, as a majority or as two-thirds of their Chamber's membership, wish to hurt or embarrass the cause of world peace or the future prosperity of the United States. Indeed, their master purpose, allowing for the conflicting motives and personalities of ninety-six men, of varying degrees of intelligence and standards of honor, was to safeguard the rights of the United States, and in connection with doing so, to teach Mr. Wilson that he, as President, could not ignore the Senate.

This was the prevailing sentiment in the Senate when the debates upon the Treaty began. Different men held different conceptions of the document and what it purported. There was no similarity of philosophical attitude, for instance, between the opposition of Borah of Idaho, a lifelong, sincere isolationist, and the jealous, pragmatical hatred of Wilson, the man, by Lodge of Massachusetts. Such a Treaty, by its very nature, was anathema to Borah, who held the President in earnest respect. It represented to Lodge an ideal commitment of the United States to assumption of her rightful place in the world, as John Hay, McKinley and Theodore Roosevelt had taught him. But it was a Democratic treaty, worse, a Wilson treaty. So it must be burdened with as many shallow, trivial amendments to the great idea of the League as might be relied upon not to harm the essentials of the League and the business interests of the United States, which Lodge served. Unfair to Germany? Bosh! That meant nothing to Lodge and the little band of Senators who served him. Germany had shown herself a menace to worldwide expansion of American trade. As for the revived prestige of the British Empire, Lodge was an Anglophile, as the Boston Irish would always tell you, despite or because of his Yankee ancestry. No, what Lodge hated about the Treaty was that he had been denied a hand in negotiating it.

To men like Boies Penrose and Philander C. Knox of Pennsylvania, old, cynical, wise politically, sniping at the Treaty meant a chance to undermine the infernal hold which Mr. Wilson had obtained upon the imagination of the people, a chance to build for a Republican victory in 1920. Penrose was dying in his chair, phlegmatically, uncomplaining, alert to the end. Outside his private life, he had no patience with the theory of idealism. He was a practical man, a rich man. The Treaty, he would admit, looked as if it would fix a world order in which Big Business might thrive; but Big Business would have a hell of a time if the Democrats stayed in power. So snipe Wilson, make him crawl, show the people how they must rely upon the vigilance of the Republican party to safeguard the country and their dividends and jobs. Brandegee of Connecticut was a man of the same stripe, who dressed like a fop, had a keen mind and debating ability which was not hindered by a peculiarly high, whining, nasal voice. He committed suicide shortly afterwards.

Then what of the jackals who fetched and carried for the strategists of Lodge's band? Albert Fall, of New Mexico, was to be convicted in his country's courts as a thief of his country's property, was to serve time in prison and die, unpardoned, deprived of the rights of citizenship, the one Senator of the United States to be punished so for a civil crime. The most pitiful of the group, big, handsome, friendly, smiling Warren Harding, was to be pushed into the Presidency by the Senate "insiders," to become the tool of the "Ohio Gang" and to die suddenly in office just before the scandal of graft and oil-lands looting in his Administration became known. Harding never had an original idea in his life, and it is doubtful if he ever had a consciously evil one; but he was the perfect example of what can happen in public life to the good-looking, plausible weakling, without self-taught convictions.* Of a different stamp from these two was Lodge's Democratic ace-in-the-hole, Jim Reed of Missouri, Hearst's spokesman on the Senate floor. A redoubtable debater, quick-thinking, pungent in speech, Reed had plenty of brains and a criminal lawyer's ability to fit his talents to any cause which paid a good retainer. In addition to these virtues, he was a machine politician, who hated Mr. Wilson, true liberalism, Mr. House and what he stood for in the Democratic organization, and the British Empire. He was a thorn in the side of his Democratic comrades, not one of whom could stand up to his powers of invective on the floor.

These were the eight men who were the activating force behind the Lodge Reservations, but Borah must be ranked apart from the other seven. His loftiness of soul, and selflessness in all he did, were on a par with Mr. Wilson's. Without his lion's voice, his power to convince all who listened to him in his disinterestedness, his gift for simplifying the most tangled questions, his blind yet honest faith in the foundations of the Republic, the Lodge clique would have had a much harder time to secure adoption of their Reservations. Of what other Senator, since the

---

* Harding's usual greeting, when I came in to see him, was to pull open a drawer in his desk. "Hullo, my boy! What will it be, Scotch or rye? Oh, Christian"—to his secretary—"let's have some ginger ale and Whiterock. You want me to say something, Smithy? What about? Oh, well, you know how I stand. I'll leave it to you."

great days of the Chamber's past, could it be written that the bare cry through the cloakrooms and galleries, "Borah's up!" would fill the empty seats, denuding even the hideaways of the bottle-tippers and poker-players, and causing demands for a quorum on the floor of the House. "If" is a mighty word, and treacherous. But if it had been possible to convince Borah that the League was a good instrument for the United States, the authority did not reside in any member of the Senate to thwart the Treaty's approval, no matter how vigorously men hated Woodrow Wilson.*

It is not the intention in anything said here to seem to deprecate the quality of the membership of the Senate of the United States in the years 1919 and 1920. It was probably a very good, run-of-the-mill Senate, of the pattern which has been prevalent since Senators were elected directly and ceased to have the character and permanence in office—on successful behavior—of ambassadors from almost sovereign States. The days of great oratory, in the early nineteenth-century tradition, passed out with the increasing complexity and quantity of business requiring the Chamber's deliberation. By the nature of its augmented responsibilities, more and more of the work has had to be done in Committee; the only way in which it can plow through the accumulated legislation of a session is to act upon bills with a minimum of debate, contrary to popular supposition. But on occasions of historical importance, such as the question of ratification of the Treaty of Versailles, the usual method is abandoned. The question is threshed out on the floor. There was no possibility of hamstringing the Treaty in the Foreign Relations Committee. It couldn't have been done, if Lodge had wanted to do it. The fight was in the open, and with all the animus the President had aroused, it ended in what was substantially a victory for him, thanks to the nonpartisan sympathy of eighty-one members for the Treaty and the Covenant in its main essentials.

This, it is fair to say, was a tribute to the commonsense and patriotism of the members of the Senate. Fall and Harding, Lodge and Jim Reed, were not typical of that membership any more than was Huey Long at a later date. It is probable that, as a body representative of a highly com-

---

* I know how firm was Borah's conviction about isolationism because I undertook to argue it with him the first time I ever talked to him alone. I came in for five minutes, and stayed three hours, which was a tribute to his willingness to learn from anyone, as well as to his unshakability. I mentioned the incident to Senator Kenyon a day or two later. Kenyon chuckled. "I wish you'd convinced him," he said. "But it wouldn't have been Borah, if you had. And I don't know but what I'm glad you missed out."

posite nation, the Senators in Washington would have shone by comparison with the contemporary Senate of France and the British House of Lords. The worst criticism that could have been brought against that Senate—and it would be relatively as true of the Senate of today—was that it included too many lawyers and rich, elderly business men, not enough agriculturists and intellectuals. It represented too heavily the vested wealth of the country, and the age average of its members was disproportionately exaggerated. But that, too, has been true of the Senate of the United States since the early days of the Republic, when successful men were farmers or petty merchants, and youth had not yet been branded as *prima facie* proof of incompetence.

It is doubtful if Iowa has ever been better represented than by her team of liberal Republicans, Cummins and Kenyon, whose open, legal minds were always on the side of constructive legislation. George Norris, of Nebraska, was the same force for radicalism as he has been ever since, although nowadays he is perhaps a shade more mellow and tolerant. The elder La Follette was setting the example his son, "Young Bob," is striving to parallel, handicapped by the same narrowness of vision and practice of political expediency. Hale, of Maine, had just been elected, and was showing himself to be quietly intelligent, a faithful worker. Capper, of Kansas, another new member, was modestly self-effacing, interested chiefly in the cause of agriculture, industrious to educate himself in problems of which he confessed his ignorance. McNary, of Oregon, a third new member, demonstrated the same canny, close-mouthed ability which has lifted him to the present leadership of his side of the Chamber. Charley Curtis was Republican floor leader, chunky, reserved, entirely partisan and uninspired, demonstrating at every turn the capacities of the political wheelhorse. Moses, of New Hampshire, also a new member, was a gabby, flip-tongued, small-town newspaper editor and product of the machine, who made himself useful to the Lodge clique by his turn for cheap wit and blind party loyalty—he cheerfully and unreservedly hated Mr. Wilson as a man who had twice triumphed over the Republican party. He was, in a way, the most obnoxious Republican in the Senate, because he represented, ungracefully, a profession which does not too often have the opportunity to reach the floor of Congress. He was not flattered by comparison with Capper, a strictly rural editor, not nearly so experienced or sophisticated.

Senator Colt, of Rhode Island, the lean, aristocratic son of the man who invented the arbiter of the Old Frontier, was a gentle, kindly man, inexperienced in politics, but whose age did not hinder him in developing an aptitude for statesmanship far in excess of that possessed by most of his fellows. Spencer, of Missouri, was a typical rich man—he had made his money, I think, in St. Louis real estate—likewise inexperienced in the craft he had assumed to practice rather late, but a fair representative of his kind, who, after all, are often sincerely influenced by the desire to use their economic independence as an opportunity for public service.

These were the Senators on the Republican side of the Chamber who stand out in one man's recollection, after twenty years, as typical of their several groups.

The Democratic minority was not so varied in composition—the usual consequence of the Solid South's custom of returning, again and again, any man who maintains party loyalty, votes right and stays out of jail. They were conspicuously lacking in debating ability, a handicap which was to tell heavily against them in the struggle over the Treaty. Their best man in this field, Reed, was a tower of strength for the Republicans. But they did possess the most distinctive, and next to Borah, certainly the ablest, Senator, in John Sharp Williams of Mississippi, last of the traditional figures of the Old South of song and story, a great gentleman, a great statesman, a scholar who put to shame, when he chose—and his favorite Bourbon allowed him—the shoddy, conventional use of stale quotations and analogies which constituted the oratory of Lodge. He spoke for our country's mighty past. We shall never see his like again. Peace to his ashes, and let nothing that has been written here reflect upon his memory, his unselfishness, his integrity of spirit.*

Very different, as a representative of the South, was "Cotton Ed" Smith, of South Carolina, who, unfortunately and by reason of Southern political methods, is still with us. Underwood, of Alabama, typified the new industrial South. In political thought there was nothing to differ-

---

* Senator Williams enjoyed the capacity of the Old School for ripe Bourbon. I have seen him interrupt debate to score a point, clinging to his desk with both hands for support, but piercing his opponent's armor with every thrust, his logic and pursuit of the thread of the argument as relentlessly intelligent as his metaphor was brilliant. I remember helping him on a street car, with the assistance of the conductor, in front of the Senate Office Building. We conversed until the conductor stopped at a certain corner. "Here you are, Senator," he said. We helped the old gentleman to the street. "May I walk with you, Senator?" I asked; "I live nearby." "I thank you, sir," he replied, "but my boy, Jim, is waiting yonder." I followed the wave of his hand to where a Negro man as venerable as the Senator stood, smiling. "I bid you good afternoon," he added punctiliously, and started to walk toward Jim. But at the curb he paused and turned around. "I should like to have had the honor of knowing your mother, sir," he said. When I climbed back on the car the conductor and all the passengers were smiling. "They don't come often like the Senator," the conductor said, giving the motorman the bell.

entiate him from a score of Republicans who spoke for Big Business. The venerable Senator Culberson, of Texas, who could remember the ante-bellum period of his State, was so crippled by palsy as to be a pathetic figure, invariably in his seat, attentive to what went on, but powerless to assume the leadership for which his experience fitted him. Senator Hitchcock, of Nebraska, was minority leader of the Foreign Relations Committee, and as such conducted the fight for the Treaty on the floor. An Omaha newspaper editor, he was an honorable and intelligent man, but seriously lacking in those qualities of personality which make for an impressive appearance in debate. He deserved, however, a greater success than that with which he met. His diligence and pains were balked by the President's stubborn refusal to listen to reason. He was not even able, in crucial moments, to gain Mr. Wilson's ear. No Senator, charged with equal responsibility, ever was rewarded with such complete failure in cooperation.

Fletcher, of Florida, was a good, uninspired politician. Atlee Pomerene, of Ohio, was a somewhat clownish man, whose outstanding virtue was an ability to get along with his opponents. Ashurst, of Arizona, new to the Chamber, was—well, the same well-meaning but inconclusive exhibitionist that he is today, intoxicated by his own voice and the use of unfamiliar words and apposite phrases. Walsh, of Massachusetts, who spoke for the South Boston Irish, was savagely anti-British, really more concerned with De Valera's fledgling Irish rebellion than with the concept of the League of Nations. Caraway, of Arkansas, and Pat Harrison, of Mississippi, were demonstrating the same routine, strictly partisan capacities they showed afterwards. With McKellar, of Tennessee, they were usual products of Southern political machines, suffering from want of effective opposition or any opposition at all. Pittman, of Nevada, was the best of the new men on the Democratic side. It would be futile to go on with the list. Other men were as good, perhaps better; but these men had personality of one kind or another, and stood forth as representative of the political conditions which had sent them to the Chamber.

Summing up, the situation in the Senate of 1919 was that the Republicans had the advantage in brains, oratory—and what counted most, numbers. What they lacked, and what would have defeated them, had the minority enjoyed adequate leadership from the White House, was a good cause. Nobody knew this better than they did. The President, in the last analysis, defeated himself. He was well served in the Senate by men, as a rule, of inferior capacity, but of unquestioning party loyalty, whatever their personal opinions.

9

While the Senate was cogitating how to make the President as miserable as possible without throwing a monkey wrench into the international machinery, and the President's frayed nerves were tightening perceptibly from day to day in the humid misery of a Washington summer, Mr. House was working as hard as ever in London and Paris to put the League in position to take over effectively the innumerable chores, direct and indirect, which were left to its discretion by the Treaty of Versailles and the companion treaties, terminating almost as troublesomely the belligerent relations of the Allies with Austria-Hungary, Bulgaria and Turkey. The wreckage of the Dual Monarchy and Bulgaria "stayed put," as we know, but in Turkey a man named Kemal Pasha, who was as unknown to the world as Lenin had been, was busily preparing to demonstrate the vitality of the Ottoman peasantry, and to wreck the chestnut-stealing tactics of Lloyd George's Greek dupes, all excited over a recrudescence of their age-old dream of re-creating a shadow of the Byzantine Empire. This was the first time anyone had made a monkey out of Venizelos, who was regarded by Mr. House as the ablest statesman in Europe; but to give Venizelos his due, it should be added that he was betrayed by the British Prime Minister's engagement to give more than moral support to the Greek attempt to conquer the Smyrna hinterland. Under political pressure at home, Lloyd George withdrew even the moral support, and the new Turkey was born, compact, revitalized and healthier for the amputation of its vexing minorities.

Nobody, in the summer of 1919, had the slightest idea that the United States would fail to ratify the Treaty, because nobody anticipated the unreasonableness of mind which Mr. Wilson was to permit to guide him after he succumbed to his illness. One of Mr. House's principal tasks was in perfecting with Clemenceau and Lloyd George the arrangements for the first meeting of the League Assembly, scheduled to convene in Washington some time in November, immediately after ratification by the Senate, with Mr. Wilson presiding over the deliberations of the instrument he had identified so earnestly with himself. As a complementary task, Mr. House spent nearly two months in London, ironing out the four possible sources of controversy in the future relations of the United States with the British Empire. These were: the question of the naval programs of the two leading sea powers—which was to be settled, along the lines he had contemplated, by the next Republican Administration through the initiative of Secretary of State Hughes; the settlement of the Irish rebellion, and Ireland's future status; the general policy of the

League toward these, and other possible sources of trouble; and the definite adjustment of the financial obligations of the Allies to the United States, and of Germany to them.

Of these, as matters developed, the most important was the last. Mr. House had perceived, from the moment of the entry of the United States into the war, that the colossal loans made by the Administration for the purpose of carrying on hostilities—loans largely spent in this country—contained infinite possibilities of harm and misunderstanding. He was under no illusions as to the probability of their repayment in whole, any more than he was as to Germany's capacity to meet the absurd claims of the Allies upon her war-strained economy. He wrote the President to this effect from London, July 30: "Do you not think also that our people should be warned not to expect complete payment of loans to the Entente? Should they not be asked to consider a large share of these loans as a part of our necessary war expenditures, and should not an adjustment be suggested by us and not by our debtors? If this is done, then it would be well to do it with a *beau geste*. For instance, I notice we have sold one billion of war material in France to the French Government for three hundred millions. Would it not have been better to have made this a gift in name, as, indeed, it is in fact? . . . If I were you I should take some early occasion to invoke the sober attention of our people to these dangers."

On September 30, he returned to this subject in a letter from Paris, in which he outlined, briefly and succinctly, an elaborate plan for weaving into one whole the complicated financial relationships of the United States and the former belligerents. He advised that the United States and Britain "should fund the interest on the Allied debts for a period of from three to five years, and agree to defer capital payments for at least five years"; that Britain should accept from France the obligations of the lesser powers to her, and that the United States, in turn, should accept these obligations; that "the United States and possibly Great Britain . . . accept some portion of the Reparation bonds received from Germany in settlement of a certain percentage of the Allied debts remaining" after the preceding transfers from France and Britain; and that, so soon as the Reparations had been defined, "there should be a scaling of the German obligations"; and finally, that "foreign exchange should be stabilized." The advantage of this plan was that it would give the United States a right to influence the mitigation of the impossible financial terms imposed upon Germany. Its disadvantage, in the eyes of many Americans, would have been that it tied the United States tightly into the Reparations problem and the whole thorny debt structure of Europe. But as against this, Mr. House argued, we were involved in this problem, in any case, whether we liked it or not; and if we wanted to collect our loans, the closer we were to the problem, the more authority we would have in enforcing methods of collection between the different nations, which might have a chance of working out with a minimum of harm and disturbance to world trade—and our trade.

There is much sense in his conclusion from the premises he established: "I believe our people will be willing to charge a part of our foreign loans to war expenditures—particularly, if they find England and France doing likewise. England has loaned Russia nearly three billion dollars, and she has loaned France and Italy together nearly four billions of dollars. She did not do this because she loved either Russia, France or Italy to any such extent; she did it merely as a part of her own war expenditures. The purpose was to defeat Germany, and she could do it best by sustaining her allies. We were actuated by the same motives, and we should be willing to take this view. If some such settlement as I have outlined is not made, it is certain we will not be able to collect our debts in full, and it is also certain that we will incur the everlasting ill-will of those to whom we have advanced loans."

The developments of the future proved him right beyond the possibility of dispute. One of the few times he ever ridiculed a public man was when he was told of President Coolidge's commentary upon the debt protests of the British and French Governments. " 'They hired the money, didn't they?' " he repeated. "Does he think he's talking about a Vermont farm mortgage? And that man is President of the United States, and Wall Street considers him sound!" A good many years after the war, Mr. House came around to the tentative opinion that the best way for the United States to have realized definitely, on at least a portion of the loans, would have been to take remuneration in the form of British and French colonial possessions in the West Indies and the Pacific. This was after Lindbergh's flight to Paris had dramatized for the public the possibilities of trans-oceanic aviation, which were to be realized so impressively within less than a decade.

"Nobody thought of it, then," he said regretfully. "Oh, a few fellers talked to me about it. I remember you did. But it didn't seem practical. Our people didn't want more colonies. We were anxious even to get rid of the Philippines. And I knew the English and French Governments would have been sour; but I'm sure it could have been done, if it had been undertaken in the right way. If they hadn't been willing to go any further than ninety-nine year leases, say, it would have been of advantage to us." As the years passed, and the probability of recovering a modicum of the readjusted debts diminished with the increase in world chaos, he became still more partial to the idea. "We need airplane bases," he insisted. "We're going to need them more and more. There's the Canal to be protected, and the air route to Asia. We've got those fellers on the hip. They have plenty of islands to spare without hurting themselves. We ought to take a strong diplomatic line toward them." *

One of Mr. House's most important achievements, during his stay in London, was to persuade his friend, Lord Grey, despite failing eyesight and ill-health, to accept the post of Ambassador on Special Mission to the United States. Ostensibly, Grey's mission had for its objective the settlement with the President and the State Department of the first three problems, which contained the germs of trouble between Britain and the United States: the naval program, Ireland, and, to a lesser extent, the formulation of League policy. Really, Mr. House wanted Grey in Washington to use his influence, as the Englishman Mr. Wilson admired and respected beyond all others, to urge upon the President the necessity, in the interests of all nations, to compromise his differences with the Senate, the gravity of which had become apparent after the Senate, at last, received an official copy of the Treaty. This, and this alone, was the reason why Grey consented to come at great personal inconvenience to himself. The Embassy was perfectly capable of handling the questions given as an excuse for his Mission, and actually did so. Grey was doomed, as will be told, to spend his three months in the United States in irritating idleness, with his only reward the opportunity to undergo an operation at Johns Hopkins, which saved him from the blindness London specialists had warned him was inevitable.

He sailed for the United States late in September, accompanied by Sir William Tyrrell as his secretary, although that title is scarcely fair to

* The Franklin D. Roosevelt Administration drove a possible entering wedge for such a policy by an agreement with Great Britain of April 6, 1939, providing for joint control and administration of Canton and Enderbury Islands, in the Phoenix Group, about halfway between Hawaii and Australia. The agreement is for fifty years, and will continue indefinitely after that period, unless previously terminated or modified. In the case of these islands there was, it is true, a dissension as to rights of ownership by discovery and occupation. The United States, apparently, discovered them, but, as so often in the history of American discoveries, failed to confirm discovery by occupation. Dissatisfaction of the Negro populations of the British West Indian islands has been recently so pronounced that a Royal Commission has made an extensive survey of the situation, with preliminary recommendations for augmentation of Imperial funds for slum clearance, education and medical relief. There is talk of federating the islands. Many of them, unless adequately defended, are potential menaces to the Panama Canal and our Caribbean possessions and Gulf coasts.

Tyrrell, who was always far more important than it would seem to indicate to the statesmen he served. He was at the time—or became soon
afterward—Permanent Under-Secretary of the Foreign Office, the key
post in the British system of government.

10

We must go back to the Missouri Compromise and the debates over
slavery to find a Senatorial crisis which paralleled in national importance
the battle over the Treaty of Versailles, or which gripped so completely
the country's interest and stirred such violent controversial emotions.
The future of the United States was in the balance, the future trend of
policy in Europe, the peace and prosperity of the world. The men who
debated in Washington, most of them with entire honesty of purpose,
were to exert a staggering influence upon men and women they had
never seen; families would be broken and scattered, boys as yet unborn
would be conscripted to die, ships undesigned would be sunk, rulers and
governments would pass, billions of wealth would be dissipated through
the abuses of peace and the exigencies of war, an obscure, psychopathic
house-painter would be spewed up from the miseries of Central Europe
to lead his people in the most terrible campaign of bigotry, torture and
oppression since the Thirty Years' War.

And mostly because two elderly Americans, Woodrow Wilson and
Henry Cabot Lodge, happened to hate each other with a vehemence
which permitted neither to see truly, in perspective, the possible consequences of what they did. For this battle in the Senate, which assumed
a meretricious semblance to an issue of high policies, was not in fact
founded on the disagreement of two opposite schools of thought, two
differing conceptions of the national interest. It was joined because
Lodge—and those Senators who agreed with him—were determined to
humiliate the President; and because the President, sick and shaken and
deprived of wise advice, was equally determined to wreck what he had
helped to create, no matter what suffering his stubbornness entailed,
rather than yield one mite of satisfaction to his adversary.

Gradually, as the struggle dragged on, week after week, in hearings
before the Foreign Relations Committee, on the floor of the Chamber,
in the newspapers, on lecture platforms, in homes and clubs, wherever
people gathered together, it took on an added accent of acrimony. It
became contentious. Where, in the beginning, men had sought to adjust
conflicting views with a measure of reasonableness, they became positive
in opinion and hostile to those who differed with them. It was the old

story: the longer you drag out a controversy, the more embittered become the participants. People grew weary of the interminable dissension, impatient with compromise. They wanted to end it, one way or the other. And Lodge and his advisers were quick to perceive this popular state of mind, and to capitalize it for their advantage. The situation was favorable to their purpose. The soldiers were pouring home on every westbound ship, sick of the war and all it had connoted, anxious to get back to their jobs. Business and industry were puzzling over the problem of shifting from a wartime to a peace basis. The war was dwindling in significance, becoming transformed into a specter people wished to forget. Prohibition and woman suffrage were looming in the offing, and nobody knew what problems they would produce to add complexity to life. National idealism, which had been flogged to a pitch of hysteria by propaganda and the excitement of great achievements, underwent a spontaneous reaction into an opposite extreme of cynical detachment. People began to think only of the burdens and hardships they had experienced, forgot the glories their efforts had made possible, became impatient with "foreigners," who had needed American help to escape the German menace and already were protesting the repayment of money Americans had gone without to lend them.

It was natural, then, that the President's attitude of non-cooperation with the Senate should arouse, first, misgivings, and finally, distrust and hostility, as the months passed, even amongst men who were inclined to favor the broad purposes of the Covenant. This was true of many influential newspaper editors, speakers and publicists. They became suspicious that some of the allegations of secret commitments abroad were founded in fact, that the League did constitute an entanglement which would react to the disadvantage of the United States unless additional safeguards were written into the Covenant. What was happening was so apparent to friends of Mr. Wilson and the League that it was not open to argument; but he refused to credit the validity of their opinions. He set his jaw, and resisted belligerently all suggestions of compromise. And yet so strong was his fundamental position, product of the patient endeavors of Mr. House and his technical advisers in Paris, that, until after he became ill, and his paralyzed hand slipped from the helm to be replaced by the inexperienced grasp of a well-meaning but mistaken woman, it was by no means certain that the Lodge Reservations to the Covenant could secure a majority in the Senate. A little conciliation, a saving sense of humor, and things might very well have gone differently, for there were many Republican Senators who did not relish the spectacle of their body engaged in a palpable effort to thwart public policy and humiliate the President of the United States.

"This is not good politics," Senator Colt declared to me. "It is not good Republican politics. It is not good Democratic politics. It is not patriotic. It is un-American. We are losing sight of what we have been fighting for: to make war as impossible as we can, and to keep on doing our share as a great nation."

Senator Kenyon said to me, after the first rejection of the Treaty, November 19—and he had tears in his eyes:

"I am ashamed and disgusted. I cannot continue a member of a body which can be so small. If this is politics, I'm out of it. I'll get out as soon as I can."

He did. One of Harding's excellent appointments, made in friendship to a man he respected without exactly knowing why, was of Kenyon to the Federal bench.*

I could go on and list other men who felt almost as strongly, but who were powerless to break the shackles of party allegiance on an issue which, after all, the President had permitted his foes to build to a false significance by his own temperamental deficiencies. But even so, had Mr. Wilson's physical strength held out it is quite possible that, unreasonable as he was, the sheer justice and rightness of his cause would have enabled him to squeeze out of the situation into which he had been maneuvered. This would certainly have been so had he been in his right mind when Mr. House returned in October, with the intention of using his masterly powers of conciliation to engineer a compromise between his friend and the Reservationists. It is true that Mr. House himself succumbed to the mental strain imposed upon him by apprehension over the evil effects produced by the President's illness. He was carried from the steamer when he reached New York, a very sick man in the realization that the friendship, which had meant so much to him, was crumbling along with the dream of international cooperation the two of them had labored to perfect. But he was not discouraged. He continued the fight, and he would have won the fight had Woodrow Wilson, who lay in the White House, crippled and inert, been able to ignore the influences which used his helplessness to further a personal prejudice.

* A Japanese correspondent for two of the great Tokyo and Osaka newspapers sat next to me in the Senate Press Gallery while the vote was being taken on the Treaty. He laughed all the time, quietly and politely. "It iss so fonny," he kept repeating. "It iss so fonny. Why do they do thiss so fonny? You excuss'? But I muss' laugh."

II

There is a note of ironic tragedy in the circumstance that physical misfortune handicapped almost simultaneously the three men, whose minds—had they been able to meet in health and amity—could almost certainly have forced a satisfactory solution of the personalized battle over the Treaty and the Covenant in the Senate. Lord Grey, wearing dark glasses, condemned to a twilight world, was at a disadvantage in performing his mission unless he had the confidence of the President, and this demanded the continuation of the President's confidence in Mr. House. Mr. House was about to leave Paris in a state of mental exhaustion. The President was so prostrated by his own efforts, and the fatigue of his Western trip, that he suffered a stroke of paralysis in the early morning hours of October 2. So, at the very moment that the Lodge cabal were driving forward the drafting of Reservations to the Covenant, these three men, who possessed the most enlightened attitude toward the world's future problems, were casualties to their joint efforts for humanity. Surely it is not an exaggeration to say that the forces of darkness were in the ascendant at this moment when the brotherhood of man attained to its last clear vision of tolerance, only to have the brief gleam consumed in the shadows of hatred and jealousy.

Washington, in those months, became a war zone, in which the weapons were secrecy, malice and innuendo. The White House was cut off from the outside world like a beleaguered fortress, and for this its occupants were to blame. There was a widespread sympathy for Mr. Wilson in his trouble. Even in the Capitol, at the other end of Pennsylvania Avenue, the hearts of most of the President's political adversaries were warm for him and eager to work out a plan for salvaging the essentials of his grandiose project. People wanted him to realize the vision which had been given him. It was only necessary for him to show a reasonable degree of willingness to compromise; but something had happened to him in recent months, or perhaps in recent weeks. And perhaps, too, others presumed to speak for him, when the time came to speak, with an assuredness not justified by the situation. We shall never know fully the processes of his mind in this period of pain and disillusionment, because the records which attempt to clarify his thoughts are manifestly warped and prejudiced.

It is difficult to re-create the Washington of the fall and winter of 1919-20, and to do so with any conviction of fairness. There was a deal of bitterness in the air. The minority of the prejudiced, on either side of the controversy, were much more vocal than the great majority, who wanted to save the organic whole of the idea for which the war had been fought and so many men had died. Again, it was the old story. A little venom, skilfully distilled, went farther than sincerity and reason. There was, so far as Mr. Wilson was concerned, a lack of leadership and exposition of his case—for which he must be held responsible, however severe the ailment which beset him. He showed, if he did not show anything weaker, a lamentable tendency to yield to light gossip, and to set the value of his own ego higher than the hopes men held for the future. With the stubborn arrogance of an invalid, he set himself against acceptance of pin-pricks to the value of the structure he had helped to create. Against the urgence of the best liberal opinion in the United States and the European democracies, he decided that the Covenant was worthless weighted down by the Lodge Reservations. He stood alone amongst men of worth in this attitude.

One of the needlessly tragic aspects of his situation was the veil of secrecy which was thrown around his capacities during his illness. It gave opportunity for countless lies and perversions of the truth—and the truth was bad enough. Mr. Wilson was not eligible to be President of the United States over a period of several months in the fall and winter of 1919-20. Article II, Section 1, paragraph 6 of the Constitution states: "In case of the removal of the President from office, or of his death, resignation or inability to discharge the powers and duties of the said office, the same shall devolve on the Vice-President." Congress, as it was authorized to do, additionally provided for the contingency of the lack of a Vice-President, by the Act of January 19, 1886, naming the Cabinet officers in order of seniority, beginning with the Secretary of State.

Mr. Wilson was so ill during this period that he could not sign State papers unaided; it was necessary for his hand to be guided through a signature. Worse than this, he was incapable of assimilating and understanding State papers and acts of legislation. He was not out of his mind, as was charged; he was simply too weak to give his attention to matters of moment involving questions of revenue, administration and diplomacy. Decisions either were put off or left to Mrs. Wilson to decide, according to her own judgment or the advice she conceived to be of value in the circumstances. She says, in her *Memoir,* that she accepted the advice of Dr. Francis X. Dercum, of Philadelphia, one of the specialists who treated the President, in permitting him to continue in office. Why did she take Dr. Dercum's advice? Dr. Dercum was not a responsible officer of the Government. The legal course for her to follow would have been to take the advice of the Attorney-General. In all probability, he would have advised a meeting of the Cabinet, with the Vice-President presiding, and the Cabinet almost certainly would have sought a ruling upon the Attorney-General's brief from the Supreme Court.

The situation presented a problem, it is true, in that there were no precedents for it. But the bulk of informed constitutional legal opinion held to the view that Mr. Wilson was, in the words of the Constitution, afflicted with "inability to discharge the powers and duties of the said office." Mrs. Wilson has stated in her *Memoir* that Secretary Lansing held this view. He did. So did Secretary of the Interior Lane.* So, I have reason to think, did Secretary of War Baker. Vice-President Marshall certainly did, but he was constrained by the manifest delicacy of his position, as next in succession, from lending the slightest support to any project to have Mr. Wilson advised to retire. Many of the best legal minds in Congress, and several members of the Supreme Court, were of the opinion that the Vice-President erred in this delicacy. As representatives of legal opinion outside the Government, I believe, both ex-President Taft and ex-Senator Root thought privately that Mr. Wilson was culpable of an indelicacy in retaining an office he was unable to execute, at least as pronounced as Mr. Marshall's excess of delicacy in refusing to intervene. Similarly, Mr. House never had any doubt that the graceful thing for his friend to have done was to turn over the reins to a Vice-President of his own party, who would have striven to carry out the President's policies for the duration of the term. The situation, to his mind, paralleled that which would have been created in November, 1916, had Mr. Hughes been elected President. And in that contingency, remember, Mr. Wilson had resolved to make way for a Republican Administration, in order that there might be no loss of energy in pressing a definite foreign policy.

It is indicative of the shift in Mr. Wilson's mental attitude that he pursued a course, in 1919, which was hostile to all that he had believed

---

* Lansing's resignation was requested by Mr. Wilson, February 7, 1920, on the ground that he had violated "constitutional law and practice" in conferring with other Cabinet officers on public affairs. There is an unconscious hint of humor in the President's letter. Lansing had long been unable to confer with the President, and being a sound lawyer and a responsible official with a multitude of international problems on his hands, it is not strange that he desired the advice of his associates. Lane resigned, March 1, in disgust with the irregularities which made impossible efficient administration of the Interior Department, as of other Government Departments. Mrs. Wilson states (*My Memoir*) that he was "very angry" over delays by the President in affixing his signature to oil leases, and she adds, without adducing any reason for her words: "When I look back upon what occurred in the Harding Administration oil scandals I thank God for my husband's wisdom."

and professed as a statesman and a student of American government. The plain truth is, that over an indeterminate period of several months the United States had no Chief Executive, in a responsible sense. Mrs. Wilson, loyally, if mistakenly, undertook to carry on a pretense of the Presidency, aided by the little group of friends and relatives who had her confidence in what was undoubtedly a most distressing time. Not even Tumulty, the President's secretary, saw him in this period. The Government ran on by the thrust of the momentum which had been built up in the war years. It is not a pleasant memory to entertain, for the dangers in such a course need scarcely be stressed. And if no worse harm flowed from it, the events consequent upon Mr. Wilson's incapacity insured the defeat of the Treaty, and the ultimate collapse of the League of Nations as a regenerative influence in a sick and weary world.

12

Immediately after Mr. House reached New York, and while he was too ill to receive callers, I sent him word that Washington was flooded with gossip of a most spiteful nature, reflecting upon members of his family and various of his intimates as well as himself. This gossip was so widespread, it permeated so many different circles, and its putative object to break down Mr. House's reputation was so transparent, that I felt he should know of it more definitely than he did, no matter how much it hurt him. He agreed with me. He was concerned, as I had been, not particularly for what was being said critically of himself and those close to him, but for the infinitely more important disruptive effect of such stories upon matters of State. I do not think that any responsible person, who happens to be ignorant of these stories, would be edified or entertained if they were repeated here. They touched a pathetic depth of human malice. It is not flattering to Mr. Wilson's memory that they were spread, ostensibly, in his behalf. They deserve mention only in so far as they influenced men's public motives and the course of events with which the American people were concerned.*

I was in close touch with the struggle, inside and outside the Senate, over the Treaty; and as it happened, by the accident of social contact,

* The slandering of Mr. House was no worse than that of the President. Mr. House, at any rate, wasn't accused of insanity. The difference between the two campaigns was that the allegations against Mr. House and his family and intimates were given credence by persons who knew the personalities involved. Those directed against the President came from sources, however high, which were irresponsible and had no knowledge about the matters they circulated. Both campaigns were utterly contemptible.

I was one of the few people in Washington who had an inkling of conditions in the White House through a kinsman of the President, who was in and out of the building once or twice a week and had access to the President's bedside as soon as Mr. Wilson could receive members of his family. This kinsman volunteered information to me, as I understood it, because he sympathized with my political views. The information was given under the old newspaper code which forbids printing or using it, except as it may guide the possessor in reaching intelligent conclusions. I should say that I repeated completely what I was told to only three people: Mr. House, Lord Grey and Sir William Tyrrell—and to the last two only at Mr. House's definite request, which was made for nonpartisan and personal reasons. I do not mean that I refrained from letting various interested people know that I possessed such information. Senator Hitchcock, in the unfortunate position of being mouthpiece in the Chamber for a leader with whom he had no contact, was appreciative of what I was able to tell him, and assured me that it was news to him. I have reason to believe that Tumulty did not know as much as I did. But all I told Hitchcock, and several other men in key positions, was that:

First, the President definitely was not insane, as was being rumored; of course, Hitchcock knew this after he and Fall, as a subcommittee of the Foreign Relations Committee, called on the President, really to determine his mentality, after the first defeat of the Treaty, November 19;

Second, he was unable to sign documents, unaided;

Third, he was dependent upon Mrs. Wilson to digest the documents sent to him for approval;

Fourth, he was more bitterly opposed to compromising with the Lodge cabal than ever;

Fifth, a rift had most certainly developed between himself and Mr. House, the reasons for which I gave Hitchcock, and to which he assented as credible and in line with his own opinion;

Sixth, that it was fairly certain that Lord Grey would not be received, and allowed to use his eloquence to persuade the President to compromise with the Senate majority.

"Just how do you come to know these things?" Hitchcock asked.

"They come to me through a channel the privacy of which I have promised to respect," I answered. "But I have been allowed to disclose the identity of my informant to Colonel House. If you care to, you might ask him what he thinks of it."

Senator Hitchcock sighed. He was wearing himself out in a thankless task.

"Oh, I scarcely think it's necessary for me to do that," he said. "Well, it looks as though the country would have to struggle along without a President, doesn't it?"

"It isn't what the Founding Fathers contemplated," I said. "If Borah will lend me the phrase."

He struck his hand on his desk.

"What a hopeless situation," he exclaimed.

The sole comment that this incident calls for, I think, is the extraordinary, no less than hopeless, situation, which it reveals in the fact that one of the great legislative officers of Government was placed in the humiliating position of having to obtain information of vital importance from a private citizen. How could the Senate function without the cooperation of the Executive, especially in a Treaty question? It was worse than a hopeless situation. It was an impossible situation. More, if the Constitution means what it seems to, it was, at the least, an extra-legal situation.

It would be erroneous to give the impression, however, that the President's feebleness continued to be as grave as it was in the early weeks of his illness. He recovered very slowly, although it is doubtful if he was ever, within the next four to six months, constitutionally able to carry out the powers and duties of his office. His irascibility and unreasonableness, certainly, remained so pronounced that he was able, on the eve of the vote on ratification, to dictate a letter advising his Senate followers that, with the Lodge Reservations, the Treaty would be nullified rather than ratified. A number of Democratic Senators murmured rebellion, but the morale had been chilled out of the minority by the mischances and tactical errors of the past year. They yielded to party discipline. Combined with the little group of "bitter-enders" who opposed ratification in any form, they defeated the Treaty by fifty-five votes to thirty-nine. If they had voted with the conservative Republicans, in violation of the President's instructions, the Treaty would have been ratified by eighty-one votes to thirteen, which would have been a fair representation of public opinion in the Senate and amongst the people at large.

So let it be said again, regretfully: Woodrow Wilson was responsible for the final defeat of the Treaty and Covenant he had helped to write and afterwards permitted his apologists to disparage, but which he regarded so highly that he would not suffer men who doubted their complete wisdom, to attempt to insert counter-checks, in the American tradition, upon the documents' possible defects. He, as much if not more than any statesman, was responsible for the failure of the League of Nations.

So unreasoning was he that, when the Treaty was reintroduced in the Senate several months later, in the hope that he would at last heed the advice of his well-wishers and collaborators in the Treaty, he persisted in his stubborn course of the self-appointed martyr. His future biographer, Baker, joined in this appeal. But Mr. Wilson reiterated his previous insistence to Senator Hitchcock that the Reservations constituted nullification, not ratification. It is a tribute to the standard of common sense and patriotism in the Senate that, once more, the men who shared with the President the treaty-making power showed overwhelmingly their desire to cooperate in establishing the new world order for which Mr. Wilson had argued. Ratification, March 19, 1920, lacked the required two-thirds assenting by only seven votes—the tally was forty-nine for ratification, thirty-five against. If the President had done what the friends of the League asked him to do, and kept his hands off, contenting himself with the assertion that any harm produced by the Reservations must rest upon their sponsors, then the vote would have been seventy-two for ratification, and but twelve opposed.

Mr. House wrote him twice, after the first failure of the Treaty, November 24 and November 27, urging this general policy upon him. The letters were never answered. "I wonder if he ever saw them," Mr. House said a couple of weeks later. "I can't understand it, I can't understand it! Lord, if I could get fifteen minutes with him I know he'd see the light. This is the greatest misfortune that ever happened. No one can say what may happen from it."

13

Lord Grey had come to the United States with the approval and sympathy of the United States Government. The President was duly notified of his arrival by the British Embassy through the State Department. Mrs. Wilson also speaks in her *Memoir* of a visit paid to the White House, September 30, by Sir William Wiseman, of whom she remarks: ". . . a secret agent of the British Government. He said he had important information for the President, and hoped Mr. Wilson would give him a private audience. I asked him to come at 11 A.M., when I told him my husband was ill and that I would receive the information and convey it to the President. If Sir William would return at two o'clock, I promised that the President's answer would be available. I had never liked this plausible little man. So I was glad my husband decided his information was not important enough for further consideration."

Now, Sir William was not merely "a secret agent." He was the Chief of the British Military Intelligence in the United States, and in this capacity had collaborated with the United States Government during the war. But beyond this, he had been—and still was—a confidential diplomatic agent of his Government, with a quasi-ambassadorial status. He had been sent here, first, it will be remembered, to act as liaison official between the British Embassy and Mr. House, prior to the entry of the United States into the war, the unusual step having been taken by the Foreign Office because of Ambassador Spring-Rice's illness and temperamental inability to get along with American officials. His call upon Mr. Wilson, September 30, was concerned with Lord Grey's visit, and inspired, in part, at any rate, by a desire to ascertain whether the announced illness of the President would interfere with it.

Whether or not he was *persona grata* at the White House—and he had lunched there a few weeks previously—it would seem that he, his Embassy, his principal, Lord Grey, and his Government were treated rather cavalierly. The British Government does not send a confidential agent to call upon the President of the United States, by special appointment, to discuss matters of trivial interest. If the President was too ill—and he probably was—to see Wiseman personally, common diplomatic courtesy suggests that he should have been referred to the State Department or invited, in view of the exigencies of the moment, to request a later appointment. Secretary Lansing, or, supposing his absence, Polk, the Under-Secretary, would have been competent to handle the subject tentatively, whatever its gravity or emergency. It speaks well for the innate tolerance and courtesy of the British emissaries involved that they refused to take offense from the incident, and that Lord Grey settled himself patiently to await the President's pleasure.

He waited for about three months at considerable personal inconvenience. He was elderly, and in bad health. He had retired from his country's service, and accepted this mission only through the urgence of his friends, including Mr. House. His failing eyesight condemned him to a lonely existence. Like all men of his age and habits, he was not too happy in unfamiliar surroundings. He missed his own woods and gardens, and the bird calls which were one of the chief solaces of his blindness. Also, it might be pointed out, he was regarded by the more liberal of his countrymen of all parties as the greatest living Englishman. He was not an ordinary Ambassador. His appointment had been made as a special compliment to Mr. Wilson.

But he waited, in hopes that he could be of service to both countries, as much as in kindly recognition of the emergency of Mr. Wilson's situation. For he, like Mr. House, perceived very soon that the President was by way of tumbling with sickening completeness from the great heights Mr. Wilson had reached. And, tired and afflicted himself, he had only sympathy for Mr. Wilson's physical condition, and understanding of the bigotry and intolerance which had helped to bring it about.

Mr. House remained in New York throughout the Treaty fight after his return home. He encouraged all those who worked for a compromise, but he refused to take any direct part in the efforts which were made. It is a tribute to him that Senator Lodge so feared the effects of a public statement by him that he was never permitted to testify before the Foreign Relations Committee, although he indicated his eagerness to do so. But he was, naturally, in close touch with Lord Grey during Grey's visit to this country, and he knew from Grey's assurances that the British Government were willing to accept the Lodge Reservations and expectant that they could win the assent of the French and other Powers. I used to stop in to see him about once a week on my periodic trips to New York, and so kept him in touch with whatever I was learning, either of the muddied currents in the Capitol or from my equally periodic budgets of White House news. I might add that other driblets of facts and allegations of facts did leak out of the White House, and those which were credible always agreed with what I learned from my own reliable informant, a man who was very fond of Mr. Wilson and deplored unostentatiously the situation in which he was involved. Mr. House and I used to put one and one together, always checking against making the result come to three. He was more anxious than ever over the implications of events in this country and abroad. He sensed the business reaction impending here, and the political drift away from a party which had been in power for two terms, and necessarily had acquired many strong enemies. But most of all, he was concerned over the international consequences of failure of the Treaty and abstention of the United States from the League.

I had just been to New York, and had told him that all I heard tended to indicate that the President was still unwilling to compromise with the Senate, while the feeling I gained from the White House news was that Mr. Wilson had no intention of seeing Grey. Immediately after returning to Washington, I saw my friend again. He said that he now knew positively that Lord Grey would not be received, and that even if the Treaty were reintroduced, and despite the pleas of the friends of the League for acceptance of the Reservations, the President would not be swayed from his position. He was so positive, his information having come from direct and indirect sources, that I telephoned what he had told me to Mr. House.

"Are you just as sure of your man?" Mr. House asked, with an edge of pain in his voice.

"As sure as I can be of anything in this crazy world," I answered. "My 'man' talks to other people who hear things in the White House. And he doesn't talk for publication, as you know, or to try to do harm to anyone."

That evening, late, Mr. House telephoned me at my home.

"Would you be willing to tell all that you've told me to Grey?" he asked.

I hesitated.

"I wish you would," he said. "It is really important, not only for me—for all of us—but for Grey. He isn't feeling so good."

I said I would.

"Then you go right around to the Embassy," he said. "Can you go right away? They'll be waiting for you. And don't let anyone know you are going or that you have been there. This is between us and the angels."

The Embassy was only around the corner. I got there slightly before midnight. It was cold and drizzly. There wasn't anybody on duty outside, and the building was dark, except for a hall light. I rang the bell—and Lord Grey opened the door. His tall figure was stooped and weary. His eyes peered blindly from behind the dark lenses, which masked them. We stood for a moment in the dim hall.

"I've sent the servants to bed," he said absently. "It was good of you to take the trouble. But just tell me this: are you as sure of what you told Colonel House as he thinks you are?"

I told him I was, and briefly why.

"Well," he said. "Well! Our friend believes you. I wonder if you would mind going into the details with Tyrrell—it will be the same as talking to me. I—I am not feeling well. If you would excuse me?"

He led the way to one of the office rooms down the hall.

"Here is Mr. Howden Smith, Tyrrell," he said. "I've asked him to talk to you about what Colonel House told us. Good night, gentlemen."

I went into what I had heard with great detail to Tyrrell, including the hopelessness of persuading even Senators most friendly to the Treaty to yield a point in their stand because of their conviction that Mr. Wilson's attitude had become childishly unreasonable. I was able to name names, and chapter and verse, and occasionally he would intervene with a curt "It's a fact. He told us as much." I told him what went on in the White House, and some of it was not too pleasant for him to hear. It was very late when we concluded, and he let me out with a cheery

"Well, it still rains, and the world goes on, some way or other, we know."

I walked away from the Embassy with a sinking feeling at the pit of my stomach. I hadn't asked any questions. That was not what I had gone there for. And I hadn't needed to ask any questions. I knew what both men were deciding as I talked to them, would decide definitely in the morning when they conferred together. The United States had come to a turn in the road. So had the unthinking world outside our borders. Ireland would drip blood for more years. The Naval Limitation Treaty would await a Republican Administration. More people would starve to death in Germany, die of typhus in the Balkans. The printing presses would be put to work printing money like cigar coupons. High tariffs would be passed by a Congress disgusted with the sour fruits of idealism. The new-born League would be lucky if it didn't die on its nurses' hands. And once again, as in the past, the world would be frustrated of a vision because a great man had not been capable of forgetting self.

Mr. House told me, afterwards, that my information had convinced Lord Grey of the hopelessness of his mission.

And ever since then I have tried to remember Tyrrell's parting word on the Embassy doorstep: "Well, it still rains, and the world goes on, some way or other, we know."

Book 10

Friendship's End

WHEN Mr. House died, March 28, 1938, a newspaper commentator wrote of him: "A silent and stooped little man, who played a powerful role in the war to end all wars, spent much of the last years of his life looking bewilderedly out of the window of his Park Avenue study at a world rushing by—rushing down the same road that led to 1914." The picture presented here is out of drawing, although it was probably the one that came to most people who did not know Mr. House personally. There was nothing of bewilderment in his contemplation of the postwar world, dancing, gambling and drinking merrily hellward during the economic turmoil and social heedlessness of the 1920's, drifting aimlessly, helplessly toward the collapse of civilization in the following decade. It was, to be sure, frequently incredible, appalling to him, that men and nations could fail so completely to comprehend the problems confronting them, the consequences of continuing inertia. But he himself had a clear perception of the basic forces at work, the greed, intolerance, racial bigotry and false pride.

Throughout the first two decades following the Armistice he was a potent factor for straight thinking in his own country and abroad. He refused to accept the privilege of age, and sit quietly and watch the "world rushing by." He wasn't so strong as he had been, and many people had forgotten him, but he continued to work on the creaky machinery of civilization whenever a chance came to him. It wasn't his fault that he was, to some extent, in his own country, the victim of a determined, persistent attempt to discredit him, in the mistaken idea that it was necessary to do so to preserve the reputation of Woodrow Wilson. On the other hand, it was distinctly his fault that he refused to permit his friends to combat this sorry campaign aggressively, for reasons which did him honor, reasons dictated by respect for Mr. Wilson's honor, which he considered his honor.

As a matter of fact, he was amused instead of annoyed by the attacks upon him, the veiled slurs, the books and articles and gossip, which represented him as someone who had never merited the power intrusted to him by a better man, a chance accident of politics. "They don't pay the President any compliment, those people," he would say. "And besides him, there must be a lot of men I worked with, who can't be exactly pleased to hear that I wasn't worth their attention."

There was scarcely a European Chief of State or Sovereign or leading statesman, educator and journalist, who did not seek his advice in the years following the war. Most of these men and women continued to regard him as the best-informed and most impartial American in world affairs. Many Americans shared this feeling, with the additional belief that his wisdom was practical in domestic questions of finance, agriculture and business. Up to the last year or two of his life, I suppose, he saw an average of a dozen to twenty people a day. People never tired him in old age, any more than they had in the earlier years. He really loved people, all kinds of people, regardless of age, creed, race or political belief. If he had any favorites, they were those who were younger than himself, for he was eager to keep in touch with new currents of thought, a reason why he was especially fond of the society of authors and journalists. One tribute to his intellectual integrity and sweetness of character was that the great men he had known abroad invariably visited him when they came to this country, and after they had ceased to come, their sons came in their places to pay respect to the man who had been a faithful friend to all who had deserved friendship. It was a part of their education.

His contacts with distinguished Americans in the latter years must have been exceeded by those of few other citizens, outside of the occupants of the White House. And this was the more remarkable because Mr. House was not one to put himself out for social life. He cared little for formal society—indeed, regarded it with good-humored scorn; but he was under a continual pressure of private invitations which he could not avoid for sentimental or friendly reasons. Men who wanted to see him, no matter how important they were, called upon him at his home, which, after the war, was an apartment at the corner of Park Avenue and Sixty-eighth Street. He remained in New York because of its convenience for keeping in contact with the personalities who were the engineers of events. But he remained an ardent Texan, and looked forward to his visits to the State he called his "real home"—his notepaper was embossed "Edward M. House, Austin, Texas."

He continued his annual trips abroad almost up to the end of his life, although less frequently, and was deeply touched by the unbroken friendship manifested for him by the men with whom he had worked and argued in the days of the war and Versailles. It pleased him, too, that, whenever he and Mrs. House were in one of the capitals, they were immediately invited to the Palace, and shown the new son or the latest grandchildren or told the gossip of the Hradchiny. I think one of the reasons why a select few Americans disliked him was that he possessed the tolerance and breadth of interest of the instinctive aristocrat, a faculty which endeared him to all Europeans and to the ordinary people he met at home, but which possibly was the reason for a certain quiet arrogance toward those who were snobbish or class-conscious.

Personally, I was amused by his reflection of the typical Western business man's or farmer's detestation of Wall Street and its works; but here, again, this feeling was directed against the atmosphere of the Street, and had nothing to do with personalities—I doubt if any Democrat could boast the friendship of as many leaders of banking and finance. It would be gratuitous to mention individuals. There were too many of them. It was next to impossible to call upon him, even after he had ceased to have influence with any Administration, without meeting some man whose name was a household word in Big Business. "My calling list still looks something like a roster of the full-page ads in the *Saturday Evening Post*," he said jokingly, one day, when we had been talking about the contemptuous hostility demonstrated toward him by the late George Horace Lorimer. I might add that this hostility was not shared by C. H. K. Curtis or the Bok family. Incidentally, one of the amusing indications of the Texan's contempt for what he referred to as "Downtown," in New York, was his pride in the fact that he hadn't been south of Twenty-third Street since, as he said, "there were good restaurants around Union and Madison Squares." One time we walked south of Forty-second Street, and he evinced a naïve curiosity in the buildings we passed and the character of business they housed. He regarded himself as an American, not a New Yorker. He was deeply conscious of the capacity of the metropolis for warping the perspectives of people who yielded too freely to its size and bounding energy.

His own energy was amazing in a man of his age. Aside from a taxing correspondence, the calling list mentioned, social engagements on many evenings or afternoons of the week, the considerable burden of organizing his papers, including a most complete diary, he was in the habit of walking for half an hour twice a day, and during these walks he carried on an animated conversation with his companion, who was selected for informative knowledge and intellectual independence. It was one of his traits that he knew and spoke to most of the doormen, shopkeepers and policemen he encountered, let alone a bewildering assortment of people who were friends of himself and his family. Another trait, which bothered me, was his utter contempt for traffic and traffic regulations. I could never understand the coordination he exhibited when he was seventy years old and older. I think it is true that he worked harder than most of his contemporaries, not excluding President Wilson; but he outlived most of them. He had no illusions as to why. "Most of them didn't know how to organize," he said. "They didn't eat properly. They either didn't have enough exercise or they had too much. They worried, which is the most killing thing a man can do. If you're going to work hard for very long you must develop the faculty of shutting off your mind every so often. You must learn to sleep properly. You must understand that once you have done something or decided a policy, you cannot save it by worrying over it."

It was typical of him that, while he was unhappy over his separation from Woodrow Wilson, he literally never worried about it. It had been an unfortunate occurrence, which had come about through influences over which he had no control. He did what he could to avert it, and to mend the breach after it had been created. Having failed in these efforts, he refused to waste sleep or concern over the situation, which, nevertheless, he always referred to with feeling.

"My conscience is clear," he said. "I would have done anything possible to avert it. Some people have much to answer for. The pity of it is that it accomplished nothing for the President, but on the contrary hastened his end, and did much to cause confusion in other people's lives." And he added: "I think you know as much about it as anyone, my friend. I refuse to judge. I don't think about it any more than I can help."

2

Mr. House only mentioned the second Mrs. Wilson to me once, directly, as having been concerned in the destruction of his friendship with Mr. Wilson. In calling upon him one day, I happened to encounter Baker, the President's biographer, who was leaving as I came in. Baker was then engaged upon the preparation of his book. I had not seen him for several years, probably not since Paris. We chatted for a moment with Mr. House, and then Baker excused himself and hastened off.

"He seemed to be in a hurry, Colonel," I commented.

"Maybe he didn't feel very well," Mr. House replied with a smile. "Here, I want to show you something." And he produced a pile of faded, cracking manuscripts, in typewriting and longhand, which were the personal correspondence of Woodrow Wilson with him—I should say some fifty or sixty separate notes, letters and telegrams, all written personally by the President. "As I've told you," Mr. House went on, "the President never took carbons of these. Under the law they are my physical property, but the right of reproduction rests with the President and his heirs. Baker asked us for copies of them for his book, which we gave him with full permission to print. Well, he isn't going to use them."

I asked Mr. House for Baker's reason for such an extraordinary attitude. Mind you, these papers constitute the only existing reflection of Mr. Wilson's feeling toward Mr. House during the period over which they were written. More than this, they are important, confidential records of how certain policies were originated and determined. They are a unique record—for one thing, they are the clearest extant record of Mr. Wilson's individuality of mind. They showed, and show, his personal attitude toward the responsibilities of his office, in that he did not think it necessary to take copies of them, an attitude which places him apart from every other President in American history. There was nothing, of course, unworthy or dishonorable or irresponsible in this attitude. It was Mr. Wilson's simply because he was a very lonely man, who, by habit, liked to work as much as possible alone. He preferred to make decisions by the guidance of his own conscience. The one person he ever consciously admitted to a full share in this habit was Mr. House.

"I'd like you to reach your own conclusion about that," Mr. House replied. "I just want to see if you agree with Miss Fanny and me."

So I sat down and read those documents through—and I was amazed. I know of no correspondence of one great man with another which is so intimate, so warm of heart, so entirely dependent upon his friend's affection and counsel. That is, up to a certain point. And I found myself fascinated in the task of trying to track down that point. When I had reread the later documents, I looked up and asked Mr. House if I had found it.

"After the President's second marriage there is a change, Colonel," I said. "It's not easy to detect. I'm not sure I'm right. They are still friendly, most of them are affectionate. But there is a certain warmth lacking. The salutations aren't as warm, although the subscriptions are. But they surely show how much he depended upon you. I wouldn't have expected them to show so much."

"That's what Miss Fanny and I thought," assented Mr. House.

That is all he said by way of comment. The rest of the conversation was concerned with having them photostated to make sure of their preservation—they were mostly on the poorest grade of scratch-paper—a work which I arranged. In view of the confidential nature of the documents, I insisted upon being present while the work was done. The originals were mounted carefully between transparent sheets of paper, and bound for security. They are in the Sterling Memorial Library at Yale University. They are the final and incontrovertible testimony to Woodrow Wilson's honorable and grateful dependence upon Edward M. House. They might fairly be called literature, too, inasmuch as they are a memorial to an unusual and beautiful friendship.

When I first saw Mr. House after the President's death, February 3, 1924, he spoke of his friend with moisture in his eyes. He said, then, what he repeated many times afterwards: "Don't ever underestimate Woodrow Wilson. Don't ever write anything to belittle him. They don't come often like him." *

* In the New York *Sun*, May 2, 1938, a few weeks after Mr. House's death, appeared a story by Bob Davis, reciting that he and Herman Kohlsaat, former publisher of the Chicago *Record-Herald*, had happened to be visiting Mr. House the day Mr. Wilson died. Kohlsaat was one of Mr. House's best friends, and Mr. House would certainly have displayed the intimacy of grief in his presence which Davis described after Kohlsaat and Mr. House were dead. But I cannot endorse Davis's following assertion that Mr. House placed responsibility for the breach between himself and the President upon an incident which occurred in Paris. The incident certainly happened. I have heard Mr. House describe it, somewhat differently, but he questioned even its importance as a contributory factor, although on that point I did not agree with him. Briefly, the President had called on Mr. House. Clemenceau dropped in, and the President excused himself, with the comment: "Let me not disturb you." A day or two later the President called again, and Lloyd George was announced, and the President excused himself again, and "this time the President's reaction . . . was indeed definite," Davis quotes Mr. House as saying.

In *The Intimate Papers,* Mr. House is quoted as saying that while the President was with him, "Clemenceau, Cecil, and one or two others sent in their cards. . . . No importance was attached by me to the incident." There are several additional garbled versions of the anecdote. The fact was, as Mr. House has said in conversation, people frequently called on him while the President was with him or just before an appointment. The Yeoman's Log for Mr. House's door, for March 18, 1919, also quoted in *The Papers,* lists no less than sixty callers by appointment that day, among them the President, Lord Robert Cecil, Sir Maurice—now Lord—Hankey, Lloyd George, Clemenceau, Tardieu, Sir Philip Kerr—now Marquis of Lothian and Ambassador at Washington; the Spanish Ambassador; M. Paul Hymans, of Belgium, Baron Makino and Count Chinda, of Japan; and many others, including "ten newspaper reporters."

3

Mr. House had his finger in the hazy, only partially recorded series of furtive negotiations which brought about the settlement of the Irish rebellion. They form a strange, not too pleasant episode in history. Mr. House refused to go into details about his part. I have reason to believe that one contribution of his was to arrange contacts between go-betweens —newspapermen and secret agents, who were usually Americans—for the Irish revolutionists and the British Government. He had a good deal to do with the preliminary negotiations leading up to the Naval Limitation Treaties of 1922, which, it will be remembered, he had envisaged during the war and the Peace Conference. He had more influence in these matters with the Governments in London and Paris than he had with the Harding Administration, which he served, not because he liked or respected it, but because it was the Government of the United States. He had some influence with the Japanese at this time. They remembered, with appreciation, his friendly cooperation at the Peace Conference, and *The Real Colonel House* had become almost a bible to the Japanese Liberals in the Diet at Tokyo. Japanese newspapermen of that day thought of him as the greatest American. They changed their opinion, some years later, when the Government of the Chinese Republic sent a Commission to the United States to obtain his advice on the details of organizing their gigantic undertaking.

His relations were so intimate with foreigners like King Albert of Belgium, King George V, Venizelos, King Alfonso, practically all the elder statesmen of Britain and France, that they often took their troubles to him. He was a good friend to the Weimar Republic, and tried all his last years, up to Hitler's advent, to do what he could to mitigate the harsh terms of the Treaty of Versailles he had so definitely disliked. Indirectly, he had much to do with the half-hearted attempts at readjustment of the abominable Reparations abuses, in the negotiations which led to the limited efforts of the United States to implement Europe's complicated debt problems. He regarded Mussolini with a mixture of disdain and admiration for Il Duce's driving determination to lift the Italian people out of their troubles. But he had absolutely no respect for totalitarianism, and declared that its perversions of human liberty and initiative would overcome its practical achievements. He heartily disliked the handling of their racial minorities by new-born Jugo-Slavia and Poland, and admired greatly the democratic achievements of Czecho-Slovakia. In all three of these countries he was a hero to their Governments and peoples, honored and celebrated. He perceived, long before most statesmen, the prolonged torment which awaited Russia, the running sore she must be in civilization's flank; but he believed, and preached, that the surest way to bring her back into the community of nations was to treat her with tolerance and consideration.*

The one hope for Europe's salvation, he thought, was an active, honorably conducted League of Nations, although he was always dubious of the success of his idea without the collaboration of the United States. The League was his great love. Most of its officers and experts were his friends. Many of them he suggested for their positions. He was always in touch with the League's work, always consulted on new plans and projects, labored tirelessly to win influential friends for it in the United States. It is doubtful if any private citizen of any nation tried more desperately than he to lift the world out of the slough of the 1920's. He hated the trends of the United States in those years, hated the hypocrisies and corruption of Prohibition, the social habits, the insane pursuit of wealth for wealth's sake, the falsity of prevailing ideas and the short-sighted policies of the Republican Administrations. He foresaw the end of Prohibition, I should say, almost ten years before most people, although he observed the law and advised his friends to do so.

In all that he did, and tried to do, he was handicapped by the secret animosity entertained for him in the ranks of his own party, a feeling which was partially produced by the enmity of the little group of Mr. Wilson's unreasonable admirers, but much more so, perhaps, by the fact that he had been identified with the last years of the Wilson Administration and the loss of the party's power. There is no doubt, too, that certain influential Democrats in Congress resented his opposition to legislation they had furthered or the fact that he had been given credit for the original ideas of bills they had been permitted to introduce. This was certainly true of Senator Glass, of Virginia, a man for whom Mr. House entertained great respect. There is a story that, when President Coolidge wanted to name Mr. House on an international commission, he was visited by Senator Robinson, of Arkansas, and warned that the

* Mr. House could see only one issue to the European situation after Hitler came into power, unless the British and French sank their differences and adopted a realistic policy. They had to admit his claims or fight them. He thought that the two countries had only themselves to blame: in the first place, for their selfishness with Germany, in the second, for not intervening decisively before Hitler attained sufficient military strength to resist them, as he did not until after the remilitarization of the Rhineland. Mr. House would have been dismayed had he lived to see the disasters to democracy and human liberty which have stemmed from Germany's successful audacity in seizing Austria some two weeks before he died.

minority in the Senate would secure the rejection of Mr. House's name on the traditional grounds of "Senatorial courtesy."

This feeling against him never concerned Mr. House. He had the same theory about himself that he had about Presidents, and to a less extent, Governors. He thought that eight years was long enough for any man to hold the power of creating or inspiring original political conceptions. He maintained that in eight years a man in a position of executive responsibility exhausted his creativeness. He thought that he had enjoyed more than his share of the privilege of advising a President and dominating a party, although he lived to alter his mind slightly. Conversely, he thought that this objection was more pertinent as to the Presidency than the so-called third term tradition, despite the fact that he was alive to the dangerous extent of sovereign authority available to a strong President. "You might put it this way," he said. "If the people ever do reelect a President for a third term, they'll be so sick of him that they'll never make the same mistake again. It will be only their own fault, if they ever do break the third-term tradition."

This comment was made in connection with President Franklin D. Roosevelt's amazing show of strength in his first campaign. Several years later, after Roosevelt had broken all political records in his reelection, Mr. House was again asked how he felt about this question. There was already beginning to be third-term talk in the air, but Mr. House asserted flatly that Roosevelt wouldn't run for a third term, whether it was offered to him or not. He had a high opinion of Roosevelt's political sagacity—and a low opinion of his wisdom in some other respects—and based his assertion partly on this; but, as will presently be told, Mr. House wasn't always correct in his expectations on this subject.*

He took no active share in the 1920 campaign because he feared his intervention would be harmful to party harmony; but prior to reaching this decision he launched two trial balloons for widely different candidates. In Paris, in 1919, he asked me to start a newspaper campaign for Hoover as the Democratic candidate—"to smoke him out," as Mr. House put it. Nobody at that time had any idea as to Hoover's party sympathies. He probably had none, as, when he was afterwards approached by newspapermen for an expression of his availability, he declined to commit himself. Which, of course, was his privilege. He had been

* At the end of March, 1940, President Roosevelt had not yet signified his intentions as to a third term, and the delegates from New Hampshire had been instructed for him. The best-informed feeling, however, was that he could be induced to enter the Convention only if the European situation became so threatening as to make him willing to seek office to give permanence to the foreign policy he had followed.

away from the United States so much that he had had no opportunities to study his personal reactions to the parties. But Mr. House felt later that if Hoover had been willing to accept the 1920 nomination, when he was at the height of his wartime popularity, and yet not tarred with any responsibility for Democratic policies, the history of the ensuing ten years might have been very different.

Mr. House had much more respect for the great Food and Relief Administrator than for Coolidge. He considered him an internationalist, in the real sense of the word, with an intelligent appreciation of international problems. As he put it, after Hoover did achieve to a very unhappy Presidency: "Hoover never knew enough about this country and its people to be a good President at a time when we were reaching the end of a crazy period of inflation. He was a great administrator, not even a good politician. He didn't know how to mix. He didn't know the mechanics of American politics. He never really learned political practice while he was in Washington. He was elected in 1928, partly because the Coolidge boom was still running, and the people didn't want to change parties; but, more than that, he was elected because his opponent was an excellent citizen, a fine Governor, who happened to be a Catholic. And one sad, unfortunate thing about this country is that it is not yet tolerant or big enough to elect a Catholic or a Jew to the Presidency."

After Mr. House returned to this country, in the fall of 1919, he asked me to approach Frank Polk, the Under-Secretary of State, and inquire how he would feel about a campaign for his nomination. Polk, who was not nearly so well known nationally as Hoover, and in all probability could not have been so good a vote-getter, was a public official of the highest capacity, who was not promoted to the Secretaryship after Lansing's enforced resignation, because he shared his chief's misgivings as to the conduct of the President's advisers and had been identified with Mr. House in the past. He, however, as he frankly said, was handicapped by the after-effects of the bullet wound in his throat, to such an extent as to make it impossible for him to undertake the sort of speaking tour which was necessary prior to the introduction of radio.* He did not feel physically capable even of the fatigue of a campaign for nomina-

---

* Mr. House was one of the first men to appreciate the significance of the influence radio would exert on politics. He predicted that, among other things, it would minimize the importance of stage orators of the Bryan and Borah type, place speakers on a more even footing and reduce the length of political campaigns, as making unnecessary the extended speaking tours demanded of candidates. He has been borne out in this prediction by the remarkable oratorical prestige gained by President Franklin D. Roosevelt, who, partly crippled as he was, would have found

tion, let alone the arduous endeavor of a swing around the country. His had been a strenuous term of service in the State Department, and he wanted to "get acquainted" with his family again. He might have had a hard time winning either nomination or campaign, but he would have been an irreproachable President for the purpose of carrying forward sympathetically Mr. House's policies and those in which Mr. Wilson believed, previously to his affliction.

By the time the Conventions had met, and considering the second defeat of the Treaty and Mr. Wilson's continued recalcitrance toward efforts for compromise, Mr. House came to the conclusion that his best course was to stay clear of the hopeless struggle. He saw only a prolonged and disastrous period of eclipse for the Democratic party. He could not do anything honorably, as he conceived, to alter the drift of events. So he stood aside. For the next ten years he devoted himself chiefly to promotion of international conciliation, and patient, tireless work to educate the leaders of American thought in the interest of the United States in cooperation with other nations. In this work he reached more Republicans than Democrats. He had the respect and confidence of both Coolidge and Hoover. Harding he regarded with puzzled disgust. It was difficult for him to understand how a man of such meager talents and questionable associations could ever have reached the Presidency. For Chief Justice Hughes, as Secretary of State, he had the same profound respect he entertained for all great Americans who serve their country. He said, more than once, that Hughes would have made a better, more efficient President than either Coolidge or Hoover.

4

The depression which started in the United States in October, 1929, was no surprise to Mr. House, although his personal fortune was so invested that he was powerless to do much to avert inconvenience to himself. All his life he had been averse to the stock market as a source of income. Most of the funds he had inherited were in land or mortgages. He had been obliged for years to live very expensively in the public service, and it was his preference that this should be at his own charges. He was jealous for Mr. Wilson's sake, as well as his own,

such tours as used to be customary most exhausting experiences; and also by the reduction in the campaigning period decided upon by both parties for 1940. Another prediction of Mr. House's was that radio would increase the size of the political audience, and hence the numbers of the popular vote. He was inclined to regard its mass influence as one of the reasons for the success of the dictators, notably in Germany.

that there should be no valid excuse for the innumerable whispers circulated about his self-interest in the power he exercised. So the depression, when it came, with its continuous and paralyzing blows at land values, its annihilation of mortgage-holders without the provision of a new market to assume the mortgages at equivalent values, wiped out equities he could never reestablish. He lost considerable money, too, in carrying men whose plight, he felt, was not their fault.

The only beneficent feature of the depression, he considered, was its ruthless success in arousing the country to the false standards of values which had destroyed the people's ethical code, as well as their sense of proportion. He had no doubt about its effect politically; but it would be erroneous to say that he anticipated such a mood of panic and despair as swept all countries. As has been shown, he had anticipated the disastrous consequences to American finances, if an effort were not made to cooperate with European debtors to enforce a sane method of collecting Reparations and balancing the international debt structure. This, however, did not reconcile him to wholesale repudiation of debts by countries with the reputations and resources of Great Britain and France. Italy and lesser countries he could understand, but he thought that it was as regrettable for the two great democracies to resort to such steps as later he held it to have been for the Roosevelt Administration to repudiate the gold value of the contracted obligations of the United States.

This statement brings forward the story of Mr. House's connection with the sustained campaign which focused national attention upon Roosevelt and procured his nomination at Chicago—a nomination adroitly and painstakingly planned, but achieved by a series of classical political trades, betrayals and plain flukes—and his impressive election, by virtue of his own personality and the country's decision to fasten upon the unfortunate Hoover complete responsibility for the economic sins of Republican predecessors.

Mr. House picked Roosevelt as a natural candidate for the Presidency long before any other responsible politician, with the exception of the late Louis Howe, who played, in a limited way, the same role with Roosevelt as had Mr. House with President Wilson. He had known Roosevelt ever since his young manhood, through Mrs. Sara Delano Roosevelt, the President's mother, who was one of the oldest personal friends of Mr. and Mrs. House. Mr. House, too, had done much to encourage Roosevelt in turning to account his first chance in national politics as Assistant Secretary of the Navy. He had taught Roosevelt the tricks of the game, had lent the remnants of his political strength to promote the young New Yorker's real emergence upon the national stage as running mate with Cox, of Ohio, in 1920. After Roosevelt's illness and recovery from infantile paralysis, Mr. House again had advised him in his essay in New York State politics, which—with the additional sponsorship of Al Smith—helped to carry him to the Governorship. Mr. House's interest throughout this phase of Roosevelt's career was to make him a national figure, with the White House as the prize ahead; and in this Mr. House's aid was perhaps as important as the faithful work of Roosevelt's household political adviser, Howe. Howe had the loyalty and devotion. Mr. House had the wisdom and experience of years, and the prestige and national connections.

After Roosevelt was nominated, with fairly certain chances of election —to which Hoover had contributed by his ill-judged, but correct, statement of the preceding summer on the danger of going off the gold standard—Mr. House assumed that he was to be the new President's closest responsible adviser. He had no desire to replace Howe or to usurp the powers or authority of James A. Farley, the National Chairman. He wanted nothing to do with patronage, of course. But he did think, and say, that he expected to be consulted upon all questions of major policy, national and international. He perceived the country's plight, and the urgent need of corrective measures. His *Philip Dru* schedule for revision of the social and economic forces had not been carried to completion in 1913-21. He had not considered the time ripe for many of "Dru's" measures, and as the years had passed and he had ripened in experience, his doubts of the wisdom of many of them had been strengthened. But he had variations or substitutions which he considered adaptable to the United States of 1932, and he took for granted Roosevelt's willingness to agree substantially with his ideas.

There were reasons to believe, after the Roosevelt triumph, that Mr. House was over-optimistic in his assumptions. It was political gossip that neither Howe nor Farley was partial to sharing influence with Mr. House. They considered that the place for an Elder Statesman was in dignified remoteness from the scene of strife—as per Prince Saionji. He should await a summons from the Palace before volunteering his advice, and not give it too often, then. The ardent young men of the Brain Trust, apostles of the New Deal, were still more firm in this conviction.* It was the ancient story of Age and Youth, and a Chief Executive who

* I shall not refer to Professor Raymond Moley's book, except as one of the products of this school of thought. It has seemed to me that Professor Moley's comments upon President Roosevelt and Secretary Hull are sufficiently comments upon himself to make unnecessary any allusion to his occasional mention of Mr. House.

was amused by it all, and determined to carry on his office in his own way, as the New Dealers ultimately came to realize. Roosevelt had no inclination to split his triumphs with Mr. House, after Woodrow Wilson's regretted example.

Not long after the election, I had an opportunity to discover the exact sentiments of Howe and Farley, exact sentiments in the sense that they expressed their minds so to newspapermen who had their confidence. What Farley said was: "Colonel House? Oh, no, we're not worried about him. A very nice old gentleman. We'll take care of him, but I don't think we'll need him." I thought this was authentic enough to convey to Mr. House. He was firmly skeptical. "I daresay certain people don't want the President to listen to me," he said. "But I'm sure I can influence him. He trusts me, and so does his mother. I've known him ever since he was a mere boy."

The next, and conclusive, indication of Mr. House's misplaced confidence occurred in connection with the pre-inauguration conference between President Hoover and the President-elect, which resulted in Roosevelt's refusal to cooperate with President Hoover to check the ominous run on the banks, the colossal losses of business and the impending "bank holiday." Mr. House was strongly in favor of such cooperation. He thought it was no time for one political party to exploit the mistakes of another. He had always believed, it will be remembered, that the outgoing party should cooperate in a time of crisis with the incoming party, and that a willingness to do so by the vanquished should be accepted by the victors.

I had an article in *Scribner's Magazine* of January, 1933, in which I said that the future policy of the Roosevelt Administration would be guided by the new President's disposition to take the advice of Mr. House or of Howe and Howe's associates. If Mr. House was heeded, the new Administration could be expected to be progressively liberal and intelligently constructive. There would be no forced radical departures from past policies. There would be an attempt to work with business so long as business was cooperative. There would be a broadening of foreign policy, and an emphasis upon naval building within treaty limits. As against this, if the advice of Howe and his friends was paramount, the country might look for a parochial attitude by the Administration, with an effort to develop every selfish political advantage.

This story was in circulation just before Christmas. President Hoover promptly telephoned Mr. House in New York, and asked him to advise Roosevelt that the President would like to meet with him in Washington as soon as possible to explore ways to work in common to avert a finan-

MR. HOUSE IN HIS LATER YEARS, WITH MRS. JAMES ROOSEVELT, THE PRESIDENT'S MOTHER

cial disaster. What happened is a matter of history. Who was right and who was wrong, of the conferees, is a subject of legitimate controversy. Mr. House accepted the rebuff to himself with his usual philosophy. He had tried, and failed. But he had no illusions left as to the closeness of his connection with the new President. He remained friendly, but, I believe, never gave advice unless it was sought, and then with detachment. He found himself increasingly out of sympathy with the ballyhoo and hustle policies of the New Deal. Much of what the Administration was trying to do he believed in, in principle; but he knew from experience that over-haste in legislation makes for frustration of valid accomplishment. He thought the Blue Eagle sensationalism of NRA was the sort of thing which might have been expected of a pack of Boy Scouts. He thoroughly disapproved of the attack upon the Supreme Court. He thought Mr. Roosevelt's purge politics against Senators who disagreed with him was nothing more than bad, cheap politics. He agreed with the fundamentals of the President's foreign policy, but he thought they were not too well applied, except as to Secretary of State Hull's web of trade treaties. For instance, he considered the conduct of the London Economic Conference amateurish and an aggravation of an already dangerous international situation. He was all in favor of the Administration's naval policy.

Now, an amusing aspect of the Roosevelt policies was that, according to internal evidence, Mr. House was mainly responsible for the most challenged and debated of them. He was hoist by his own petard. And the petard was *Philip Dru* and its radical preachments delivered two decades previously. I do not know whether Mr. House gave one of the original copies of his book to Mrs. Roosevelt, senior, or to the young man who was to become President of the United States. But he most certainly presented a copy to Professor Felix Frankfurter, of Harvard Law School, who found much to admire in Mr. House's rough conceptions for whittling out a better system of social justice. Professor Frankfurter —who is now Mr. Justice Frankfurter, of the Supreme Court—was scheduled to duplicate with Mr. Roosevelt, more than anyone else, including Howe, the part played by Mr. House with President Wilson. But whoever interested the new President in Philip Dru's ideas for remodeling the United States, it is impossible to compare Dru's suggested legislation with Mr. Roosevelt's and not be impressed by their similarity.

Dru considered the Constitution "not only outmoded, but grotesque." He asserted that "every man or woman who desires work shall have it, even if the Government has to give it." He demanded an eight-hour, six-day week, which, of course, has been outmoded, typical of the way in which the New Deal outran Dru. He was for "adequate wages," while an attempt to reduce wages would give an employee the right to take legal proceedings against an employer. He was for compulsory recognition of unions, old-age pensions, laborers' insurance laws and cooperative loan societies under Government supervision. He wanted, rather vaguely, "reformation of the study and practice of medicine." He wanted reform of all the courts, and the Supreme Court in particular, which held a "Damoclean sword," and he was for compulsory retirement of all judges at seventy. He foresaw the Securities and Exchange Commission in a decree for Federal regulation of Stock, Cotton and Produce Exchanges; and he was most drastic in his projected regulation of Public Utilities. The Nation and States were to share in the earnings of all corporations, including Utilities, with the right of access to their books and the figures of salaries paid to high officials. Above and beyond this, Dru wanted to dissolve all holding companies. And, finally, Dru believed in "fireside talks" to discuss politics!

These are but a few of the policies Franklin D. Roosevelt took over from *Philip Dru*. Many of the phrases conceived by Mr. House echo in the speeches and "fireside talks" of the man who studied politics under him for more than twenty-two years. Others, it is true, words and ideas, were transmuted by Mr. Wilson into his sonorous prose.

So, perhaps, Mr. House had a secret reason for the amused detachment with which he accepted his relegation to the status of an aged Samurai noble. He had only himself to blame for the fact that the disciple, as usual, outdistanced the preceptor. There had been a time when he, himself, might have gone farther than President Roosevelt. The main point is that when Mr. House came to put his startlingly revolutionary ideas into practice he slammed the brakes on them. "I didn't know as much then," he said, smilingly. "You know, I wish it had been a better book. I wrote it too fast, on the south porch at Austin, to forget that I was getting over an illness. And by the way, how did you know I'd written it?"

"That, Colonel, is one thing you'll never know," I told him, grinning. "But you forgot your politics when you thought of yourself as an author, and some people think it's a better book than you do."

5

After he became convinced that President Roosevelt preferred to employ the theoretical conceptions of Philip Dru rather than the trial-and-error adaptations of them advocated by Dru's creator, Mr. House accepted placidly the honorable retirement of an Elder Statesman's lot. He didn't retire into the shades. He continued to be interested in all the facets of life which came under his observation. I doubt if any old man ever enjoyed a wider circle of friends, and he had a still wider circle of acquaintances. He kept his health remarkably. His one serious affliction, which became periodically more painful as he grew older, was a mysterious inflammation of the nerves around the chest. The only doctor he discovered who could relieve this ailment was a rural practitioner in France upon whom he stumbled in the course of one of the wandering journeys he loved to go upon with Mrs. House. This inflammation crippled him occasionally, and kept him housebound, which he detested, and interrupted the steady stream of callers, an affliction he detested still more.

Contrary to what Walter Lippmann has written about him, he read a good deal in his later years; but he read for the most part lighter books, works dealing with episodes in which he had participated, articles upon similar subjects in historical journals, and magazine articles upon contemporary politics. I never gave him anything to read, or suggested a subject to him for survey, which he did not comment upon with the clarity he brought to every subject which interested him. That he read casually some lurid modern fiction I know, because he would comment upon such work with unusual prejudice. Mr. House hated cruelty and vulgarity. But to return to his intellectual ability, which Lippmann dismissed rather cavalierly: It was of a high order. He had read, when he was young, the sound books upon those subjects valuable to the career he fashioned for himself. He grasped subjects quickly.

Lippmann says: "Two well-spaced typewritten pages were about the limit of what he cared to take in by reading; the rest had to be filled in by oral explanation." Certainly, this was true during the days when he worked under inconceivable pressure, and when the range of activities he was obliged to span surveyed the industry, the politics and the military developments of a world at war. It would have been impossible for him to spare the time to go into all the details which distract the mind of the pundit, the limited expert or the subordinate executive. No Chief of Staff could do otherwise. Nor would any great corporation executive. He was fanatical, much more so than Mr. Wilson, on the fact that most people took too much time to explain their ideas. "Put the essentials in a page or two," he would say. "Then I'll send you to someone who can help you work out the details or find the man you need to do it."

Lippmann also has written—and I single him out simply because he was typical of many who worked under or for Mr. House, and who, for one reason or another, deprecated him: "The career of Colonel House was like that of an actor or of a singer in that there is no record left by which posterity can form an independent estimate of his worth. There are, to be sure, some memoirs, some letters and some papers. But no one who knew the Colonel will make the mistake of thinking that they reveal the man or define the part he played in the history of these times. . . . The work he did was done in private talks with President Wilson and with a highly selected circle of influential men here and abroad. . . . So the man displayed in the memoirs, and even more the man of the post-war legends, is a fiction, almost unrecogizable to those who knew the Colonel when he served Woodrow Wilson."

These statements are simply not borne out by the facts. Mr. House left a mass of papers, including a diary which has been only partially published. His work was not done solely with President Wilson or with "highly selected" groups of men. He was at pains to meet all and sundry, to touch as many levels as he could. I doubt if any man of his time had as extensive an acquaintance with the best of the world's journalists or intellectual thinkers, upon whose opinions he frequently placed more reliance than upon those of statesmen or political leaders. Furthermore, there was nothing fictional or indefinite about Mr. House, his character or his beliefs. A man of reticence, he was entirely frank with those he trusted. He had the heart of a child, and the sharp zest of a child for stimulating experience and success in undertakings.

As I have tried to show in this book, Mr. House's difficulty in playing a part in public life was conditioned by his personality and his limited fund of physical strength, which were products of illness in his youth. He could not hope to be master alone of a situation, unless he went out on the hustings and subjected himself to the amorphous detail which crushes almost all men in public office, no matter how strong they are, in the course of years. He had to depend upon someone else to carry his ideas and objectives to the voters—and it was no disgrace to Woodrow Wilson that most of the best of what he said or thought, in the term of their friendship, either came from Mr. House or was molded by him. The counterpoise to this is that the moment Mr. House ceased to be able to use the personality of Mr. Wilson to advance his ideas, he became relatively obscure and his ideas failed—and Mr. Wilson became a saddened spectator of the collapse of his dreams. The two were necessary to each other; the fact is unescapable. It is not palatable to many persons, but it was a tribute to both of them that for some years they understood their mutual dependency and accepted it without resentment on either side.

It was the quality which made them both truly great. Each accepted service from the other, in order that each could give more complete service to his country.

6

I should like to tell one more story about Woodrow Wilson's friend, Mr. House. He was not a man who talked about creed because he accepted and honored and held in respect all creeds alike. He did not mention the Deity or discuss Him or take His name in vain.

One of the last times I walked with him on a beautiful day in spring, he remarked, clutching my arm—not for support, but in a fashion of his of pure affection:

"I like this kind of a day, bright and sunny. Let's walk over to the park." And then, quite cheerfully matter-of-fact: "You know, I shan't be here much longer."

I protested—and stopped at the light in his face.

"Oh, no, I'm not sorry," he said. "I don't want to live too long. I'd rather go out running."

Index